THE HIDDEN PLACES

of Yorkshire and Humberside

Written by ***JAN RICHARDSON***

SECOND EDITION

Acknowledgements

This book would not have been compiled without the dedicated help of the following:- Elaine & Adele - Administration; Sarah, Les & Albert - Artists; Jan Richardson - Writing and finally Bob, Chris, Vic, Jim, Harvey, Simon, Gerald & Jody - Research.
All have contributed to what we hope is an interesting, useful and enjoyable publication.

OTHER TITLES IN THIS SERIES

The Hidden Places of East Anglia
The Hidden Places of Somerset, Avon & Dorset
The Hidden Places of Southern & Central Scotland
The Hidden Places of Nottinghamshire, Derbyshire & Lincolnshire
The Hidden Places of Oxfordshire, Buckinghamshire & Bedfordshire
The Hidden Places of Northumberland & Durham
The Hidden Places of Gloucestershire & Wiltshire
The Hidden Places of Hampshire & Isle of Wight
The Hidden Places of Lancashire & Cheshire
The Hidden Places of Hereford & Worcester
The Hidden Places of Devon & Cornwall
The Hidden Places of Cumbria
The Hidden Places of Sussex

Printed and bound by Guernsey Press Channel Islands.

Tryfan House, Warwick Drive, Hale, Altrincham, Cheshire. WA15 9EA

Introduction

THE HIDDEN PLACES is designed to be an easily used book. Taking you in this instance, on a gentle meander through the beautiful countryside of Yorkshire & Humberside . However, our books cover many counties and will eventually encompass the whole of the United Kingdom. We have combined descriptions of the well-known and enduring tourist attractions with those more secluded and as yet little known venues, easy to miss unless you know exactly where you are going.

We include hotels, inns, restaurants, caravan parks and camping sites, historic houses, museums, gardens and general attractions throughout each of these fascinating counties: together with our research on the local history. For each attraction there is a line drawing and a brief description of the services offered. A map at the beginning of each chapter shows you each area. and there is also a reference guide giving you full details of all the hotels, inns, etc., detailed.

We do not include firm prices or award merits. We merely wish to point out *The Hidden Places* that hopefully will improve your holiday or business trip and tempt you to return. The places featured in this book will we are sure, be pleased if you mention that it was *The Hidden Places* which prompted you to visit.

THE HIDDEN PLACES

of

Yorkshire and Humberside

Contents

Staithes

CHAPTER 1

North Yorkshire Captain Cook Country

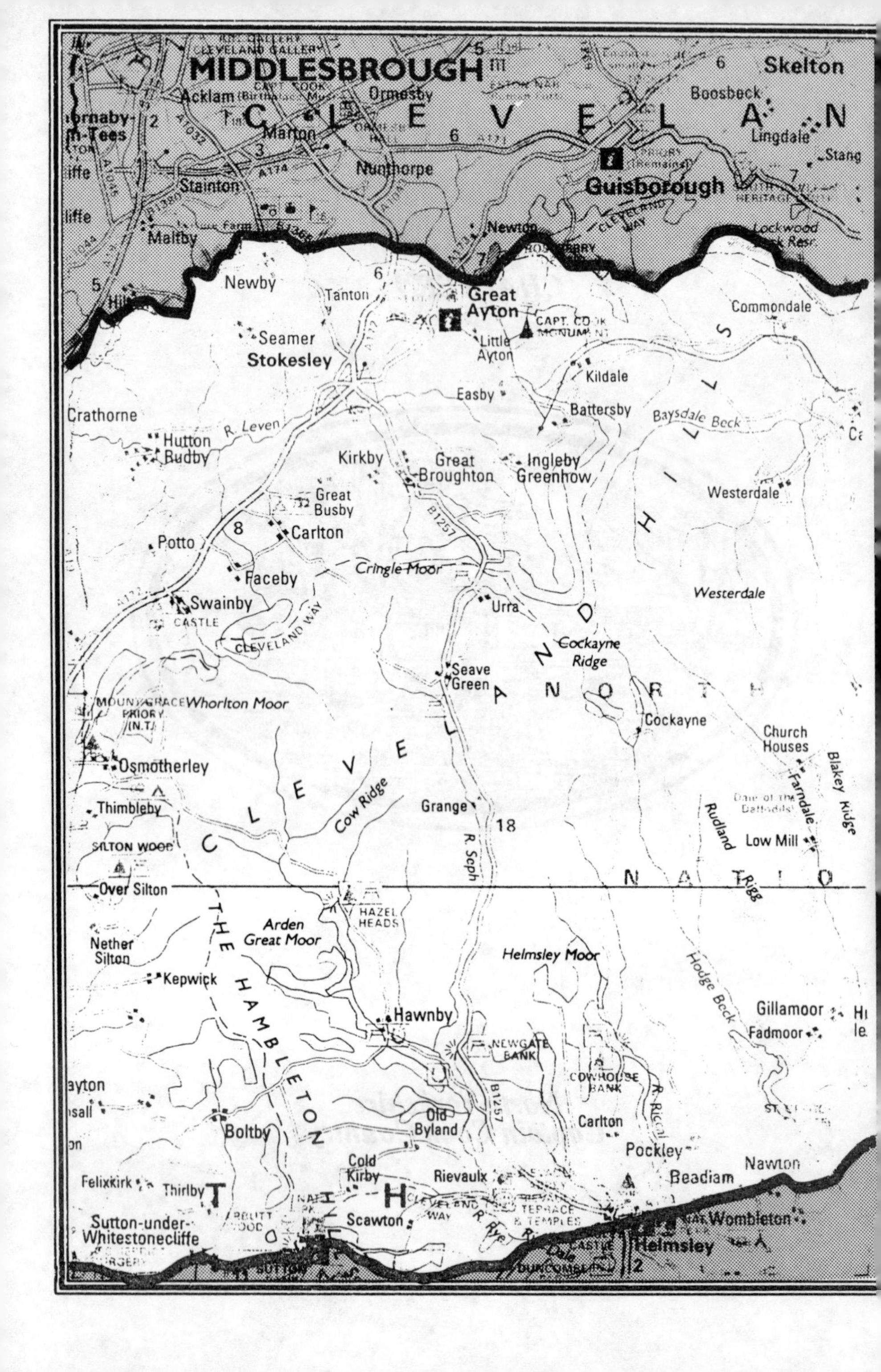
MIDDLESBROUGH
CLEVELAND
Skelton
Acklam
Ormesby
Boosbeck
Marton
Lingdale
Nunthorpe
Stainton
Guisborough
Maltby
Newton
Lockwood Beck Resr.
Newby
Tanton
Great Ayton
Commondale
CAPT. COOK MONUMENT
Seamer
Stokesley
Little Ayton
Kildale
Easby
Crathorne
Battersby
R. Leven
Baysdale Beck
Hutton Rudby
Kirkby
Great Broughton
Ingleby Greenhow
Westerdale
Great Busby
Carlton
Potto
Cringle Moor
Faceby
Westerdale
Swainby
CASTLE
Urra
CLEVELAND WAY
Cockayne Ridge
Seave Green
CLEVELAND NORTH
MOUNT GRACE PRIORY (N.T.)
Whorlton Moor
Cockayne
Church Houses
Osmotherley
Blakey Ridge
Farndale
CLEVELAND HILLS
Thimbleby
Cow Ridge
Grange
Rudland Rigg
Low Mill
SILTON WOOD
R. Seph
NATIO
Over Silton
HAZEL HEADS
Arden Great Moor
Nether Silton
Helmsley Moor
Hodge Beck
Kepwick
THE HAMBLETON
Gillamoor
Hawnby
Fadmoor
NEWGATE BANK
COWHOUSE BANK
B1257
Old Byland
Boltby
Carlton
Pockley
Cold Kirby
Rievaulx
Nawton
Felixkirk
Beadlam
Thirlby
Scawton
Wombleton
Sutton-under-Whitestonecliffe
Helmsley
R. Rye
DUNCOMBE

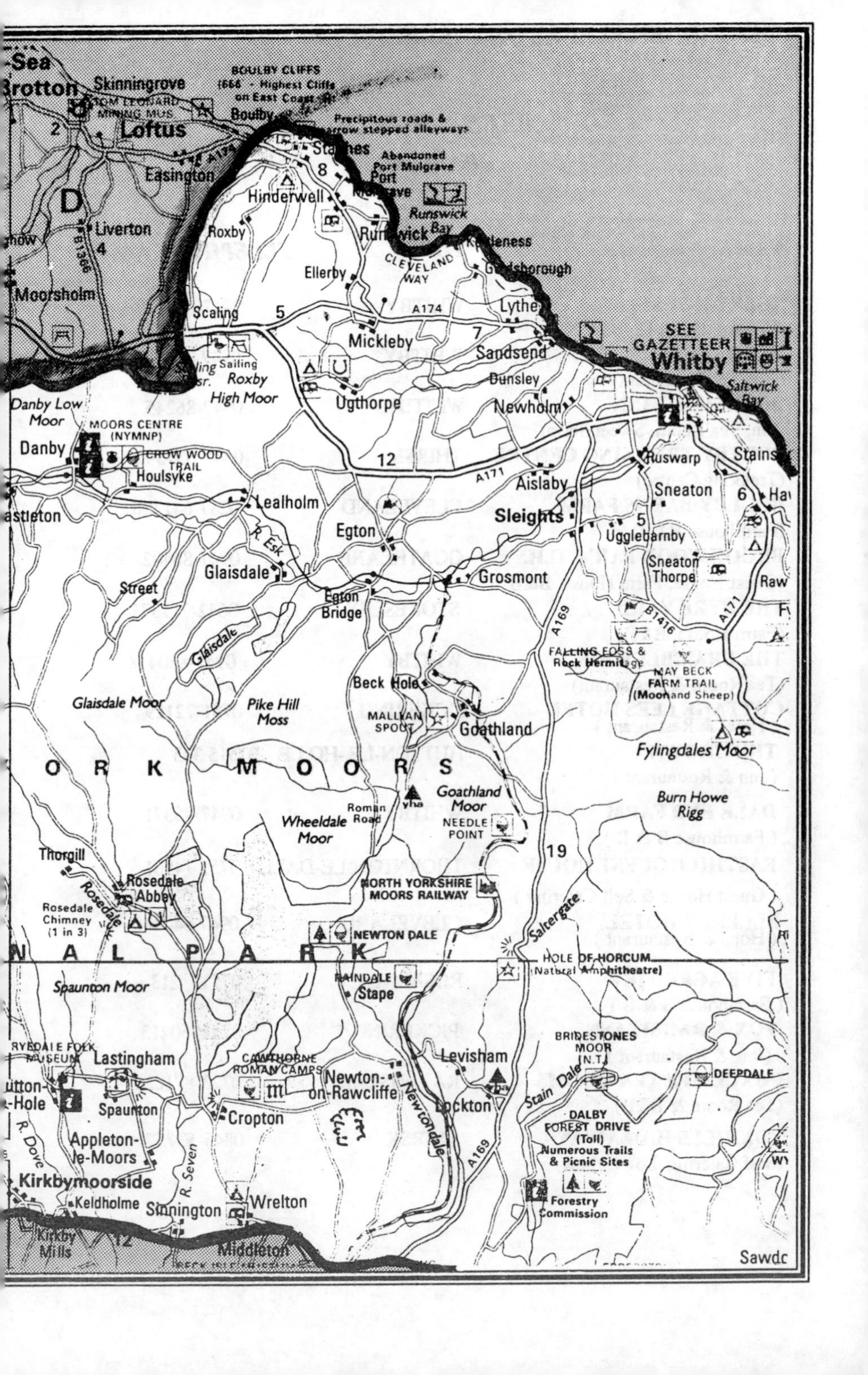

Sea
Brotton
Skinningrove
TOM LEONARD MINING MUS.
BOULBY CLIFFS
666 - Highest Cliffs on East Coast
Boulby
Precipitous roads & narrow stepped alleyways
Loftus
Staithes
Abandoned Port Mulgrave
Port Mulgrave
Easington
Hinderwell
D
Liverton
Roxby
Runswick
Runswick Bay
Kettleness
B1366
CLEVELAND WAY
Goldsborough
Ellerby
Moorsholm
Scaling
A174
Lythe
Mickleby
Sandsend
SEE GAZETTEER
Whitby
Sailing
Roxby High Moor
Dunsley
Saltwick Bay
Danby Low Moor
Ugthorpe
Newholm
MOORS CENTRE (NYMNP)
Danby
CROW WOOD TRAIL
Houlsyke
A171
Ruswarp
Aislaby
Sneaton
Lealholm
Castleton
Sleights
Egton
Ugglebarnby
R. Esk
Glaisdale
Sneaton Thorpe
Grosmont
Street
Egton Bridge
B1416
A169
Glaisdale
FALLING FOSS & Rock Hermitage
MAY BECK FARM TRAIL (Moon and Sheep)
Beck Hole
Glaisdale Moor
Pike Hill Moss
MALLYAN SPOUT
Goathland
Fylingdales Moor
O R K M O O R S
Goathland Moor
Burn Howe Rigg
Roman Road
Wheeldale Moor
NEEDLE POINT
Thorgill
Rosedale Abbey
NORTH YORKSHIRE MOORS RAILWAY
Saltergate
Rosedale
Rosedale Chimney (1 in 3)
NEWTON DALE
N A L P A R K
HOLE OF HORCUM (Natural Amphitheatre)
RAINDALE
Stape
Spaunton Moor
BRIDESTONES MOOR (N.T.)
RYEDALE FOLK MUSEUM
Lastingham
CAWTHORNE ROMAN CAMPS
Levisham
DEEPDALE
Newton-on-Rawcliffe
Newtondale
Lockton
Stain Dale
Spaunton
Cropton
DALBY FOREST DRIVE (Toll)
Numerous Trails & Picnic Sites
R. Dove
Appleton-le-Moors
R. Seven
Kirkbymoorside
Keldholme
Sinnington
Wrelton
Forestry Commission
Kirkby Mills
Middleton
Sawdon

REFERENCE GUIDE
CHAPTER I

NAME	*TOWN*	*TELEPHONE NO.*
ABBEY HOUSE (Hotel & Guest House)	WHITBY	0947-600557
BAGDALE HALL (Hotel & Restaurant)	WHITBY	0947 -602958
BIRCH HALL INN (Inn, Tea Room, Sweet Shop)	WHITBY	0947-86245
BOLTBY TREKKING CENTRE (Trekking Centre)	THIRSK	0845-537392
BOULBY BARNS FARM (Farmhouse B&B)	CLEVELAND	0287-641306
BROOKWOOD FARM G.H. (Guest House, Farm House, B&B)	GOATHLAND	0947-86402
THE BYRE YARD (Farm House, B&B)	STOKESLEY	0642-711371
THE BRAMBLEWICK (Tea Room & Restaurant)	WHITBY	0947-880418
COTTAGE LEES HOTEL (Hotel & Restaurant)	PICKERING	0751-72129
THE CROWN (Inn & Restaurant)	HUTTON-LE -HO LE	07515 343
DALE END FARM (Farmhouse B & B)	WHITBY	0947-85371
EASTHILL GUEST HOUSE (Guest House & Self Catering)	THORNTON-LE-DALE	0751 74561
ELLERBY HOTEL (Hotel & Restaurant)	CLEVELAND	0947 840342
FIVE ACRE VIEW (Farmhouse B & B)	ROSEDALE	07515 213
FOX & RABBIT INN (Inn & Restaurant)	PICKERING	0751 60213
FOXCLIFFE TEA ROOMS (Tea Room & B&B)	RAVENSCAR	0723-871028
FOXHILLS HIDEAWAYS (Self Catering, Log Cabins)	THIRSK	0845-537575

Reference Guide
Chapter 1

FRIARS HILL RIDING CENTRE (Riding Centre)	SINNINGTON	0751-32758
GARDEN HSE GRINKLE CARAVAN PARK Static Caravan Site	GRINKLE	0287-640401
GRINKLE PARK HOTEL (Hotel)	EASINGTON	0287-640515
GOLD CUP INN (Inn)	NETHER SILTON	060983 -416
HARKER HILL (Farm House B&B)	STOKESLEY	0642-710431
HOME OF THE WREN (Place of Interest)	THIRLBY	0845-597453
HIGH FARM (Farm House, B&B, Self Catering Cottage)	CROPTON	07515-461
INGLE HILL (B&B)	STOKESLEY	0642-712449
LASTINGHAM GRANGE (Country House Hotel)	YORK	07515-345
THE LION INN (Inn, Restaurant & Accomodation)	KIRBY MOORSIDE	07515-320
THE MAGPIE CAFE (Cafe & Restaurant)	WHITBY	0947-602058
THE MALLYAN SPOUT (Hotel & Restaurant)	WHITBY	0947- 86206
MELHOUSE BIRD GARDEN (Place of Interest)	PICKERING	0751 -76538
MILBURN ARMS HOTEL (Inn, Hotel & Restaurant)	ROSEDALE ABBEY	07515-312
NORTH YORKSHIRE MOORS RAILWAY (Place of Interest)	PICKERING	0751-73799
NORTHFIELDS FARM (Farm House B&B)	MICKLEBY	0947-840343
OLD SMUGGLER (Restaurant)	WHITBY	0947-602637
THE PIER INN (Inn, Restaurant and B&B)	WHITBY	0947-605284

Reference Guide
Chapter 1

POETS COTTAGE SHRUB NURSERY (Place of Interest)	WHITBY	0947-87424
PRUDOM HOUSE (Guest House)	WHITBY	0947-86368
QUAKER COTTAGE (B & B)	HUTTON-LE-HOLE	07515-465
RECTORY FARM HOUSE (Country House Accomodation and Self Catering Cottages)	LEVISHAM	0751-60304
THE RED LION (Inn with Accomodation)	LYTHE	0947-83300
RED HOUSE FARM (Farm House B & B, Holiday Cottages)	GLAISDALE	0947-87242
ROSALIE'S (Farm House Accomodation, Holiday Cottages & Tourist Atttraction)	HARWOOD DALE	0723-870288
ROSEDALE CARAVAN AND CAMPING PARKS (Caravan & Camping Parks)	ROSEDALE ABBEY	07515-272
SANDFIELD HOUSE FARM (Caravan Park)	WHITBY	0947-602660
SMUGGLERS ROCK (Country Guest House & Self Contained Holiday Cottages)	RAVENSCAR	0723-870044
SYCAMORES FARM (Farm House and B & B)	ROSEDALE ABBEY	07515-448

Reference Guide
Chapter 1

TERRAFAUNA HOUSE OF FOSSILS (Place of Interest)	WHITBY	0947-600058
TRENCHERS LICENSED RESTAURANT (Restaurant)	WHITBY	0947-603212
TROUTSDALE LODGE (Country Guest House)	TROUTSDALE	0723-882209
VALLEY VIEW FARM (Farm House and B & B)	OLD BYLAND	04396-221
THE WASH HOUSE (Pottery)	WHITBY	0947-604995
WELLFIELD TREKKING CENTRE (Trekking Centre)	RAVENSCAR	0723-870182
WETHERCOTE FARM (B & B)	BILSDALE	04396-260
THE WHEATSHEAF INN (Inn & Restaurant)	WHITBY	0947-85271
WHITBY GLASS LTD (Place of Interest)	WHITBY	0947-603553
THE WHITE SWAN (Hotel)	PICKERING	0751-72288
THE WHITE SWAN HOTEL (Inn with Food, Accomod., Caravan & Camping Park)	NEWTON-UPON RAWCLIFFE	0751-72505
WHITFIELD HOUSE HOTEL (Hotel)	GOATHLAND	0947-86215

Whitby Abbey

CHAPTER 1

A Voyage in Captain Cook Country

The North Yorkshire Moors is an area of approximately 650 square miles, and most definitely holds more than enough of interest to occupy the most avid tourer of our sceptred isle.

Many of the preconceptions of the area we had at the outset of our travels were changed somewhat, especially the expectations of a rather inhospitable, bleak terrain, which could not, as it happens, be farther from the truth. We found ourselves travelling through pretty cottaged hamlets, kept in a style reminiscent of the typical English rural scenes one might associate with more southerly counties, surrounded by the more characteristic heather-clad hills. Visiting it as we did in mid-August, the flowers and greenery were profuse, and set a quite magnificent backdrop to our journey.

We also discovered that there is something about this area that seems to create a sense of that pioneer spirit, hence the title we decided on. The region is famous for its greatest son, Captain James Cook, who learnt his skills in seamanship at Whitby, but a whole range of other enterprising individuals have, through the ages, originated here, from the early Christian settlers through to more recent times with the now world-famous Yorkshire veterinary surgeon, James Herriot, created to almost legendary status through the continuing popularity of the books and television series.

Throughout this book, I have attempted to create a series of structured journeys, dotted along the way with the best of the various stop-offs and hostelries we were privileged enough to find. The tourist traps of this particular area are for the most part compelling, but the little gems we discovered off the beaten track served to make this a truly memorable holiday by anyone's standards.

We started our journey at the historic fishing port of **Whitby,** which serves as an excellent base for jaunts around this varied and interesting area, and is, in itself, worthy of several days exploration on its own.

Visitors stopping here might be forgiven for imagining, as we did, that it would be shrouded in mist and have a distinctly gothic air to it. We can, of course, blame the Dublin-born novelist Bram Stoker for this, who based part of his Gothic horror "Dracula" rather incongruously, so it may seem, in this little town, as well as in his more typical "haunt" of

Transylvania. Sitting by the busy harbour, with its bright fishing boats and "cobles" (traditional rowing boats) bobbing about on the sheltered waters, surrounded by the friendly red and white cottages that characterise the port area, all thoughts of rolling mists and looming figures in black cloaks will be instantly dismissed (although those wishing to perpetuate the myth are welcome to participate in a Dracula Walk which takes place on a weekly basis!)

The historical background of Whitby carries more romantic interest than one might also presume, if you can draw your attention from the stalls advertising "chip-butties" and other dubious delights, that is. Its traditions as a Christian settlement and whaling port are ancient and inspiring indeed.

In 657 AD, St Hilda, a Northumbrian princess, founded a community for monks and nuns here. The imposing ruins of the Abbey dedicated to her dominate the cliff views and certainly set the scene as one might imagine the many fishermen of bygone days gazing up at it whilst heading out to the fishing and whaling grounds.

Two monks, Elfwy and Reinfrid were said to have founded the present day Abbey, having found themselves both impressed and moved by the sight of the original and ancient abbey, the foundations of which these days are all that remain. The main part of the building we see today dates mainly from the 13th century.

Reinfrid was reputed to have formerly been one of William the Conquerer's soldiers who took part in the massacres known as the Harrowing of the North. No doubt his stalwart efforts to promote Christianity in the region were by way of penance for his involvement in these terrible events.

Amongst the other interesting and charming historical stories is that of Caedmon, the swineherd, celebrated as the first English poet, who lived here in pre-Norman times and famous for his translation of the scriptures. The legend of the Penny Hedge is another fascinating tale and a must for avid collectors of folklore memorabilia.

The story goes that three local noblemen were out boar-hunting and during this, cornered and wounded a large boar. The creature managed to escape, and was consequently given shelter by a local monk. On discovering this, the young lords were moved to anger, and mortally wounded the kind-hearted friar. The local Abbot would have caused the three to have been put to death, but for the dying wish of the monk. He had forgiven them, on the condition that they should make a pilgrimage each year on Ascension Eve, to the forest where the deed occurred, cut down branches of a tree, and then construct a wall of these branches on the Whitby shore that was strong enough to resist three tides. The tradition is still carried on today by the Mayor of Whitby and the Lady of the Manor, who is said to be a descendant of one of the noblemen.

For those with tastes of a more nautical flavour, one can visit the cottage in Grape Lane where James Cook served his apprenticeship. In fact reminders of the great man are never far away in one's ramblings through Whitby. A handsome monument to him stands on the West Cliff, looking down towards the Abbey, not far from the whalebone arch which is another famous landmark. Nor do you need to go very far to see shops, teahouses, etc. that are named after the famed explorer or one of his ships which were built in the shipyards here.

Another thing that one will notice in exploring Whitby, are the lovely sepia-tone photographs by Frank Meadow Sutcliffe, a nostalgic record of the sailing ship traditions and lives of the local fisherfolk of days gone by. A trip to the Whitby museum in Pannet Park will provide more information as to the lives and industry of these people, as well as more detailed documentation on Cook's endeavours.

For those who may wish to take home a print of one of Sutcliffe's original photographs, one can visit the **Sutcliffe Gallery** on Flowergate. The gallery is a fascinating documentation of this remarkable man's life and works. The great love and respect he held for the hard-working locals is evident for all to see, and his portraits of such local characters as Lizzie Alice Hawksfield collecting mussels and Isobel Batchelor posing in her tattered skirt are a tender and haunting reminder of a populace that would have passed unnoticed into obscurity, were it not for Sutcliffe's efforts with his cumbersome and primitive photographic equipment. For more in-depth information as to the life of this talented man, and a greater selection of his work than is normally available, a visit to the gallery is a must.

Those interested in the even more ancient world of palaeontology should make a point of visiting the **Terrafauna House of Fossils** . This unusual business is located in the heart of the old part of town at No. 4 Market Place. Proprietors, David and Nathalie Manning, specialise in fossils and minerals of every shape, size and description. Visitors are welcome to browse around their fascinating two-storey premises with its remarkable range of mineral specimens, some of which have been found on the Whitby coast. The recent upsurge in interest in geology, palaeontology and dinosaurs has made this a popular and rewarding place to spend an hour or so. Many items are for sale and provide unusual souvenirs of the area.

The areas around Whitby are rich in such fossil deposits, and were of

great attraction to Victorian collectors who frequented the area in those days. The mining of alum, potash and most notably, jet, were and still are a large part of the region's economy, and the ports of Whitby and Staithes were at one time kept extremely busy with the export trade this brought in.

Terrafauna House of Fossils

For another of Whitby's famous exports, we made our way to the ancient part of **Whitby** known as Sandgate, where we called in at the renowned glass studio, **Whitby Glass Ltd**, home of the world famous 'Whitby Lucky Duck'. The studio was founded in the early 1960s by Peter Rantell and today is personally run by Dorothy Clegg, twice former mayor of Whitby and current deputy mayor of Scarborough. Visitors are invited to call in at the 400 year-old building to observe the skilled crafts people as they draw, bend and fashion coloured glass into the intricately shaped good luck talismans. These have been exported to places are far apart as Mexico and Japan, with their alleged successes including financial windfalls and the ending of a drought in southern France.

Just off Church Street in the old part of **Whitby**, we called in at the **Wash House Pottery** in Blackburns Yard. This unusual studio was created with the help of her family and friends by potter Laureen Shaw from the shell of an old wash house which stood near her home. Much of Laureen's work is influenced by Mexican and American-Indian pottery which she

Whitby Glass

studied whilst at university in Arizona. She specialises in hand-painted tiles, nameplates and planters made using techniques handed down through generations. Designs include birds and fish painted in oxides onto tinglazed earthenware using the Spanish Maiolica technique. Other pots are slipped, burnished and pit-fired to give wonderful metallic finishes.

Wash House Pottery

Of course, the appeal of Whitby to many of the tourists who come here, is the lure of the seafaring community, the hustle and bustle of port life, and

Street Scene, Whitby

so many Whitby establishments retain that nautical appeal about them.

In the heart of the town, at No. 29 Baxtergate, we called in at the restaurant and cafe, **The Old Smuggler.** This fine establishment can either be reached along Baxtergate, or via Loggerheads Yard which is situated directly opposite the railway station. For most of its long life (parts date back as far as 1401), this historic timber-framed building was used as an inn. Originally known as the 'Ship Launch', it was the regular haunt of shipwrights who built and launched ships on the site directly behind the inn. During the 18th- and early 19th-centuries, the inn also became known as a centre for local smuggling activities (hence the present

The Old Smuggler

name). Having relatively poor land links with the rest of the country, the part of the coast around Whitby became a favourite area of operations for smugglers and at the entrance of the building, a figurehead of a smugglers' vessel was fixed to the wall after it was broken up by excise men as a warning to those who challenged their authority. The figure is called a *loggerhead*, and the alley which leads down to the quay, Loggerhead Yard, derives its name from it. The inn was also frequented by press gangs who forced unwilling sailors into service in the Royal Navy. Unsuspecting victims would sometimes be encouraged to consume too much ale, then were bundled down to the quay and onto a ship before they had a chance to work out what was happening.

The inn relinquished its licence shortly after the Second World War, and since then it has operated as a café and restaurant. The present owner, Pat Chambers, has been here since 1971 and in that time has made many improvements to the interior whilst ensuring that the building's original style and character have been retained. Today, the low beamed ceilings, panelled walls, uneven floors and historic atmosphere remain. Pat's house speciality is 'uppercrust pastry', served with a choice of fillings which include chicken and ham, Italian pepper, spicy lamb cobbler, chicken and apricot and a number of tasty vegetarian options. (Special children's meals are also available.) The dishes are beautifully prepared and the food just melts in the mouth. The Old Smuggler is licensed to serve alcoholic drinks with meals and is open daily for morning coffees, lunches and afternoon teas. Closed evenings.

Leaving this particular establishment, and feeling in the mood for exploration of the quayside area, we passed the site of the Old Custom House, now rather paradoxically a bookmakers, which no doubt would have amused the smugglers of Whitby were they alive today.

On walking through the old town, on the east side, the cobbled streets and yards, with their alleys running down to the waterfront, convey a strong sense of a fishing community united by the power of the sea. From the old town, you can climb the famous 199 steps to the church of St Mary, the place of worship for fishermen and seafarers for centuries. The interior has a distinctly nautical feel to it, due to alterations carried out by local shipwrights in the 17th century. Today, Whitby still retains its air of a seafarers' town, with the fishing boats and cobles anchored alongside more modern keel boats, and the yachts that one can see heading towards the marina situated upriver.

In a splendid position on Whitby's bustling quayside, we found the first-rate eating house, **The Magpie Cafe.** The building dates from the 18th century and was once the home of the renowned whaling family, the Scoresbys. It was then used as a shipping office for many years before being reopened as a cafe in the 1950s. The Magpie is more a first-class restaurant than a cafe, being *Egon Ronay* recommended and mentioned in

The Magpie Cafe

Whitby Harbour

the *Good Food Guide, Wholefood Guide* and *British Relais Routier Guide*. Owners Alison and Ian Robson have built their reputation on quality; the house speciality is fresh local fish and seafood and it is said they serve the best fish and chips in the area. The seating areas have an atmosphere which is relaxed and welcoming with flowers on the tables and prints of old Whitby on the walls. The upper level also has magnificent views of the harbour. Open daily March to November. Last orders 6.30 pm.

The Scoresbys were a family of great note in the colourful annals of Whitby, and can be termed alongside James Cook as great historical figures linked to the region.

Between 1753 and 1833, Whitby was the capital of the whaling industry, with the rather dubious distinction, by today's standards, of bringing home 2761 whales in 80 years. Much of that success was due to the skills of the great whaling captains William Scoresby and his son. William Scoresby Senior was renowned for his great daring and navigational skills, as well as for the invention of the crow's nest or mast-head lookout. His son, William, possessed leanings of a more scientific nature, and occupied himself with various experiments during his long days at sea in the icy Arctic waters. He is most noted for his discoveries of the forms of snow crystals, and the invention of the "Greenland" magnet, which made ships' compasses more reliable.

The whaling industry is now, thankfully, long dead, but fortunately, the fishing industry is not, as many of Whitby's restaurants will prove, being famous for their seafood menus.

Those looking for a restaurant serving the very best in fresh locally-caught fish and seafood should on no account miss **Trenchers Seafood Restaurant** which is situated opposite the quayside in **Whitby**'s New Quay Road.

Since 1981, Trenchers has been owned and run by three siblings, Terry, Judy and Nicky Foster, and between them they have managed to create a thriving restaurant which is a genuine pleasure to visit. From the outside, Trenchers has an elegant façade with colourful awnings and an almost Edwardian quality.

Inside, the atmosphere is friendly and welcoming; the colour holly green dominates and the seating is arranged in low booths creating a feeling of relaxed intimacy. One of the restaurant's greatest assets is its staff. Some members of the team have been here for almost ten years (always a good sign), and although sometimes they have to work under great pressure, they always go about their business with a smile and give the impression that nothing is too much trouble.

Trenchers Restaurant

Trenchers other main asset is its menu. This is dominated by freshly caught fish and seafood dishes, and as well as freshly prepared entrées, includes salads and freshly-cut sandwiches. The 'secret ingredient' which is featured in many of the fish dishes is Trenchers special light and crisp savoury batter. When the freshest haddock, cod, skate or lemon sole is prepared in this delicious coating, the result is truly mouthwatering. As well as fish and seafood, the menu features traditional English dishes such as homemade steak pie and cottage pie, continental dishes such as lasagne and vegetarian dishes. Children are very welcome, and with this in mind, the restaurant offers a good choice of specially-priced children's meals. Trenchers also has a full restaurant licence and a wide selection of aperitifs, beers, house wines and non-alcoholic drinks is available from the cocktail bar. Trenchers Seafood Restaurant is renowned throughout Yorkshire, and it is well worth making a detour to experience its charming atmosphere, first-class service, excellent value for money, and above all, its wonderful food.

In a wonderful position overlooking the harbour, we discovered the **Pier Inn**, one of the oldest inns in **Whitby**. Downstairs, the bar retains much of the building's original character and charm with beamed ceilings and walls decorated with fine examples of local memorabilia. A varied selection of bar meals is available at lunchtimes and in the evenings, and on Sundays, a first-rate roast lunch is served. Since 1988, the inn has been run by Les and Janice Metcalf, and during this period, they have remodelled the upstairs to make seven beautifully appointed guest rooms. These

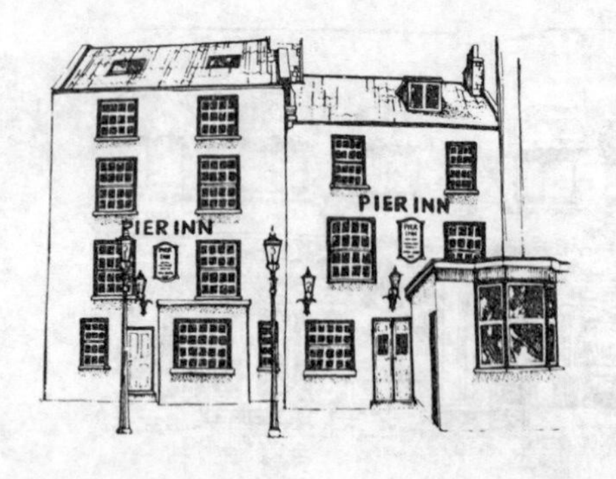

The Pier Inn

all have superb views of the harbour or sea, and are equipped with colour televisions and tea/coffee making facilities.

Near the centre of **Whitby**, we also found one of the most outstanding hotel-restaurants in the county, **Bagdale Hall**. (It is easy to find a short distance from the rail and bus stations on the A171 Guisborough road.) Originally constructed by James Conyers in 1516, Bagdale Hall is a converted medieval manor house which is said to the be the oldest

Bagdale Hall & Restaurant

inhabited building in Whitby. (Only the parish church and the Abbey are older.) During its lifetime, the building has undergone a number of major renovations. In the late 1880s, the then owner, Henry Power, began a project to restore Bagdale Hall to its former glory after it had fallen into disrepair following a sixty-year period when it had been used as tenements. A further scheme in 1914 completed Henry Power's work, and then in 1990, the present owners, Barry and June Josey, carried out a major refurbishment to convert the building to a modern first-class hotel and restaurant.

Today, the hotel has six magnificent guest rooms, all individually designed and equipped with en-suite bathrooms. All rooms have a pleasant sitting area and are splendidly equipped with colour televisions, tea/coffee making facilities, hair dryers and trouser presses. The three spacious suites on the first floor (two of which have four-poster beds) also contain sofas which convert to beds allowing them to be used as family rooms if required.

Bagdale Hall's elegant restaurant is renowned for serving one of the finest á la carte menus in the North of England. Chef Bob Shackleton's career has taken him to Kensington Palace where he cooked for Princess Margaret and to Abbey Road Recording Studios where he was a chef during the Beatles' era. He specialises in steak, duckling and lobster dishes, each prepared to the individual wishes of the diner. The hotel also has an impressive lounge and bar with original timber beams and a beautiful decoratively carved fireplace.

The building has a long reputation for being haunted by friendly spirits. Unexplained noises have been heard emanating from the kitchen and household items have been known to move of their own accord.

Unearthly characters, said to be the ghosts of 17th-century adventurer, Captain Browne Bushell, and his wife whom he returns to find, have also been seen to appear and disappear in the upper rooms and staircase.

Enjoying a stunning location perched on East Cliff in the grounds of Whitby Abbey, with magnificent views across the bay, you will find **Abbey House**. Originally the home of the Cholmleys, a prominent north country family, this beautiful Elizabethan house provides traditional home comforts and is a charming base from which to view the breath-taking scenery that surrounds it, and to discover the fascinating history of the Abbey itself. Abbey House is one of thirteen houses in the British Isles belonging to Countrywide Holidays Association, which 100 years ago, pioneered walking and special interest holidays. The Association offers excellen t value bed and breakfast accommodation for one or more nights which is booked directly with the house, whilst the special interest and walking holidays can be arranged by phoning 061 225 1000

Abbey House

One mile northwest of **Whitby** town centre along the A174 coast road, we visited the **Sandfield House Farm Caravan Park**. This quiet and friendly twelve-acre caravan park is set within lovely undulating farmland and has magnificent views over the surrounding countryside and coastline. Martin and Christine Warner have been running the site since 1985. They provide first-rate facilities for touring caravans, including electrical hook-ups, water points, coin-operated laundry facilities and a recently opened shower and toilet block.

Sandfield House Farm

Holidaymakers looking for more rustic accommodation will also not be disappointed in their travels around this area.

On the A174 midway between Whitby and Loftus, we came to the delightful hamlet of **Ellerby**. Here is located the **Ellerby Hotel**, which is owned and run by David and Janet Alderson.

Ellerby Hotel

Thanks to their vision and a great deal of hard work, a ramshackle collection of buildings has been transformed into a truly outstanding inn, hotel and restaurant. There are now nine well-appointed letting rooms, each with en suite facilities, and to the rear, an impressive residents' conservatory looks out over a beautiful flower-filled garden to breathtaking countryside beyond. The hotel restaurant serves an excellent range of meals (including lunch on Sundays) and has become particularly renowned for its sumptuous twice-monthly Chinese banquets. The Ellerby Hotel is situated a mile inland from the picturesque fishing village of Runswick Bay and is open all year round.

If you are looking for restful self-catering accommodation in the beautiful northeastern corner of the National Park, you should consider the first-rate static caravans offered by Ged and Val O'Neill at the **Grinkle Caravan Park** in **Grinkle**. This small attractive site can be found two miles south of the A174 at Easington (it may be helpful to telephone the owners (0287) 640401 for exact directions). The two-and-a-half acre site stands on part of the old Grinkle estate and is surrounded by thirty-five acres of beautiful parkland which is open to the public. There are eight spacious static caravans available which are all fully equipped with televisions, gas cookers, fridges, flush toilets, and mains water and electricity. Open March to October. Unsuitable for pets.

Grinkle Caravan Park

Also forming part of the same estate, is the **Grinkle Park Hotel**, a splendid country house hotel situated at the end of a long meandering tree-lined drive. The present house was built in 1881 by Sir Charles Mark Palmer MP, ship-builder and ironmaster, to replace the original manor house which had stood on the estate for centuries. For over sixty years, it was the Baronetcy of Grinkle, but changing times necessitated its conversion to a hotel following World War II. Today, this handsome, stone-built house stands in the 35 acres of the Grinkle estate and is the ideal place for those seeking a peaceful and luxurious break.

Grinkle Park Hotel

The hotel has excellent sports facilities including an all-weather tennis court, a croquet lawn and a billiard room with a full-sized table. It also has a fine wood-panelled entrance hall with an open fire, a delightful restaurant which is also open to non-residents, and the charming Camelia Room where guests can take afternoon teas and light meals in a relaxed and elegant atmosphere. The hotel's twenty bedrooms are individually named and decorated (two have four poster beds) and are appointed to the highest modern standard. Each has an en-suite bath or shower, colour television, direct-dial telephone, tea/coffee-making facilities and superb views over the surrounding countryside.

Three miles east of Loftus, and just to the north of the A174 Whitby to Saltburn road, we called in at **Boulby Barns Farm**, near **Boulby**. At the heart of this seven-acre working smallholding stands a renovated 18th-century stone-built farmhouse which is owned by David and Jenny Blyth. As well as running the smallholding, David and Jenny provide top quality farmhouse bed and breakfast accommodation; they have four spacious and beautifully decorated guest rooms available and offer a wonderful breakfast menu which usually includes yogurts and cheeses that are actually made on the farm.

Boulby Barns Farm

For those interested in the mining industry of the area, near to Boulby, is the mine owned by Cleveland Potash Ltd. Members of the public are invited to take a ride in the lift that services thė mine, which descends a staggering 4000 feet, said to be 4 times as long as the Empire State Building!

Despite the mining links of this area, a thriving farming community is much in evidence, and the roads are dotted with signs selling farm produce.

Northfields Farm, near **Mickleby**, also provides excellent quality farmhouse bed and breakfast accommodation from May to early October. This 330-acre working cereal farm is situated in the country approximately one mile from the A174 Whitby to Staithes road and it may be advisable to telephone the owners, Christine and Peter Prudom (0947) 840343, for directions. Their 260 year-old listed farmhouse is unusual in that, instead of being stone-built, it is constructed of handmade red bricks. Northfields Farm offers two spacious and charmingly decorated letting rooms (one double, one family), as well as traditional farmhouse breakfasts and friendly atmosphere. The course of the former coastal railway passes nearby and offers magnificent views over the surrounding countryside and coastline.

Northfields Farm

At the summit of Lythe Bank, three miles northwest of Whitby on the A174 Loftus road, we came to the charming village of **Lythe**. In a splendid position set back from the main road, we found the **Red Lion**, a traditional English inn which is run by two fine hosts, Christine and Mark Harrison. Inside, they have been successful in creating an atmosphere which is truly relaxed and friendly. They serve a good range of traditional ales, and at lunchtimes and in the evenings, a wide selection of first-rate bar meals. The Red Lion also has five letting rooms available (one family, three double, one twin), all spacious, comfortable and equipped with colour televisions and tea/coffee making facilities.

The rustic fishing port of **Staithes** is situated 9 miles up the coast

The Red Lion

from Whitby, and is a must for day trippers staying in the area.

Cars are not allowed down the exceedingly steep road into the main port area, and so you will be required to disembark and get your walking shoes on!

Staithes is notable as the place where the 17 year old James Cook worked in William Sanderson's haberdashery shop, before he set off to start his apprentice-ship for Thomas Scottowe, a friend of Sanderson.

American tourists may be interested to discover that the renowned privateer John Paul Jones launched a raid on the port for supplies before his battle with the British navy off Bridlington.

As you descend towards the famous wharf and its characteristic enclosing cliff-face, the stone chapels and rather austere architecture bear witness to strong links with its Methodist past. As you near the harbour, look out for the walkway called Slippery Hill; you don't need too much imagination to know why it was given this name, as the gradient will attest.

After a short break in this area, we headed back down the B174 and then on to the A171, in the direction of another of the region's great beauty spots, **Robin Hood's Bay**, or Baytown, as we were informed its true name was. There are several theories as to why it was given this rather unlikely name. Some claim that the famous hero hid here once, although why he would be so far from his native Sherwood Forest could be anybody's guess. A more likely explanation are the bronze age burial mounds located a mile to the south of the village, called "Robin Hood's Butts" ,which, being very distinctive, gave rise to its naming.

Although fishing is no longer the mainstay of the town, in the 18th and 19th centuries the village thrived on it. By 1920, however, there were only two fishing families left in the Bay, mainly due to lack of harbour facilities, and the industry died out. Today the interest is being revived, due to this being renowned as one of the best crab grounds on the north coast.

The reputation of the young seamen in this area was held very highly indeed, and press gangs from the Royal Navy were sent here to procure men for their vessels. Apparently the local women had different ideas, and were reported to have discouraged the gangs by means of pans and rolling pins!

Because of the natural isolation of the bay, smuggling played a great part in the prosperity of the town in the 18th and 19th centuries, much of it reputedly financed by the local squires, who risked hanging for lucrative gains. In 1856 the coastguards were given the task of tracking down the miscreants, but soon found the task too difficult, and the Whitby-based excise-men and dragoons were brought in to assist. The houses and inns in the Bay were said to have connecting cellars and cupboards, and it is reported that "a bale of silk could pass from the bottom of the village to the top without seeing daylight"

Shipwrecks play another major role in the history of the Bay, as the many reefs that surround the coast would indicate. A notable episode occurred in 1881, when a large brig called "Visitor" was run aground. The seas were so rough that the lifeboat from Whitby had to be dragged eight miles in the snow to Robin Hood's Bay to be launched. In the end, it was the brave people of the village who rescued the crew, a much lauded event in the history of the community.

The town itself has not escaped totally from the ravages of the sea, and on several occasions parts of it have been swept into it. The construction of the sea-wall in 1975, at a cost of £578,000, has however since prevented any such repetitions of this occurring.

The view of the Bay from the top of the hill is breathtaking indeed, and the buildings with their adjoining byways, with such interesting names as Jim Bell's Stile, Covet Hill and the Stocks are charming. In fact, the whole of the town exudes an air of cosy tranquility, and this is to be found in many of the inns and boarding houses that can be found there.

Those looking for an excellent morning coffee, light lunch, afternoon tea or evening meal in this lovely place should look for **The Bramblewick** on the quayside.

Formerly an old fisherman's cottage and bakery (at one time, the baker used to charge the locals one penny for heating their roasts), parts

The Bramblewick

Staithes

of the building date back over 400 years. Owners, Linda and Andrew Carter, concentrate on preparing fine home-cooked dishes, especially those using fresh local fish and seafood. All the cakes and puddings are homemade and include such tempting offerings as 'Temple of Doom' and 'Tombstone pudding'. Evening booking advisable.

Some small way out of Baytown, is the cliff-top village of **Ravenscar**, noted for its views and wildlife walks.

Whilst on the main road into the village, we also stopped off at the **Wellfield Trekking Centre**, which is run by Carol and Mick Foulds. The centre specialises in riding holidays for unaccompanied young people of between eight and sixteen years of age, and is an ideal place for those keen to combine horse riding with a great deal of fun. Wellfield lies within an area of great scenic beauty and is surrounded by bridlepaths which lead onto the nearby moors, through woodland and down to the beach. The centre caters for all levels of riding experience and provides tuition if required. At the start of the holiday, each person is allocated their own horse or pony and is encouraged to take personal care of their mount for the duration of their stay. Other activities at the centre include trips to nearby towns, swimming pools and fun parks, and judging by the comments of the participants, an excellent time is to be had by all.

Wellfield Trekking Centre

In a magnificent position near the southern end of Robin Hood's Bay, we found the **Smuggler's Rock Country Guest House**. This handsome Georgian House stands on the approach to the village of Ravenscar, and is well situated for those wishing to explore the the surrounding countryside and coastline.

This former coaching inn once had links with smugglers and in the east wall, there is a small window through which a light was shone when it was safe to bring up contraband through the tunnels that led to the house.. Today Smugglers Rock has been tastefully renovated and offers ten en-suite guest rooms, all with colour televisions and tea/coffee making facilities. Open March to mid-November. Two well-equipped holiday cottages are also available all year round.

Smugglers Rock

In a superb position overlooking the surrounding countryside and coastline of this particular area, we found the **Foxcliffe Tea Rooms**. Standing adjacent to the old Scarborough to Whitby railway line, the building was constructed in 1891 as the Station Hotel. Today, these charming tearooms are personally run by Mrs Diana Wicks. She is renowned for her home baking and prepares most of the items on the menu herself. The tearooms are open for light lunches and afternoon teas from 11.30am to 5pm daily, Easter to September.

Diana also provides year-round bed and breakfast accommodation with an optional evening meal. She has four spacious letting rooms available, all tastefully decorated and equipped with first-rate modern facilities. Unsuitable for smokers or pets.

Anyone seeking bed and breakfast or self-catering accommodation on the eastern side of the North York Moors National Park should make a point of finding **Rosalie's Farmhouse Accommodation and Holiday Cottages at Chapel Farm**. Rosalie's is situated in a tucked-away location on the western edge of Harwood Dale Forest between the A171 Scarbor--

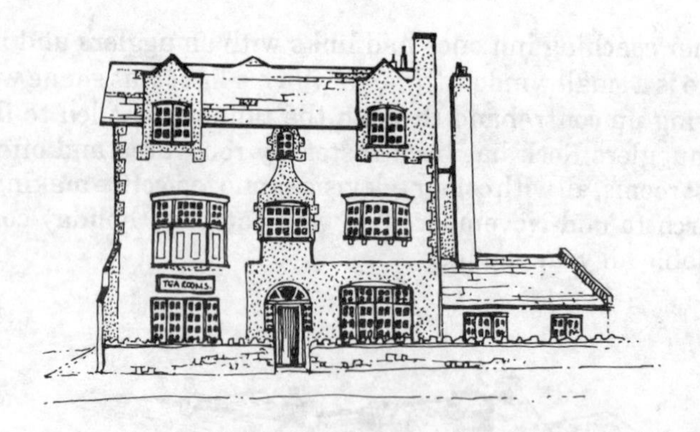

Foxcliffe Tearooms

-ough to Whitby road and the village of Harwood Dale (5 miles south-west of Ravenscar), so it may be advisable to telephone the owners, Rosalie and Howard Richardson (0723) 870288, for directions. Surrounded by superb countryside and standing within its own thirty-acre estate, Chapel Farm dates from the reign of Elizabeth I. The historic remains of St Margaret's Chapel lie within the grounds a short distance to the south of the main house and are definitely worth a visit. The present-day farmhouse has been tastefully modernised and offers top quality bed and breakfast accommodation. There are three comfortable guest rooms available, one large double, one double and one twin. The large double is equipped with en suite facilities, a king-size bed, colour television and tea/coffee making facilities. It is also suitable for use as a family room. The other rooms both have hot and cold washbasins and beverage making facilities. Guests are welcome to use the comfortable drawing room and are served splendid Yorkshire breakfasts each morning.

Rosalie and Howard also have two attractive self-catering holiday cottages available. The Barn Cottage has been converted from an original cow byre and sleeps up to six people in two bedrooms, one with a double bed, the other with four singles. The kitchen is equipped with a dishwasher, split level cooker and washing machine, and the sitting room has a colour television and a gas fire to supplement the central heating. Outside, there is a large private garden equipped with tables, chairs and a barbecue. Cruck Cottage has two bedrooms (one double, one twin), plus two Z-beds. An unusual stone arch entrance leads into a large living room which has a wood-burning fire and colour television; the fully-fitted kitchen has a microwave oven and is appointed to a high standard. On summer weekday afternoons, the farmhouse opens as a tea shop serving delicious homemade cakes, pastries and drinks. A range of handmade pottery, locally-painted pictures and a selection of Howard's home-grown dried flowers is also available.

Rosalie's Farmhouse Accommodation

Travelling further down towards **Scarborough** (Detailed in chapter 2), we came across **Scalby Close Park**. It is situated in a sheltered position surrounded by mature trees on the A165 Burniston Road. This family-run site is owned and personally run by Peter and Maureen Bayes, and although small-scale, offers a standard normally only to be found on larger impersonal sites.

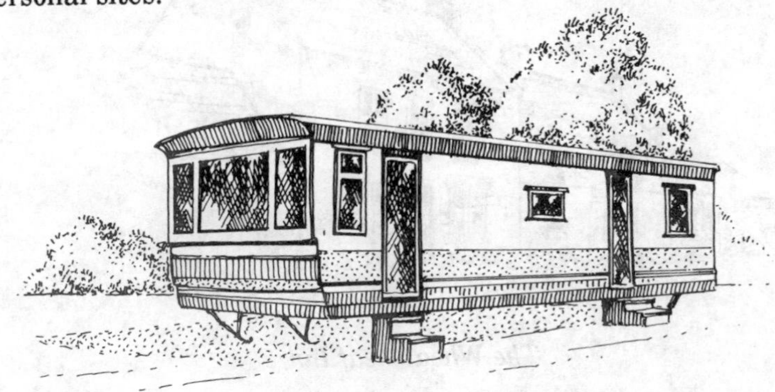

Scalby Close Park

On-site facilities include a well-stocked mini-market, modern shower/ toilet block, washerette and electrical hook-ups. A number of two and three-bedroomed self-catering holiday homes are also available. These sleep five to seven people and have fully-equipped kitchens with fridges and microwave ovens, and spacious lounges with colour televisions.

Returning to the A171, we travelled back up towards Whitby, in order to gain access to the increasingly popular but nonetheless very lovely Eskdale and moorland areas.

Eskdale is renowned for its salmon fishing, and such placenames as Great and Little Fryupdale certainly stimulate one's appetite, although the term "fry" is more likely to be due to the term used for young fish, rather than to methods of cooking them!

It is worthwhile noting, that should anyone wish to travel to the area with the intention of taking advantage of the abundancy of salmon, the inland waters are not public property, and permission must be obtained from the land-owner first. A rod license and permit will also be required (Details of these are obtainable from the local branch of the National Rivers Authority).

Between the A171 and the River Esk six miles to the southwest of Whitby, we came to the delightful Eskdale village of **Egton**. Here we found the impressive traditional inn and guesthouse, the **Wheatsheaf Inn**, which has been owned since 1978 by Albert and Susan Latus, and is now managed by their son Michael.

The Wheatsheaf Inn

Parts of this fine inn date back 450 years and inside, much of its original character and charm have been retained with beamed ceilings, open fires and a wood-panelled bar area. A good selection of bar meals is served here, and a splendid collection of bank notes from all over the world decorates the room.

A first-class restaurant has been created in the adjacent building which at one time was a cowshed. This has magnificent stone walls, a relaxed and stylish atmosphere, and a menu which offers an extensive range of dishes. On the day we visited, the daily specials included pheasant braised with spring vegetables, lemon marinated chicken and homemade vegetarian chilli.

The residents' lounge is spacious and elegant, and the guest rooms all have en suite facilities and are appointed to the highest modern standards. Look out for the superb room at the top of the house which has a truly unique atmosphere. The Wheatsheaf caters for fishing and shooting parties, and being situated only a mile-and-a-half from the North Yorkshire Moors Railway terminus at Grosmont, provides the ideal base for exploring the nearby moors and coastline.

In our wanderings around Eskdale, we came to **Lealholm**, a picturesque village set on the side of the moors, where we discovered a delightful and unusual shrub nursery owned and run by Hilda Rees. **Poet's Cottage** is built on the site where the poet John Castillo lived, hence the name. It is situated on the bank of the river Esk and is an example of something "that just grew".

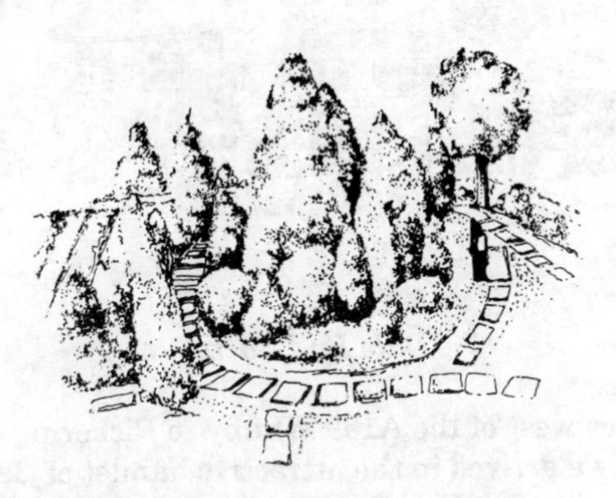

Poets Cottage Shrub Nursery

Started in 1978 by Mrs Rees and her late husband, the nursery developed as a result of locals and visitors asking to look round what, originally, was the Rees' private garden. Now several years later, Poet's

Cottage offers a mature setting for the many trees and shrubs that fill the beautiful landscaped garden with their ever-changing colours. A garden made for retirement has become a treasure trove of interesting specimens. Hilda Rees and her qualified and knowledgeable staff welcome not only buyers but also visitors who just want to browse around this unusual nursery.

Holidaymakers looking for top quality farmhouse accommodation in beautiful Eskdale should look for **Dale End Farm** at **Green End**. This delightful working hill farm is truly well-hidden between the villages of Grosmont and Goathland, so it may be advisable to telephone the owner, Marion Cockrem (0947) 85371, for directions. The stone-built farmhouse enjoys magnificent views of the Esk Valley, and inside, the open inglenook fireplace, oak-beamed ceilings and traditional furnishings help to retain much of its original 18th-century character. Mrs Cockrem's traditional Yorkshire breakfasts and evening meals are delicious and generously proportioned. The farmyard is full of fascinating animals including lambs, calves and unusual Vietnamese pot-bellied pigs. Open all year round.

Dale End Farm

Three miles west of the A169 Whitby to Pickering road and a mile from Goathland,we arrived in the attractive hamlet of **Beckhole**. Set in the heart of spectacular Yorkshire countryside, Beckhole was once a thriving industrial community with its own blast furnace. Today, only an inn and eleven cottages remain, one of which is a charming guesthouse owned and run by Lesley Holland. The **Brookwood Farm Guest House** offers four spacious and delightfully decorated letting rooms, and provides

Beggar's Bridge, Eskdale

guests with excellent hospitality and delicious Yorkshire breakfasts and evening meals. It is open all year round and welcomes children and pets. The farm has its own fishing rights for guests and also keeps a small collection of rare animals.

Brookwood Farm Guesthouse

Standing near to the Thomasson Fosse waterfall is the unique inn and teahouse, the **Birch Hall Inn**. The inn has been licensed since the early-1700s and gives the impression of having changed little since. Inside, there is a bar with room for only a handful of people, a seated area where customers are served through a hatch, and between the two, a charming sweet shop.

The Birch Hall Inn

The inn is decorated with old toys, tins and other evocative memorabilia, and conveys the feeling that time has stood still. The bar offers sandwiches, pies and other simple fare, and in the tearoom above, delicious afternoon teas are served in an atmosphere which has hardly changed for a century.In the delightful Eskdale village of **Glaisdale**, we found an exceptional bed and breakfast and self-catering establishment, **Red House Farm**. This handsome farmhouse has parts dating from the 17th-century and a number of alterations and extensions dating from the 18th-century. The present-day house stands within six acres of land and has been carefully modernised so as to retain as much of its original character and charm as possible. The interior has low beamed ceilings, stone slab floors, a fine inglenook fireplace and has been decorated with great attention to detail.

Owners, Tom and Sandra Spashett have been here since 1987 and in that time have built up an establishment with truly first-class facilities. They have three letting rooms available (two double, one single); all have en suite facilities and are furnished to an extremely high standard. As well as delicious farmhouse breakfasts, by arrangement they also serve evening meals using fresh local ingredients wherever possible. (Fresh cow's milk and dairy produce are available from the farm each day.) In addition to the farmhouse accommodation, an 18th century threshing barn, itself a listed building, is being converted, the aim being to provide first-rate self-catering holiday accommodation and lie within easy reach of the moors and the coast at Whitby.

Red House Farm

Look out for Tom and Sandra's collection of traditional farmyard animals including geese, ducks and rare breeds of poultry, and also for the duck pond and herb garden which they were in the process of completing when we visited.

We found a particularly peaceful and relaxing hotel in a very quiet location in the heart of the North York Moors called the **Whitfield House Hotel**, near **Goathland**. The hotel is situated on the edge of the delightful hamlet of Darnholm and it may be advisable to telephone the owners, John and Pauline Lusher (0947) 86215 for directions. The handsome hotel building is a former farmhouse dating from the 17th-century. Much of its original character and charm have been retained and inside, the atmosphere is truly relaxed and welcoming.

Whitfield House Hotel

The cottage-style bedrooms all have bathrooms en-suite and are equipped with radio-alarms, hair dryers and tea/coffee making facilities. The standard of service is high and the full English breakfasts and four-course table d'hôte dinners offer the very best in country cooking. The hotel lies a short distance from the stepping stones at Darnholm and within easy reach of many superb woodland and moorland walks. Open March to October inclusive.

Goathland, well served by train, car or bus, describes itself as a moorland resort as indeed it is. Sheltered by the surrounding moorlands from cold winds, it has a surprisingly mild climate for a village so high above sea level, and a beautiful situation. Many of the houses have wonderful views of the moors and this is especially true of **Prudom House**, a renovated farmhouse owned by Ian and Viv MacCaig.

Prudom House

The house stands on the second oldest site in the village, the original building going back to the 12th century. The name "Prudom" was probably that of a sheep-stealer who, it is believed, was hanged for his activities! The sheep now wander safely across the green in front of this lovely old house which provides comfortable, homely accommodation. Whilst preserving the farmhouse "feel" with exposed beams, log fires, oak panelling and stone-work, the MacCaigs have incorporated modern features. Some bedrooms have en-suite shower and toilet and tea and coffee facilities. There is central heating in all rooms. The food is home-cooked to produce out-of-the-ordinary country dishes and the house has a residential table license. In addition, the MacCaigs have a small tea-room alongside the house serving morning coffee, snacks, soup, granary rolls and afternoon teas. Within the tea room you will find local products on display and for sale such as glassware, woodwork and metalwork.

Our main impressions of Goathland were that it had that definite air of "getting away from civilisation" that most of the avid hiking enthusiasts we met were seeking. That is not to say that the facilities on offer are anything less than excellent, but the horned moorland sheep that wander along the roads, with not a care for any of the cars whose progress they often hinder, are a constant reminder of this fact. There is a Brigadoon-type quality about the place, which, on suddenly coming across this little haven after driving (or walking) across miles of wild and isolated moorland, you cannot fail to notice.

As one might imagine with an isolated community such as this one, the traditions go back far, and none so far as the origins of the Plough Stots Service, a ritual sword dance performed in the town every January. The Nordic settlers brought this particular ceremony to these parts over a thousand years ago, the "stot" being derived from the Scandinavian word for a bullock. In the ancient procession, young men of the village drag a plough through the street, in place of the bullocks that would normally perform the task. The dancers follow, brandishing 30 inch swords, in a pagan ritual that the Norsemen were keen to retain after their invasion of the area (and who would argue with them!)

The main items of local interest to note are the famous Roman road, trodden by thousands of hiking enthusiasts each year, the steam train route from Goathland to Grosmont, (part of which follows the original route built by George Stevenson in 1845), the 70ft Mallyan Spout Waterfall, reached by a footpath close to the hotel (there are other waterfalls also in the area, including Nelly Ayre Foss and Thomasson Fosse), and of course the many varied walks through the breathtaking countryside that surrounds the village.

In a splendid position overlooking the wide expanses of Goathland Moor, we found the **Mallyan Spout Hotel**, named after the waterfall previously mentioned, which flows into a wooded valley a short distance away. This handsome ivy-clad, stone-built hotel provides a perfect base for those interested in outdoor pursuits or the peaceful pleasures of fine food, good wines and charming hospitality.

Inside, the atmosphere is friendly and the surroundings luxurious. There is a cocktail bar and three spacious guest lounges with views over attractive gardens to the moors and beautiful Esk valley beyond. Each of the 24 individually decorated bedrooms has a private bathroom, colour television, telephone and radio. Most are decorated in cottage style and have breathtaking views over the surrounding countryside and moorland. In the coach house, two double and two twin rooms are available at ground floor level for those finding stairs a problem.

The hotel has been owned and personally run by Judith and Peter Heslop since the early 1970s. They ensure their guests receive a professional standard of service which makes them feel instantly at home. The hotel restaurant is renowned for its cuisine and is open to residents and non-residents alike. The menu is long and adventurous and features freshly caught seafood from Whitby. On the day we visited, the chef's specialities included the starter, 'fresh pear poached in rosemary and lime with fresh coriander, stilton and creme fraiche mousse', and the main course, 'sauteed medallions of monkfish with a pink and green peppercorn sauce served on a bed of wild rice'. All dishes are freshly cooked to order and they may require a short while to prepare. The results, however, are mouthwatering and well worth waiting for.

Mallyan Spout Hotel

The Mallyan Spout Hotel provides an ideal base for exploring the many nearby beauty spots and places of historic interest. The privately-owned North Yorkshire Moors Railway stops at nearby Goathland station and offers a fascinating excursion through heather-clad hills, wooded valleys and charming moorland villages. The hotel also runs a programme of special weekends for the gourmet or for those interested in such activities as hill-walking and fishing.

If you were to take an excursion on the B169 towards Pickering, your attention would be drawn to three huge objects that dominate the skyline on **Fylingdales Moor**. You may well be forgiven for believing yourself to be viewing something straight out of a science-fiction movie. The structures, each some 150 feet in height stand, in a row, like immense golf-balls, lined up, ready for some giant golfer to tee-off; the scene is bizarre, to say the least. The moor at this point is rather bleak and foreboding, and the inclusion of these objects only intensifies this feeling. In the 1950s, at the height of the Cold War, the structures were erected as part of a nuclear early warning system by the American air-force, although they are now deemed redundant, or at least out-moded. These signal receivers have, however, become so much part of the landscape, that there is a debate currently taking place to decide whether they are of sufficient architectural merit to be kept on.

Driving along the B169 towards Pickering leaves one with an impression of the grand isolation of this place. It would be advisable, however, not to run out of petrol at this point! The most environmentally-friendly way to view it, though, must be on foot, and should one's resolve run out, a ride for the remainder of the journey can be taken on the steam train route.

Deciding to make tracks back towards civilisation, we made our way back to the A 171, and travelled west, past Danby and Guisborough. Just outside Danby, we called in at the **Danby Lodge National Moors Centre**, an excellent facility for those who might wish to take full advantage of the recreational value of the moors. Here they organise all manner of walks, for wildlife enthusiasts right through to those with more active requirements. There are good parking facilities here, as well as those for disabled visitors.

We then headed off down the B173, through Great Ayton, famous as the place where James Cook spent his youth. Passing through the village we passed the place commemorating the former site of the Cooks' family home, which was transported in 1934, brick by brick, creepers and all, to Point Hicks in Australia. An obelisk in Australian stone is all that remains in Great Ayton today. The skyline at Great Ayton is made distinctive by the peculiarly shaped hill known as **Roseberry Topping**, sometimes called the Matterhorn of Yorkshire, which rises to 1000 feet above the village. Beyond that, one can also see the Captain Cook Monument up on Kildale Moor. We carried on then towards the attractive market town of **Stokesley**.

Those wishing to participate in a painting, drawing or arts-related course should make a point of discovering **The Byre Yard** at nearby Tanton Hall Farm. This fascinating centre is located in a group of 18th-century farm buildings in the hamlet of **Tanton**, one mile north of Stokesley. Arranged around an enclosed courtyard, the buildings have been carefully transformed by Barbara and Richard Agar into a peaceful studio and learning facility.

Day, weekend and holiday courses are offered, with residential participants being welcome to stay in the first-class accommodation situated in a private wing of Barbara and Richard's home. When not being used by course participants, bed and breakfast is available to outsiders. Good access for the disabled.

Stokesley itself is a charming, quiet little town, the peacefulness only broken on Fridays, which is market day. The town consists of the market square, rows of elegant Georgian houses and a number of old

Byre Yard

bridges which span the River Leven. An old water wheel marks the entrance to the town. 700 years ago, the town was owned by the Balliol family, one of the descendants of which is remembered as the founder of the Oxford college of that name.

As the B1257 starts to climb towards the Cleveland Hills, we reached the pleasant moorside community of Great Broughton. On the eastern edge of the village, we dropped in on Margaret and Len Sutcliffe who provide first-rate bed and breakfast accommodation at their home, Ingle Hill.

Ingle Hill

This attractive modern Dormer bungalow was built to a high specification by Len in 1977. (Nowadays Len puts his skills to work tending the delightful flower-filled garden which surrounds the house.)

Inside, the atmosphere is relaxed and welcoming; the guest rooms are spacious, homely and tastefully decorated, and enjoy magnificent views over the surrounding countryside. Ingle Hill is well located for reaching dramatic Bilsdale and the nearby Cleveland Way and Coast to Coast long-distance footpaths.

Whilst travelling on the minor road midway between the A19 and A172, we came across **Harker Hill** farmhouse bed and breakfast, near **Seamer**. This 250 year-old farmhouse is set at the heart of a thirty-acre working mixed farm with magnificent views over the surrounding country-side.Mrs Pam Thompson provides her guests with the warmest of welcomes and a first-rate farmhouse breakfast. She also prepares delicious evening meals by prior arrangement.

There are four spacious letting rooms available, all comfortably appointed and equipped with hot and cold washbasins. An attractive garden surrounds the house where guests are welcome to sit and sunbathe. Harker Hill is located within easy reach of Teeside, the Cleveland Hills and the North York Moors.

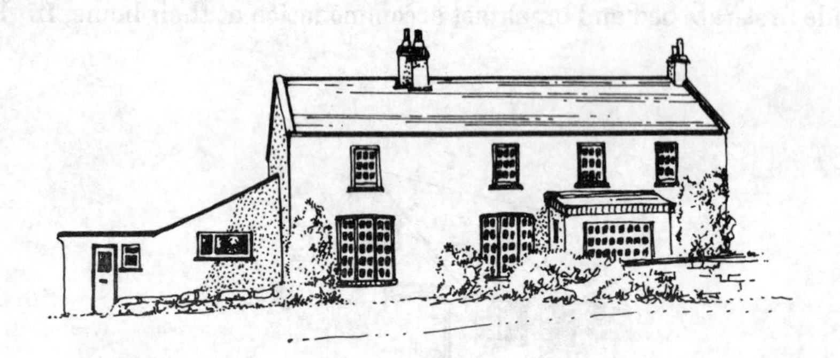

Harker Hill

On the edge of the Hambleton Hills two miles east of the A19 Thirsk to Middlesbrough road, we came to the charming village of **Nether Silton**. Here, we found the impressive freehouse and restaurant, the **Gold Cup**

Inn, which has been owned since January 1992 by Linda and Graham Makin. The inn was named in commemoration of one of the earliest flat races to be run in England in 1715. Inside, the atmosphere is cosy and intimate, with Chef Graham personally preparing the dishes for the excellent restaurant menu. The bar serves fine traditional ales. There are also two double guest rooms available, one of which has en suite facilities.

Around this particular area, the countryside seems very intimate and cosy, an impression created by the closeness of the surrounding hills and trees. Of all the places we travelled through, the areas around Nether and Over Silton and Osmotherly gave the closest impression of a "hidden place" that we had found so far. Places of note around here worth a visit are; the country park area above Osmotherly that offers splendid views over Stockton and Darlington, the lovely village of Osmotherley itself, famous as the starting point of the famous Lyke Wake Walk and the pretty church of St Mary, Over Silton, accessible only by walking across two fields.

Gold Cup Inn

On the western edge of the National Park four miles northeast of Thirsk, a minor road led us to the lovely village of **Boltby**. Here, we called in at the first-class riding centre, the **Boltby Pony Trekking Centre**, which has been run since 1987 by Jim and Sheila Ashby. The trekking centre is part of a 120-acre working mixed farm whose 200 year-old farmhouse was formerly a local pub, the Johnstone Arms. Jim and Sheila have around sixteen ponies and horses available for one- and two-hour accompanied rides, and for longer forest and moorland hacks through the delightful

Hambleton Hills. All levels of age and experience are catered for, including special provision for the disabled on shorter rides. Open all year round. Booking advisable.

Boltby Trekking Centre

We turned north off the A170 Thirsk to Helmsley road at Sutton-under-Whitestonecliffe and after one mile arrived in the charming village of **Thirlby**, home of the internationally renowned furniture workshop, **Pear Tree House**.

Home of the Wren

In 1979, Bob Hunter and his family acquired some farm buildings in the centre of the village which, after several months of hard work, were converted into woodworking and carving workshops. These are now known as the **'Home of the Wren'** after the little birds which frequented the buildings during their restoration and which later became the trademark which is carved onto all pieces of finished oak furniture. Visitors are invited to tour the workshops and to view the completed work. Open Monday to Saturday, 10am to 5pm.

Not far away, in nearby **Felixkirk**, a short walk from the centre of the village led us to **Foxhills Hideaways,** a real find for those looking for good self-catering accommodation. Gill Mayne and her daughter Andrea have four impressive Scandinavian-style log cabins available which are carefully sited in beautiful wooded grounds. Each cabin is appointed to a high modern standard and contains lounge. kitchen and dining area, two bedrooms, and shower room. Also within the grounds is a 'winter garden" with table-tennis and pool table and an attractive children's play area surrounded by trees. Free pony-trekking is included in holidays at Foxhills.

Foxhills Hideaways

After Felixkirk, we made our way back on to the A170, and made a detour to the marvellous remains of **Rievaulx Abbey**, a sight definitely not to be missed in a tour of this area. The setting for this wonderful example of Gothic architecture, nestling as it does in a sheltered and deeply wooded valley, only serves to emphasise the size and magnificence of the construction. It is said to be one of the most beautiful of any monastry in the country, and visiting it as we did in the evening, just as the sun was setting, we were inclined to agree. The original Abbey was founded in 1132 and was the first Cistercian Abbey in the north of England. The stone used in it's construction is Corallian limestone, quarried at nearby Hollin Wood and transported by means of the small canal built for this purpose. The most famous Abbot of Rievaulx was Aelred, originally an Anglo-Saxon nobleman from Hexham in Northumberland, and a statue dedicated to him stands in the centre of Helmsley, three miles from here. The most pleasant approach to the abbey is possibly via the terraces and temples, created for Thomas Duncombe in the mid 18th century, and many of the postcard views are taken from this route.

Like many of the ruins in the area, the Abbey is occasionally used for musical events, and the what's on section of local newspapers and tourist guides should be viewed to find out when these occur.

Two miles west of Rievaulx Abbey, between the A170 Thirsk to Helmsley and B1257 Bilsdale roads, we came to the picturesque village of **Old Byland**. Set in the heart of the village with stunning views over the surrounding North Yorkshire countryside, we found **Valley View Farm**, a traditional working farm which also offers first-rate farmhouse accommodation.

Valley View Farm

There are four spacious guest rooms in all, two in the house and two in the tastefully converted adjoining barn. All have en suite shower- or bathrooms, colour televisions and tea/coffee making facilities. The owner, Mrs Sally Robinson, provides excellent Yorkshire hospitality and superb farmhouse breakfasts and evening meals. Valley View Farm is open all

Rievaulx Abbey

year round and welcomes children and pets.

Those looking for honest farmhouse accommodation in the heart of beautiful Bilsdale should look for **Wethercote Farm**, near **Laskill**. Situated in a rural position half-a-mile west of the village, it may be advisable to telephone the owner, Mrs Winnie Wood (04396) 260, for directions.

Wethercote Farm

This working hill farm is set amongst spectacular moorland scenery making it the ideal base for walkers. There are three spacious guest rooms available, all with access to a bathroom and a shower-room (both with WCs). There is also a comfortable guests' sitting room with a colour television and a roaring coal fire on cool evenings. Mrs Wood provides her guests with delicious breakfasts, packed lunches by arrangement, home-baked cakes and the warmest Yorkshire hospitality.

We stopped off briefly at nearby **Helmsley**, possibly most notable for the famous **Duncombe Park**, dating from 1713, and home of the Duncombe family for that time. It was described by Arthur Young in 1770 as,

"The place in this country by far most worth the attention of the curious traveller, it cannot be viewed without the most exquisite enjoyment."

The building and its gardens were designed in 1713 by William Wakefield for the afore-mentioned Thomas Duncombe, a great lover of the grand, classical style of architecture. His descendants, Lord and Lady Feversham still own the property today. Another landmark of the area is Helmsley Castle, which is located not too far from the market square. The

Helmsley

tower still stands to its full height, despite the fact that half of the castle was blasted away during the Civil War.

The countryside around Helmsley is beautiful indeed and two-and-a-half miles north of the A170 Pickering to Kirkbymoorside road at Keldholme, we stopped in the lovely hillside village of **Hutton-le-Hole**, home of the famous **Ryedale Folk Museum**.

In a splendid position overlooking the village green, we found the **Burnley House Country Hotel**, an elegant Georgian pantiled building which dates from 1787. Inside, many of its original features have been retained, including stone-flagged floors and beamed ceilings. The hotel is furnished with fine locally-made furniture and all of the seven delightfully-decorated bedrooms have en suite facilities, remote-control colour televisions and tea/coffee making facilities.

Burnley House Country Hotel

Owners, Jean and Bryce Benson, specialise in traditional English cooking using fresh locally-sourced ingredients wherever possible. The hotel is unsuitable for young children, smokers and pets.

Standing adjacent to the Ryedale Folk Museum we found the fine country inn, **The Crown**, which has been run since 1986 by Phil Mintoft. The present inn was built in the 1940s on the site of the old Crown Inn, and during its construction a number of coins were found which dated back to 1770. The Crown has built up an excellent reputation for the quality of its food and drink; as well as a fine range of traditional hand-pulled beers, an extensive restaurant menu is served which offers a choice of over twenty main courses including those suitable for vegetarians. The Crown also has

The Crown

first-rate facilities for five touring caravans within its attractive grounds

Almost next door to the Folk Museum and certainly looking very photogenic is **Quaker Cottage,** built over 300 years ago as a traditional Yorkshire "longhouse".

Quaker Cottage

The building was unique in that it had only one third dwelling with two thirds byres. Up to 1920 there were only two windows, one to each storey. After renovation (1920), the cottage became a teashop - "The Golden Teapot" but prior to this it's history is fascinating. Between 1695 and 1745,

John Richardson, one of the best known members of the Quaker movement, lived in the cottage and from here travelled to America three times, to Ireland, Wales and extensively throughout England,no mean feat during this era.

Quaker Cottage is now a small, licensed guesthouse, owned and run by Maureen and Bill Campbell-Trotter who offer their guests a warm welcome and individual attention.

The Campbell-Trotters spent considerable time working in the Far East before settling in the lovely old village which they now regard as home. On more than one occasion guest have been tempted back to the cottage by Maureen's cooking and have recommended it to their friends. Bills' passion is golf with oil-painting a close second - something he shares with others in the village by running the local Art Club.

We found it a charming and friendly guest house with open fires, easy chairs and enchanting bedrooms - old fashioned surroundings with modern facilities, including central heating. A four-course breakfast is served with the option of a four-course evening meal in the guest's lounge-dining room. The high standard, traditional home cooking is something not to be missed.

On the dramatic cross-moor road between Hutton-le-Hole and Castleton, we came to the fine 16th-century freehouse, the **Lion Inn** at **Blakey**.

The Lion Inn

The inn stands in a superb position on the ridge between Rosedale and Farndale at the highest point in the North Yorkshire Moors National Park. It is thought the inn was founded in the 1550s by local friars keen to supplement their meagre monastic income. Two centuries later, farmers established a market here to sell surplus corn to the horse breeders and stable owners of Ryedale, then in the mid-19th century the inn flourished during a time of increased mining activity in the area. Following a period of decline at the beginning of this century, the Lion has undergone a renaissance thanks to wider car ownership and an increased interest in the rural environment.

The Lion Inn has been run since 1980 by Barry and Diane Crossland. Together, they have been successful at retaining the historic atmosphere of the inn whilst still providing a high modern standard of hospitality. The bar offers an extensive selection of top quality bar meals, including vegetarian and children's dishes and a special three-course lunch on Sundays. There is also a delightful candlelit restaurant serving a superb á la carte menu. The inn has nine well-appointed letting rooms available (including a romantic honeymoon suite with four-poster bed) and outside, there are facilities for campers with breakfast provided if required

A particularly peaceful haven on the southern edge of the North York Moors can be found at the **Lastingham Grange Country House Hotel** in the historic village of **Lastingham**. Built around an attractive courtyard, this fine establishment stands in ten acres of landscaped grounds on the northern side of the village, five miles northeast of Kirkbymoorside.

Lastingham Grange

Originally a 17th-century farmhouse, the Grange was transformed into a country house in the 1920s, then following World War II, it became a hotel which has remained under the personal ownership of the Wood family since the mid-1950s. There are twelve comfortable guest rooms, all with private bathrooms, and a spacious lounge and dining room overlooking the terrace and rose garden

The village of **Rosedale Abbey** must be one of the loveliest in the National Park. It is situated on a minor moorland road seven miles north of the A170 Pickering to Kirkbymoorside road (turn off at Wrelton) and is a perfect example of a North Yorkshire moorland settlement. The village stands at the heart of beautiful Rosedale and is surrounded by wild open moorland, fast-flowing streams, attractive woodlands and rolling farmland. In a splendid position overlooking the green in the centre of the village, we found the first-class hotel and inn, the **Milburn Arms Hotel**. With parts dating back 350 years, this former manor farmhouse was the centre of a working farm until the 1950s. Inside, it still retains much of its original character and charm with stone-flagged floors, low beamed ceilings and an atmosphere which is friendly and welcoming. The hotel has twelve superb bedrooms, all individually designed and furnished to give each its own special character. All are appointed to a very high standard and are equipped with en-suite bathrooms, colour televisions, telephones and beverage making facilities. Downstairs, residents can relax in the elegant drawing room with its log fire, soft sofas and interesting collection of books.

Milburn Arms Hotel

Good food and wine is an essential part of a visit to the Milburn Arms and owners, Terry and Joan Bentley, pride themselves in the quality and range of their cuisine. The chef uses fresh local produce wherever possible, including fish from Whitby and local game in season.

The emphasis is on traditional English cooking presented with flair and imagination and accompanied by a selection of fine wines from most of the wine-producing regions of the world. In addition to the restaurant menu, homemade bistro-style meals are served every lunchtime and evening in the bar. The Milburn Arms is also known as Rosedale Abbey's village pub and is a lively meeting place for locals and visitors alike. With its low beams and log fires, the atmosphere is relaxed and friendly and it is an ideal place to chat with the regulars or enjoy a traditional game of darts or dominoes. The bar offers a choice of around twenty different malt whiskies, a dozen different cognacs, and for the real-ale drinker, a fine selection of traditional beers which are kept in first-class condition and served by hand-pump.

If you are searching for good quality farmhouse bed and breakfast accommodation in this beautiful part of Rosedale, look for **Sycamores Farm**, one mile from the village. (Telephone the owners, Lorraine and Trevor Dale (07515) 448, for directions.) This modern centrally-heated farmhouse is part of a working dairy farm. The bedrooms are all equipped with hot and cold washbasins and tea/coffee making facilities, and the comfortable guest lounge has a colour television and breathtaking views over Rosedale. Lorraine and Trevor provide hearty Yorkshire breakfasts and excellent value evening meals by arrangement. Children and pets are welcome.

Sycamores Farm

In a splendid rural position a short distance nearby, one can also find first-rate farmhouse accommodation at **Five Acre View**. (For directions, it may be best to telephone the owners, Alison and Malcolm Dale (07515)

213.) The house is situated at the heart of a 150-acre dairy farm and was constructed on the site of an old miner's cottage using the stone from the original building. Alison and Malcolm have been providing hospitality for their guests since the mid-1980s. They provide comfortable accommodation, first-class breakfasts, and evening meals by prior arrangement. The centrally-heated guest rooms are decorated in a country style and all have hot and cold washbasins, colour televisions and tea/coffee making facilities. Downstairs there is a comfortable lounge where guests can relax and watch satellite television in front of an open fire. For those interested in angling, trout fishing is permitted along a nearby stretch of the River Seven. Open all year round.

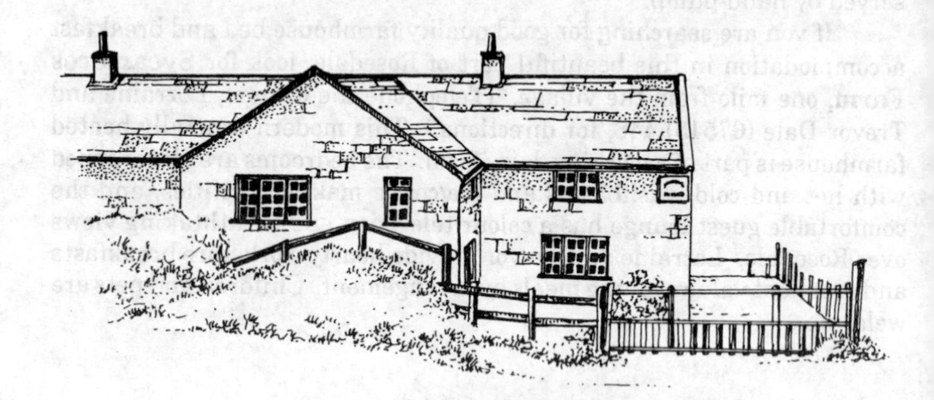

Five Acre View

Those dedicated campers amongst yourselves might find **Rosedale Caravan and Camping Parks**, four miles northeast of Hutton-le-Hole more to your choice. Maureen and Barrie Doughty have owned and personally run this picturesque 30-acre park since 1987 and can accommodate up to 100 touring caravans and 150 tents.

The site facilities include a modern shower block, laundry facilities, a popular club and restaurant, and a shop selling groceries, gifts and camping accessories. A limited number of electric hook-ups are available which should be booked in advance. There is also a splendidly-equipped children's play area, and in the village, a post office, newsagents and two inns.

Four miles west of Pickering, we turned north off the A170 Kirkbymoorside road to reach the pleasant Ryedale village of **Sinnington,**

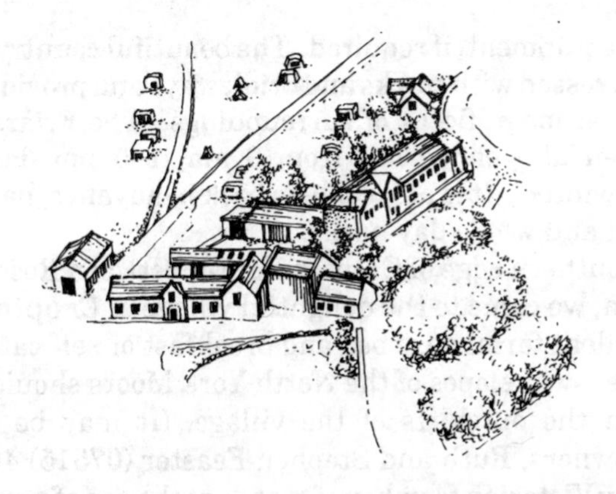

Rosedale Caravan Park

and discovered the **Friars Hill Riding Stables** which can be found on the eastern side of the road into the village. This British Horse Society approved riding centre has been open since 1984 and has around twenty horses and ponies available for one and two hour rides, and half and whole day hacks through the superb local countryside. The proprietor, Mrs Christine Gamble, provides lessons for riding enthusiasts of all ages and levels of experience.

Friars Hill Riding Stables

There are even lessons in sidesaddle riding and four sessions each week for disabled riders. The facilities at the stables include a splendid outdoor arena with an all weather surface and the provision of riding hats and equipment, if required. The beautiful countryside of lower Ryedale is crisscrossed with tracks and bridleways and provides wonderful riding in the most magnificent of surroundings. The Friars Hill Riding Stables are open all year round from 9 am to 5 pm daily. (Closed Wednesdays in winter). It is advisable to book in advance, particularly for lessons and half and whole day hacks.

On the southern edge of Cropton Forest, between Rosedale and the A170 at Wrelton, we came to the delightful village of **Cropton**. If you are looking for excellent farmhouse bed and breakfast or self-catering accommodation on the lower slopes of the North York Moors should look out for **High Farm** on the outskirts of the village. (It may be advisable to telephone the owners, Ruth and Stephen Feaster (07515) 461, for directions) This lovely Victorian farmhouse stands at the top of a sweeping drive in a magnificent position overlooking surrounding farms and woodland.

High Farm

Once part of a working farm, the house is now encircled by a large open country garden, and despite being fully modernised, it still retains much of its original character and charm. The spacious letting rooms all have en-suite showers/bathrooms, tea/coffee-making facilities and are appointed to a very high standard. There is also a separate dining room and a guests' lounge with colour television. Ruth and Stephen also have a delightful stone cottage adjoining High Farm which has been recently converted for use as self-catering accommodation. The fully centrally-heated cottage has three ample bedrooms (two double, one twin) and has been equipped to the highest standards.

The fitted oak kitchen/dining room contains such equipment as a dishwasher, an automatic washing machine and a microwave oven, and there is also a comfortable lounge with a gas coal-effect fire and a colour television.

Pickering is situated some 12 miles east of Helmsley in the heart of Ryedale and is the larger of the two towns. It has its own castle, originally a motte and bailey type, dating back to William 1's attempts to dominate the area.

Originally, the town's reputation was based on its pigs and horses, the pork being transported to Whitby, salted, and used aboard the ships that sailed from there. Horse-breeding was very important also, and the famous Cleveland Bay which was extensively bred in the area, was much in demand for the pulling of handsome cabs and street-cars.

The story connected with the original naming of the town is interesting, if ratherfar-fetched. In 270BC, the town as it was then, was presided over by a certain King Peredus. The king lost a ring that he treasured in the River Costa, and accused a maiden of stealing it.

Pickering Castle

One of his cooks was preparing his favourite dish of freshly-caught local pike, and discovered the ring in the belly of the fish. The king was intrigued with this, and believing it to be an omen of some sort, promptly married the maiden. He also decided to call the town Pike-ring to commemorate the event! As the locals would say, would you believe it?

In 1106, Henry 1 visited Pickering Castle and founded the Royal Forest of Pickering, which at this time was a vast domain, covering most of the southern region of what is now the North Yorkshire Moors.Many reminders of the town's medieval past still remain, including the famous 12th century murals in the local parish church of Saints Peter and Paul, and of course, the castle, which is a popular tourist attraction.

Walking along the main road in Pickering, you may recognise the building called **Skelgate House** as the one used in the film of "All Creatures Great and Small". Those interested in the history of the surrounding rural communities should make a point of visiting the **Beck Isle Museum**, which is open March to October.

Opposite the old Post Office in the market place, one will also come across the historic inn, **The White Swan**. Here, there are thirteen delightful guest rooms, each with a private bathroom, colour television and direct-dial telephone. The restaurant is renowned for the quality of its cuisine and takes pride in using locally-sourced produce, including pink-fleshed trout, duckling, game and Farndale goat's cheese. The owner, Mrs Dierdre Buchanan, is a knowledgeable wine buff and has put together an extensive list which includes over seventy bins from St Emilion, probably more than any other establishment in the country.

The White Swan

One of the most outstanding attractions of this area is the privately operated, steam-hauled **North Yorkshire Moors Railway** which runs between **Pickering** and **Grosmont**. This spectacular line passes through some of the most dramatic landscapes in the National Park including several Sites of Special Scientific Interest. The railway was designed before the age of steam by the great railway engineer, George Stephenson, in order to provide Whitby with a modern land link with the outside world.

North Yorkshire Moors Railway

One particularly noteworthy hotel and restaurant we discovered with superb views over the Vale of Pickering is the **Cottage Leas**, near **Middleton**. This delightful 18th-century converted farmhouse stands in a truly peaceful position one mile north of Middleton village along a quiet country lane. The hotel offers thirteen luxurious guest rooms (one with a four-poster bed), all equipped with private shower- or bathrooms, colour televisions, telephones and tea/coffee making facilities. There is also a delightful lounge with an open log fire, a relaxing bar and the pleasant 'Jug and Platter' dining room.

Four miles north of Pickering along the route of the North Yorkshire Railway, we came to the pleasant moorland village of **Newton-upon-Rawcliffe**. In a fine position overlooking the village pond and green, we found the **White Swan Hotel** (not to be confused with the one previously mentioned), a splendid family-run establishment which offers the best in traditional Yorkshire hospitality. The bar offers a warm

Cottage Leas Hotel & Restaurant

welcome to visitors and locals alike, there is a separate lounge, the 'Brass Room', with a cosy open fire, and a dining room serving traditional fare in relaxed and homely surroundings. Upstairs, there are five comfortably appointed guest rooms, each with hot and cold washbasins and fine views of the moors. Behind the hotel, there is also an attractive caravan and camping park.

White Swan Hotel

An attraction in nearby Newton Dale which should not be missed is the **Mel House Bird Garden** at **Newton-upon-Rawcliffe**, four miles north of Pickering. This three-acre working wildlife haven operates a breed and release scheme for native owls under the careful stewardship of owner, Caroline Rudland.

Mel House Bird Garden

Five miles northeast of Pickering on the A169 Whitby road, we stopped at the fine roadside pub and restaurant, the **Fox and Rabbit Inn**, at **Lockton**.

There has been an alehouse on this site since the 14th-century, when the local lords of the manor would stop for refreshment whilst hunting game in the forests of Newton Dale.

Fox and Rabbit Inn

The present building dates from the late 18th-century and probably derives its name from the extensive rabbit warrens which covered the nearby Dalby Moors at the time. Today, this impressive country inn is run by Ann and Gordon Wheldon. They provide their customers with first-rate ales and an excellent selection of home-cooked bar meals including children's meals, vegetarian dishes and special Sunday lunches.

Still touring around this area, we came to the village of **Levisham** where first-class guesthouse and self-catering accommodation can be found at **Rectory Farm House**, situated one mile west of the A169 Pickering to Whitby road at Lockton. This handsome former farmhouse retains much of its original character and charm; the delightful residents' lounge has a log fire and the bedrooms (some with en-suite facilities) are individually-decorated and appointed to a high standard. Owners, Mr and Mrs Richardson, also offer two superbly-appointed self-catering holiday cottages in their converted stone barn. These sleep four or six people, and being open all year, are ideal for special off-season breaks.

Rectory Farm House

Two-and-a-half miles east of Pickering on the A170 Scarborough road, we came to **Thornton-le-Dale** with its delightful market square. At the eastern end of the village, we called in at the **Easthill Guest House**, a first-rate private hotel run by Carol Fitzgibbon and her brother Martin. All eight tastefully-decorated bedrooms have en suite facilities.

Downstairs, there is a spacious lounge and an attractive dining room where delicious home-cooked meals are served. The guesthouse is surrounded by superb landscaped grounds. Hidden in an adjoining pine wood

Easthill Guest House

you will find three Scandinavian-style 'A frame' self catering chalets. Built in 1989 each sleeps from 4-5 people and are fully centrally-heated and equipped with every modern amenity. Unsuitable for pets.

Whilst staying here, we paid a visit to nearby Dalby Forest ,which is managed by the Forestry Commission, who enforce a toll fee of £2 for those who wish to drive through. For holidaymakers looking for the ideal spot for a picnic, this particular location offers excellent facilities.

Those amongst you looking for accommodation which offers something very special and out of the ordinary should make a point of finding **Troutsdale Lodge** in the heart of beautiful **Troutsdale**. It is situated in a peaceful rural position in the southeastern corner of the National Park, five-and-a-half miles north of the A170 at Snainton. (It may be advisable to telephone the owner, Clive Palmer (0723) 882209, for accurate directions.) The Lodge was built in 1912 by Indian diplomats as an Edwardian country bungalow and later was used as a shooting lodge. Today, the refurbished house stands at the end of a sweeping driveway in two acres of beautiful shrub-filled gardens and has magnificent views over the green forests of Troutsdale. Thanks to the vision and hard work of the proprietor, much of the Lodge's Edwardian style and grandeur has been revived. The present-day building has five outstandingly appointed guest rooms, all equipped with private en-suite shower/bathrooms and beverage-making facilities.

Clive Palmer and his staff serve first-rate English breakfasts, and can also provide lunches by arrangement. In the evenings, excellent quality dinners are served (to residents only) in the elegant dining room.

These are prepared to traditional Yorkshire recipes using fresh locally-sourced ingredients wherever possible. Troutsdale Lodge is licensed to serve alcoholic beverages to diners and residents and offers an interesting list of wines. Look out in the dining room for the unusual table which converts into an original Riley billiard table with cues and billiard balls to match. Before or after the meal, guests can sit out on the charming veranda and enjoy wonderful views of the Dale. Those preferring to be inside can relax in the fine guests' sitting room with its mellow atmosphere and fine collection of books, including many on the flora, fauna and history of the surrounding area.

Troutsdale Lodge is open all year round and offers a warm and genuine Yorkshire welcome to those looking for a truly secluded haven in this charming sector of the National Park. As it lies within convenient reach of the moors, coastline and many nearby places of historic interest, it also provides an ideal base for those wishing to explore the area on foot or by car.

Troutsdale Lodge

Robin Hoods Bay

St. Gregory's Minster - Kirkdale

CHAPTER 2

The Howardian Hills

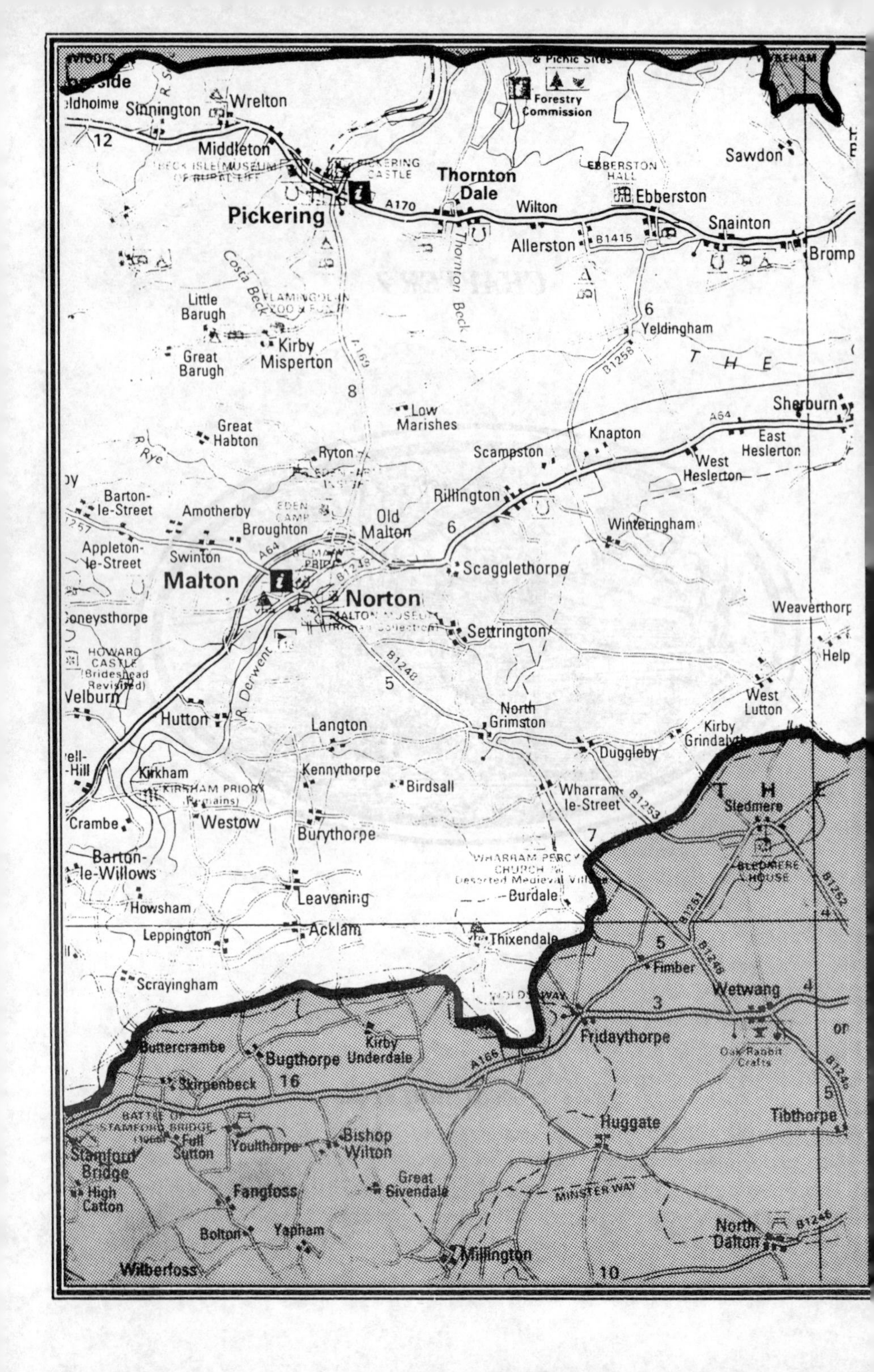

Sinnington
Wrelton
Forestry Commission
Middleton
Pickering
Pickering Castle
Beck Isle Museum of Rural Life
Thornton Dale
A170
Wilton
Ebberston Hall
Ebberston
Snainton
Sawdon
Allerston
B1415
Thornton Beck
Costa Beck
Little Barugh
Great Barugh
Kirby Misperton
A169
Yeldingham
B1258
Low Marishes
Great Habton
R Rye
Ryton
Knapton
Scampston
Sherburn
A64
East Heslerton
West Heslerton
Rillington
Barton-le-Street
Amotherby
Broughton
Eden Camp
Old Malton
Winteringham
Appleton-le-Street
Swinton
Malton
Norton
Scagglethorpe
B1248
Malton Museum
Settrington
Weaverthorpe
Coneysthorpe
Howard Castle (Brideshead Revisited)
Help
R. Derwent
West Lutton
Welburn
Hutton
Langton
North Grimston
Kirby Grindalyth
Duggleby
Kirkham
Kirkham Priory (Remains)
Kennythorpe
Birdsall
Wharram le-Street
B1253
Sledmere
Crambe
Westow
Burythorpe
Sledmere House
Barton-le-Willows
Wharram Percy Church
Deserted Medieval Village
B1251
B1252
Howsham
Leavening
Burdale
Leppington
Acklam
Thixendale
Fimber
B1248
Scrayingham
Wolds Way
Wetwang
Fridaythorpe
Buttercrambe
Bugthorpe
Kirby Underdale
Oak Rabbit Crafts
A166
Skirpenbeck
Battle of Stamford Bridge
Full Sutton
Youlthorpe
Bishop Wilton
Huggate
Tibthorpe
Stamford Bridge
High Catton
Fangfoss
Great Givendale
Minster Way
Bolton
Yapham
North Dalton
B1246
Wilberfoss
Millington

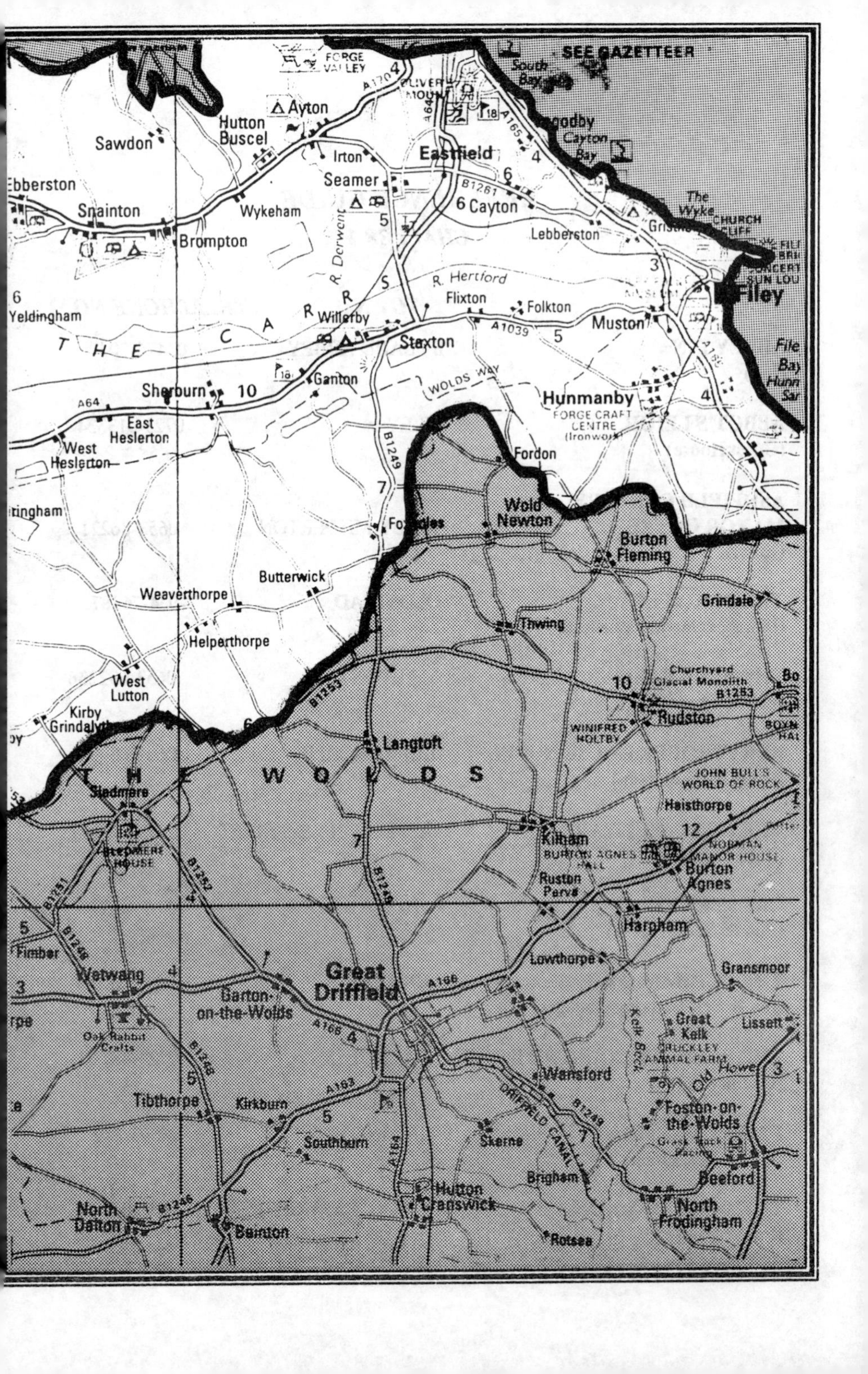

SEE GAZETTEER
FORGE VALLEY
South Bay
Ayton
Hutton Buscel
Sawdon
Irton
Eastfield
Cayton Bay
Ebberston
Seamer
Snainton
Wykeham
Cayton
Brompton
Lebberston
The Wyke
CHURCH CLIFF
R. Derwent
R. Hertford
Filey
Yeldingham
Flixton
Folkton
THE CARRS
Willerby
Staxton
Muston
Ganton
WOLDS WAY
Sherburn
Hunmanby
FORGE CRAFT CENTRE
East Heslerton
West Heslerton
Fordon
Wold Newton
Foxholes
Burton Fleming
Butterwick
Weaverthorpe
Grindale
Thwing
Helperthorpe
West Lutton
Churchyard Glacial Monolith
Rudston
Kirby Grindalythe
WINIFRED HOLTBY
Langtoft
THE WOLDS
JOHN BULL'S WORLD OF ROCK
Sledmere
Haisthorpe
Kilham
NORMAN MANOR HOUSE
BURTON AGNES HALL
Burton Agnes
Ruston Parva
Harpham
Fimber
Wetwang
Lowthorpe
Gransmoor
Great Driffield
Barton-on-the-Wolds
Great Kelk
Lissett
Oak Rabbit Crafts
Kelk Beck
Old Howe
Wansford
DRIFFIELD CANAL
Tibthorpe
Kirkburn
Foston-on-the-Wolds
Southburn
Skerne
Brigham
Beeford
Hutton Cranswick
North Frodingham
North Dalton
Bainton
Rotsea
A64
A165
A1039
A166
A163
A164
B1249
B1253
B1252
B1251
B1248
B1246
B1261

REFERENCE GUIDE

CHAPTER 2

NAME	*TOWN*	*TELEPHONE NO.*
ABBEY INN (Inn)	BYLAND ABBEY	03476-204
ABBOT'S LEIGH (Guest House)	FILEY	0723-513334
ASHFIELD COUNTRY MANOR HOTEL (Hotel)	KIRBY MISPERTON	0653-86221
THE BLACK SWAN (Inn, Accomod., Restaurnat)	OLDSTEAD	034-76387
THE BLUE BALL (Public House)	MALTON	0653-692236
BURYTHORPE HOUSE HOTEL (Hotel & Restaurant)	BURYTHORPE	0653-85200
THE CRESSWELL ARMS (Public House)	APPLETON-LE-STREET	0653-693647
CROSS KEYS (Pub & Guest House)	THIXENDALE	0377-88272
THE DURHAM OX (Inn & Self Catering Cottages)	CRAYKE	0347-21506
THE EVERLEY COUNTRY INN (Country Inn)	HACKNESS	0723-882202
FAIRFAX ARMS (Pub & Restaurant)	GILLING EAST	04393-212
THE GOLDEN LION (Public House)	GREAT BARUGH	0653-86242

HEADON FARM HOLIDAY COTTAGES (Self Catering Cottages)	WYDALE	0723-859019
KILLERBY OLD MALL (Self Catering Cottages)	CAYTON	0723-583799
THE OAK WHEEL (Pub & Restaurnat)	BURNISTON	0723-870230
THE PHEASANT HOTEL (Hotel)	HAROME	0439-71241
THE RED HOUSE (Guest House & Self Catering)	WHARRAM-LE-STREE	09446-455
ROBERT THOMPSON'S CRAFTSMEN (Furniture Manufacturers/)	KILBURN	03476-218
ROUND THE BEND (Tea Rooms & B & B)	THIXENDALE	0377-88237
SANDS FARM GUEST HOUSE & COUNTRY COTTAGES (Guest House & Self Catering Cottages)	WILTON	0751-74405
SEDGWICK GUEST HOUSE (Guest House)	HOVINGHAM	0653-628740
SPROXTON HALL (Farm House B&B)	SPROXTON	0439-70225
THE STAR INN (Country Inn)	WEAVERTHORPE	09443-273
THE WHITE SWAN (Country Inn)	AMPLEFORTH	04393-239
WOMBWELL ARMS (Inn & Accomodation)	WASS	0347-6280

Kirkham Priory - Malton

CHAPTER 2

From the Howardian Hills to the Yorkshire Riviera

The busy market town of **Malton** sits at the most eastern edge of the Howardian hills, with the twin village of Norton facing it across the River Derwent. Its Roman name was Derventio, a settlement of some note, even acting at the time as an inland port via the river. There was a Roman fortress based here, situated within some 8 acres of settlement, although the only indication of this that remains is a cross that marks its location on Orchard Field. In the museum, just off the market square, are many Roman relics that have been excavated from this era, including flints and stone weapons used by older civilisations, Roman implements, plaster from the walls, sandals, bone wool-combers, buttons, pins, knife-handles, skeletons and fragments of Roman glass and pottery. In fact, the whole area is something of a honeypot to archaeological buffs, including the medieval site at Wharram Percy, some seven miles to the south-east.

The town's present name is said to have been given to it 800 years ago on its rebuilding after it had been burned to drive off the Scots.

Malton today is comprised of a number of yellow houses, narrow streets, a spacious market place and the old church of St Michael. Another building of note is Malton Lodge, a charming folly, with battlements and mullioned windows. Much of the stone with which it is built is said to have come from Lord Eure's house, which was pulled down in Stuart days in an attempt to settle a dispute over the property by two heiresses.

Less prominent than St Michael's is the church of St Leonard, with its mixture of Norman and Jacobean architecture. Over the high arches in the nave are many grotesque carvings and the East window displays some wonderful examples of stained- glass art. In the cemetery lies one of the unsung heroes of Malton, Dr G.C. Parkin, who devoted all his energies to fighting a typhoid epidemic in 1933 and who died as a consequence.

Old Malton is another place to visit, situated a mile from Malton itself, a collection of quaint houses, thatched cottages, the Church of St Mary and the gabled Abbey, nestling amongst meadows and rows of yew trees. St Mary's is part of the Gilbertine priory founded by Eustace Fitzjohn in the 12th century. Within the church is a curious blend of Norman architecture, 15th century additions, up to the present day. There is a round arch, adorned with zigzags and other designs, which holds a stout oak door on which we can see the famous mouse design of Robert Thompson of Kilburn. His work is also evident on the pulpit and lectern. Most of the wooden furniture and stalls are carved elaborately with all manner of wondrous beasts and historical/mythical scenes.

In St Mary's churchyard is the grave of Charles Smithson, one of Charles Dickens' closest friends, who lived at nearby Easthorpe Hall. It was with Smithson that Dickens hatched his scheme to create an imaginary boy, in order to gain access to the schools where he was to research Nicholas Nickelby.

The area around Malton is also notable for the number of racing stables and stud farms in the surrounding countryside, which service the many racecourses in the Yorkshire area.

Near the centre of town, we found the splendid inn and eating house, **The Blue Ball**, which is run with great flair by Elaine and Brian Rey. Parts of this fascinating old building date from 1302, though it is for its more modern attributes that the pub is renowned: the Blue Ball stocks over 450 different bottled beers from around the world, it has won awards for 'Best Ploughman's Lunch in Ryedale', has been voted 'Best Decorated Pub in Malton' for five years in succession, and has twice been a regional finalist in the Pub Caterer of the Year Award. Recommended.

The Blue Ball

Three miles northwest of Malton on the B1257 Hovingham road, we came to **Appleton-le-Street** with its fine Saxon church, one of the few left untouched by Cromwell's forces in the 17th-century. In the village, we dropped in at the first-rate pub and eating house, the **Cresswell Arms**. Built in 1845 as a farmhouse, the original bread oven can still be seen in the wall of the bar. This traditional Yorkshire inn has been run for the past 26 years by Mr and Mrs Raine. Their 30-seater dining area is open all day for good home-cooked meals and refreshments, and they also offer first-rate overnight accommodation and caravan and camping facilities in their two acre park at the rear.

The Cresswell Arms

Most famous of this area's attractions must surely be Castle Howard, the main location of the popular series "Brideshead Revisited", not so much a stately home, more a magnificent baroque palace.

Charles Howard, third Earl of Carlisle, commissioned Sir John Vanburgh, who consequently made his reputation on the project, to build Castle Howard on the site of a former castle. The main part of the construction took place between 1699 and 1726, when Vanburgh worked in close association with Nicholas Hawksmoor. Between them they designed the first private house with a dome. Also in the main hall are some beautiful frescoes; the originals unfortunately were destroyed in a fire in 1940, but were repainted by Canadian-born artist Scott Nedd in 1962-63.

Horace Walpole in 1772 wrote, " Nobody had told me that I should see such a place, a town, a fortified city, temples on high places, woods worthy

Castle Howard

of being each a metropolis of the Druids, the noblest lawn in the world fenced by half the horizon and a mausoleum that would tempt me to be buried alive; in short, I have seen gigantic places but never a sublime one."The interior is rich with all manner of art treasures; paintings by Holbein, Van Dyck, Kneller, Lawrence, furnishings by Adam, Sheraton and Chippendale. In the chapel is the alter from the Temple at Delphi which Nelson wrested from the French at Naples.

In the Stable Court are the Costume Galleries containing fashions from the 18th to the 20th centuries.

Travelling north of Malton, on the B163, we came to the village of **Kirkby Misperton**, near the Flamingo Land Zoo and Fun Park (a useful stop-off point should you have any younger members of the family in tow). Opposite the handsome 15th-century church of St. Lawrence in the heart of the village, we found the **Ashfield Country Manor Hotel**, a spacious country farmhouse which has recently been converted into a seven-bedroomed hotel. Proprietors Noel and Molly Bulmer and their staff provide guests with a high standard of comfort and service. The bedrooms all have en suite facilities and are appointed to a high modern standard, and the restaurant offers a first-rate á la carte menu which includes a choice of vegetarian dishes. Adjoining the hotel, there is also a small and pleasant caravan park which is under the same ownership.

Ashfield Country Manor Hotel

Six miles north-east of Kirkby Misperton, the A170 Scarborough road passes through the picturesque village of **Wilton.** Here, we discovered the **Sands Farm Guest House and Country Cottages**, a former working farm , whose farmhouse, chapel and outbuildings have been beautifully converted to provide modern luxury holiday accommodation.

Sands Farm

The restoration has been successful in retaining the traditional character of the buildings whilst achieving an extremely high standard of cleanliness and comfort. The farmhouse guest rooms are equipped with colour television and tea/coffee making facilities, and there is also a lounge and dining room where delicious evening meals are served by prior arrangement. The four superbly appointed holiday cottages have high beams and open fireplaces, and provide luxurious self-catering accommodation for four to eight people.

In nearby **Great Barugh** (pronounced 'Barf'), two miles west of Kirby Misperton, is the fine traditional guesthouse, **The Golden Lion**, which is run by Pat and Jim Collier. The pub building dates from around 1630 and has white-painted walls, a pantiled roof and is surrounded by an attractive beer garden. Inside, the log fires and heavily beamed ceiling help to create an atmosphere which is cosy and welcoming. Pat and Jim serve a selection of fine country ales including Tetley and Double Chance bitter from Malton. They also offer traditional home-cooked bar meals including fish from Whitby and the house speciality, steak pie.

Golden Lion

Taking the country roads back to the B1257, and heading west, we came to the peaceful village of **Hovingham**. In a splendid position overlooking the village green, we found the **Sedgwick Guest House** which is owned and personally run by Mr and Mrs F J Smurthwaite. The building's Victorian façade hides a much older structure, and during its recent refur-bishment, the owners were careful to preserve the original features and character of the house. There are now seven well-appointed bedrooms, all with en-suite facilities, comfortable beds, colour televisions and tea/coffee making facilities. With its restful atmosphere and wonderful views over the surrounding countryside, the Sedgwick Guest House provides a perfect base for exploring this delightful part of North Yorkshire.

Sedgewick Guest House

Still in Hovingham is the famous **Hovingham Hall**, built on the site of a Roman villa. It was built by Thomas Worsley, a friend of George III, who gave him the statue by Giovanni, depicting Samson slaying the Philistine.

The 18th century house is surrounded by larch and beech, with a Saxon tower still attached to it.

Hovingham itself is well-known for the annual cricket festival which has been held here for over a hundred years. The ancient church has been here from Saxon days, and contains a carved Saxon stone with the figures of Mary and Gabriel on it.

About 2 miles out of Hovingham is the village of Cawton, where there is a spa house with three springs, which was popular in the 19th century.

Bearing north-east of Cawton, and about 3 miles north of Hovingham is the village of Nunnington and the 17th century manor house of **Nunnington Hall**. It looks down on the River Rye, with a picturesque pack-horse bridge nearby. Nunnington Hall is a mixture of architectural styles. The original house was tenanted in the mid-sixteenth century by Sir Robert Hinckes, who served as physician to Henry VIII, Catherine Parr, Edward VI and Queen Elizabeth. It was Sir Robert to whom the task fell to inform Elizabeth that she would never have children.

Gateway, Nunnington Hall

A subsequent owner was the 1st Viscount Preston, who married Anne Howard, daughter of the Earl of Carlisle. The viscount was chosen as Charles II's ambassaador to the court of Louis XIV, but rather foolishly chose to involve himself in various political intrigues. He was forced to spend the latter years of his life at Nunnington, after being saved from execution by William III's pardon. The Hall was later tenanted by farmers and fell into dilapidation, until 1870 when it was restored.

On a minor road, near the Hall and two-and-a-half miles southeast of Helmsley, we came to the charming village of **Harome.** In a superb position overlooking the village green, we found the extremely well-appointed **Pheasant Hotel.** This splendidly renovated and extended country hotel occupies the former village blacksmith's workshop, a shop and two cottages. Today, it has twelve bedrooms, all with private bathroom, colour televisions and tea/coffee making facilities, as well as two self-contained suites and two attractive cottages which are run as a fully-serviced part of the hotel. A large garden and paddock provide fresh produce for the hotel kitchen where the preparation of the finest English food is supervised by the owner, Mrs Tricia Binks. The hotel has a heated, indoor swimming pool. Unfortunately, credit cards cannot be accepted.

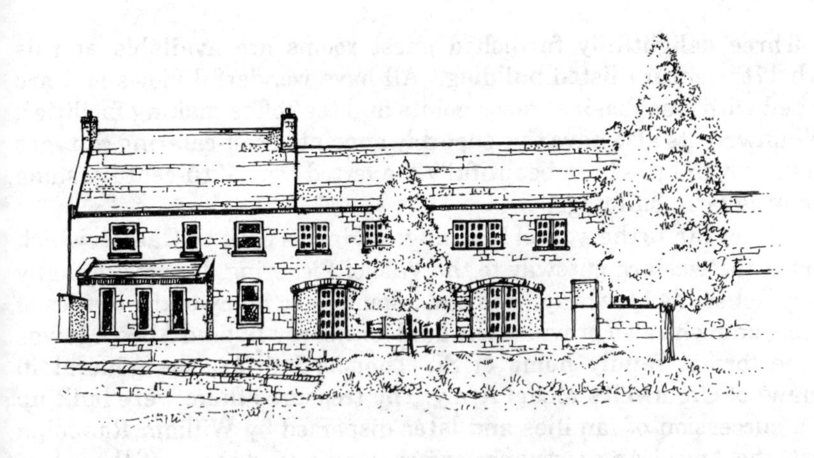

The Pheasant Hotel

One mile south of Helmsley on the A170 Thirsk road, we came to the village of **Sproxton**, a small neighbour to Helmsley that crowns a hilltop situated in a big bend of the River Rye. The tiny church of St Chad in the village was built in the 17th century and was once the private chapel of a great house at nearby West Newton Grange.

Those looking for exceptional bed and breakfast or self-catering accommodation in this part of the North York Moors should make a point of finding **Sproxton Hall**, a short distance from the centre of the village. (It may be advisable to telephone the owners, Mr and Mrs Wainwright (0439) 70225, for directions.)

Sproxton Hall

Three delightfully furnished guest rooms are available at this superb 17th-century listed building. All have wonderful views and are equipped with washbasins, razor points and tea/coffee making facilities. The Wainwrights also have five superbly appointed self-catering cottages available which have been beautifully converted from 17th-century stone and pantile farm buildings.

Not too far, to the west of Nunnington Hall, is **Gilling Castle,** which stands at the western gateway to the Vale of Pickering. It was originally built by Robert de Mowbray, who had a hand in so many of the castles of the area, and who also provided the land for nearby Byland Abbey. It was also the former family home of Sir Thomas Fairfax, the general in command of Cromwell's Model Army. The treasures there were built up from a succession of families and later dispersed by William Randolph Hearst, the American newspaper owner, who moved many of them to a castle he owned in Wales. Since 1929, Gilling Castle has been used as a preparatory school for Ampleforth, a nearby public school. It still has its original Norman keep, with additions from the 16th and 18th centuries.

Nearby is the delightful village of **Gilling East**. Whilst here we called in at The **Fairfax Arms**, a handsome stone-built free house which stands beside a stream a short distance back from the main road. The present owners, Sandra and Neville Kirkpatrick, have successfully managed to retain the inn's traditional atmosphere and character despite carrying out a series of major interior improvements. They have also built up an excellent reputation for serving a fine selection of first-rate bar meals and traditional hand-pulled beers.

Fairfax Arms

The village itself rests in a picturesque location in a narrow valley between the Hambleton and Howardian Hills. there is a famous green amidst its avenues of pine and chestnut where the great batsman Prince Rahjitsinhji practised at one time. He was renowned as a hero of the Great War, raising an Indian battalion and leading his men into the firing line, and was later given a seat on the League of Nations council as a result of this. The Prince lived at the Rectory for many years, with the tutor he had met at Cambridge. During his years here, he also donated the now famous Church clock-tower.

Three miles west of the B1363 Helmsley to York road at Oswaldkirk, a minor country road led us to the attractive village of **Ampleforth**, home of the famous Roman Catholic school which was founded by Benedictine monks shortly after the French Revolution. In a fine position on Ampleforth's long main street, we found the charming inn and eating house, **The White Swan**, which is run by Graham and Norma Davies. This splendid free house serves a range of traditional hand-pulled beers (including Everards Old Original) and for whisky drinkers, there is a choice of over sixty single malts. However, it is for its food that the White Swan is particularly renowned. Chef Jon Entwistle has worked in the area for over twenty years and in that time has built up a reputation for preparing the very best in English and continental cuisine.

The White Swan

The inn claims to serve the best steaks in North Yorkshire, with meat is taken from local grass-fed cattle and then hung for the correct period before being freshly cut and cooked to order. A wide selection of

Byland Abbey

other dishes is available which, on the day we visited, included rack of lamb, Barbary duck breast, homemade rabbit pie and a range of imaginative fish dishes. On Sundays, the inn also serves an excellent three-course roast lunch. Diners can choose to eat in the pleasant fifty-seater restaurant or in the recently extended lounge and patio which can comfortably accommodate up to eighty people.

Whilst exploring this area, one of the greatest tourist attractions must be **Byland Abbey**, reputed to be the largest Cistercian abbey in England. The story behind its founding is an interesting one. In 1134, Abbot Gerold and 12 monks from Furness Abbey set out for Calder in Cumberland, marking the beginning of 43 years of wandering. Driven out by the Scots, they returned first to Furness, then to Old Byland, where Robert de Mowbray granted them land. This site was in turn deemed to be too close to Rievaulx, and they moved on yet again to Stocking where they stayed for 30 years. In 1177, they moved to their final location, on the beautiful wooded ridge where the Abbey is located today.

Today there are only fragments of the north transept remaining and the south transept, dating back to 1225, stands like a great pinnacle, tilting at a dangerous angle. The north aisle has traces of a medieval wall-painting depicting the Madonna. Other artefacts are now kept in a small museum, with a fine collection of Norman and 13th century fragments, carved capitals with traces of paintings, gargoyles and bosses.

The battle of Byland in 1322 is believed to have been fought at Shaw's Moor to the north of Oldstead and Scot's Corner. While Edward II was dining at the Abbey on his return from an unsuccessful invasion of Scotland, the Scots made a surprise attack, and routed the English forces camped hereabouts. The king managed to escape, but the Scots captured his jewels, ransacked the Abbey and scattered the monks.

Directly opposite the famous abbey in the village of the same name, we found the fascinating pub and eating house, the **Abbey Inn**. From the outside, the inn is a handsome, stone-built, ivy-clad building. (Look out for the two stone dogs which sit guarding the front door.) The interior, too, has traditional elements including stone-flagged floors and polished wood surfaces, but here the owners, Peter and Gerd Handley, have added a number of highly unusual artefacts to create an atmosphere which is both original and extremely congenial. Apart from its wonderful interior, the inn is famous for the quality of its food, and the imaginative dishes prepared by Norwegian-born Gerd attract a steady flow of diners from far and wide. Recommended.

Abbey Inn

On the edge of Ampleforth Forest, half a mile northeast of Byland Abbey, we came to the delightful village of **Wass.** Here, we found the **Wombwell Arms,** an exceptional inn and bed and breakfast establishment which is owned and personally run by Mr and Mrs Evans. Several years ago, they set their hearts on owning their own country inn and so gave up their teaching posts to undergo a training in hotel and catering management with Grand Metropolitan. They then proceeded to search the length and breadth of the country in an attempt to find the perfect location for their business; several months and 24,000 miles later they settled upon the Wombwell Arms.

Wombwell Arms

Since taking over, much of their efforts have gone into the complete refurbishment of the inn's interior. This has been done with great care and taste so as to retain as much of the building's original character and charm as possible. The present day atmosphere is relaxed and welcoming with Scrabble, Trivial Pursuit and glossy books on country sports on hand to brighten the dreariest winter day. As well as a good range of traditional hand-pulled beers, the inn offers an impressive wine list and a tempting range of single malt whiskies. A first-rate lunchtime and evening menu is also served which features top quality local game and venison dishes. The Wombwell Arms also offers a number of extremely well-appointed guest rooms which are all equipped with en suite facilities and tastefully decorated in coordinated country style.

In the shelter of the famous White Horse escarpment in the south-western corner of the National Park, is the delightful hamlet of **Oldstead**.

Here, we visited the charming pub, restaurant and guesthouse, the **Black Swan Inn**. For those seeking accommodation, there are six comfortable guest rooms here, all with en-suite shower rooms, colour televisions and spectacular views of the Hambleton Hills. There is also an elegant first-floor restaurant which offers a tempting á la carte menu, and the Drovers Bar which serves a selection of traditional ales, first-rate bar meals, and features hand-carved woodwork from the renowned 'Mousey' Thompson workshop. With its blazing log fires, central heating and cosy atmosphere, the Black Swan is perfect for an off-season break.

The Black Swan

Whilst staying here, we made a point of visiting the White Horse at **Kilburn**, about six miles south-east of Thirsk, certainly a sight worth recording on camera. It was said to have originally been the idea of one Thomas Taylor, who had seen the White Horse at Uffingham in Berkshire, although the actual work was engineered half a century later by local schoolmaster John Hodgson, with the help of his pupils and local villagers. It is 314 feet long and 228 feet high and can be seen from as far away as Harrogate and Otley.

The Horse has one drawback from the ones in Berkshire, in that whereas they are carved in chalk, which remains white, the one at Kilburn is set on limestone, which means it has to be "groomed" regularly by means of lime-washing and covering in chalk chippings to prevent it going grey.

The White Horse is and always has been viewed with some pride by the local inhabitants. The following verses regarding its beginnings are an extract from a poem written in 1923 by local lad Thomas Goodrick, who remembered the event in 1857:

When the master had gone out,
The children were delighted
To romp about and shout.
But soon John Hodgeson came
With a letter in his hand
And the drawing of a horse
Which he had closely scanned
From Mr Thomas Taylor
Who in London did reside,
Saying "Please can you make a horse
On Rolestone Scarr hillside?"
I've just come back from Berkshire
A pretty sight I've seen,
A big horse on the hillside
With a coat so white and clean."

Six miles east of Thirsk, between the A170 and the A19 York road, we also took the opportunity of visiting the workshops of **Robert Thompson's Craftsmen** in the village of Kilburn. These world-famous workshops were founded early this century by Robert Thompson, a gifted local craftsman who took his inspiration from medieval ecclesiastical carvings. He always insisted on working with naturally seasoned English oak, a practice which

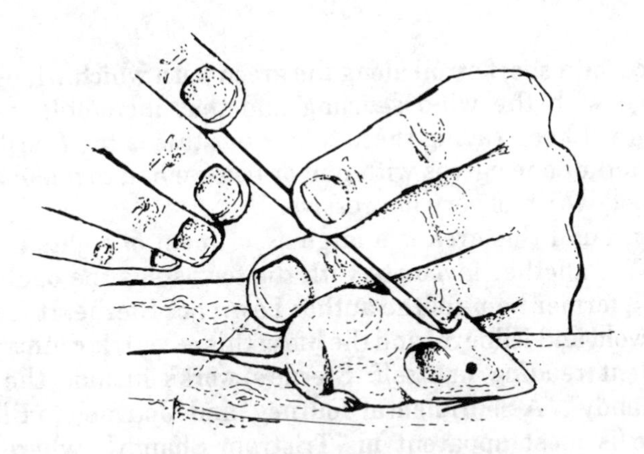

Robert Thompson's Craftsmen

is continued to this day. The organisation carried on after his death in 1955 and today, thirty highly-skilled craftsmen continue to produce classic pieces of furniture and carved items in the workshops which stand behind his ancient timber-framed cottage, now the company's showroom and offices. Over the years, the workshops have become renowned for the carved 'mouse' trademark which can be found in churches and public buildings throughout the world. Visitors to the workshops are welcome to view the craftsmen and carvers at work during normal working hours, from 1st October to 1st April.

Also in this area is **Sutton Bank Top**, famous as one of the most gruelling legs of the Milk Race, and arguably one of the most beautiful views in Yorkshire. James Herriot is quoted as saying:

" Sutton Bank Top. This is the scene, which, during forty years I have observed in all its moods. I must have stopped at this very spot thousands of times because there is no better place for a short stroll along the green path which winds around no better place for a short stroll along the green path which winds around the hill's edge with the wind swirling and that incredible panorama beneath. I know I keep saying these things but this *is* the finest view in England." Whether one agrees with him or not, we had to make a special visit to the spot, which is very impressive.

In fact, around this area is a large assortment of sights to see and places to go. Yet another favourite with the tourists is the oddly named **Shandy Hall**, former home of the author Lawrence Sterne. It is situated between Coxwold and Kilburn, and the life of this eccentric country pastor makes excellent reading in itself. Sterne's works include the famous "Tristram Shandy", "A Sentimental Journey" and "Journey to Eliza" The wit of Sterne is most apparent in "Tristram Shandy", where we are introduced to such characters as the redoubtable Uncle Toby, Corporal Trim and the amorous Widow Wadman. The Reverend Sterne must have been quite an interesting personality, and must have been a common topic of conversation and gossip amongst his small community of parishioners.

The parson came to live at Shandy Hall in 1760 when Lord Fauconberg of nearby Newburgh Priory conferred the parish to him. He wrote of his new home,

"'Tis within a mile of his lordship's seat and park. 'Tis a very agreeable ride out in the chaise I purchased for my wife. Lyd (his daughter) has a pony which she delights in. Whilst they take these diversions I am scribbling away at my "Tristram". My Lydia helps to copy for me, and my wife knits and listens as I read her chapters."

Tudor in origin, the house has several peculiarities, one being a tiny eye-like window in the huge chimney stack, located in the study to the right of the entrance. Standing in this room, one can imagine Sterne sitting there - one day he would be there writing a sermon, the next another rollicking chapter of "The Life and Opinions of Tristram Shandy".

Questioned once on the appropriateness of such humour for a man of his station, he replied,

"Sorrow is better than laughter - for a cracked-brained order of Carthusian monks, I grant, but not for men of the world."

Sterne was possessed of a particularly sharp and off-beat sense of humour, never more manifest than in his letter (now kept at Newburgh Priory) regarding the seating arrangements in his church. He advised that those who approved of the vicar "can face him, and those who don't can face the other way".

The house, with its own eccentricities seemed tailormade for him, with such peculiar features as the strangely shaped balustrades on the

the bedroom powder-closet, whereby Sterne (or 'Yorick' as he nicknamed himself) could reach through a hatch and draw pails of water for his ablutions, by means of an old well-rope in the adjoining room.

Shandy Hall has other interesting features, including the beautiful old church, visible from its windows, with its octagonal perpendicular tower, three-decker pulpit and the Fauconberg family tombs.

One item in the church that has caused some amusement, regards the floor-brass in the nave recording the death of Sir John Manston in 1464. A space was left encouragingly for his wife Elizabeth's name to be added at a later date, but after all these years, the space is still blank. One can almost hear Lawrence Sterne's voice observing that Sir John must be rather tired of waiting for her by now!

Newburgh Priory

We travelled on to nearby **Easingwold**, some nine miles away on the A19 Thirsk -York road.

It is a very pretty market town with creepered houses, old inns and shops clustered around the village green.

Within the town is an old bull-ring, dating from the days when bull-baiting was a popular pastime. On the way to Uppleby is a timbered house on which can be read "God with us in 1666", presumably left there by one of the old campaigners who remembered the battle-cry on Marston Moor.

There is also a lovely avenue of beeches that leads to the 14th century church, which is well worth a visit.

Within its walls, one feels a great sense of antiquity, echoed in the old roofs, carved chests, alms-boxes, an old chained Testament and a parish coffin, a sad reminder of the days when the poor of the area would only be carried to their graves in the communal coffin and then buried in a sheet. One might also note the leaning pillars, the chancel with its bulging walls and gallery drooping at one end, which challenge one's views on perspective.

Two miles east of Easingwold, a country road led us to the charming village of **Crayke**. In the centre of the village, we called in at the fine 18th-century inn, **The Durham Ox**, an excellent find for those looking for good food and traditional Yorkshire hospitality. Inside, the inn has stone-flagged floors, old-fashioned settles and an impressive inglenook fireplace. A varied range of well prepared home-cooked dishes is available seven days a week (excluding Sunday evenings), and upstairs there are a number of clean and bright guest rooms equipped with colour televisions and tea/coffee making facilities. The Durham Ox also has three self-catering holiday cottages available which are grouped around a courtyard at the rear.

The Durham Ox

Crayke itself is an interesting little village, situated on the crest of a hill with the houses clustered around the church and castle on top, visible right across the vale of York. A Saxon fortress was said to have marked this spot many years ago. There is also little left of the Norman castle once sited here, save the foundations; the battlemented house we now see amongst the trees behind the church is the tower house known as the Great Chamber built in the 15th century. It has a beautiful garden and a splendid view from its windows. By it are the remains of the New Tower, a majestic ruin cloaked in ivy.

The church is said to mark the place where St Cuthbert's body was finally laid to rest after his long wanderings, the origins of the inn's name date back to this. There are many fine features in the church, including two stone figures, said to be Sir John Gibson and his wife who lived here in Elizabethan days.

From Easingwold, we travelled back east along country roads, towards Malton, stopping off briefly on the B1363 at **Sutton Park**, well worth a visit if you are in these parts.

The house was built in 1730 by Thomas Atkinson, and was almost certainly one of the regular haunts of such notable local people as Lawrence Sterne. It contains some exceptionally fine examples of Sheraton and Chippendale furniture and magnificent plasterwork by the Italian craftsman Cortese. One notable feature is the collection of fans, some of them originating from the collections at Buckingham Palace. The gardens and parkland are particularly attractive, having been designed by the grand master of landscape, Capability Brown. There are many unusual and interesting plants, the present plantings having been established over the last 25 years; you will come across a Georgian ice-house, beautiful woodland walks and nature trails on your visit here, and you may also notice that the house itself is always full of flowers from the gardens. There is a gift shop and cafe, which sells wonderful home-made cakes and scones and lunches and teas are catered for if you are travelling as a party, booking in advance.

After stopping here, we continued east, through West Lilling, Bulmer, Thornton-le-Clay and on to **Kirkham Priory**.

Kirkham, unlike other priories and abbeys already mentioned was presided over by the Augustinian order of monks. The founder in the early 1120's was Walter Espec, who was also responsible for Rievaulx, and there are many similarities with the Cistercian house, in particular the integration of a waterway as a part of the design. Espec at one time had threatened to give Kirkham over to the Cistercian order, but this fortunately came to nothing and in the 13th century the Order were made custodians of the De Roos family sepulchres (at this time the De Roos were the lords of Helmsley Castle), a responsibility which gave them this influential family's patronage and ensured their survival. The family's heraldry is prominent on many of the remaining structures we can see today.

Gateway, Kirkham Priory

Hidden in the country lanes three miles east of Kirkham, we made a point of finding the village of **Burythorpe**, home of the exceptional country house hotel and restaurant, **Burythorpe House**. This outstanding George II residence was built around 1750 and stands within large, delightfully wooded grounds. All the bedrooms are individually decorated, sumptuously furnished and equipped with en suite bathrooms, colour televisions and beverage making facilities.

Burythorpe House Hotel

The oak-panelled restaurant (open to non-residents) offers an extensive á la carte menu, and after dinner guests can relax in the lounge or enjoy a game of snooker on the full-sized table. There is also a tennis court and a large heated indoor swimming pool with an adjoining sauna, solarium and fitness room.

For those who are drawn to the world of archaeology, the deserted village of **Wharram Percy,** six miles south east of Malton, and within striking distance of the hotel, is a fascinating place of historical interest. If you wish to actually watch the team of diggers go about their business, then you will be able to do so for three weeks in July of each year, when professor Maurice Beresford and John Hurst, Inspector of Ancient Monuments organise their stalwart teams of volunteers.

The village excavations began 25 years ago, when Professor Beresford obtained permission from Lord Middleton to investigate the site. The findings have been of continual interest to the world of archaeology ever since, for below the remains of the medieval village have been found artefacts of both the Saxon and Roman eras.

For many years it was assumed that Wharram Percy was one of the many casualties of the Black Death, but in fact, it was merely the more expedient measure of providing land for intensive sheep-farming that led to its demise as a population centre.

At the site one can see peasant houses that date from the 13th - 16th centuries, the manor house of the Percy family who gave the village its name, a 12th century church, cemetery (complete with exposed skeletons!), medieval and tudor vicarages, a mill, as well as the older Anglo-saxon and Roman sites.

The minor roads to the south of Wharram Percy led us to the charming village of **Thixendale**, three miles northwest of the A166 at Fridaythorpe. Here, we visited the 200 year-old country free house, the **Cross Keys**, which is run by the Clooneys and the Ansteys. They describe the inn as serving 'proper beer and proper cooking', and we certainly found the range of Tetleys traditional hand-pulled beers and freshly prepared bar meals to be first-class.

On the day we visited, the daily blackboard specials included such delicacies as stout hare, rabbit casserole and braised pheasant. Inside, the inn retains much of its traditional character and charm, while outside, there is an attractive lawned garden with picnic tables and hanging baskets of flowers.

Also in **Thixendale**, Mrs Anstey owns a listed 17th-century cottage, **'Round the Bend'**, which she runs as a tearoom and bed and breakfast

Cross Keys

establishment. We can personally recommend the tearoom's enormous homemade scones, baked to a secret recipe and piled high with cream. When we visited in early May, we were able to enjoy our tea in the attractive garden, observed by Mrs Anstey's cats as they lazed in the evening sun. Tearoom open daily 10am to 6pm, Good Friday to end October, closed Thursdays. Mrs Anstey also has three letting rooms available, all tastes catered for.

Round the Bend

Also in this area, north of Wharram Percy on the B1248 Beverley road, is the delightful village of **Wharram le Street**. Here, we visited the highly recommended guest house **The Red House**, which is owned by former farming couple, Stella and Richard Scott. Their handsome red-brick house stands in an acre of gardens with a grass tennis court; it dates from 1807 but incorporates a stone building which is considerately older. Inside, the guest lounge has a roaring log fire and the bedrooms all have private bathrooms, colour televisions and tea/coffee-making facilities. Stella and Richard provide excellent traditional cooking using many of their own

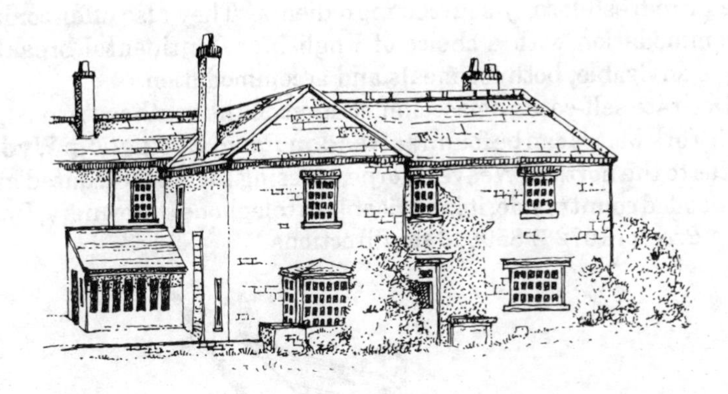

The Red House

organically produced ingredients. They also have an attractive self-catering holiday cottage available which sleeps up to five

Those looking for an exceptional Yorkshire Wolds' inn should make a point of finding the **Star Inn** at **Weaverthorpe**.

Star Inn

(It is located thirteen miles east of Malton and worth making a detour to find). The Star is one of only two establishments in North Yorkshire to be included in the *Independent's* list of 100 best pubs. It is full of local character and serves a fine selection of traditional regional hand-pulled beers. It is also renowned for the excellence of its pub food, with owners, Susan and David Richardson, specialising in traditional country recipes which require fresh locally-sourced ingredients. They also offer comfortable accommodation with a choice of English or Continental breakfast. Booking is advisable, both for meals and accommodation.

First-rate self-catering accommodation on the southeastern edge of the North York Moors can be found at **Headon Farm Cottages** in **Wydale**, eight miles to the north of Weaverthorpe, crossing the A64 (Situated in the heart of wooded countryside, it is advisable to telephone the owners, Denise and Clive Proctor (0723) 859019 for directions.)

Headon Farm Holiday Cottages

Originally forming part of the Wydale Hall Estate, the farm provides easy access to the nearby moors, Heritage Coast and Vale of York. The five spacious stone-built holiday cottages are grouped around a sunny courtyard and have been tastefully converted from 19th-century farm outbuildings. Inside, they are spotlessly clean and extremely well-furnished and appointed. All 'extras' including bedlinen, heating, video and microwave are included, and being fully centrally-heated, they are especially suitable for off-season lets.

Heading towards the coast, we stopped off at **Killerby Old Hall** near **Cayton**. Situated midway between Scarborough and Filey on the B1261, this elegant late 16th-century manor house is set in lovely grounds a mile-and-a-half inland from the sandy beach at Cayton Bay. The beautifully restored Hall contains early wood panelling and an inglenook fireplace, and offers extremely comfortable accommodation for up to ten people. Three further well-appointed cottages are available in the converted stables, each sleeping four-five. All properties have full central heating, log fires and year-round access to a heated indoor swimming pool making them particularly suitable for off-season breaks. Nearby attractions include a riding school and Valerie Green's stained glass studio/ showroom.

Killerby Old Hall

Travelling a small distance further up the A64, we headed towards probably the best known and most popular resort in Yorkshire, **Scarborough**.

Visitors to the resort could not fail to be impressed by the panoramic setting of the cliffs and bays here, and the buildings, in their latter-day splendour, seem appropriately in proportion with their setting.

In fact, the popularity of Scarborough did not begin with the attractions of its seaside, but from people flocking to sample the benefits of its spring water, discovered in 1626 by Mrs Tomyzin Farrer, and later popularised in a book published by a certain Dr Wittie, who named it "Scarborough Spaw".

Whenever I think of Scarborough though, a mental image of ladies in huge and unflattering Victorian swimming costumes, being wheeled to the water's edge in cumbersome bathing machines, immediately springs to mind. These may be images of the resort that are long gone, but many of the legacies remain in the form of Punch and Judy tents, donkey rides,

Victorian bandstands and pleasure-gardens, abundancies of candy-floss and lettered rock.

The connecting of the railway from York in 1846 was the factor that really transformed Scarborough into the resort we know today. People from the industrial towns of the West Riding could travel out to escape the grime and pollution caused by the Industrial Revolution, to breathe the cleaner sea air.

There is more to Scarborough though, than the candy-floss stalls and brightly painted Regency and Victorian buildings. Parts of it, notably the Castle and its environs, date back to medieval times, and were themselves built on the site of a Roman fort and signal station. Scarborough Castle dates from the 12th century, in the reign of Henry II, and in its time was twice beseiged by Parliamentarian forces in 1643 and 1648. The renowned Quaker George Fox was also imprisoned here in 1665. The gaunt remains of the structure stand high on Castle Rock headland dominating the two bays. Staged battles to commemorate the invasions of the Danes, Saxons and more latterly the Napoleonic incursions are often held here, along with other events, and are a popular attraction for the tourists.The cliffs around the area are also well worth exploring, and form the final part of the famous Cleveland Way.

Those visiting the resort around Shrove Tuesday might be forgiven for wondering as to the sanity of the inhabitants of Scarborough. The sight of people exercising the ancient right to skip along the highways, in competition with the more usual methods of getting from A to B, may be witnessed, although the local authorities do attempt to restrict the avid and eccentric exponents of this quaint and peculiar custom to the area along Foreshore Road. Another tradition upheld by the locals at this time is the sounding of the Pancake Bell, a custom started by the wives of the town to alert their menfolk in the fields and in the harbour that they were about to commence the cooking of the pancakes. The local gas and electricity companies are no doubt relieved that such a mammoth and concerted effort is not in practice today!

Scarborough, as is fitting for such a well-established holiday resort, is primed for entertainment of all kinds, from the intellectual attractions of the **Rotunda Museum** on Vernon Road and the art collections at the Scarborough Art Gallery, right through to the futuristic world of holograms at **Corrigans Arcade** on Foreshore Road. **The Stephen Joseph Theatre in the Round** is another lively venue, where playwright Alan Aykbourn is the director.

Another place worthy of a visit is the **Wood End Museum of**

Scarborough Castle

Natural History on the Crescent, once the home of the famous Sitwell family. There are permanent displays of their books and photographs, as well as changing exhibitions of local wildlife. Particularly worth a visit is the double-storied conservatory and aquarium.

Should you wish to escape the noisy arcades and crowds of tourists consuming vast amounts of candyfloss and toffee-apples by the van-load, one might try to head west across Seamer moor towards the lovely Forge Valley.

A short distance from the village of **Hackness** on the southeastern edge of the moors, we found the fine inn and hotel, the **Everley Country House**. This handsome mid-19th century building is situated at the head of the beautiful Forge Valley to the north of the A170 at Ayton.

Everley Country House

Owners, Richard and Jill Taylor, have successfully retained the building's original character and charm; the lounges have outstanding views of the gardens and surrounding countryside, as do the four comfortable and well-appointed letting rooms. First-rate bar meals are provided, as well as good facilities for children. Look out for the trademark of the 'Gnome Man' on the carved oak bar. The Everley Country House is open all year and offers special off-season breaks.

Whilst in this area, you will probably see the ruined remains of **Ayton Castle** at the side of the road, situated near the junction of the A170 and B1261. This was once one of the many pele towers built in the region when there was great danger from invading Scottish marauders. Some of these towers took the precaution of having the entrance at first floor level, in order to make a forced entrance difficult. Others, like Ayton, had a strong door at ground level, leading to a narrow interior staircase with a bend in it suitable for easy defence. The living quarters were located on the first floor and the sleeping quarters on the second.

In more peaceful years, many of these towers had a more comfortable mansion added and became stately homes, but their defensive origins are easily recognisable. The fear of the Scottish invaders in these parts was once very real, and in one of the invasions, Scarborough was almost destroyed. A body of Scots under Robert the Bruce once marched as far as Beverley.

If you are looking for somewhere to eat in this area, the delightful **Oak Wheel** inn and restaurant is situated not far away, three miles north of Scarborough, close to the junction of the A165 **Burniston** Coastal Road with the A171 Whitby road. Since taking over a few years ago, Jim and Fiona Warren have transformed the place into a top class establishment which is popular with both visitors and regulars alike. The bar serves a fine selection of Tetley's and Cameron's ales, along with an extensive range of good value bar meals including homemade pies, vegetarian dishes and special children's meals.

The Oak Wheel

Upstairs, the separate Oak Wheel Restaurant offers a choice of more elaborate dishes including char-grilled steaks and fresh lobster in season. Outside, there is an attractive beer garden with a charming pet's corner.

Built on high ground, nearby **Filey** looks down on a large, crescent-shaped bay that has consistently retained its attraction for the tourists over the years, and for those seeking a quieter resort than Scarborough, it presents the perfect alternative. The bay is sheltered by the protective promontory known as Filey Brigg, which offers the greatest protection from the ravages of the North Sea. It was once a fishing village, despite the fact that it had no harbour, which necessitated the boats and cobles having to be hauled across the beach.

Looking at the friendly, bustling little resort these days, it is hard to imagine that once a leading primitive methodist preacher said of Filey,

"It is a place noted for vice and wickedness of almost every description; drunkeness, swearing, Sabbath-breaking, cock-fighting, card-playing and dancing have been the favourite diversions of this place for many years". One cannot help but surmise that this damning report on the town had the consequence of attracting the tourists by the cart-load, hence its popularity today !

Filey was once a resort filled with ornate hotels to whom wealthy visitors came with their families and nannies, it was considered the perfect holiday place for children, although, as is the trend with so many of these older resorts, the grandeur has been replaced by glitzy bingo halls and shops selling the usual seaside paraphernalia. Some of the vestiges of its past role as a fishing village remain, however, and one may still glimpse the occasional fishing boat beached on one of the slipways. There are also still quiet streets of traditional cottages, one of which houses the local Folk Museum, mainly around the Queen Street area.

The border between the East and North Ridings once crossed right through Filey, separating the town from the area where the parish church was situated. This unusual situation was regarded with the typical Yorkshire brand of dry humour - should you be taken seriously ill the wry comment was often heard that you might well be "Off t'North Riding" if you didn't recover!

As with all well established seaside resorts there is a wealth of hotels and bed-and-breakfast accommodation available.

One which we can recommend is **Abbot's Leigh** in Rutland Street, close to the town centre and only five minutes' walk from the beach. This warm and comfortable private hotel is English Tourist Board Three Crown Commended with all bedrooms having en-suite bathrooms, colour televisions, clock radios and tea/coffee making facilities.

Owners Mike and Pat Carter provide their guests with a first-rate Yorkshire breakfast and a satisfying fiv e course evening meal. Unsuitable for pets and children under three years of age.

This particular area of Yorkshire well deserves its popularity, due to the fact that the surrounding countryside and coastline offers so many

Abbot's Leigh

attractions. Travel south of Filey to Flamborough Head, and you will pass some of the highest cliffs in the British Isles. The huge chalk sweep of the Head is a familiar sight to most people, who will have seen it featured in a number of Victorian seascape paintings.

Whether you pursue such interests as bird-watching, wildlife walks, archaeology, historical facts or simply just looking for some fun in the well-chaptered seaside manner, this area will open them up to you.

Reminders of those less popular tourists, the Saxons and Danes, are evident wherever you may go. Look out for placenames that can give one an indication of their origins. Key words such as ' ton' (Saxon word for a family farm on open land, enclosed by a fence), 'ley' (Saxon word for a clearing in woodland) and ' ham', indicating a farm or homestead, tell us whether the land we now see was once either forest or agricultural land.

The Norse invaders introduced the ' thorp's and 'by's into the vocabulary - as in Fridaythorpe, Kirkby and, of course, Scunthorpe. The Danes also gave us the ' erg' or ' burgh' at the ends of placenames such as Sedburgh and ' Scarthi's Burgh', now known as Scarborough.

CHAPTER 3

Flamborough Head To Humberside

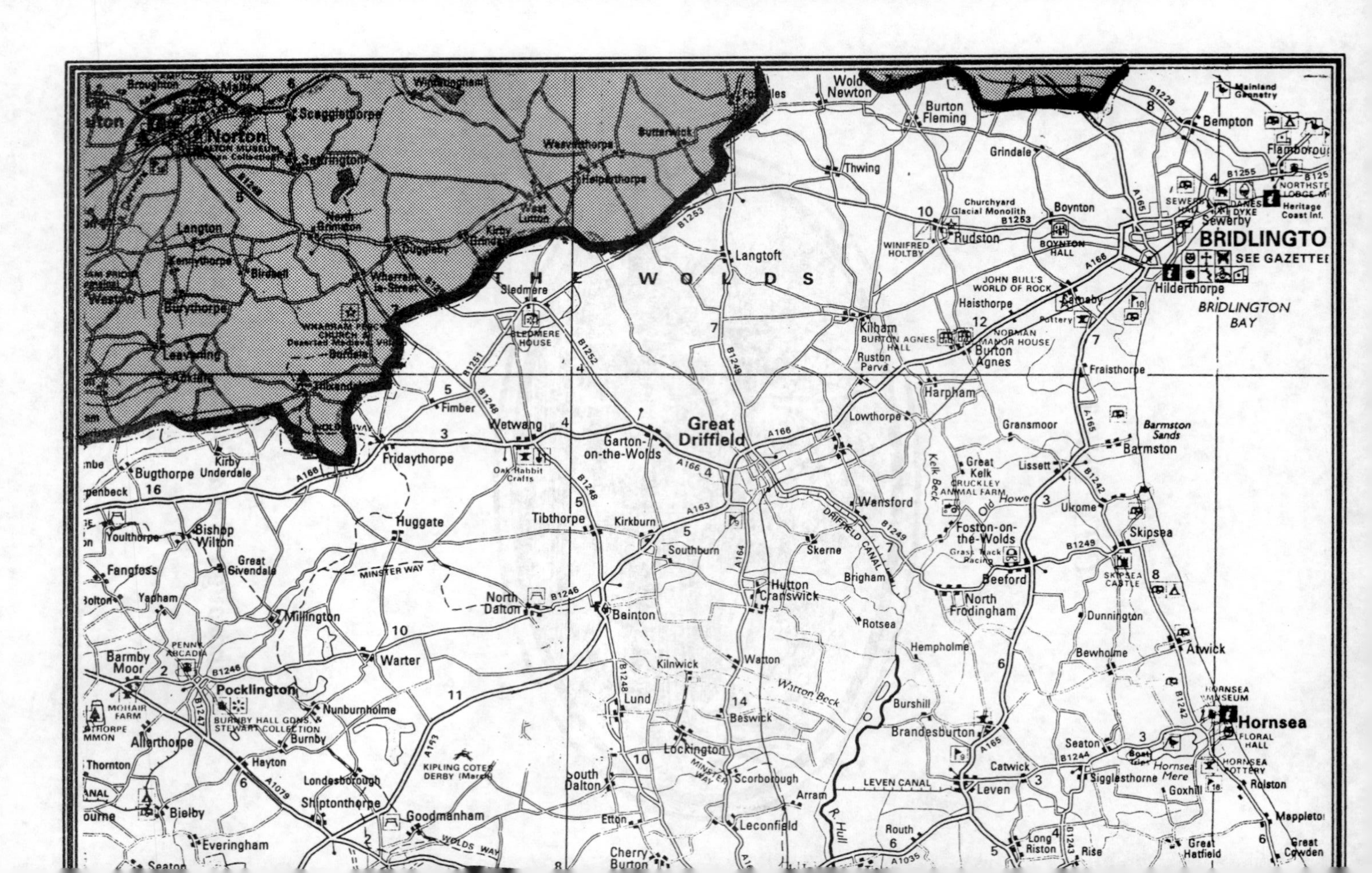

BRIDLINGTON
SEE GAZETTEER
BRIDLINGTON BAY
Hilderthorpe
Sewerby
Bempton
Mainland Gannetry
Flamborough
Heritage Coast Inf.
DANES DYKE
SEWERBY HALL
Boynton
BOYNTON HALL
Churchyard Glacial Monolith
Rudston
WINIFRED HOLTBY
Grindale
Burton Fleming
Wold Newton
Thwing
Langtoft
THE WOLDS
Kilham
BURTON AGNES HALL
Burton Agnes
NORMAN MANOR HOUSE
Haisthorpe
JOHN BULL'S WORLD OF ROCK
Carnaby
Pottery
Fraisthorpe
Barmston Sands
Barmston
Ruston Parva
Harpham
Lowthorpe
Gransmoor
Great Kelk
CRUCKLEY ANIMAL FARM
Kelk Beck
Old Howe
Lissett
Ulrome
Skipsea
SKIPSEA CASTLE
Foston-on-the-Wolds
Grass Track Racing
Beeford
North Frodingham
Dunnington
Bewholme
Atwick
HORNSEA MUSEUM
Hornsea
FLORAL HALL
HORNSEA POTTERY
Hornsea Mere
Goxhill
Rolston
Mappleton
Great Cowden
Great Hatfield
Sigglesthorne
Seaton
Catwick
Leven
LEVEN CANAL
Long Riston
Rise
Routh
Brandesburton
Burshill
Hempholme
R. Hull
Great Driffield
Wansford
DRIFFIELD CANAL
Skerne
Brigham
Rotsea
Hutton Cranswick
Watton
Watton Beck
Beswick
Kilnwick
Lockington
MINSTER WAY
Scorborough
Arram
Leconfield
Lund
South Dalton
Etton
Cherry Burton
Bainton
Southburn
Kirkburn
Tibthorpe
North Dalton
Garton-on-the-Wolds
Wetwang
Oak Rabbit Crafts
Fimber
Sledmere
SLEDMERE HOUSE
Fridaythorpe
Huggate
Warter
Millington
Nunburnholme
Burnby
BURNBY HALL GDNS. & STEWART COLLECTION
Pocklington
PENNY ARCADIA
Barmby Moor
MOHAIR FARM
Allerthorpe
Hayton
Londesborough
Shiptonthorpe
Goodmanham
KIPLING COTES DERBY (March)
WOLDS WAY
Thornton
Bielby
Everingham
Seaton
Bugthorpe
Kirby Underdale
Bishop Wilton
Youlthorpe
Fangfoss
Great Givendale
Yapham
Norton
Malton
Broughton
MALTON MUSEUM
Scagglethorpe
Settrington
Wintringham
Wharram-le-Street
Duggleby
Kirby Grindalythe
West Lutton
Helperthorpe
Weaverthorpe
Butterwick
North Grimston
Langton
Kennythorpe
Birdsall
Burythorpe
Westow
Leavening
Acklam
Thixendale
WHARRAM PERCY CHURCH & Deserted Medieval Village
Foxholles
A165
A166
A163
A164
A1079
A1035
B1229
B1255
B1253
B1249
B1252
B1251
B1248
B1246
B1247
B1242
B1243
B1244

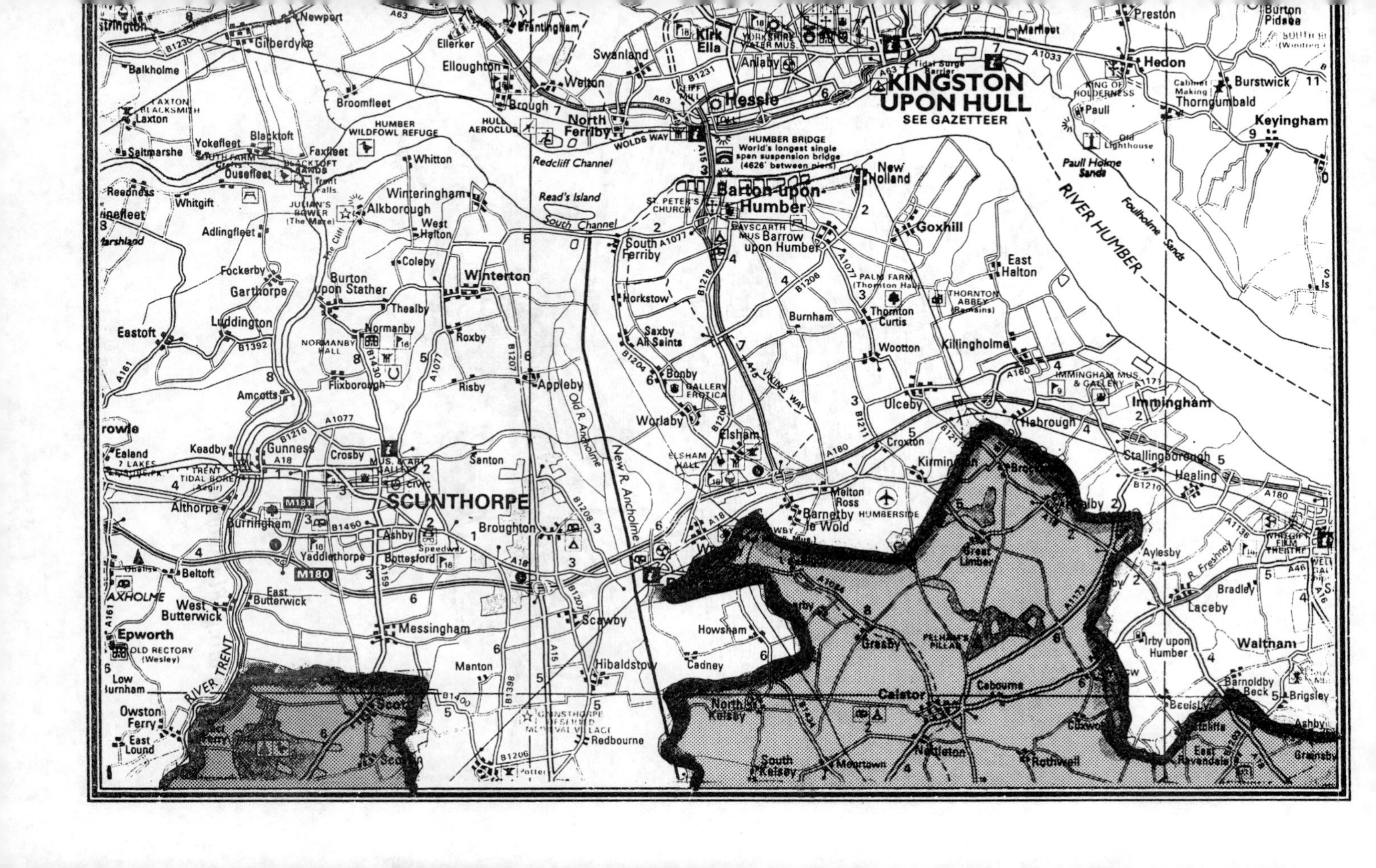

KINGSTON UPON HULL
SEE GAZETTEER
HUMBER BRIDGE
World's longest single span suspension bridge (4626' between piers)
RIVER HUMBER
Paull Holme Sands
Foulholme Sands
Redcliff Channel
Read's Island
South Channel
HUMBER WILDFOWL REFUGE
HULL AEROCLUB
WOLDS WAY
VIKING WAY
Barton upon Humber
BAYSCARTH MUS
Barrow upon Humber
ST. PETER'S CHURCH
THORNTON ABBEY (Remains)
PALM FARM (Thornton Hall)
IMMINGHAM MUS. & GALLERY
GALLERY EROTICA
ELSHAM HALL
NORMANBY HALL
JULIAN'S BOWER (The Maze)
OLD RECTORY (Wesley)
HUMBERSIDE
SCUNTHORPE
MUS. & ART GALLERY
CIVIC
Speedway
Old R. Ancholme
New R. Ancholme
RIVER TRENT
TRENT TIDAL BORE (Aegir)
7 LAKES
AXHOLME
Hessle
Anlaby
Kirk Ella
Swanland
Welton
Elloughton
Brough
North Ferriby
Brantingham
Ellerker
Newport
Gilberdyke
Balkholme
Laxton
Broomfleet
Blacktoft
Yokefleet
Saltmarshe
Faxfleet
Ousefleet
Reedness
Whitgift
Adlingfleet
Whitton
Winteringham
Alkborough
West Halton
Coleby
Winterton
Burton upon Stather
Thealby
Normanby
Roxby
Fockerby
Garthorpe
Luddington
Eastoft
Amcotts
Flixborough
Risby
Appleby
South Ferriby
Horkstow
Saxby All Saints
Bonby
Worlaby
Elsham
Burnham
Thornton Curtis
Wootton
Goxhill
New Holland
East Halton
Killingholme
Ulceby
Croxton
Kirmington
Habrough
Immingham
Stallingborough
Healing
Melton Ross
Barnetby le Wold
Great Limber
Aylesby
Laceby
Bradley
Waltham
Irby upon Humber
Barnoldby Beck
Brigsley
Ashby
Grasby
Howsham
Cadney
Caistor
Cabourne
North Kelsey
South Kelsey
Nettleton
Moortown
Rothwell
East Ravendale
Keadby
Gunness
Crosby
Santon
Burringham
Althorpe
Ashby
Bottesford
Yaddlethorpe
Broughton
Scawby
Messingham
East Butterwick
West Butterwick
Beltoft
Epworth
Low Burnham
Owston Ferry
East Lound
Manton
Hibaldstow
Redbourne
Ealand
Preston
Hedon
Paull
Thorngumbald
Burstwick
Keyingham
Marfleet
Burton Pidsea
Old Lighthouse
RING OF HOLDERNESS
R. Freshney
A63
A15
A1077
A18
A180
A160
A1173
A159
A161
A1033
A1136
A46
A16
M180
M181
B1218
B1206
B1204
B1211
B1207
B1208
B1398
B1400
B1430
B1392
B1216
B1450
B1231
B1230
B1210
B1434

North Landing, Flamborough

REFERENCE GUIDE

CHAPTER 3

NAME	*TOWN*	*TELEPHONE NO.*
'AND ALBERT' (National & International Art & Crafts)	BEVERLEY	0482-871251
BURTON LODGE HOTEL (Hotel)	BRANDESBURTON	0964-542847
DUKE OF CUMBERLAND (Public House)	NORTH FERRIBY	0482-631592
THE KINGS HEAD (Hotel)	BEVERLEY	0482-868103
OAK HOUSE (Accomodation)	BEVERLEY	0482-881481
SARGENTS DAIRY ICE CREAM (Ice Cream Parlour)	HIBALDSTOW	0652-654339
SPRINGFIELD WATER GARDEN CENTRE (Water Garden Centre & Fish Farm)	BURSTWICK	0482-896770
STRIDES GALLERY (Gallery/Framing)	DRIFFIELD	0377-241512

The Bayle

Bridlington Priory

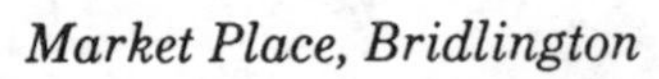

Market Place, Bridlington

CHAPTER 3

From Flamborough Head to Humberside

Any visit to the east coast of Yorkshire would be incomplete without a trip to the high cliffs of **Flamborough Head** and the huge expanse of Bridlington Bay.

Flamborough Head must be one of the most famous sights in England, as distinctive as the cliffs at Dover. The chalk that it consists of probably covered most of Yorkshire at a time when this part of the world was a vast sea, the remains of which are evident in the fossil deposits that can be found in abundance all along this coastline.

Flamborough itself, is another place where the sword-dancing festival, introduced by the Nordic settlers, has been retained. Originally it was the fishermen, in their white trousers and blue guernseys, who performed the rite, but now, with the decline in the fishing community, it is the boys of the local Primary School who have taken over. The dances, to the merry strains of melodian playing, comprise of such movements as the Fling-off, Single Parade, Swing Through and the final Lock of the wooden swords, which have replaced the 20 inch steel blades which were once used.

Another reminder of this region's ancient past, is the deceptively named **Dane's Dyke**, which is, in fact a much older site of an Iron Age entrenchment. A rather interesting legend connected with the place concerns the Constable family, who resided here throughout several centuries of early recorded history. The story goes that each year they kept the tradition of paying a token rent to the King of Denmark by firing an arrow bearing a gold coin from the headland into the sea. It is worth noting that at one time more than 40% of the placenames in the area were of Scandinavian origin, due to the fact that the Danes during their invasions had laid claim to much of the area over a long period, and therefore such rents were often required to be paid by the local families.

Travelling west, along the B1255, is the well-known seaside resort of **Bridlington**, noted particularly for its sands, which stretch along the coast for at least ten miles.

There are still some places of historical interest and charm in Bridlington, including the priory and busy harbour, although they are somewhat lost amidst the more modern trappings of a typical east coast resort.

Not so long ago, it was still the traditional Yorkshire fishing harbour, with rows of terraced stone-built houses and mile upon mile of uncluttered beaches. The bustling harbour thronged with the strong dialects of local fishermen conducting their sales of the day's catch, and holiday-makers could entertain themselves aboard the large steam-boat, or hire their own small rowing skiff.

Nowadays it is the bingo hall and fruit-machine arcade that beckons, and the tourist trade these attractions bring in has lured the off-spring of the old fishermen away from their original livelihood.

The surrounding coastline itself has suffered over the years from the devastations of erosion caused by the sea. Huge sections of this coastline as far as Withernsea have disappeared in an alarmingly short period of time.The owners of weekend bungalows which cluster together at various locations along this stretch are well aware of the risk that they may arrive one bank holiday weekend to discover that their garden or front door has disappeared, and that they may do so themselves whilst sleeping, should they be unprepared for this eventuality! Complete towns with names such as Auburn, Hartburn and Owlthorne, spoken of in old records as "places of fair fame" now lie beneath the waves of the North Sea, never to be seen again.

This process is due to the geological tilting which is lifting the west side of the British Isles and lowering the east, which has necessitated the construction of the protective sea walls in various seaside towns on the East coast.

Bridlington has been the site of various historical events throughout the ages and one very notable episode involved Queen Henrietta-Maria, the wife of Charles I.

The story goes that her ship was once forced into Bridlington Harbour by a savage storm at sea. During the height of the storm, she apparently attempted to calm her maidservants by rather optimistically proclaiming that "Queens of England are never drowned"

The house in which she took shelter afterwards was bombarded by enemy cannonballs during the night; she was forced to flee, clad only in a flimsy nightgown, and hid in a nearby ditch, having first run back to her lodgings to rescue her pet dog.

When the captain of the offending vessel was eventually captured by Royalist forces and condemned to death, the Queen intervened, protesting, "But I have forgiven him all that, as he did not kill me, he shall not be put to death on my behalf."

The next day, she departed with her retinue to Boynton Hall, travelling to it via the ancient Wold Gate.

The Hall grounds are watered by the quaintly named Gypsey Race, a chalk stream that has the peculiarity of disappearing underground for long periods, leaving a dry watercourse behind. In fact, the ditch Henrietta Maria had hidden in had been this very watercourse, and it was fortunate for her during her adventure, that it had not been further added to by a rather unpleasant and wet surprise!

There are many other interesting and eccentric stories in the history of Bridlington. It is a curious fact that, during the reign of King Stephen, the town was granted a peculiar source of revenue - the right to the goods and chattels of all fugitives and felons coming to the town, together with all the goods aboard any ship wrecked on its shores. As one may imagine, this statute was subject to a great deal of abuse by various corrupt individuals.

One story latched on to by the tourist industry, is the famous sea-battle between the American privateer, John Paul Jones, and several merchant ships led by Captain Pearson, which is a common theme in many of the holiday entertainments offered.

In the old town, one can see the Bayle or gatehouse of 1388, one of the only monastic buildings left in Bridlington. In its time, it has been used as a jail and a courtroom, and is now used as a museum for priceless antiques and memorabilia of the local East Yorkshire Regiment, the Green Howards.The Church and Priory of St Mary's are other buildings of interest, easily overlooked amidst the entertainment halls that surround it.

At **Sewerby**, nearby, is a magnificent Georgian mansion that is set in 50 acres of garden and parkland. The house was built in 1714-20, with later additions in 1808. There is an elegant Italian-style clock tower (1847) and the neo-Norman church was designed by Sir Giles Scott. Particularly lovely is the old-English style walled garden with a colourful and rich variety of flowers, a joy to walk through on a summer's day.

The house was first opened in 1936 by Amy Johnson and it was fitting that in 1958 her father presented the Museum with mementoes of the Yorkshire-born aviator. Johnson was the first woman to fly solo between England and Australia in 1930 and later made several epic journeys to South Africa and India. The museum has her flying jacket on exhibition, as well as her navigation instruments and an amazing collection of exotic gifts she was presented with from all over the world. There is also a small zoo with flamingoes, llamas and monkeys. The Museum and Art Gallery has a varied and rich collection with displays of motor vehicles, 'climmers' activities and archaeological finds, including Anglian bronze and gilded jewellery.

Sewerby House also has a famous portrait of Queen Henrietta Maria, wife of Charles 1. The picture has a particularly interesting history. In February 1643, Henrietta Maria visited Holland to pledge her personal jewellery in order to buy arms and ammunition to help the Royalist cause. She left Holland, escorted by seven Dutch vessels under the command of Admiral Van Tropp, hoping to make Newcastle. As previously mentioned, a storm prevented her. During her stay at Boynton Hall, she persuaded, or forced, the resident Strickland family to give her their gold and silver, which was melted down for her husband's cause. As a receipt, the Queen left the painting - one can imagine the fury of the staunch Parliamentarian Walter Strickland at this constant and cheeky reminder of his loss! Later, the painting was removed to Sewerby, and is on exhibition today, for all to see.

Seeking fresh air, one might wish to take a walk along Sewerby Cliffs, which have a remarkable geological feature - a buried cliff, another product of the geological tilting of the region.

Another of the town's famous attractions is **Burton Agnes Hall**, six miles out of the town on the A166, a fine example of a Tudor hall, built on an elaborate scale at the turn of the 16th century, towards the end of Elizabeth's reign.

The Hall has a broad recessed front between projecting wings with graceful bowed windows. A long gallery once stretched the full length of the building, with fine Venetian windows at each end. The hall has rosy brick walls and stone mullioned windows, and is surrounded by formal gardens and topiaries. It is particularly famous for its Jacobean gatehouse, with ceilings and overmantles carved in oak, plaster and alabaster. Its valuable collection of paintings are also worth viewing, if only for one of the least flattering portraits of Cromwell ever painted.

Close by, in comparison, is the old hall, some parts of which date back to Norman times. Behind is an old donkey wheel, used as a primitive means of power, and in these days of dwindling resources, who is to say that it might not be back in use some time in the future!

The Wolds, to the east of Bridlington, were once described by Daniel Defoe in his travels, as "very thin of towns and people", although he recorded a great number of sheep, cattle and horses. The Sykes family were largely responsible for its civilisation and reclamation; before then, as recently as the 17th century, there were recordings of wolves roaming the region, ravaging the local sheep folds and villages.

Rudston House, near to Boynton, previously mentioned, is famous as the childhood home of Winifred Holtby, well-known authoress and avid believer in the fairies she claimed to be able to communicate with at the bottom of the garden here. No wolves here, although not too far away at Hunmanby, the local church ran a hospital for travellers who had been savaged by the beasts whilst crossing the then inhospitable Wolds; in fact the name of the village is said to have been derived from "House of Dog Maw", a place where hounds were kept for hunting down the same pestilential beasts.

Further on, down the A166, is the busy agricultural town of **Great Driffield**, with its popular riverside area and converted warehouses. It is a town of ancient origins and was once the capital of the kingdom of Deira. The famous Saxon king Ethelred is also said to be buried here.The Parish Church is a good example of Perpendicular architecture, parts of it dating back to the 12th century.Inside, it has beautiful stained glass windows, medieval in origin, portraying local nobility.

In Exchange Street, a small thoroughfare running directly off the town's main street, we found an unusual and fascinating establishment, **Strides Gallery**, which is run by two sisters Alison Botten and Karen Cross. The name of the gallery originates from the previous owners, a

Strides Gallery

butcher's family who occupied the premises for over a hundred years. At one time, parts of the building were used as a slaughterhouse and holding area for cattle and sheep, and when at the turn of the century there was a serious flood in Driffield, the animals were saved from the rising floodwaters by being dragged up into the family's living quarters on the upper floors. Since the shop had become so well known as the home of the Strides' family business, it was decided to retain the name for the gallery. Today, there is a fine selection of artwork on show which is produced by both new and well-known British artists/craftspeople. The gallery specialises in hand-made contemporary glass, studio ceramics, jewellery, wood and original watercolours, and also offers a carefully chosen selection of etchings and limited-edition prints. As well as providing helpful and knowledgeable advice, Alison and Karen operate an efficient on-site picture framing service. Open Monday to Saturday, 9.30am to 5pm. Closed Wednesday.

Ten miles north-west of Great Driffield is the popular **Sledmere House** (situated north of the rather curiously named village of Wetwang). It is a magnificent Georgian mansion that has belonged for many years to the Sykes family, its gardens having been landscaped by Capability Brown. When one enters the village of Sledmere, one might be forgiven for thinking that one has been dropped into a masterpiece of classical fantasy. It might be true to say that different generations of the Sykes family had set about creating a decorative playground for themselves - statues of tritons blowing horns herald you through gates, past pillars and even through the doors of the village inn! Robert Manners, MP for Hull was once quoted as saying to Sir Richard Sykes,

Carved Figures, St Mary's

"Till Sledmere is quite completed, the delight you take in that pretty place I dare say will not let you stop your hand, but afford you daily employment and the most delightful amusement."

There is indeed a wonderful sense of fun around this place - there are humorous friezes by Joseph Rose in the Hall, and lovely little carved parasols above the cresting of a Chinese-style bed. For those of more studious direction, there is a huge library over a hundred feet long.

Those of musical tastes may be interested in the large pipe organ, that is played daily between 2.00 - 4.00pm. There is also an Exhibition Centre and a Waggoners Museum, as well as special events throughout the summer.

Travelling down the B164, we visited the ancient market town of **Beverley**, a place of curious and eccentric place-names steeped in history. It gained its power as the centre of trade and industry that served the port of Hull during medieval times. This was tightly controlled by the 38 trade guilds that implemented a complex set of ordinances. Some of these included the ordinance that saddlers were not allowed to make reins, and that bakers were not allowed to employ Scotsmen- whether or not this was due to the bad feelings generated by the many invasions by their more northerly neighbours, or whether it was simply because their culinary abilities were considered rather inadequate, we will never know!

As a centre of trade, it naturally was an important market centre. This is approached from the south by Toll Gavel, the ancient toll-gate that was controlled by the guilds.

The market is separated into three sections. The south side is South Market, Cornhill on the north side and there is also Butterdings pavement in the centre, in the middle of which is the 18th century market cross. As the name may imply, this area was reserved for the sale of butter and dairy produce.

A pleasing blend of different centuries' architecture has shaped the Beverley we know today. The town is surrounded by 'common pastures', which are still supervised by pasture-masters and a 'regular neat-herd'.

As might be expected, Beverley is notable for it's antiquaries - which include the Minster, St Mary's church and the 18th century Guildhall. The Guildhall still houses a court-room which deals with offenders even today. The figure of Justice overlooking the building is unusual in that she does not wear a blindfold, contrary to the norm. A town clerk was said to have replied, in answer to a query about this, that "In Beverley, justice is not blind."

Under the shadow of the minster in **Beverley**'s Highgate, we came across a real find, the labyrinth of shops and small retail units collectively known as **'...and Albert'**. We were first attracted to this fascinating Victorian arcade by the imaginative 3D sign which hangs on the wall to the right of the doorway. This shows a dozen of the shop units in miniature and has a charming 'doll's house' quality reminiscent of one of Richard Hamil-

Beverley Minster

ton's pop art creations. Inside, the building has the compelling atmosphere of an Arabian souk. The air is filled with such evocative aromas as freshly-ground coffee, perfumed candles and newly-worked leather, adding to the feeling that one is entering a vast Aladdin's Cave.

All three storeys are overflowing with a fascinating array of crafts and artefacts, some produced locally and some originating from as far away as Africa and the Far East. Altogether, there are twenty-five shop units offering an astonishing variety of high quality products of every description. The shop known as Magpie stocks a beautiful selection of cards, clocks, candles and gifts, and within its upstairs room a fascinating range of etchings from the antique print shop. An interesting range of plants, terracotta pots and frostproof planters can be found throughout the whole building. Those interested in studio glass and crystal cutting should look out for the Little Glass Studio, and upstairs, a unique range of handmade and imported jewellery is on view at Sirocco. The Africana Room imports batiks from Uganda, paintings from Tanzania and tapestries from Losotho and Transkei, and the Turning World, sells top quality hand-worked wooden bowls and giftware.

Leather Craft specialises in belts and leatherware made from the finest British hides, and at Quilling Cards, beautiful handmade stationery and cards can be personalised by their helpful staff. Those interested in minerals and semi-precious stones should head for Merlin's Crystal Cave, and collectors of secondhand books should seek out Books on the first floor. Also on this floor can be found the Honey Pot and Reflections, shops which offer a varied choice of original gifts including framed prints, mirrors and clocks. Anyone interested in fine linen, lace and beadwork should make a point of finding Broderies, and those with a fascination for beautifully detailed miniature buildings should look for the premises run by M. James.

The Sugar Craft Shop stocks everything for the cake decorator and sugar craft artist, and mouthwatering handmade fudge and chocolates are available at Hideaway Wood. Also on view is a display of kitchens and kitchen furniture by Stirling and Jones Traditional Interiors. Those in need of refreshment after all this hard work, should then head for the Butler's Parlour Victorian Tea and Coffee Rooms to enjoy a delicious homemade cake, sandwich or light meal accompanied by a cup of speciality tea or coffee.

The proprietor of '...and Albert' is Cottingham-born David Murden. After completing a master's degree in clinical psychology, his intention was to return to the area to practise his chosen profession. His plans were changed, however, when he discovered that in Beverley, a number of small traders were being prevented from obtaining retail premises due to the inflated rents brought on by the property boom. He then took up the offer to purchase the premises in Highgate and set out to convert the building for use as a Victorian arcade whilst still practising as a psychologist. However, this plan was not without its problems; the building turned out to require a substantial amount of reconstruction work which led to a great deal of financial pressure being placed on David's shoulders. However, by the end of 1987, the project was successfully completed and the building opened its doors for to the public for the first time.

...And Albert'

Such has been the success of the project since then, that David has opened a second '...and Albert' in York's Stonegate, although this new operation differs from the first in that it is run as a large single retail unit rather than as a number of small ones. The York shop also acts as a showroom and test-market for David's latest project, the '...and Albert' World Crafts' Trade Warehouse at Market Weighton, where a huge variety of traditional crafts and modern artefacts are imported from the Third World to sell to the trade. What is perhaps even more incredible is that David is not satisfied merely to involve himself with the UK end of the operation. We discovered that he also personally travels to such countries as Nigeria, Morocco, Java and Bali on buying expeditions for the warehouse. Part entrepreneur and part adventurer, David's exploits will undoubtedly lead to further successful and worthwhile enterprises in the future.

One place in particular we would recommend if staying in this popular tourist spot is the splendid **Kings Head Hotel**. This historic inn dates from Georgian times and during its recent refurbishment, great care was taken to preserve the genuine character and atmosphere of the building. There are now twelve beautifully appointed bedrooms, all furnished in an attractive country style and equipped with en-suite

The King's Head Hotel

bathrooms, colour televisions, trouser presses and tea/coffee making facilities. On the ground floor, there is a pleasant hotel bar offering a wide range of traditional beers, wines and delicious bar meals. The hotel's charming country kitchen restaurant is open both to residents and non-residents and serves an excellent range of continental and traditional English dishes which are prepared using fresh locally-sourced ingredients wherever possible. (On Sundays, excellent traditional roast lunches are available.) There is also an excellent wine list offering selections from most wine-producing areas of the world. The Kings Head also has an attractive conservatory room where guests can enjoy a drink or light meal in relaxed plant-filled surroundings. Adjacent to the hotel, we found an attractive coffee shop and bistro serving a range of tasty sandwiches, snacks, pastries and cakes, along with a selection of specialist coffees and teas.

Also in **Beverley**, in the charmingly named road 'North Bar Without', we called in at the first-rate bed and breakfast establishment, **Oak House**. Owners Mr and Mrs Hindle have lived in this fascinating house for over thirty years. The older, rear half of the building is Georgian and dates back to 1780; the front half was a later addition in 1880 by James Elwell who was responsible for the extensive wood carving which was

Oak House

hand-crafted in Victorian Tudor style both outside and inside the house. The old metal bell-pull still operates at the front entrance, although it no longer summons a butler from some distant downstairs room. On entering the house, the wood panelling, block flooring, carved oak architraves and impressive staircase not only create a warm and friendly atmosphere, but also evoke a great sense of history. The Hindles have been offering their guests a genuine welcome and warm hospitality for many years. (They also offer a full English breakfast which has to be seen to be believed.) The guest bedrooms are traditionally decorated and equipped to a good standard, and the public rooms are spacious and comfortable. The owners take great pride in offering friendly personal service and like to think of Oak House more as a private home which offers good quality, restful accommodation.

One of the famous sons of Beverley was James Edward Elwell, the creator of the Gothic-style screen, as well as some of the house frontages in North Bar Without. The house once occupied by him has carvings of his, based on subject matter from Punch magazine. In conservative Beverley, these created a stir in their day, as one can see such national leaders as Disraeli and Gladstone graphically and irreverently depicted. His son Frederick W.Elwell R.A. was another famous and versatile artist.

Lewis Carroll was familiar with Beverley, and in fact claimed to have been inspired with his idea for the White Rabbit on seeing a statue of a rabbit carrying a satchel in the grounds of St Mary's Church.

The Minster is possibly best viewed from Westwood, one of the common pastures that encircle the town, its twin west towers rising in pale splendour from the plain that surrounds it.

North Bar Without, Beverley

Its wonderful and distinctive Gothic lines provide excellent material for photographers, and good views are also to be found from the neighbouring streets that lead up to it.

The interior is notable for its splendid carvings - in the west front are the figures of Adam and Eve in the Garden of Eden, and inside medieval queens stand alongside packmen and farmers, choristers and a man playing the bagpipes. There is a rather wry scene of a fox, robed as a cleric, preaching to a congregation of geese. All of these were produced by the Ripon school of woodcarvers before the Reformation took place.

Near to the High Altar is the chair used by malefactors to seek sanctuary, a strangely evocative sight. Carved out of the solid stone, it is also known as the Frith stool, and may once have been John of Beverley's episcopal seat in the 8th century. There are only two others in existence in the British Isles, one at Hexham Priory, the other at Sprotborough Church, near Doncaster. It was originally designated for the purpose it is known for today by King Athelstan in 937 AD.

Offenders using this cold, unyielding seat, whilst the Church authorities decided what to do with them, usually found they were given board and lodging for 30 days, and then given a safe escort to the county boundary or the nearest port.

Another favourite tourist attraction is the tomb of Lady Eleanor Percy, adorned with its wonderful canopy of angels, saints and knights. Its splendour must surely be a sign of the high regard both her family and others held for her, although her actual lifespan was both short and quiet, not at all indicative of the flamboyant decoration of her resting place.

The magnesian limestone that the Minster is built from, as are so many of the stone structures in this region, often seems to glow, especially in the evenings, bringing the wonderful carvings within and without to life. Try not to overlook the quirky representations of the ailments Stomach Ache, Toothache, Sciatica and Lumbago, surely more terrifying to any medieval or modern onlooker than the most grimly threatening gargoyle, more often seen in such settings.

One hidden place within the Minster that we would recommend, if you can obtain permission, is the section in the roof that houses the 18th century crane. It is used by workmen effecting repairs on the inner cicumference for hoisting materials, etc. It can be approached by a spiral staircase in the south transept, and then up some curious steps flanked on either side by the ancient buttresses, strange by the fact that they are constructed from bleached, twisted tree branches.

A mile to the north of the point where the A165 Hull to Bridlington road meets the B1244 Hornsea road, we called in at the **Burton Lodge Hotel** near **Brandesburton.**

Burton Lodge Hotel

Set within two acres of landscaped grounds, this splendid country house hotel has its own pitch and putt course and grass tennis court. It also adjoins an attractive parkland golf course where guests can enjoy reduced green fees. All the beautifully decorated guest rooms in this recently extended and remodelled hotel have private bathrooms, colour televisions, telephones and tea/coffee making facilities. There is also a delightful dining room which serves the very best in English country cuisine. The hotel has been designated English Tourist Board 'three crown highly commended'.

Travelling toward the coast, is the resort of **Hornsea**, most famous for its pottery factory, which is the largest visitor attraction in Humberside, providing all year activities for the family. Hornsea is a quieter resort than Bridlington, but still has plenty to offer the active tourist.

The Mere is a well-known nature reserve, with facilities for boating, sailing and angling. It is Yorkshire's largest freshwater lake, formed by glacial action, and is the refuge for over 170 species of birds. Also nearby at Hornsea Bridge is the North Holderness Museum of Village Life, with carefully recreated period rooms, and an exhibition of agricultural equipment and tools of local trades.

The quaint church of St Nicholas is a charming example of a fisherman's church, built mainly of sea-cobbles. One local character of note was the Parish Clerk in the 1700s, who apparently used the crypt to hide smuggled goods. The church was unroofed one night during a terrifying storm, and so troubled was the miscreant by the ominous nature of this sign from above, that he suffered a fatal stroke as a result.

Nearby **Burton Constable Hall** was originally built in 1570 by Sir John Constable, with parts of the previous structure dating back as far as the reign of King Stephen in the 1100s. The Hall was also completely remodelled in the 18th century on Jacobean lines.

The ubiquitous Capability Brown also designed these grounds, inspired by the gardens at Versailles. Indeed King Louis XVIII of France was invited to live here during his exile after the Revolution, and perhaps the Constables decided it might make him feel more at home!

There are some wonderful portraits adorning the walls here, including Zucchero's Mary Queen of Scots and Holbein's portraits of Sir Thomas Cranmer and Sir Thomas More.

The magnificent Chinese room is a glory to see, and the many dragons that skulk around it are a favourite with all visitors. Some are constructed of Chinese paper, others of more robust nature hold little Chinese lanterns, there are others climbing to the windows and clawing at the window jambs.

There are baby dragons that glower at us in endearing hostility - what pleasure the Constable family must have had in inviting friends to view this room! It does in fact pre-date the Prince Regent's similar extravaganza at the Brighton pavilion, and Thomas Chippendale himself designed the distinctive Dragon chair, fit for a Ming Emperor.

This region of Holderness is a place of great contrasts, with the old towns of Market Weighton andBeverley on one hand and the garishly tacky resorts, such as Cleethorpes on the other.

The farthest place of interest down the Holderness coast is the lively, traditional resort of **Withernsea**. As with all the resorts on this coastline, the beaches are long, golden and sandy, and their cleanliness has earned them praise from the European community commission. Notable tourist attractions are the bird sanctuary at Spurn Point, the Lighthouse Museum, and the popular Sunday Market. There is also the Pavilion Leisure Centre, (when the weather does not live up to expectations) equipped withswimming pools, water flume, sauna, solarium, as well as dry sports facilities.

The Withernsea Lighthouse Trust accomodates a museum dedicated to the RNLI, the adjoining building housing the Kay Kendall Memorial Museum and local history section.

Spurn Point does not appear, at first glance, to be a place of great attraction to tourists, but should you be searching for a desolate and uninhabited wilderness, then you would find the ideal location. It is a region of sand-dunes and flats, where no-one but the lighthouse crew and the life-boat men and their families live. The only other denizens are the hundreds of species of rare and solitary wild-fowl that take sanctuary here, and are the fascination of the avid bird-watcher. It is, in fact, the very isolation of the place that has provided the ideal home for these birds, and one hopes that it will remain so.

There are some other villages and hamlets in this region that are also worthy of a visit. **Patrington** is a collection of picturesque dutch-style cottages that surround a 14th century church considered so beautiful, that it is titled "the Queen of Holderness" The tower and spire are considered to be particularly fine, along with the nave arcades, south transept, and the Easter Sepulchre. The coastal erosion around these parts works out at about two yards per year, which, though a constant threat, means this particular Queen will safely reign for at least another 2000 years!

A look by the curious historian will discover many places of note in this area alone that have, as with previously named cases, fallen prey to the encroaching sea.

Ravensrodd was one of these, noted as the place where Henry

Bolingbroke erected a sculptured cross to mark his landing in 1399. It now resides in Holyrood House at Hedon, a sad reminder of the once prestigious port.

Patrington Church

The descendents of the Constable family, who still bear the title Lords of Holderness, retain the dubious privilege of ownership of any flotsam and jetsam that comes to shore on this peninsula. On being lauded on his fortune in this, the late Brigadier Chichester Constable was heard to reply,

"I also have to pay for burying or otherwise disposing of any whale grounded on the Holderness shore - and it costs me about £20 a time!" - a not insubstantial sum in those days. The huge bones of one such whale are still on show in the grounds of the hall today.

The tiny village of **Paull** is worth visiting for its wonderful view across the Holderness plain and that afforded from its short promenade of the Humber estuary. Nearby **Hedon** is yet another ancient borough, and sports a church that companions the one at Patrington called the "King of Holderness'

Three miles east of Hedon, we came across the **Springfield Fish Farm and Water Garden Centre**, located near the pleasant village of Burstwick, south of the B1362. Springfield Fish Farm consists of a large and attractive area of landscaped grounds, which in addition to a large variety of

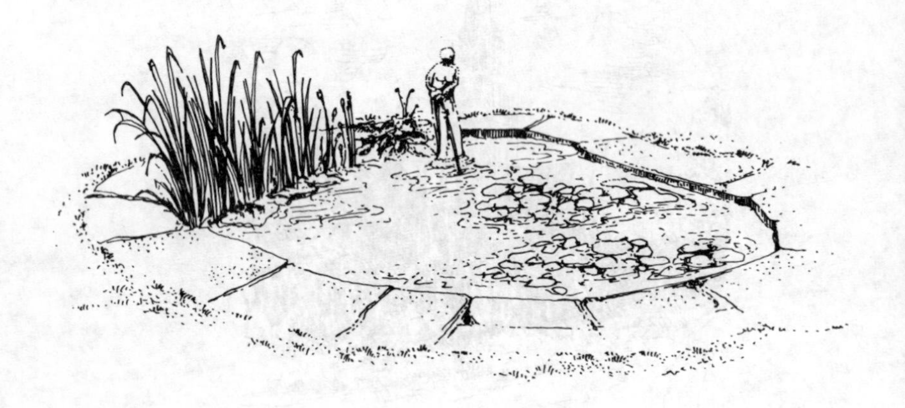

Springfield Fish Farm and Water Garden

specimen trees, shrubs and plants, contains twelve natural ponds. These ponds are home to many thousands of ornamental freshwater fish, perhaps the most spectacular of which is the splendid Koi fish that can grow up to three feet long. Visitors are welcome to wander around the gardens and fish farm, to sit and view the special display ponds and, at certain times, to even feed the fish. The Springfield Garden Centre supplies everything that could be required by owners of garden ponds and aquariums. Apart from the many interesting species of fish, items available include an enormous selection of water-loving plants, water-pumps, pond-linings, books and specialist equipment. The family are true enthusiasts and are always on hand to provide helpful and knowledgable advice on anything relating to the fascinating world of the freshwater garden.

Hull, officially known as Kingston upon Hull, lies on the southern margin of the plain of Holderness, its port and harbour washed by the tidal flow of the Humber, whose mouth is at Spurn Head.

The area was presided over in medieval days by the war-like Lords of

Holderness, the land here much prized due to its accessibility for shipping and trade. The Romans had used it as a port to supply the fortresses and garrisons in the area, although it really only started to take on real significance in the 1200's. A medieval chronicler wrote,

"Hull, a town of seamen and merchants, scarcely heard of in Saxon days, outport of York and Beverley, was drawing to itself the trade of the great waterways that converged on the Humber, shipping thence wool, hides, lead and small amounts of cloth."

In Tudor days, it was a well known and prosperous town, as the many period houses and mansions in the area will attest.

It is hard for us to imagine, with our modern, stereotyped view of the county, and living in days of centralised government, just how important a role Yorkshire has played during many historical/political interludes. Hull's significance as a port attracted the most powerful of families, and many political and religious upheavals occurred here that were to reverberate throughout England. The infamous Pilgrimage of Grace during Henry VIII's reign took place here, the closest to civil war England was to come to, prior to the conflict between the Royalists and Parliamentarians two centuries after.

It involved several notable families in the region, including the Lords of Holderness. Henry's reply to the insurrection was swift and terrible, and ended the lines of many of these ancient houses.

During the Civil War in Charles I's reign, Hull again became a focal point, and the Royalists spent much time and effort, mostly wasted, on attempting to wrest the control of the Humber from the Parlimentarian forces.

There were many well-known coaching houses here in the 18th century, most of which no longer exist. There were the Crosskeys and the Reindeer in the Market Place, the Crosskeys in Whitefriargate, Moor's (now the George Hotel) in the Land of Green Ginger and Wellburns in Lowgate. By the 1830's most of the trade had gone to the Vittoria Tavern in Queen Street, the Bull and Sun in Mytongate (an ancient reference to the worship of the god Mithras by the Romans in this area) and the Black Horse in Carr Lane. Of these only the George remains.

Hull is perhaps mostly known for being the birthplace of that most famous of reformers, William Wilberforce, noted for his campaign to abolish the slave trade.

There is an impressive Elizabethan house in High Street where he was born, now used as a museum to commemorate his life and works.

The Transport Museum, just a few yards down the road is also

Humber Bridge

worth a visit. Here one can see such curiosities as the Velocipede and "Automobile a Vapeur" - a steam driven car. Tourists visiting the museum invariably cluster around Lady Chesterfield's ornamental sleigh, caparisoned with ornamental swan and rearing unicorn, with its panoply of bells to herald her approach. She must have longed for the snow to come in order to venture forth in this fanciful mode of transport!

Many of the oldest parts of Hull were bombed out of existence in the second world war, but fortunately the subsequent rebuilding has not resulted in so much of the urban, concrete replacements that other such towns and ports have suffered. There is still a wealth of beautiful, ancient and grand architecture, of which the area around the Queen's gardens, the Maritime Museum and the Holy Trinity Church are but a few. The old town, much of which dates back 800 years ago, is full of narrow cobbled streets and quays and old waterside inns which are popular with visitors to the city. The high-rise tower-blocks of so many cities are fortunately lacking here, offering clear views of the city's old architecture and the Humber estuary, spanned by the famous bridge.

The entertainments are many, but for those especially interested in the arts, theatre and music, as well as the pageantry associated with the area, the Spring might make a good time to visit, as this is when the Hull Festival takes place, which offers an excellent selection of events.

Hessle, lying closest to the great Humber Bridge, is an excellent point to either take a train or the car through the picturesque Wolds villages on this side of the Humber, inland towards Selby. Those interested in geology will be interested in the chalk cliffs in this region - to be found nearly 20 miles inland. These are relics of the original coastline, which ran from this point to Bridlington.

Like its neighbour, **Kirkella**, the town was founded by the heathen son of the Saxon King Ida, who invaded in AD547 and who established the kingdom of Northumbria, which stretched from the Humber to the Firth of

Forth. Hessle is an attractive market town these days with some fine Georgian houses.

Three miles out of Hessle, we turned off the A63 to reach the former Viking settlement of **North Ferriby**. Set back from the main road in the High Street, we found the **Duke of Cumberland**, an imposing Tudor-style pub and eating place run by Dan and Julie Hallas, two charming hosts whose approach is young and informal. They both started working here as part-time bar staff until within two years, they were made an offer to run the pub. Since they have been in charge, they have successfully created an atmosphere which is welcoming both to regulars and visitors alike. The spacious lounge and bar are full of character and provide a comfortable and relaxing place to enjoy a quiet drink or an appetising bar meal from the extensive range available.

The pub also has an impressive function room and a large attractive play area to the rear. On Sundays, Dan and Julie organise very popular and enjoyable quiz evenings.

The Duke of Cumberland

Nearby, is the pretty village of **Welton**, with its stream that flows past the green, under bridges and into a tree-lined duck pond. The imposing Welton Grange was built in 1741 for a Hull merchant, complete with its Venetian style windows. In fact the whole of Welton was a retreat for the wealthy shipping merchants of Hull, and the architecture reflects this.

The Church of St Helen here, dates from Norman times, but was almost totally rebuilt by Sir Giles Gilbert Scott in 1862-3, the Victorian architect who designed St Pancras station. It is particularly noted for its13th century doorway and the intricate Pre-Raphaelite windows made by William Morris' company of craftsmen. In the graveyard is the memorial of Jeremiah Found, a resilient local reputed to have out-lived eight wives!

The Green Dragon Inn at Welton is famous as the place where the highwayman Dick Turpin, residing here under the alias of John Palmers, was finally arrested in 1736, not for his crimes of highway robbery, but for the misdemeanour of drunkenly shooting a cockerel and threatening a labourer.

Further up the A65, is **Brantingham**, with its church that nestles between two hillsides. The village's war memorial is particularly unusual, and of heroic proportions, and was built from masonry rescued from Cuthbert Broderick's Guildhall in Hull during its reconstruction in 1914. Various stone urns located around the town were also part of the salvage.

Here, also on the edge of the Wolds is the village of **South Cave**, the name of which is said to be a corruption of South Cove, due to its southern parish being located in a back-water of the Humber. It was granted a town charter in 1291, and it has a Town Hall and market place that were built in 1796. Whilst here, one might make a point of looking out for **Cove Castle**, a splendid Gothic building once the home of George Washington's great grandfather.

Travelling back through **North Ferriby**, we crossed the Humber Bridge, and journeyed south-east, to the well-known towns of **Grimsby** and **Cleethorpes**, the former with the tradition of being the foremost North Sea fishing port, the latter one of the busiest east coast resorts.

Cleethorpes' popularity grew as a result of the weekend-break requirements of the Humberside masses, with a tradition for the freshest cod and chips in Yorkshire, due to it's proximity to neighbouring Grimsby, less than three miles up the coast.

The front is tightly packed with all manner of diversions for the traditional family holiday, so characteristic of the English seaside; donkeys, crazy golf, funfairs, winter gardens, shows and exhibitions - they are all here, dominated by the not-unattractive pier, which looks out to a broad sweep of the North Sea as it enters the Humber estuary, with the occasional deep-sea trawler and cargo ship heading for Grimsby and the Hull Docks.

Grimsby's entertainments are possibly more hidden that most, especially if one is constantly distracted by the all pervasive aroma of the fishing industry, which is king here. The town has its own peculiarly industrial skyline, dominated as it is with the derricks of the cargo handling cranes, lighthouses and masts of the many trawlers that still operate from here, despite the economic handicaps imposed on them through recent fishing quota regulations, which do not appear to have dimmed the spirit of those whose families have carried on the trade here for generations.

Its history, as with so many of these east-coast towns, starts with the Danes. The story goes that a Danish fisherman called Grim landed on the south bank of the River Humber after fleeing Denmark with the heir to the Danish throne, Havelock, who had been in danger from those who wished to usurp his inheritance. Grim settled here, and the subsequent village became known as "Grim's Place", or Grimsby as it was later known.

The sustaining of Grimsby in relatively modern times has relied, first on the canal system, which helped in the transporting of the fishermen's wares to the rest of the North, then the excellent road system, which now ensures that the many fish-mongers and the mobile outlets that one sees dotted around the north of England (and possibly further) can boast 'Fresh fish from Grimsby '. The huge demand for fish and chips from the east coast resorts, such as Cleethorpes, Mablethorpe and Skegness has also aided the perpetuation of the industry.

Grimsby also, predictably, offers some of the best seafood restaurants in the North, so lovers of this particular form of cuisine might like to stop off in order to investigate this claim.

The cultural focal point in recent times, has centred on the impressive **National Fishing Heritage Centre** - no-one can say that the people of Grimsby are not proud of their fishing industry, as a visit to this remarkable centre will prove.

The centre comprises of a walk-through, theatrical documentary on the history of fishing in the region. It is a sensory experience, enhanced by simulated ships' decks that roll and pitch in an uncomfortably authentic way, and icy blasts of arctic- style gales, in an attempt to simulate the trawlermen's progress through the Arctic fishing grounds. One will also learn about the fishing communities' superstitions, how the skipper knew where to start fishing, how many boats were lost, how much was earned, what their first port of call was when they first arrived home, and so on.

A further attraction is the **Perseverance**, the last all sail fishing smack to operate from Grimsby, still rigged and floating in a large indoor marina.

The Centre has four galleries that have an ever-changing programme of exhibitions, a gift shop called **The Bonded Stores** and a cafe titled **The Ice Barrel**. There are also a range of music, dance and arts exhibitions and craft markets throughout the summer.

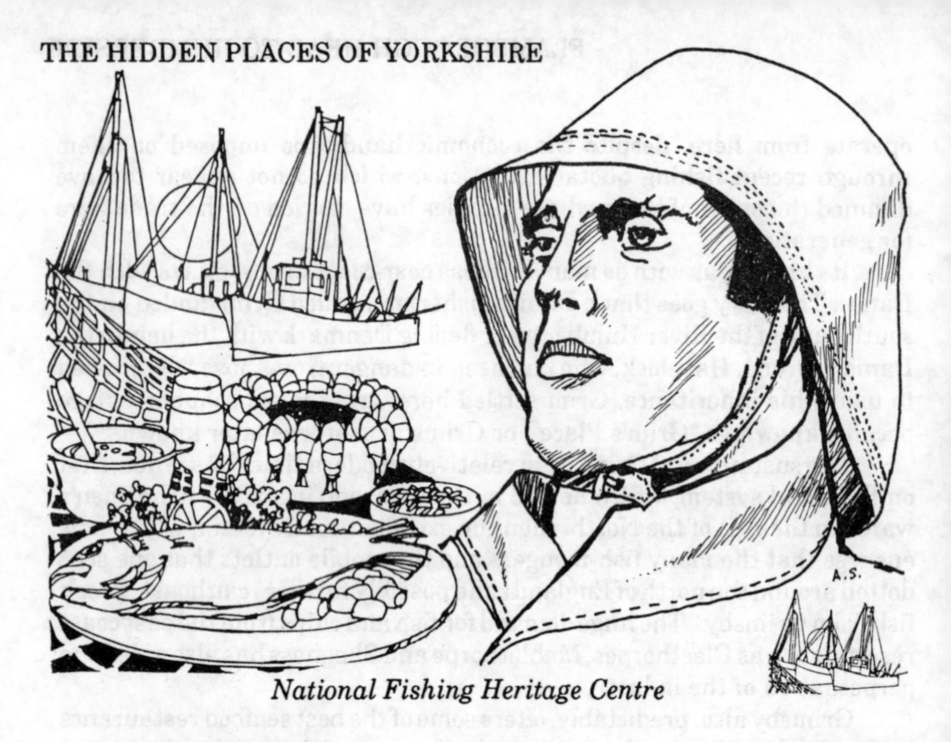

National Fishing Heritage Centre

Visitor participation is encouraged throughout, which the Centre describes as a Share and Shiver experience!

One will leave this place with a fascination for this dangerous and romantic occupation, that much is guaranteed. Those Saturday night fish-and-chips will never taste the same again!

The Alexandra Dock is another focus of activity, with a range of water-borne activities, a folk club that operates from the **P.S. Lincoln Castle** - a finely restored paddle steamer moored there and a jazz festival that takes place in the summer.

There are other musical events of repute that take place, including lunchtime concerts that take place at the historic Town Hall, orchestral and choral concerts of national repute and an international singing competition.

Other leisure attractions include an excellent golf course, **the Peoples' Park,** well-equipped Leisure Centre, various activities in the Weelsby and Bradley Woods, charming Victorian and modern shopping streets and malls and, of course, those inns frequented by the fishing and trawlermen, and definitely to be visited by those looking for the real Grimsby, that cannot be supplied by the tourist industry!

Nearby attractions include the east coast resorts, watersports on offer at **Barton Clay Pits**, an interesting reclamation project, the 12th century

Thornton Abbey, Waltham Mill, with its museum and miniature railway, the 900 year old Alvingham Watermill, the award-winning Elsham Hall Country Park, equipped with craft shops and falconry centre, and the Regency-style Normanby Hall, which is set in 350 acres of magnificent parkland. Details of all these venues are available from the Tourist Information centre at the Heritage Centre in Grimsby.

Travelling west, is the town of **Brigg**, and on recommendation, we went in search of **Sargent's Dairy Ice Cream Parlour**, which is situated at Wheelgate's Farm near **Hibaldstow**. This impressive family-run firm can be found four miles southwest of Brigg, and a couple of miles south of junction 4 on the M180.

Sargent's Dairy Ice Cream

Wheelgates stands within a pleasant country area whose main economic activity is agriculture. It was here that in 1922, the Sargent family founded their manufacturing operation which today still produces old-fashioned dairy ice-cream according to traditional methods and using recipes which utilise only fresh natural ingredients. Since the ice-cream parlour at Wheelgates was opened in 1988, it has proved to be a great success. Visitors are welcome to tour the farm before trying a home-made afternoon tea or ice-cream from the extensive choice available (in recent years, a number of mouth-watering speciality ice-creams have been added to the range). The Sargents also have a landau available which can be hired for weddings and special occasions. This is drawn by a pair of handsome grey horses which can often be seen around the farm. Children are welcome to meet the animals and to try out the farm's children's play area.

ANTIQUE

CHAPTER 4

Selby and the Vale of York

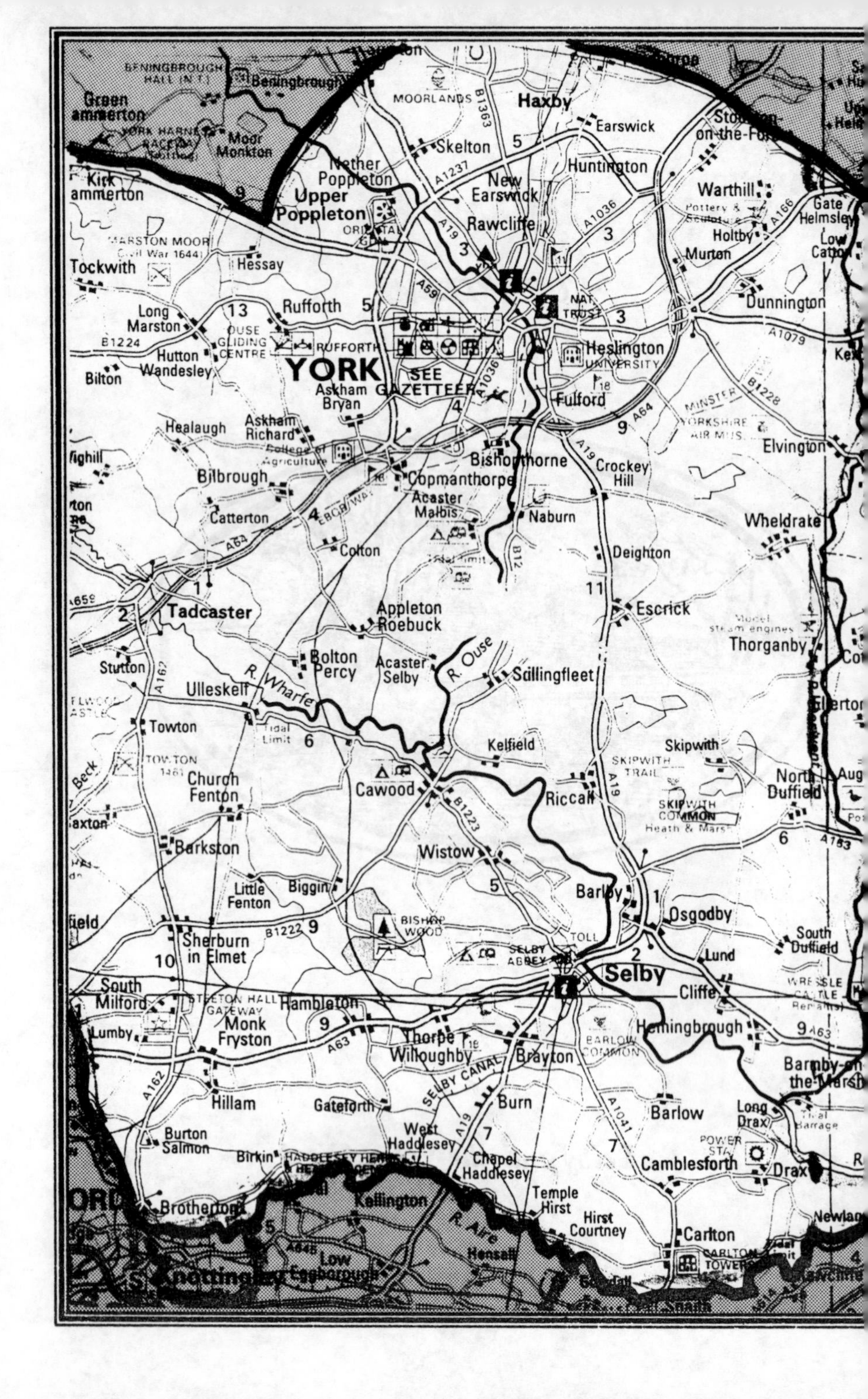

Beningbrough
Green Hammerton
Moor Monkton
Kirk Hammerton
Nether Poppleton
Upper Poppleton
Skelton
Haxby
Earswick
Huntington
New Earswick
Rawcliffe
Warthill
Gate Helmsley
Holtby
Murton
Low Catton
Dunnington
Marston Moor Civil War 1644
Tockwith
Hessay
Long Marston
Rufforth
Ouse Gliding Centre
Hutton Wandesley
Bilton
YORK
SEE GAZETTEER
Heslington
University
Fulford
Askham Bryan
Askham Richard
Healaugh
College of Agriculture
Bishopthorpe
Copmanthorpe
Acaster Malbis
Crockey Hill
Yorkshire Air Mus.
Elvington
Bilbrough
Catterton
Colton
Naburn
Deighton
Wheldrake
Tadcaster
Appleton Roebuck
Escrick
Model steam engines
Thorganby
Stutton
Bolton Percy
Acaster Selby
R. Ouse
Stillingfleet
R. Wharfe
Ulleskelf
Towton
Tidal Limit
Kelfield
Skipwith
Skipwith Trail
Skipwith Common
Heath & Marsh
Church Fenton
Cawood
Riccall
North Duffield
Barkston
Wistow
Little Fenton
Biggin
Barlby
Osgodby
Bishop Wood
Sherburn in Elmet
South Duffield
Lund
Selby Abbey
Toll
Selby
South Milford
Steeton Hall Gateway
Hambleton
Cliffe
Wressle Castle
Lumby
Monk Fryston
Thorpe Willoughby
Brayton
Barlow Common
Hemingbrough
Barmby-on-the-Marsh
Selby Canal
Hillam
Gateforth
Burn
Barlow
Long Drax
Burton Salmon
West Haddlesey
Chapel Haddlesey
Power Sta.
Birkin
Camblesforth
Drax
Kellington
Temple Hirst
Brotherton
R. Aire
Hirst Courtney
Carlton
Carlton Towers
Low Eggborough
Knottingley
Hensall
A19
A59
A64
A1036
A1237
A1079
A166
A162
A63
A1041
A163
B1363
B1224
B1228
B1222
B1223

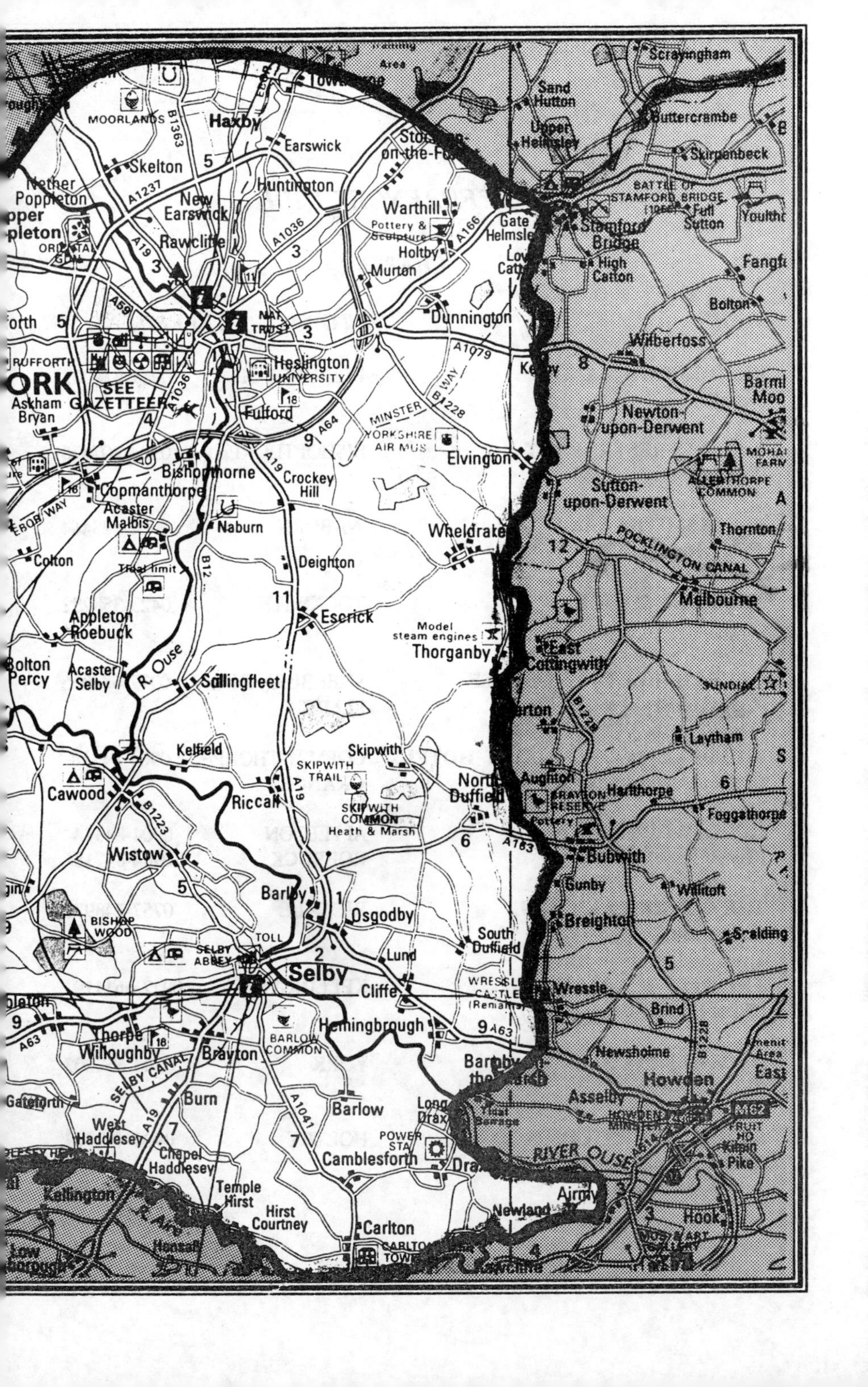

Scrayingham
Sand Hutton
Buttercrambe
Upper Helmsley
Skirpenbeck
MOORLANDS
Haxby
Earswick
Skelton
Huntington
Nether Poppleton
New Earswick
Warthill
BATTLE OF STAMFORD BRIDGE
Full Sutton
Pottery & Sculpture
Gate Helmsley
Stamford Bridge
Rawcliffe
Holtby
High Catton
Murton
Dunnington
Bolton
NAT TRUST
Wilberfoss
RUFFORTH
Heslington
UNIVERSITY
SEE GAZETTEER
Askham Bryan
Fulford
Newton-upon-Derwent
MINSTER WAY
YORKSHIRE AIR MUS
Elvington
Bishopthorne
Crockey Hill
Copmanthorpe
Sutton-upon-Derwent
ALLERTHORPE COMMON
Acaster Malbis
Naburn
Wheldrake
Thornton
POCKLINGTON CANAL
Colton
Deighton
Melbourne
Tidal limit
Escrick
Appleton Roebuck
Model steam engines
Thorganby
East Cottingwith
Bolton Percy
Acaster Selby
R. Ouse
Stillingfleet
SUNDIAL
Laytham
Kelfield
Skipwith
SKIPWITH TRAIL
Cawood
Riccall
North Duffield
Harlthorpe
SKIPWITH COMMON
Heath & Marsh
Foggathorpe
Bubwith
Wistow
Barlby
Gunby
Willitoft
Osgodby
Breighton
BISHOP WOOD
Spalding
South Duffield
TOLL
SELBY ABBEY
Lund
Selby
Cliffe
Wressle
WRESSLE CASTLE (Remains)
Brind
Hemingbrough
Thorpe Willoughby
Brayton
BARLOW COMMON
Newsholme
Barmby on the Marsh
Howden
SELBY CANAL
Gateforth
Burn
Barlow
Asselby
Long Drax
Tidal Barrage
HOWDEN MINSTER
West Haddlesey
POWER STA
FRUIT HO
Chapel Haddlesey
Camblesforth
RIVER OUSE
Kilpin Pike
Temple Hirst
Kellington
Airmyn
Hirst Courtney
Newland
Hook
Carlton
Hensall

REFERENCE GUIDE

CHAPTER 4

NAME	*TOWN*	*TELEPHONE NO.*
BILBOROUGH MANOR (Hotel)	BILBOROUGH	0937-834002
BISHOP'S RESTAURANT (Restaurant)	BISHOPTHORPE	0904-707878
BLSCKSMITHS ARMS (Public House)	NABURN	0904-623464
THE BOOT & SHOE (Inn)	TOCKWITH	0423-358232
CHURCH HILL GUEST HOUSE (Guest House)	SHERBURN IN ELMET	0977-684965
THE DUKE OF CONNAUGHT HOTEL (Hotel & Holiday Cottages)	COPMANTHORPE GRANGE	0904-84318
HOLLY LODGE (Guest House)	APPLETON ROEBUCK	0904-84314 0904-84718
THE OLD RICCALL MILL (Restaurant)	RICCALL	0757-248972
THE OLD VICARAGE (Guest House Accomodation)	KELLINGTON	0977-661119
OSCARS WINE BAR (Wine Bar-Bistro)	YORK	0904-652002
SALLY ARNUP STUDIOS (Pottery Bronze Studios)	HOLTBY	0904-489377

SCARTHINGWELL CENTRE (Antique Arcade)	TADCASTER	0937-557877
VILLA NURSERIES (Guest House)	RICCALL	0757-248257

Askham Richard

CHAPTER 4

Selby and the Vale of York

Lovers of beautiful architecture, archaeology and ancient churches will find no end of such commodities in the area in and surrounding the triangle of Selby, Tadcaster and York.

Travelling from Hull to Selby, following the line of the Ouse, one may glimpse the graceful spire of Hemingborough's St Mary's Church, and the tower of the ancient Saxon church at Drax.

The skyline at **Drax** is more noticeably dominated by the cooling towers of the power station located there, but the church of St Peter and Paul is well worth stopping off for. It has, over the years, been added to and rebuilt, but the original structure is apparent in the shape of the chancel arch and an ancient font was once unearthed in the churchyard that dates from the Saxon period. The church was once connected to an Augustinian Priory nearby, and after this was demolished, several artefacts from the priory, including the finely carved bench-ends, some of the bricks used in the re-built sections and the statues of St Peter and Paul one can see inside. There is a legend that there are as yet undiscovered tunnels below that once led from the Priory and a castle that also once stood here.

The church of St Mary at **Hemingbrough** is prominent, not only for its 190 ft spire, but also for the pale rosy colour of its brickwork which, nestling amidst fields and trees as it does, makes it look extremely attractive indeed. As with Drax, this has been the site of a church since Saxon days, and the nave bears most evidence of this. In 1426, the church became a collegiate under the jurisdiction of the Prior of Durham until the Reformation in Henry VIII's reign. The church was refurbished during this period with the impressive spire that is such a landmark today. St Mary's also possesses the oldest misericord in the country, dating back to 1200, as well as many other fine features.

Those touring this area can find truly delightful bed and breakfast accommodation at **The Old Vicarage** in **Kellington**. This peaceful little village lies six miles southwest of Selby just off the A19 and within easy reach of the main M62 and A1 trunk routes. The Old Vicarage is a substantial white-painted house with unusual arched window frames and a crunching shale driveway. The immaculately-maintained building dates from the 17th-century, and inside, it retains much of its original character and charm. There is an elegant period drawing room with comfy sofas, chairs and a chaise longue, all finished in a warm shade of rose pink. The bedrooms are all centrally-heated and equipped with hot and cold wash-basins, shaver points, colour televisions and tea/coffee making facilities. Most also have magnificent views over the beautiful lawned gardens which surround the house. Four further bedrooms, all with ensuite facilities are planned. The Old Vicarage has been the family home of Mrs C Abraham for many years. She is a delightful host and provides her guests with charming hospitality and delicious home-cooked breakfasts. Her splendid house maintains an atmosphere of relaxed luxury and is ideal as a place to break a journey or as a base for exploring the many nearby places of interest.

The Old Vicarage

The town of **Selby** began as a small Anglo-Saxon settlement of fishermen and farmers, marked by a great oak called the Stirhac which was used as a meeting place

All of this changed in 1069 when a young monk from Auxerre in France called Benedict, having had a vision of Saint Germanus, sailed from East Anglia and up the Ouse. When three swans flew in formation across the bows of his craft, the monk saw this as a sign of the Holy Trinity, and promptly set up a preaching cross under the Stirhac, which drew a number of followers. His community went from strength to strength, and attracted the attention of the Sherriff of York, who granted them land and permission to build a monastery. It was also at around this time that Selby began to flourish as a port, as well as a religious centre, possibly due to the fact that William's son Henry (later Henry 1) was born here.

The beautiful building we can witness today is the product of several centuries of additions to the initial rather heavy Norman style, although one rather quirky feature is that two of the high arches within the church are badly distorted, due to building the great tower too quickly on its soft clay foundations. Even so, Benedict would no doubt be very pleased by the splendour of the present-day Abbey, in many ways as graceful as the swans he was so inspired by. The three swans are also featured on the town's coat of arms.

Sadly, there was a fire in 1905, which caused extensive damage, but careful restoration enabled much of the original 13th and 14th century work to survive. One of the most famous surviving features is the coat of arms of John de Washington, Prior of the Abbey around 1415, and ancestor of George Washington. It is distinguished by the now famous stars and stripes charges, and is a popular attraction for the American tourists visiting here.

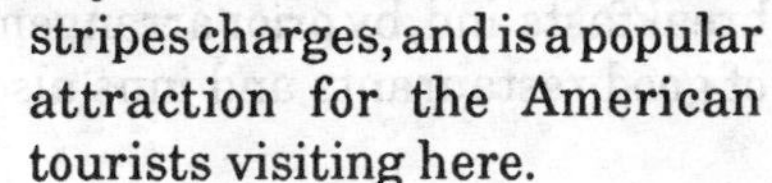

Selby Abbey

Apart from Selby's significance as a trading and religious centre, the Industrial Revolution brought other changes to the town, in the shape of the railway and some of the deepest coal-mines in Britain.

The railway station dates from 1834 and is the oldest surviving station in the United kingdom. The mines produce coal for the giant power stations at Ferrybridge, Eggborough and Drax, which in turn produce power for the national grid, as well as pumping waste heat to the local horticultural centres. Major products grown in the area as a result include mushrooms, wheat, barley, potatoes and sugar beet. It is impossible to drive along the A19 without the sight of these megalithic structures looming into view - but should you happen to take a wrong turning down one of the country lanes in this area, they do provide an excellent point of reference to help get you back on route!

Whilst touring the area around Selby, we came to the attractive village of **Sherburn-in-Elmet**, situated west of the town, on the junction of the B162 and the B1222. In a fine hilltop position facing the village church, we found the **Church Hill Guest House** which is owned and run by Mrs Joan Moody. A well-appointed modern annexe to the rear of her traditionally-built house was completed in 1991. This purpose-built extension contains two twin-bedded guest rooms with en-suite facilities, and two single bedrooms with hot and cold washbasins. These are all newly decorated and equipped with tea/coffee making facilities. The design of the new extension takes into account the needs of disabled guests and provides easy access for wheelchairs. There is also a separate residents' lounge and a pleasant dining room where Mrs Moody serves excellent Yorkshire breakfasts and, by prior arrangement, first-class evening meals. A number of good restaurants and inns also lie within easy reach.

Church Hill Guest House

We found Mrs Moody to be a very friendly and welcoming host who is rightfully proud of her clean and newly-appointed guesthouse. Being situated only 20 minutes drive from York, Selby and Leeds, and with its easy access to the main A1, M1 and M62 trunk routes, Church Hill Guest House provides a good stopping place for both through travellers and those seeking a convenient base to explore the area.

Travelling north up the A 19, we came to **Riccall**, just eight miles out of York.This village was mentioned in the Domesday Book, and still has a Norman Church, which stands in the centre of the village. It is also recorded as the site where the Norwegian king Tostig anchored his fleet of ships in 1066 before marching on to battle at York. Nowadays, its only noteable feature is its coalmine, a companion to the others at Stillingfleet and Selby.

On the northern edge of Riccall, we called in at the first-rate bed and breakfast establishment, **Villa Nurseries**, which lies just off the A19 York road four miles north of Selby. This pleasant guesthouse is run by Judith Parish and her son, David, and is attached to the family's wholesale nurseries business. (Though not a garden centre, guests can view and purchase plants by arrangement.) The house dates from the 1700s, and despite recent modernisation, still retains much of its original character and charm. Inside, there are seven well-appointed bedrooms and a comfortable private television lounge. Guests are also welcome to sit in the attractive sun lounge which has recently been constructed within the old walled garden.

Turning west at the village church, we drove into Landing Lane, (so-called because the landing site where Tostig landed his fleet is said to be located nearby), and here found the unique **Old Riccall Mill Restaurant** which is housed in a converted 19th-century windmill. The present brick tower was constructed in 1811 to replace the mill which had stood on the site since 1290. Later, the original four-sailed mechanism was superseded by steam-powered equipment which continued to grind corn until 1911. The mill was then converted to a private residence before being taken over in 1989 by Spanish-born Manolita Brage who extensively refurbished and extended the building so as to transform it into a first-class restaurant.

Not only has Mrs Brage been successful in creating an extremely pleasant and welcoming atmosphere, but she also offers her customers the very best in imaginative Spanish, continental and English cooking. The menu lists a wide choice of delicious main courses, including fish, steaks and the traditional Spanish delicacies, *Zarzuela*, a dish consisting of shellfish served in a brandy, cream and lobster sauce, and *Paella*, the classic rice and seafood dish. There is also a wide selection of starters, pasta dishes, vegetarian dishes and tempting desserts. We personally spent a very pleasurable evening enjoying some of the most charming hospitality and best Spanish cooking which we have so far experienced.

The Old Riccall Mill

Four miles south of York on the B1222 Cawood road, we came to the pleasant village of **Naburn**. At one time, a ferry on the River Ouse operated between here and Bishopsthorpe, a mile-and-a-half to the north. A short distance from the riverbank, we found the well-recommended pub and eating house, the **Blacksmith's Arms**. Parts of the inn date back several hundred years and throughout its long history it has been extended and remodelled many times. The present owners have been successful in retaining the pub's traditional atmosphere. They also offer an excellent selection of top quality pub meals, both at lunchtimes and in the evenings, and in fine weather, customers can sit outside in the pleasant walled garden.

On the western bank of the River Ouse, two miles south of York city centre, we made a point of visiting the pleasant riverside village of **Bishopthorpe**. Visitors can either arrive here by car, or by boat from King's Staith in York. A short distance from the riverbus terminus, we found the first-rate **Bishop's Restaurant** which is run by John Elgie, a former manager of the Mansion House Hotel in Roundhay, Leeds. This modern octagonal building is set in a quiet garden in an unrivalled position overlooking the River Ouse. Outside, there is an attractive children's play space and a special area where barbecues are held every Sunday lunchtime, weather permitting.

Bishops Restaurant

John Elgie's policy is to offer 'the best value in quality for the price'. He and his staff serve an extensive bar meals' menu every lunchtime and evening, Tuesdays to Saturdays, with such items on offer as homemade steak and kidney pie, sauteed Nidderdale trout, and casserole of chicken in mushroom and red wine sauce. There is also a special children's menu. As well as bar meals, Bishop's serves full four course á la carte dinners between 7pm and 9pm, Tuesdays to Saturdays. Main courses on offer include Chateaubriand, swordfish kebab and 'duck fillets Vietnamese'. A full range of starters, steaks and desserts is also available. Bishop's also specialises in afternoon teas which are available until 5pm, Tuesdays to Sundays, and traditional three-course roast lunches which are available every Sunday between 12pm and 3pm.

At last, we came to the fascinating city of **York**. There is so much to do and see in this wonderful and ancient town , that a one day stop-off is not really enough.

The Romans came here first in AD 71, when the Roman governor, Quintus Petilius Cerealis chose it as the best military strong-point for his invasion of Brigantia, due to its proximity to the juncture of the rivers Ouse and Fosse. He called the new fortress-city Eboracum, and it was soon to become the capital of Lower Britain and a major city within the Roman Empire.

Several Emperors visited Eboracum and Severus held his Imperial Court here until he died in AD 211.

The Legions occupied Eboracum until AD 410, their headquarters standing on the site where the Minster is today. Parts of their building are evident in the foundations that are on view to the public, and a 31 ft Roman pillar, part of the garrison, can be seen near the south entrance.

The withdrawal of the Romans left the way clear for the invading Anglo-Saxons, who occupied the city and set it up as Eoferwic. Their most famous ruler was Edwin, King of Northumbria, who married Princess Ethelberga of Kent. She helped to bring Christianity to the area, with the help of her chaplain, the Bishop Paulinus. He baptised Edwin and some chosen subjects in a small well on the site where he was to found the first cathedral of St Peter.

Christianity also brought learning to the North, and by the 8th century, Eoferwic was the most important centre of learning in this part of Britain.

The Vikings took advantage of the unrest in the 9th century to invade and York was again the centre of their attention. They named the city Jorvik, settling down to a peaceful existence - remains of their settlements can be viewed at the Jorvik Centre in Coppergate.

Such interestingly named characters as King Halfdan and Eric Bloodaxe make this a particularly fascinating period for the modern-day tourist, certainly names to stimulate the imagination!

The area was constantly in turmoil throughout the 11th century, with the Norwegian invasion, constant bickerings between Saxon lordlings and kings, and culminating with the Norman Invasion.

So troublesome were these Northern lands that William 1 embarked on a terrible solution to the problem, beginning the dreaded Harrowing of the North. He decided that his most effective policy was to lay the land barren, kill the cattle and thereby drive the Northerners into submission by means of starvation.

York eventually re-established itself as a major centre, which was helped by the birth of William's son, Henry 1, at nearby Selby.

By the Middle Ages over a hundred crafts were being practised here, bringing about the founding of the many guilds. The wealthiest of these were the Company of Merchant Adventurers, or overseas traders.

York was by now the second largest and most important city in England. The bars, or gates were built at this time, and many kings and queens were frequent visitors. In 1397, a Royal Performance of the York Mystery Plays was staged, an event which has since taken place every 4 years.

Richard III was the monarch most closely associated with the city.

The long standing Wars of the Roses centred on the houses of York and Lancaster, only being resolved through the marriage of Henry VII and Elizabeth of York.

York, however, suffered during the Reformation of Henry VIII, losing its Abbey, priories and friaries and countless treasures were lost.

Paradoxically, though, it was the Tudor monarch who did York its greatest favour by setting up the Council of the North, which brought back power to the region.

The Council increased York's importance to such a degree that it became the centre for so many of the battles between the Royalists and the Parliamentarians in the Civil War almost a century later.

The turning point of the war happened at the battle of Marston Moor, just to the west of York, after which Prince Rupert was forced to hide within the city walls until the surrender to Sir Thomas Fairfax in 1644.

The village of Tockwith lies one mile north of the B1224 York to Wetherby road, midway between York and the main A1, in the heart of historic Marston Moor. It was a short distance from here that Prince Rupert's forces suffered the crushing defeat mentioned previously. Today, it seems hard to imagine that this peaceful village was once the centre of events that changed the course of the nation's history.

If you would be interested in finding out more about past events surrounding the village and the famous battle, make a point of visiting the village pub, **The Boot and Shoe**, and talking to Mr and Mrs Warren who run it.

The Boot and Shoe

Both have a keen interest in local history, a fact which is reflected in the internal decoration of the main bar, which is covered in old photographs of the village, antique lamps, hand-polished horse brasses and perhaps most absorbing, an account of life in the village at the time of the Battle of Marston Moor. As shown in an early photograph, the Boot and Shoe originally had a thatched roof, and to the rear, there was an old forge building which had its own mounting steps and farrier's equipment(this building is to be restored in the near future). The exterior of the present-day building is painted white and covered in beautiful hanging baskets of flowers which Mrs Warren lovingly attends to. The Warrens provide a range of fine hand-pulled ales and the traditional country fare is based on old 17th century recipes, such as bacon and egg pie, the old farm labourers' favourite.

The other historical events connected with York are numerous, and so many of them are centred around **York Minster** itself, the City's cathedral that dominates the skyline from any angle in the town's streets.

When we visited York in the Autumn, it was a clear, crisp day, and the cold atmosphere lent the cream/pink brickwork an ethereal air, a splendid vision of great ecclesiastical influence and power. The low medieval houses and shops seemed to huddle together, in deference to the huge structure. No wonder John Evelyn, the Jacobean diarist wrote,

"Which of all the greate chirches in England has been best preserved from ye furie of ye sacreligious - it is a most intire magnificent piece of Gothic architecture."

So many notable people have written great eulogies to the beauty of the Minster, but the modern attitude was rather humourously summed up in an observation in a book I recently read on York. The author observed two wealthy American tourists, a man and his wife, halt in front of the great edifice in their car - the husband eventually deciding on a plan of action, saying,

"I'll do the inside, you do the outside, and we'll meet here in half an hour".

The origins of the Minster stretch back so far, that it has always been in contention with Canterbury itself for ecclesiastical precedence.

This spirit of competition was never more heated than at the Council of Westminster, when Robert of Canterbury placed himself on the right side of the papal legate. Roger of York, in an attempt to out-manoeuvre him, vied for the position, the outcome leading to the York envoy ending up on the Archbishop's lap - an act of affrontery that caused him to be seized and beaten. The fiasco must have been amusing for onlookers to witness -one

York Minster

can almost imagine the two great figures of power wrestling in a flurry of crumpled vestments and fallen mitres!

Roger was not the only interesting character to have attained the prized title. Consider the fascinating tale of Lancelot Blackburne, Archbishop of York between 1724-43, whose hair-raisng exploits as a buccaneer aboard a pirate ship would make wonderful material for a novel, a fact successfully kept hidden from public knowledge at the time. The Fiddler statue in the crypt represents the roguish Blackburne, seen here playing the instrument he " borrowed" from his college tutor before he headed off for more stimulating exploits on the high seas. The grinning figure, clad in tam o' shanter, is placed by the horrific sculpture of the Hell Cauldron, almost as a warning, which he appears to hold in laughing disregard. Blackburne's statue is a favourite with the public and holds a degree of fascination that only the notorious can have.

One should be prepared to spend some time here, as there is a lot to see, from the substantial foundations, right up to the guided tour of the Great Tower, which of course gives breathtaking (not to mention dizzy) views of the city.

The streets are fascinating, and the charmingly eccentric lines of the Shambles, Stonegate and Goodramgate, to name but a few, are essential viewing. The streets are also interspersed with lovely little churches - I would hazard a guess that there are more ecclesiastical buildings per square mile here than anywhere else in the North, if not Britain. St Mary's Abbey is the venue of the famous York mystery plays, which have been carefully preserved in their curious blend of high Latin and Yorkshire dialect.

One wonderful scene from the Harrowing of Hell, once performed by the town's saddlers guild, reveals Jesus standing at the mouth of Hades, first shouting grandly in Latin,

"Attolite portas principes" and finishing with "Oppen uppe!" in broad Yorkshire, which usually causes a few chuckles in the audience.

A place well worth finding whilst travelling the streets of York's bustling city centre is **Oscar's Wine Bar** in Little Stonegate. This busy wine bar and bistro can be found in a narrow passage leading off Stonegate, the main thoroughfare leading down from York Minster. Outside, an attractive courtyard provides an ideal place to sit in fine weather; inside, there is a large L-shaped bar and a number of smaller rooms decorated in a relaxed informal style. Here, both visitors and local business people rub shoulders in an atmosphere which is pleasant and unpretentious. As well as a wide selection of good value wines, Oscar's offers an impressive menu of freshly prepared dishes which are both wholesome and delicious. Open daily, 11am to 11pm.

The Jorvik Centre, on Coppergate, is one of the many prides of York, a fascinating experience for museum-goers of all ages.

Visitors are required to step aboard a time-car and travel back through representations of real-life Viking Age Britain. You can witness a bustling market, full of Danes bartering for chickens, corn and other esential provisions and wares, dark smoky houses (no central heating in those days!), and a busy wharf, when goods were transported along the Ouse and Foss and deposited here from other regions. All have been recreated in accurate detail, complete with authentic sights, sounds and smells to the minutest detail, and this centre is a great favourite with adults and children alike.

Nearby is the **York Heritage Centre** with its impressive collectiion of exhibits, including a towering reconstruction which gives one a real insight into the precarious nature of medieval cathedral construction. A visit to this centre will provide one with an educational and enjoyable way to explore over 1000 years of York's history and architecture.

The Arc is located in a beautifully restored church close to the Shambles, and is an award-winning hands-on exploration of archaeology for visitors of all ages.

Here one can meet practising archaeologists who will advise you on how to sort and identify genuine finds and to try out ancient crafts. For the more technically minded, there are a series of inter-active computer displays which demonstrate the value of modern technology in uncovering the past - a fascinating educational experience. The City considers this as its pride and joy, and it must be visited by all those who value the part archaeology has played in presenting the history of this oldest of places.

Others interested in the history of York and its mysteries will no doubt feel compelled to go on the **Original Ghostwalk of York**, which starts at the **King's Arms** pub on **Ouse Bridge**, and takes place at eight pm. every night. It is not for the faint-hearted - for the most part, York's history is full of torture and intrigue. There are, predictably, many haunting and mysterious stories connected with York and these are related against a backdrop of memorable scenery. For those with a romantic and curious nature, this is a must.

Railway enthusiasts will be similarly drawn to the **National Railway Museum** on Leeman Road (voted Museum of the Year in 1991), where one can see nearly two hundred years history of the technical and social changes brought about by the invention of railways and their contribution to the civilisation we know today. Here, you can see a replica of Stephenson's Rocket, explore a simulated section of the Channel Tunnel, view a display of objects which demonstrate the workings of the railway system, and take a glimpse into the future of rail travel with British Rail's up-to-the-minute exhibits.

There is a collection of historic carriages used by past and present royalty and an impressive collection of steam locomotives, which include

Monk Bar, York

the famous Mallard. If seeking refreshment, one may take a break in the Brief Encounter Restaurant in the South Hall, for fans of that particular classic movie and there is a barbecue in the summer months held outside.

Seekers of information on anything to do with railways can also use the extensive reference library here, with a reading room attached (booking may be necessary for this).

Stonegate, York

The black and white timbered **Merchant Adventurers' Hall** on Fossgate is another magnet for tourists, who are drawn by the history that is associated with this powerful guild. It dates from the 14th century, when York's merchants were granted a licence to form a fraternity and possess property and thus the Company of Merchant Adventurers came into being and this great hall, symbolising the power and wealth they amassed over the centuries. It comprises of the Great Hall where all their affairs were transacted, a hospital or almshouse and their own chapel of worship. The guild controlled the trade in all "goods bought and sold foreign", and indeed, is still in operation today. The building with its beautiful and complex timbered roof exhibits the many colourful banners of York's Medieval guilds. In a similar vein, there is also the **Merchant Taylors' Hall**, originally constructed by the Confraternity of St John the Baptist.

The York **Museum of Automata** holds an appeal for children and adults alike. I must admit myself to having a childish fascination for these ingenious mechanisms, and found this particular venue bewitching.

The definition of automata is of man-made objects that imitate the movement of living things through a mechanism that is concealed, so as to make them appear to move spontaneously.

The Museum traces the history of automata, from the simple articulated figurines from ancient civilisations, through to the displays of modern robotics.

The French Gallery contains a throng of animated musicians, clowns artists and eccentrics from Parisian Cafe Society, displayed throughthe latest video, sound and lighting techniques. Some of these pieces are grimly fascinating, the sorts of objects that one would see occasionally on the Antiques Road Show, fetching a very high price indeed, and due to their extreme fragility, modern technology can help to bring them to life for the many visitors to the museum.

The Contemporary Gallery and Seaside Pier provide one with the opportunity to get some hands-on involvement, where one can crank modern exhibits into action. There is a reconstruction of a 1950's saucy postcard seaside pier with a collection of humorous automata performing the sort of bawdy behaviour one might expect. The Automata Shop provides one with an opportunity to buy contemporary pieces, music boxes, mechanical toys and craft kits suitable for all ages.

The York Castle Museum is a goldmine of nostalgic memorabilia and reconstructions not to be missed. It was opened in 1938, based on the collections of Dr John Kirk, a country doctor from Pickering, who acquired the objects to represent a way of life that was fast disappearing. Today, the Museum has extended to fill the former Female and Debtor's prisons that used to be here. Amongst the collections of memorabilia, the period reconstructions are perhaps the most fascinating, from the Jacobean and Georgian Dining rooms, through to an authentic representation of Victorian Kirkgate.

The range and number of galleries and museums in York are staggering and would in all probability take weeks to visit in their entirety.

Those interested in York's Roman heritage may wish to view the **Roman Bath Inn**, where one can see the remains of the steam baths used by the occupants of the garrison here, or the **Roman Corner Tower**, located behind the Merchant Adventurers' Hall. Parts of the stone walls the Romans built to surround their fort are most evident at this point, where it rises to a height of 16 ft.

The medieval bars, or gates, stand at the old four corners of the city, and were reconstructed in the middle ages from the old Norman fortifications. These edifices are impressive enough, but standing back seem small in comparison with the mass of York Minster that stands within their protection.

It has to be the sheer range and breadth of history encompassed in the architecture that this city is comprised of, that remains in one's memory forever and provides endless avenues of exploration.

Any season is full of surprise and entertainment here. Even in the normally dull months of January and February, here, in York, the streets come alive with Viking Warriors carousing and carrying flaming brands to set their funereal launches ablaze on the Ouse, in the exciting **Jorvik Festival**.

As far as sheer variety of ancient historical interest goes, York must surely be the city of cities.

Other places to visit include **the Guildhall**, **St William's College**, **the Mansion House**, **the City Museum and Art Gallery**, **the University** buildings and grounds, **the Theatre Royal** in **St Leonard's Place**, **Clifford's Tower**, **Fairfax House** and **the York Dungeon** (for those with a stout heart and a strong stomach!). There are of course many other curiosities and places to visit whilst here, many of them hidden away, not all of them located within the city walls - purchase of a good tour guide with map is essential to discover these hidden places, and a good day's walk around the streets will reveal much. One particularly memorable way to view the city might be to walk the length of its Roman/Medieval walls, which are often beautifully illuminated at night, especially in tourist season.

The main tourist office is located on **St Leonard's Place**, not far from Bootham Bar.

Four miles east of York, and just to the north of the A166 York to Stamford Bridge road, we took a break from the city, and visited the attractive hamlet of **Holtby**. Here, we called in at the fascinating sculpture and pottery studios run by **Sally Arnup** and her husband Mick Arnup. Sally Arnup became a full-time art student at the tender age of thirteen and later, at the Royal College of Art, worked under John Skeaping, becoming acquainted with Sir Jacob Epstein. She specialises in bronze sculptures of animals and birds, always working directly from the live creature rather than using sketches or photographs. Work by Sally and her potter/painter husband, Mick,

Merchant Adventurer's Hall

Sally Arnup Studios

can be viewed in their charming studio showroom.

Located within easy reach of York and the main trunk routes to London, Edinburgh and beyond is the **Duke of Connaught Hotel** at Copmanthorpe Grange, near **York**. This relaxed and friendly establishment is situated in a peaceful rural location four miles southwest of York city centre and it may be advisable to telephone the owners, Jack and Josie Hughes (0904) 84318, for accurate directions. Copmanthorpe Grange is a former specialist stud farm which was set up to supply Hackney horses to draw the Royal Mail carriages between York, London and Edinburgh.

The Duke Of Connaught Hotel

Bootham Bar, York

Indeed, the Duke of Connaught Hotel is named after one of the most famous stud stallions, Garton Duke of Connaught, who was a great Hackney champion winning the National British Championship and Paris Championship in Victorian times. In recent years, the old stud farm has been gradually converted into a modern hotel and a number of self-contained cottages. The interior of the hotel retains much of the building's original character and charm with beamed ceilings and a pleasant country cottage atmosphere. There is a relaxing bar and dining room, a comfortable guests' sitting area, and a number of spacious bedrooms which are all equipped with en suite facilities, central heating, colour televisions and tea/coffee making facilities. The self-catering cottages accommodate from two to eight people and have fully-equipped kitchens, modern bathrooms and well-furnished sitting rooms with colour televisions. 3 crowns, AA & RAC listed.

The minor country roads to the south west of York nearing Tadcaster, led us to the peaceful village of **Appleton Roebuck**, six miles from the centre of the city. Situated just outside the village, we found the extremely well-appointed modern guesthouse, **Holly House**, which is owned and run by Mr and Mrs W Whitehead. Their large and comfortable house has been constructed in recent years to a high specification; they have five guest-rooms available, three with en suite facilities and other two with access to a luxurious bathroom with a bidet and corner bath. All the rooms are clean and newly decorated, and most have open views across the large landscaped garden to the fields and woodland beyond.

The most exceptional feature of Holly House is the magnificent

Holly House

indoor heated swimming pool which is housed in a newly-constructed building within the grounds. This building is also equipped with showers, laundry facilities, hair dryers and a number of fitness machines which guests are welcome to use. Guests can also enjoy splendid views of the garden from the tables and chairs which are set around the pool. Holly House is situated within easy reach of the ancient city of York and provides an excellent base for exploring the Vale of York with its many historic places of interest.

Three miles to the north of Appleton Roebuck, on the other side of the A64, is the pretty conservation village of **Bilbrough**, home of the renowned country house hotel and restaurant, **Bilbrough Manor**. For seven centuries, Bilbrough was the family seat of the Fairfax family, the most famous of whom was 'Black Tom', the founder and commander of Parliament's New Model Army which defeated the forces of Charles I during the English Civil War. He resided at Bilbrough Manor for many years and was eventually buried in the local cemetery. The present house was constructed in 1901 to replace the decaying Tudor manor; it stands in beautiful landscaped gardens surrounded by 100 acres of farm-and woodland with magnificent views over the Vale of York.

Bilbrough Manor

In 1986, Bilbrough Manor was purchased by Colin and Susan Bell who began a major refurbishment programme in order to transform it into a modern, first-class country house hotel. In 1990, the beautifully restored hotel won the award for 'Best Northern Newcomer' and today, it welcomes guests from all over the world. Bilbrough Manor has twelve spacious and individually furnished bedrooms, each beautifully appointed and equipped with private bathroom, colour television and direct-dial telephone. On the ground floor, there is a reception hall with a welcoming log fire, a large and elegant guest lounge, and a magnificent oak-panelled dining room where outstanding New Classical French cuisine is served by a skilled and enthusiastic team of chefs.

Compared to the many diversions of York, nearby **Tadcaster** would appear to have little to offer - but it does have the memorable distinction of being one of the foremost brewing centres in Yorkshire.

In medieval days, Tadcaster was a major route centre and port for locally quarried limestone which was its main means of prosperity. By 1341, the brewing industry already had a firm foot-hold, with two breweries being recorded as in existence.

Before this, Tadcaster had been significant as the site of a Roman settlement called Calcaria, which means simply "limestone", indicating that quarrying had taken place as early as then, if not earlier.

After the Norman Conquest, Tadcaster was given to William de Percy and there are the remains of a motte and bailey castle here where he is said to have lived.

It was again of vital strategic importance during the Civil War, and later was a main stop-off point on the main coaching routes between London and York. This had the consequence of increasing the need for ale to keep the travellers and merchants happy.

Today, there are 3 well-known breweries based here, the skyline easily distinguishable by the brewery chimneys one sees as one approaches.

Four miles south of **Tadcaster**, we went in search of Scarthingwell Farm, home of the renowned centre for antique and contemporary arts and crafts, the **Scarthingwell Centre**. The Centre can be found by turning east off the A162 Tadcaster to Pontefract road just north of the village of **Barkston** and is a truly fascinating place to visit for all those interested in antiques, crafts and much, much more.

The heart of the Centre is its unique antique arcade. This consists of a number of individual retail units which together form a fascinating Aladdin's Cave around which visitors are welcome to browse. Here, we saw books, period furniture, art deco pieces, original paintings, fine linen and lace, and antique jewellery, lamps and porcelain. We also came across an interesting collection of penny slot-machines, wind-up gramophones, old 78s and items of classic clothing including 1920's and 30's dress suits and pantomime costumes. Prices were unusually good and it is not surprising that the arcade draws collectors and specialist buyers from all over the country.

The Centre is also home for a number of contemporary craftspeople. In her **Glass House** workshop, Jenny Gregory designs, makes and repairs wonderful stained glass panels to her customers' specifications. She also makes mirrors, lampshades, firescreens and other decorative glassware and always has a stock of interesting pieces available for visitors to purchase. Elaine Hall exhibits her own wide range of watercolour paintings and also offers an efficient picture-framing service. Children are not forgotten, as Alwyn's Book Corner boasts a fascinating colection of books and toys.

There are also over 300 items of reproduction pine furniture on view at the showrooms of **Scarthingwell Replicas**. Here, finished pieces of furniture are stained and waxed to the client's individual requirements, or they can be purchased in the basic whitewood condition for the customer to finish at home.

Scarthingwell Centre

Also on sale is a huge selection of modern and traditional pottery from China, Italy and the Staffordshire potteries, natural toiletries, greetings cards and dried flowers. The Scarthingwell Centre is constantly evolving; manager Gill Brier tries to offer something different each year and is always open to fresh possibilities. The Centre is open 10am to 5pm daily including weekends, and is serviced by an excellent cafe offering homemade hot and cold fayre.

Fountain's Court - Harrogate

CHAPTER 5

Harrogate & Knaresborough

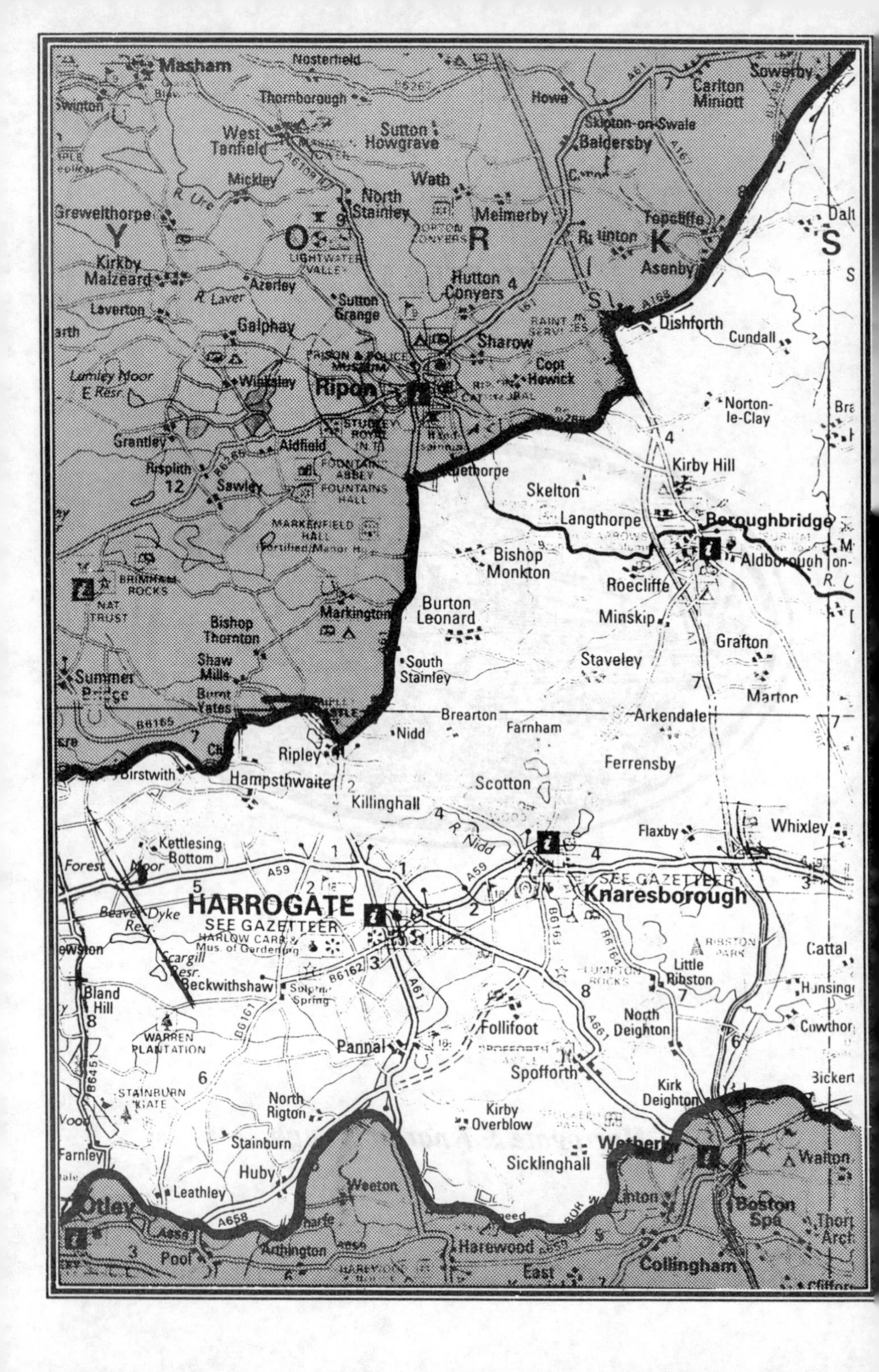

Masham
Nosterfield
Thornborough
Howe
Sowerby
Carlton
Miniott
Swinton
West
Tanfield
Sutton
Howgrave
Skipton-on-Swale
Baldersby
Mickley
Wath
R. Ure
Grewelthorpe
North
Stainley
Melmerby
Topcliffe
Y
O
R
K
S
LIGHTWATER
VALLEY
Kirkby
Malzeard
Azerley
Hutton
Conyers
Asenby
R. Laver
Laverton
Sutton
Grange
Dishforth
Cundall
Galphay
Sharow
Lumley Moor
E Resr.
Ripon
Copt
Hewick
Norton-
le-Clay
Grantley
Aldfield
Risplith
Sawley
FOUNTAINS
ABBEY
FOUNTAINS
HALL
Kirby Hill
Skelton
Langthorpe
Boroughbridge
MARKENFIELD
HALL
Bishop
Monkton
Aldborough
BRIMHAM
ROCKS
NAT
TRUST
Roecliffe
R. L
Burton
Leonard
Markington
Minskip
Bishop
Thornton
Grafton
South
Stainley
Staveley
Shaw
Mills
Summer
Burnt
Yates
Brearton
Arkendale
Farnham
Nidd
B6165
Birstwith
Ripley
Ferrensby
Hampsthwaite
Scotton
Killinghall
R. Nidd
Flaxby
Whixley
Kettlesing
Bottom
Forest
Moor
A59
HARROGATE
SEE GAZETTEER
Knaresborough
SEE GAZETTEER
Beaver Dyke
Resr.
HARLOW CARR &
Mus. of Gardening
RIBSTON
PARK
Cattal
Scargill
Resr.
Beckwithshaw
B6162
Little
Ribston
Bland
Hill
A61
B6161
B6163
B6164
North
Deighton
WARREN
PLANTATION
Follifoot
A661
Pannal
Spofforth
B6451
STAINBURN
GATE
North
Rigton
Kirby
Overblow
Kirk
Deighton
Stainburn
Wetherby
Walton
Farnley
Sicklinghall
Huby
Weeton
Leathley
Otley
Boston
Spa
A658
Arthington
Pool
Harewood
Collingham
East

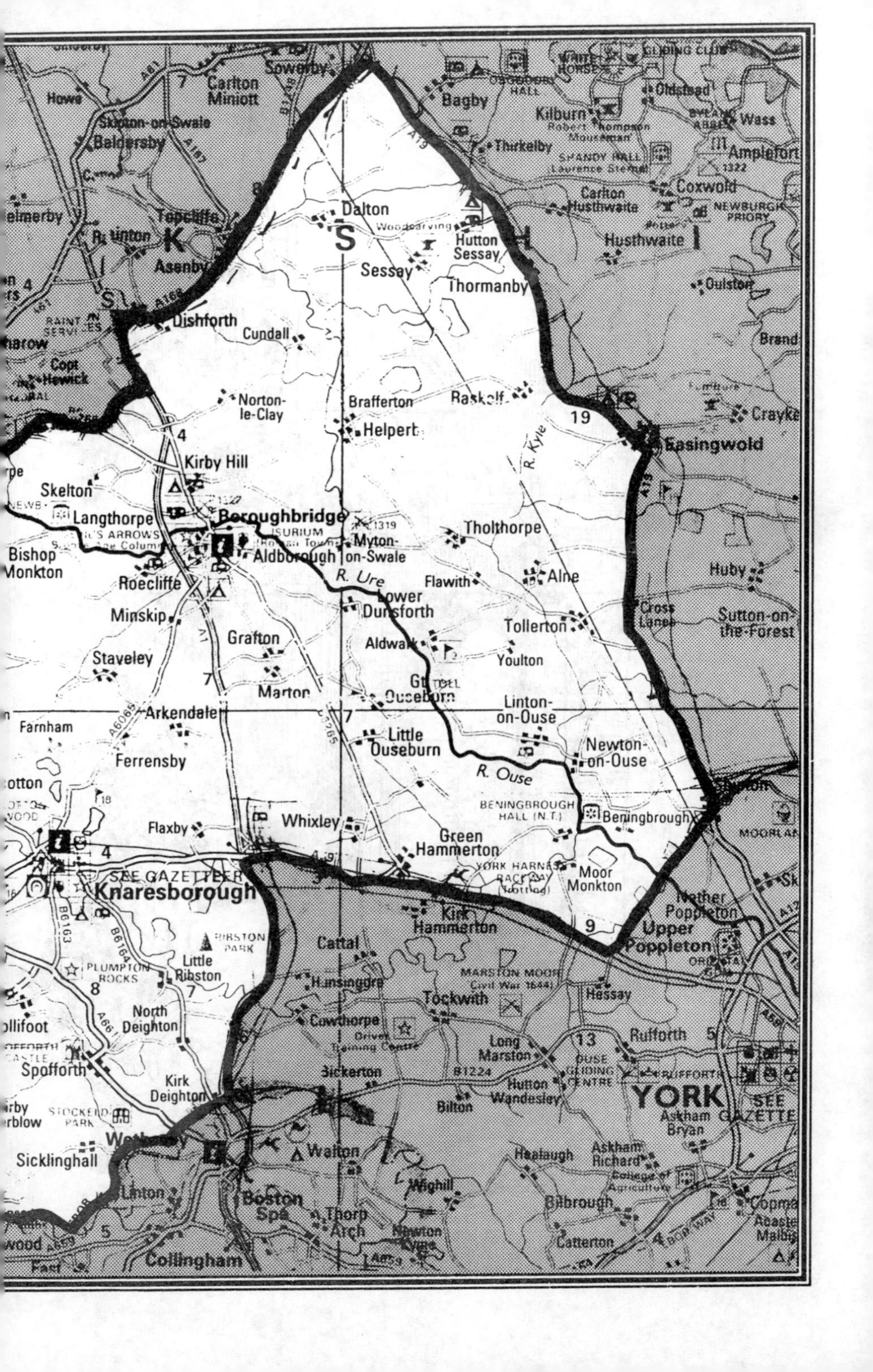

Knaresborough

RERERENCE GUIDE

CHAPTER 5

NAME	*TOWN*	*TELEPHONE NO.*
THE ANGEL INN (Country Inn & Restaurant)	TOPCLIFFE	0845-577237
BAY HORSE INN & REST. (Country Inn)	BURNT YATES	0423-770230
EBOR MOUNT (Guest House)	KNARESBOROUGH	0423-863315
GARTH HOUSE (Farm House B & B)	DALTON	0845-577310
LA BERGERIE (Restaurant)	HARROGATE	0423-500089
THE OLD BLACK BULL (Pub with Accomodation)	RASKELF	0347-21431
VALLEY HOTEL (Hotel)	HARROGATE	0423-504868
THE WHITE HOUSE (Hotel)	HARROGATE	0423-501388

The Royal Pump Room
Harrogate

CHAPTER 5

Harrogate and Knaresborough

Tourists travelling out of the Vale of York should by no means miss out on visiting the famous historic towns of **Knaresborough** and **Harrogate.**

Knaresborough is an ancient town, with pantiled cottages, Georgian houses and narrow streets, which occupies a hillside by the quaintly named River Nidd. It has many unusual and attractive features that include steep-stepped narrow streets leading down to the river, a 14th century castle standing on a cliff-top near the ancient market-place, the famous Petrifying Well, which has to be seen to be believed, and of course the world-renowned Mother Shipton's Cave.

The Petrifying Well is a constant source of curiosity to the passing tourist. The effects that its lime-rich water has on objects are truly amazing, and an array of paraphernalia, from old boots to bunches of grapes are on view, seemingly turned to stone. It is little wonder that these were considered magical properties by the superstitious over the centuries and the Well connected with witchcraft and various other interesting tales.

The foremost tale concerns Mother Shipton, who was said to have been born in the cavern that is situated by the well, on 6th July 1488, and who has the reputation of being England's most famous prophetess. How much of her story is true and how much the exaggeration of legend, we will never know.

The story says that she was born in the cavern in the midst of a terrible storm, and was soon found to have a strange ability to foretell the future. As she grew older, her prophetic visions became more widely known and feared throughout England.

However, the most singular feature about Mother Shipton has to be the fact that she died peacefully in her bed, as opposed to being burnt at the stake as most witches were wont to do. She had been threatened with burning by, amongst others, Cardinal Wolsey, when she had warned him on a visit to York that he might see the city but never enter it. Wolsey sent three of his men, deliberately disguised, to tell her of his intention. It seems indicative of the awe in which she was held, that one of these men was Lord Henry Algernon Percy himself. Somehow the witch saw through their disguises, fed them cakes and ale and after unnerving them by calling each of them by their name, sent them on their way.

True to her prediction though, Wolsey never did enter York, for he was arrested at Cawood for treason by the same Lord Percy, and died soon afterwards at Leicester. A strange tale indeed!

Amongst her many prophesies, she was reputed to have foretold the invasion and defeat of the Spanish Armada in 1588 and Samuel Pepys recorded that it was Mother Shipton who prophesied the disastrous Great Fire of London in 1666.

Whether or not one believes in such things, the stories, which are based on fact, are fascinating, and even more curious is an indefinite prophesy made by her regarding the far future, which goes,

"Carriages without horses shall go,
And accidents fill the world with woe,
Around the world thoughts shall fly
In the twinkling of an eye.
Iron in the water shall float
As easy as a wooden boat.
Gold shall be found, and found,
In a land that's not now known"

One might almost surmise that Mother Shipton could have made a fortune, had it been possible to take out shares in British Telecom, Ford Motors and the larger shipping companies at the time! However, her prediction that the world would end in 1981 would seem to cast doubts on the overall reliability of her visions, but for those people drawn to the mystery surrounding this intriguing character, visit the place to reveal more!

There are many places to stay whilst visiting this most curious of towns, and one that we can recommend is the **Ebor Mount Guest House** in York Place, a handsome 18th-century town house which is thought to be partially constructed of stone taken from Knaresborough Castle. The guesthouse is owned and personally-run by Stuart and Margaret Kneeshaw who actively take part in the annual 'Knaresborough in Bloom' competition so that in summer, driving through the unusual archway not only takes you into the private car park, which in itself is a bonus when the town is crowded with visitors, but here you will also find a walled garden covered in hanging baskets and ablaze with colour. Inside, the atmosphere is warm and welcoming; the eight spacious and tastefully decorated guest bedrooms each contain en suite facilities, colour televisions, radio-alarms and beverage making facilities. (Some rooms are specially reserved for non-smokers.) There is also an attractive diningroom where the Kneeshaws serve their renowned full English breakfast, a meal for which they have received a great many compliments over the years. Guests are offered a good choice of dishes and are able to eat as much as they wish. Ebor Mount lies within easy walking distance of the market place, Knaresborough Castle and the Nidd Gorge, and is also conveniently located for both the bus and railway stations. The guesthouse is English Tourist Board two crown rated and is open all year round.

Ebor Mount Guest House

Whilst in Knaresborough, take the opportunity to visit **the House in the Rock**, also known as **Fort Montague**, a curious dwelling hewn out of the solid rock over some sixteen years by a father and his son, and the now infamous **St Robert's Cave**, where Eugene Aram was said to have hidden the body of Daniel Clark.

Aram was hanged in 1759 after one of the most puzzling murder mysteries in Yorkshire's history.

He was the village school master at Ramsgill in upper Nidderdale, reputed to have taken up bad company with local miscreants Daniel Clark, Richard Houseman and Henry Terry, landlord of the Barrel Inn.

One day, Clark, who had obtained a quantity of goods on credit, went

Knaresborough

missing, never to be seen again. The goods were eventually found in Aram's garden, which seemed to implicate him, but a charge of complicity in the crime fell through.

Fourteen years later, a skeleton was unearthed at nearby Thistle Hill, which was presumed to be Clark. Aram's wife accused Houseman, Houseman accused Aram, and revealed that the body was in fact in St Robert's Cave, the ancient hermitage on the banks of the River Nidd. The eventual outcome was that Aram was tried and hanged , although there is still doubt as to his guilt. After his execution, his body was taken to Knaresborough to hang in chains. One wonders if the greatest crime in the eyes of the people of Knaresborough was the murder of Clark, or the profaning of the cave from where their favourite local saint performed so many of his legendary miracles.

St Robert was the son of a Mayor of York, born in 1160, who died in 1218. On his death, so beloved was the saint, that the people of Knaresborough would not allow the monks of Fountains Abbey to bury him, instead keeping his bones and finally interning him in a place near the altar in the chapel of Our Lady of the Crag. It is guarded by the statue of a larger than life-size figure of a knight, in the act of drawing a sword. The saint is yet another of the colourful characters in the magical history of this singular town.

In the tradition of this town's reputation for exceptional and odd characters, is Blind Jack of Knaresborough. Jack Metcalfe was born in 1717, and lost his sight at the age of six, but went on to achieve fame as a roadmaker. He was a remarkable person, who never allowed his blindness to bar him from any normal activities - he rode, climbed trees and swam, and was often employed to guide travellers through the wild Forest of Knaresborough. He was a talented fiddle player and one of his more roguish exploits was the elopement with Dolly Benson, the daughter of the inn-keeper of the Royal Oak in Harrogate, on the night before she was due to marry another man.

But his most memorable achievement was the laying of roads over the surrounding bogs and marshes which he achieved by laying a foundation of bundles of heather down, a feat which had never been done before.

Between Knaresborough and York, one can find **Beningbrough Hall**, a delightful 18th century house, with 7 acres of gardens, wilderness play area (which should keep restless children occupied for a good while), pike ponds and scenic walks. The hall has a fully working Victorian laundry - we felt extremely grateful for 20th century technology, following our visit there! Another item of interest is the permanent exhibition of 18th century

Beningbrough Hall

portraits, on loan from the National Portrait Gallery. There are often other exhibitions that take place here, for which there is usually an additional charge.

Nearby **Harrogate** is renowned for other things, notably its spa waters. Around 400 years ago, there were said to be about 88 different springs to be found in Harrogate that pinpointed it as a venue for the rich and influential to visit, in order to partake of the healing properties of its waters. The original spa was discovered in 1576 by William Slingsby. The growth of the town due to these resources began to accelerate in the last century and reached a climax early in this one. These days, Harrogate is a very attractive town, with many quieter diversions for the discerning tourist, notable for its Victorian and Edwardian architecture. The many old-fashioned shops are typified by Montpelier Parade, a crescent of shops surrounded by trees and flower-beds, and the popular Valley Gardens and Stray (200 acres of open grassland) make this a very green tourist spot indeed.

Harrogate's excellent shops, hotels and restaurants, as well as exhibition and meeting halls, make it a popular cultural and conference centre. Its main impression is that of a lively, light-hearted town, which illuminates its crescents and streets with fairy-lights all year round.

In Mount Parade, on the fringe of **Harrogate**'s bustling town centre, we made a point of finding the first-class French restaurant, **La Bergerie**. This fine establishment is owned and personally-run by Luchon-born chef Jacques Giron who settled in Yorkshire after serving his apprenticeship in London. Jacques takes great pride in the personal attention given both to his customers and to the dishes he prepares. The menu offers a choice of two- and three-course dinners and is changed every six weeks. On the day we called, starters included pigeon breast garnished with Chanterelle mushrooms, and main courses fillet of sole garnished with lobster strips. The puddings too were superb. Expect to pay around £25 per head including wine. Open Monday to Saturday evenings.

La Bergerie

There will be few natives of Harrogate who have not heard of Betty Lupton, the almost legendary Queen of the Wells. For over 50 years, she dispensed the spa waters, dishing out cupfuls of the odious smelling liquid to paying visitors, who were then encouraged to walk off the dubious effects of the "medicine" by taking a trip around the Bogs Fields, known today as **Valley Gardens**. She conducted her business in the ostentatiously named Royal Baths, which in their heyday, were full of rich visitors sampling the waters, which had been described as similar to bad eggs, beaten up in paraffin. Nowadays, the tourists, rather more wisely, prefer to sip cups of tea in its tall, pillared room, with a pianist or string quartet playing in the background. Gone today are the visitors to the chalybeate springs, elegantly "promenading" through the walks and gardens of the popular resort; instead, Harrogate is the haven of the business-man and sales executive, filling its conference centres.

The family-run **Valley Hotel** stands in a splendid position overlooking **Harrogate**'s attractive Valley Gardens which, with their concert stage, eighteen-hole miniature golf course, bowling green and tennis courts, are one of the principal attractions of the town. This English Tourist Board four crown and AA two star rated hotel can be found in Valley Drive within easy reach of the conference centre, theatre and town centre shops and so provides an excellent base for both business guests and holidaymakers alike. Inside, the proprietors have managed to create a relaxed and informal atmosphere, bridging the generation gap by successfully making the very young through to the very old, at home in their surroundings. Proof of this is contained in the comments written in the visitors book. The bedrooms are all spacious (most are family rooms) and equipped with en suite bath/shower rooms, colour televisions, direct-dial telephones and tea/coffee making facilities.

Valley Hotel

There is also a lift to all floors which dates from the 1950s and which has an old-fashioned sliding gate and fine inlaid veneers. This is regularly maintained in its original condition and is a great favourite with residents. The food is home-cooked and delicious (even the bread, marmalade and desserts are home-made); the menu always features vegetarian dishes, as well as such house specialities as braised beef in orange sauce, Indian samosas and regular daily specials on the blackboard. As you enter the hotel, look out for Snoopy the family dog who often stands with her front paws behind the reception desk ready to give the guests a friendly greeting.

One place worth visiting, if staying in Harrogate, is **Rudding Park and Gardens**, an attractive Regency House with splendid lawns, gardens and woods outside and a wonderful selection of paintings, tapestries and antiques inside.

We also took the opportunity of visiting the old part of town known as **'High Harrogate'**, where we found the outstanding **White House Hotel.** This splendid establishment is owned and personally run by former interior designer Jennie Forster and stands overlooking the grass and trees of the Stray. Built in 1836 in the style of a Venetian villa, the hotel was constructed by the then mayor of Harrogate who was involved in the supply of the town's famous panacean 'sulphur water'. The present-day hotel offers the most luxurious of surroundings whilst never appearing over-formal or oppressive; all the furnishings have been carefully and tastefully chosen to create an atmosphere which is extremely relaxed and comfortable. Mrs Forster and her staff go to great trouble to make their guests feel like this is their second home. Personal service is the key and

White House Hotel

there are no lengths to which they will not go to provide that extra special touch. The food too is imaginative and of a similarly high standard. The restaurant has been awarded the AA's coveted *Rosette* and is believed to be one of only three establishments in Harrogate to have been granted this prestigious accolade. A sample dinner menu might include the starter 'mixed leaves with grilled goats' cheese and raspberry vinegar', and the main course 'breast of Grassingham duck with pink peppercorns, wild mushrooms and port'. With its unique atmosphere and superb service, the White House Hotel is a wonderful place for those wishing to spoil themselves in exceptional style.

Spofforth Castle, a couple of miles south-east of the town on the A661, is another place of note, an historic building whose sight stirs the imagination, despite its ruined state.

The powerful Percy family originally founded the castle, which is, amongst other events that took place here, said to have been the birthplace of Harry Hotspur. Its crumbling walls and wind-blown chambers and passage-ways, hewn out of the solid rock, hold an eerie fascination for all who come here.

Spofforth Village nearby has retained a great deal of old-world charm, with its old mill on the tiny River Crimple and the old church, where the legendary Jack Metcalfe is buried; this area, so close to Harrogate, is well worth devoting a half-day of one's visit to see.

If travelling by Beningbrough Hall, one may happen upon the picturesque village of **Nun Monkton**, worthy of being pictured on a chocolate box, with its distinctive red-roofed cottages that nestle around a village green and duckpond.

This village was once known chiefly for its ducks, believe it or not, for the large village pond drew a great many of them at one time and the problems of random egg-laying and over- population of the birds reached nearly epidemic proportions! However, the stalwart members of the local Women's Institute took matters firmly in hand, and a crisis was narrowly averted - Alfred Hitchcock would have possibly been quite interested in the problem as material for a film, had he been aware of the incident (called "The Ducks"...?). However this may amuse readers, the problem was a pressing issue at the time, and the local paper featured the developments for some weeks.

One cannot blame the feathered menaces for being attracted to the place, with its lovely cottages, gardens, the beautiful and ancient buildings of Red House Preparatory School and of course the famous Church, built from the former remains of the old Priory.

The Priory was founded in the 12th century, as the home of Benedictine nuns, by William de Arches and his wife Ivetta. The arch theme in the architecture is apparent, a charming indulgence and perhaps culminating in the splendid window with its William Morris designs. The nun's choir was demolished during the Dissolution, but fortunately what was salvaged presents us today with a very attractive building, built in stages, due to the poverty of the local community, who were unable to complete their project all at once, lacking the larger income of the great Cistercian priories. Among the prioresses of Nun Monkton, two were of the distinguished local family, the Slingsbys, whose chief memorial is Red House across the river at **Moor Monkton**, another idyllic location, which amongst other features, has a windmill.

Nun Monkton Church

Red House was the hiding place for Sir Henry Slingsby at various stages of the Civil War, who despite his best efforts was spotted here by Sir John Bourchier of Beningbrough, who informed his Parliamentarian friends. There is still a gateway at the house, where Slingsby was captured and led off to his execution on the 8th of June 1658. It is said that the present adventuresome occupants of the school now here still fill their leisure hours in search for the secret room the unfortunate Slingsby was forced to hide in.

Should one get the opportunity to look around Red House, one might wish to search for this oneself, or at least guess where the entrance might be, or visit the beautifully preserved Jacobean family chapel, mentioned so affectionately in Sir Henry's diary. The school, in fact have gone to great lengths to preserve the house as it was, although the same cannot be said for another Slingsby residence in Knaresborough, Scriven Hall, which was demolished some time back, along with its contents so lovingly commissioned and collected by the family, and the village it fathered absorbed into the environs of the larger town.

The town of **Ripley**, which is reached via the A61, is a quiet, pretty place, with cobbled streets, and a part in the Civil War that makes interesting reading.

One will notice, on walking through the town, the oddly named Hotel de Ville, which is in fact, the Town Hall. It is said that Sir William Amcotts

Ingilby was responsible for this, being an avid Francophile, he remodelled the entire town in 1827/8, on one he had seen in Alsace Lorraine, replacing the original thatched cottages with those in a more Tudor style.

The estate was granted to Thomas Ingilby in the 1300's, for diverting a wild boar from the King's person in Knaresborough Forest, and a boar carved out of stone in the fountain in the town square commemorates this event.

In the outer walls of the parish church, built around 1400, are holes said to have been caused by musket balls from Cromwell's firing squad, who executed Royalist prisoners here after the battle of Marston Moor. Inside, at the end of a eulogy to Sir William Ingilby, Cromwell made a further mark by adding " No Pompe nor Pride, let God be honoured"

The castle is open to the public, with beautiful gardens, lake and an avenue of tall beeches that its attractive towers only just seem to peek over.

Its tranquility belies the events that happened here after Marston Moor, when Cromwell, exhausted after his day's slaughter, camped his Roundheads here and chose to take sojourn in the castle.

The Ingilbys were Royalist, and at this time Sir William was away, leaving only his sister, Jane Ingilby, dubbed "Trooper Jane", due to her fighting skills, to deal with Cromwell's intrusion. She dealt with the general with as much ill-will as possible, offering no food or bed, and even spent the evening glaring across the hall-table at her unwelcome guest, who had slumped on the sofa in uncomfortable cicumstances, pointing two pistols at his head!

After the self-styled Lord Protector of England left the castle in a fume the next morning, she was heard to declare "It was well that he behaved in so peaceable a manner; had it been otherwise, he would not have left the house alive." One is left wondering how history would have been changed, had Cromwell been foolhardy enough to step out of line.

However, the sad postscript to this story is that, Cromwell, his pride damaged by being bettered by a woman, on leaving the castle, ordered the immediate executions of his Royalist prisoners, within earshot of Mistress Ingilby, causing the musket-ball holes in the church walls previously mentioned. One can imagine that, forced to listen to Cromwell's revenge, Jane Ingilby may have had reason to regret staying her hand the previous evening.

Ripley Castle has held its share of secrets over the years. A priest-hole was discovered in 1963 behind the wainscotting in the Knight's Chamber, where Catholic priests were hidden to prevent them from suffering terrible reprisals.

Ripley Castle

The Chamber is the topmost room in the tower of the castle, dating from 1555. Despite this hiding place, Francis Ingilby, the priest of the family in Elizabethan days, was arrested, and hung, drawn and quartered at York in 1586.

A couple of miles to the west of Ripley, the B 6165 Nidderdale road passes through the village of **Burnt Yates** with its charming village green, school and church. In a splendid position overlooking the cricket pitch on the green, we found the exceptional inn and restaurant, **The Bay Horse** which is owned and personally run by the Donockley family.

Originally constructed in the 18th century, this lovely old building retains much of its traditional character and atmosphere. The interior has been tastefully remodelled by Mrs Donockley and her daughters, benefiting from their past experience in the design world. The rooms are furnished with antique furniture and the walls covered with fine old pictures and prints. The Bay Horse is also renowned for it's food and offers a truly imaginative menu, both at lunchtimes and in the evening. On the day we visited, the lunchtime dishes included "catfish steak" (a Louisiana fish fillet marinated in herbs and spices) and in the evening the main course included "wild boar and venison pie" (traditional country meats cooked in a 'jus roti' of onions, mushrooms, red wine and finished with brandy).

All dishes are freshly prepared and so may involve a moderate wait, however, they are well worth waiting for. The inn also provides an ideal base for those wishing to stay in this beautiful area and offers sixteen attractively furnished bedrooms, all equipped with en-suite facilities and appointed to the highest modern standards.

The Bay Horse Inn and Restaurant

The small villages and ham-
ets surrounding Ripley are a tonic
or any city-weary visitor, and
Iampsthwaite is particularly so.
Iere one can see St Thomas a
Beckett's Church, where Peter
Barker, "Blind Peter", a character
n the tradition of Jack Metcalfe, is
uried. Despite his blindness,
Barker was a skilled cabinet-maker,
lazier and musician; by the font is
mysterious portrait of a bearded
nan, painted by the local vicar's
aughter, which may well be Blind
Peter himself. Not far from his por-
rait is the richly decorated tomb of
Amy Woodforde Finden, composer
f the "Indian Love Lyrics", who
ied in 1919. The novelist
Thackeray was also said to have
riginated here.

Two miles from Aldborough, one may decide to visit the village of **Myton in Swale**, which was once the site of one of the strangest battles ver fought of British soil.

In 1319, Berwick-on-Tweed had fallen into the hands of the Scots, and he English under Edward II, 'The Hammer of the Scots' as he was dubbed, ad held them under siege in retaliation. Robert Bruce, by means of a iversion decided to mount an attack on York, the plan being to capture Queen Isabella.

News of the plan reached York, Queen Isabella was moved from the ity and the Scots probably would have withdrawn, their plan thwarted, ave for the attack, rather imprudently mounted by William de Melton, rchbishop of York, to teach them a lesson.

An army of priests and tradesmen was hurriedly assembled, and the abble marched on up the Swale valley to meet with the Scottish forces. The ntrained volunteers, though thousands strong, were no match for the attle-hardened Scots, and after crossing the Swale at Myton were slaughtered, priests and all in a tragically uneven foray, called the White Battle, lthough the Scots, surprised by the sight of so many war-like priests, ubbed it "The Chapter of Myton".

Travelling west, is the ancient Roman town of Isurium Brigantum, or **Aldborough**, as it is known today.

The town's significance is perhaps identified by the fact that it is signposted from York, on the posts that indicate the city's interesting historical features. It was once the home of the 9th Legion, who wrested it from the Celtic Brigantian tribe.

The modern-day focal point is the tall maypole on the village green, around which traditional dances take place each May. At one end of the green is a raised platform which is all that remains of the Old Court House. An inscription on it recalls that up to 150 years ago, this very spot was the place from where the elections of members of Parliament were announced. Below, are some well-preserved stocks, that are, in fact, only replicas of the originals.

There is a small museum in Aldborough, which houses relics of the town's Roman past. This was once a thriving Roman city of vital strategic importance and close by to the museum are some of the original walls and pavements of that city.

The church of St Andrew in Aldborough was built in 1330 on the site of a Norman church that was burnt down by the Scots in 1318. This in turn was built on the site of the ancient Temple of Mercury. Modern archaeologists no doubt reel in horror at the fact that parts of the present church were built with stones from the Temple's walls.

One ancient relic, however, that is still preserved in the Church's grounds is the Anglo-Saxon sun-dial called the Ulph-stone. A cryptic message on it reads,

"Ulph ordered the church to be built for his own and Gunware's soul".

Its partner town of **Boroughbridge** is an historic town with large roomy hotels, a cobbled market-place and the famous bridge. Once a main thoroughfare for the Celts of Brigantia, then the Romans, through to the coaching days and traffic passing from the West Riding to the North, Boroughbridge has returned to its former unassuming role of a wayside village, due to the by-pass (A19) that takes most of the 20th century traffic from it's streets. The great **Devil's Arrows** bronze-age monoliths stand like guardians, uncomfortably close to the new road, seeming to warn the intrusive vehicles to move on quickly, an enduring symbol of the town's ancient past.

Its bridge is perhaps most famous by association with the murder of the Earl of Hereford by one of Edward II's loyalist forces, which took place during a battle on the bridge itself. A soldier of the king was said to have hidden during the foray in the timbers of the original bridge and took the opportunity to thrust a long spear through the Earl's armour as he galloped past. The rebels of whom Hereford had been one, fled in disarray. John de Mowbray, one of their number, was captured within sight of his castle at Upsall near Thirsk and killed in a lane now rather grimly called Chop Head Loaning - which gives us some idea as to the grisly nature of his death.

Near Boroughbridge is **Newby Hall**, a small but beautiful Adam house, adorned with tapestries, pictures and antique furniture, with gardens that sweep down majestically to the banks of the Ure.

Its architectural history is prestigious indeed. The original Hall was designed by Sir Christopher Wren, and in 1766, two extra wings were added by Robert Adam, one of which was intended to house the current owner, William Weddell's collection of statuary. Weddell also commissioned Adam to buy the beautiful Gobelin tapestries which have made Newby Hall world-famous.

Newby Hall

The old-world villages around Newby Hall are well worth touring for their hidden charms. **Bishop Monkton**'s origins are probably episcopal. It is watered by a tiny stream that chatters its way around little streets, necessitating numerous stone bridges. Nearby **Copgrove** is another lovely location, and was once the home of an important spa, it's popularity eventually waning against the competition from its much larger neighbour, Harrogate. The memories of this are commemorated in a window in the local church, which depicts St Mungo, patron saint of the town's well, blessing a crippled boy and girl, who are about to throw aside their crutches. In the next panel, we see St Francis surrounded by various members of the animal kingdom, including an ox, a cockerel, a partridge, some rabbits, a squirrel and an otter.

On country roads, some eight miles west of Boroughbridge, is the old village of **Raskelf**, mentioned in the Domesday book, and renowned for its 15th century church (which boasts one of the few wooden towers remaining in the country). Also, at the crossroads in the centre of the village stands an eighteenth century pinfold. **The Old Black Bull** dates back to the 16th century and many original ships' timbers are still exposed. Horse bits and brasses adorn the walls and an open fire enhances the olde worlde atmosphere. The four modern and spacious letting roomsare in an annexe at the rear of the pub with their own separate entrance. They are all en-suite with central heating and equipped with colour television and beverage-making facilities.

The Old Black Bull

On a pleasant country road between the A19 and A168 four miles south of Thirsk, we found the busy rural village of **Dalton**. Those looking for accommodation on a typical working farm should look here for **Garth House**. Set back from the main road within a large attractive garden, this substantial Yorkshire farmhouse offers bed and breakfast accommodation of an unusually high standard. Owner Barbara Ramshay provides her guests with genuine Yorkshire hospitality and the finest traditional country cooking. As well as hearty English breakfasts, she serves mouth-watering homemade afternoon teas and delicious farmhouse suppers. The lounge and dining room have recently been knocked into one spacious room with an open fire and a pleasant relaxing atmosphere.

Garth House

Nearby **Topcliffe** is probably better known to tourists as the venue for the famous annual gypsy fairs. The village is set in one of the most beautiful locations, where the sparkling Swale rushes past charming churches, an old inn and a series of huddled cottages, sheltered by the east bank or "cliff". No wonder the gypsies chose this as the most suitable place to congregate!

The church dates back to the 14th century, the Topcliffe family brasses being its greatest treasure, although a visit to nearby **Maiden Bower** reminds us that it was the powerful Percy family that shaped this land before the Topcliffes resided here. The castle that once stood proudly on its brow was constructed soon after the Battle of Hastings, the precursor to such strongholds as Wressle, Spofforth and Leconfield.

In Topcliffe, a short distance from the river, is the delightful 17th century former coaching inn, **The Angel Inn**.

The Angel is owned and managed by Tony and Trish Ardron who have carried out a number of important improvements since taking over in 1986. There are now three bar areas, a restaurant serving an impressive range of English and Continental dishes, a games room and an attractive beer garden with a barbecue patio. Private river fishing is also available.

There are also a number of tastefully decorated letting bedrooms, all of which have en-suite facilities, satellite televisions, mini-bar, radio alarms, direct-dial telephones and beverage-making facilities.

The Angel Inn

CHAPTER 6

Ripon to Darlington

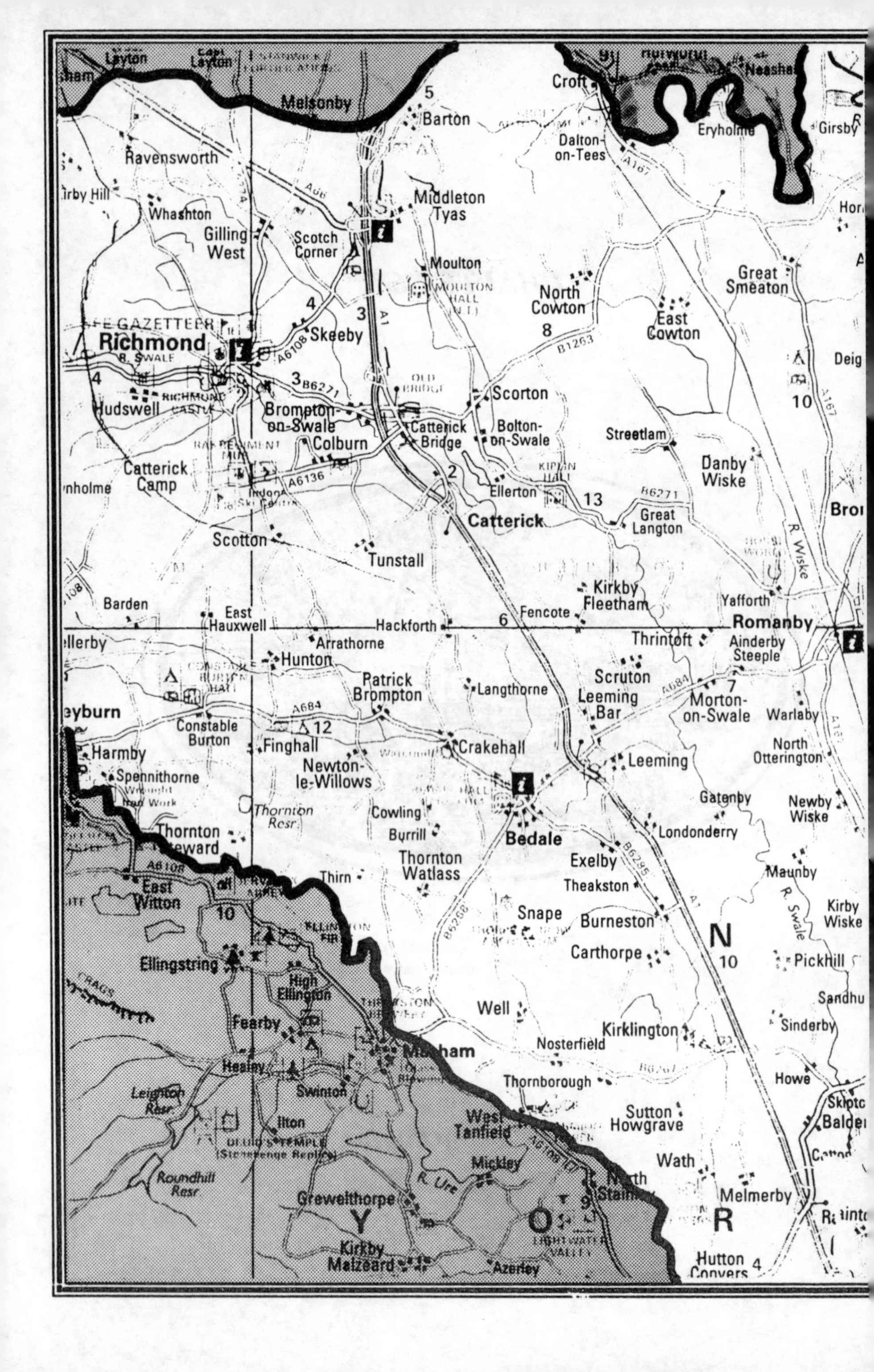
Melsonby
Barton
Croft
Neasham
Eryholme
Girsby
Dalton-on-Tees
Ravensworth
Middleton Tyas
Whashton
Gilling West
Scotch Corner
Moulton
Moulton Hall
North Cowton
Great Smeaton
East Cowton
Richmond
Skeeby
Hudswell
Scorton
Brompton-on-Swale
Catterick Bridge
Bolton-on-Swale
Colburn
Streetlam
Danby Wiske
Catterick Camp
Ellerton
Catterick
Great Langton
Scotton
Tunstall
Kirkby Fleetham
Barden
East Hauxwell
Hackforth
Fencote
Yafforth
Romanby
Arrathorne
Thrintoft
Ainderby Steeple
Hunton
Scruton
Patrick Brompton
Langthorne
Leeming Bar
Morton-on-Swale
Warlaby
Constable Burton
Finghall
Crakehall
North Otterington
Harmby
Spennithorne
Newton-le-Willows
Leeming
Thornton Resr.
Cowling
Gatenby
Newby Wiske
Burrill
Bedale
Londonderry
Thornton Watlass
Exelby
Maunby
Thirn
East Witton
Theakston
Snape
Burneston
Kirby Wiske
Ellingstring
Carthorpe
Pickhill
High Ellington
Well
Fearby
Kirklington
Sinderby
Nosterfield
Healey
Swinton
Thornborough
Howe
Leighton Resr.
Ilton
Sutton Howgrave
West Tanfield
Druid's Temple
(Stonehenge Replica)
Roundhill Resr.
Mickley
Wath
Grewelthorpe
Melmerby
Kirkby Malzeard
Azerley
Hutton Conyers
A1
A66
A167
A6108
B6271
A6136
B1263
A684
B6285
B6268
B6267
R. Swale
R. Wiske
R. Ure

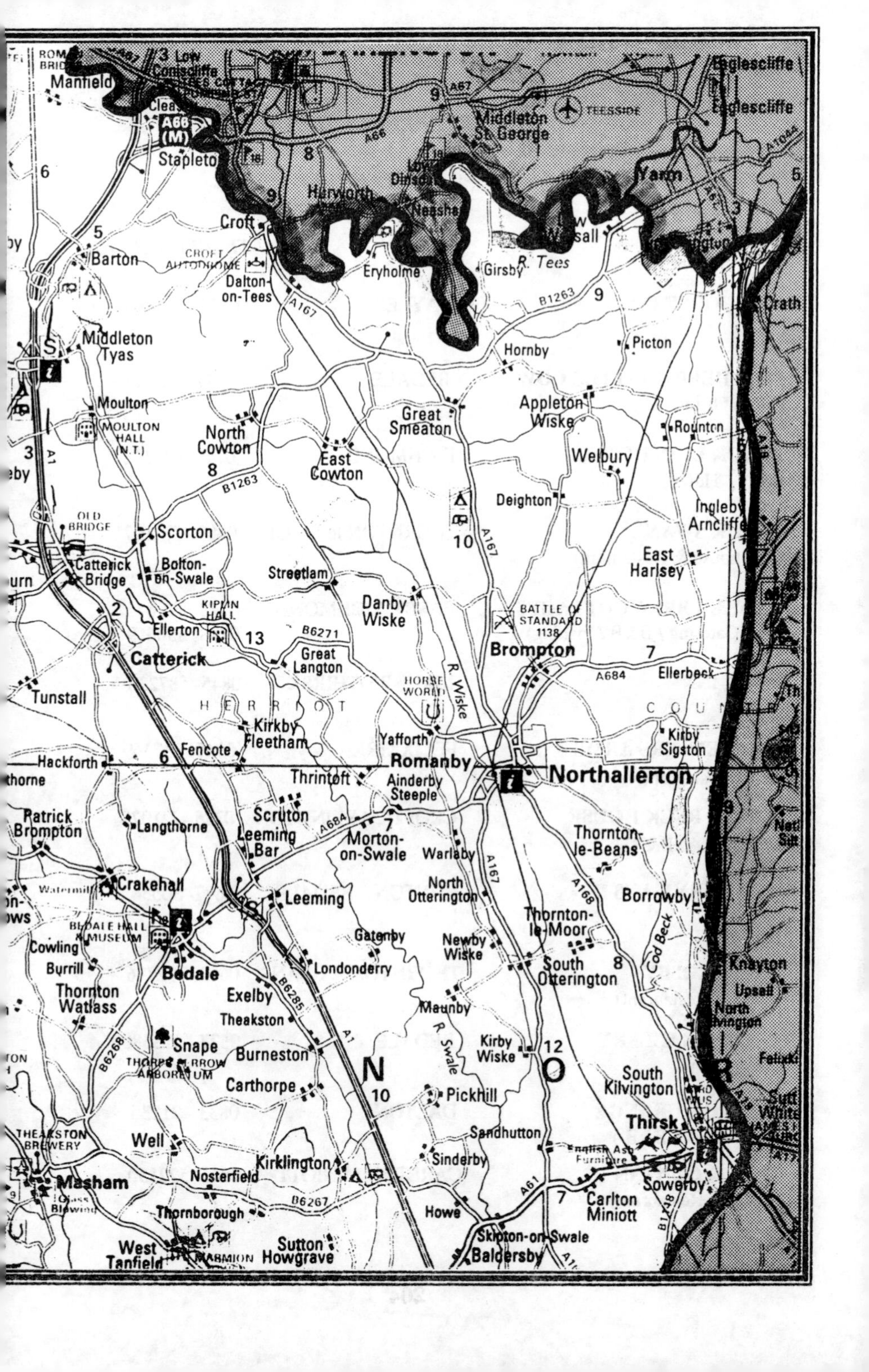

Manfield
Low Coniscliffe
Middleton St George
Teesside
Eaglescliffe
Stapleton
Hurworth
Low Dinsdale
Neasham
Yarm
Low Worsall
Croft
Croft Autodrome
Barton
Dalton-on-Tees
Eryholme
Girsby
R. Tees
Middleton Tyas
Hornby
Picton
Moulton
Moulton Hall (N.T.)
North Cowton
Great Smeaton
Appleton Wiske
Rounton
East Cowton
Welbury
Deighton
Old Bridge
Scorton
Ingleby Arncliffe
Catterick Bridge
Bolton-on-Swale
Streetlam
East Harlsey
Danby Wiske
Kiplin Hall
Ellerton
Battle of Standard 1138
Catterick
Great Langton
Brompton
Ellerbeck
Tunstall
Horse World
R. Wiske
Herriot
County
Kirkby Fleetham
Yafforth
Kirby Sigston
Hackforth
Fencote
Romanby
Northallerton
Thrintoft
Ainderby Steeple
Patrick Brompton
Langthorne
Scruton
Leeming Bar
Morton-on-Swale
Warlaby
Thornton-le-Beans
Crakehall
Watermill
Leeming
North Otterington
Borrowby
Bedale Hall & Museum
Gatenby
Newby Wiske
Thornton-le-Moor
Cod Beck
Cowling
Burrill
Bedale
Londonderry
South Otterington
Knayton
Upsall
Thornton Watlass
Exelby
Maunby
North Kilvington
Theakston
R. Swale
Snape
Burneston
Kirby Wiske
Thorp Perrow Arboretum
Carthorpe
South Kilvington
Pickhill
Thirsk
Theakston Brewery
Well
Sandhutton
Kirklington
Sinderby
Masham
Glass Blowing
Nosterfield
Carlton Miniott
Sowerby
Thornborough
Howe
West Tanfield
Marmion
Sutton Howgrave
Skipton-on-Swale
Baldersby
A1
A66 (M)
A66
A67
A167
A684
A61
A168
A19
B1263
B6271
B6285
B6268
B6267
N
O
R

REFERENCE GUIDE

CHAPTER 6

NAME	*TOWN*	*TELEPHONE NO.*
BAY HORSE INN (Inn)	GAYLES	0833 -21468
BIG SHEEP & LITTLE COW (Place Of Interest)	BEDALE	0677 -422125
BLACK LION HOTEL (Inn / Hotel)	RICHMOND	0748- 823121
BLACK SWAN (Freehouse & Restaurant)	THORNTON le MOOR	0609 -774117
BROKEN BREA COTTAGES (Self Catering / B&B / Fishing)	EASBY RICHMOND	0748 -825647 0748- 850619 **(fax)**
BUCK INN (Inn)	MAUNBY/THIRSK	0845- 587236
CARPENTERS ARMS (Inn & restaurant)	FELIXKIRK	0845- 537369
CLOW BECK HOUSE (Farmhouse B&B)	CROFT/DARLINGTON	0325 -721075
COUNTRYMANS INN (Inn)	HUNTON / BEDALE	0677- 50554
THE CROSBY -(Inn & Restaurant)	THORNTON le BEANS	0609- 772776
DALES GALLERY (Gallery)	BEDALE	0677 - 423580
DALTON GRANGE (Farmhouse B&B)	DALTON	0833 - 21235
DOG & GUN INN -(Inn & Restaurant)	CARLTON MINIOTT	0845- 522150

Reference Guide
Chapter 6

DOXFORD HOUSE (B&B)	SOWERBY / THIRSK	0845 -523238
ELMFIELD HOUSE (Country House Hotel)	ARRATHORNE / BEDALE	0677 -50558
FOX & HOUNDS (Inn)	PICKHILL	0845 -567384
FRANK JOBLING (Place of Interest)	W TANFIELD / RIPON	0677- 70481
HOWE VILLA (Country House Hotel)	RICHMOND	0748- 850055
HYPERION HOUSE (B&B)	BEDALE	0677-- 422334
INDUSTRIOUS COTTAGE (Place of Interest)	BEDALE	0677- 70386
JERVAULX HALL (Country House Hotel)	RIPON	0677 - 60235
KIRK CURIOS (Place of Interest)	BEDALE	0677 -425713
LITTLE HOLTBY FARM (Farmhouse B&B)	LEEMING BAR	0609- 748762
LOVESOME HILL FARM (Farmhouse B&B)	NORTHALLERTON	0609 - 772311
Mc COYS (Hotel Restaurant Bistro)	STADDLEBRIDGE	0609- 82671
MOUNT PLEASANT FARM (Farmhouse B & B)	WHASHTON	0748- 822784
OLD BREWERY (Guest House)	RICHMOND	0748 - 822460

Refernce Guide
Chapter 6

OLD MILL (Place Of Interest)	BALK / THIRSK	0845- 597227
OLD OAK TREE (Inn & Restaurant)	S. KILVINGTON	0845 523276
OLD RECTORY (B & B)	THORNTON WATLASS	0677 -423456
OLD RED HOUSE (Hotel)	CARLTON MINIOTT	0845 -- 24383
OLD VICARAGE (B & B)	CRAKEHALL / BEDALE	0677- 422967
PLUMP BANK (B& B)	THIRSK	0845- 522406
PORCH HOUSE (Guest House)	NORTHALLERTON	0609-779831
SION HILL HALL (Place of Interest)	KIRBY WISKE	0845-- 587206
SUNDIAL HOTEL (Hotel)	NORTHALLERTON	0609 - 780525
THORNBOROUGH HOUSE FARM (Farmhouse B & B and Self catering)	S.KILVINGTON	0845 - 522103
THORPE PERROW ARBORETUM (Place of Interet)	SNAPE / BEDALE	0677- 425323
TRESKE SHOP (Furniture Makers)	THIRSK	0845-522770
TUDOR HOTEL (Hotel & Restaurant)	BROMPTON on SWALE	0748 -818021
TURF HOTEL (Hotel & Restaurant)	RICHMOND	0748 822673

Reference Guide
Chapter 6

VILLAGE INN (Inn Restaurant B &B)	BROMPTON	0609 771660
WELLFIELD HOUSE FARM (Farmhouse B & B)	OTTERINGTON	0609- 772766
WELLINGTON HEIFER (Inn)	AINDERBY STEEPLE	0609 - 775542
WEST END GUEST HOUSE (Guest house & Self Catering)	RICHMOND	0748 - 824783
WHITE HEIFER (Inn)	SCARTON / RICHMOND	0748- 811357
WILLOWS (Coffee Shop & Restaurant)	RICHMOND	0748 -824874
WINDSOR HOUSE (Guest House)	RICHMOND	0748 823285
WOODHILL GRANGE (Farmhouse B &B)	THIRSK	0845 522237
WOODHOUSE ANDREW (Place Of Interest)	BEDALE	0677 423573
YAFFORTH EQUESTRIAN CTR (Equestrian Centre)	YAFFORTH	0609 780258
YORKSHIRE GLIDING CLUB (Place of Interest)	SUTTON BANK THIRSK	0845 597237

CHAPTER 6

From Ripon to Darlington

When we hear the names of certain towns, we immediately think of their common associations. We therefore think of the races when we hear of Ripon, and Darlington conjures up thoughts of steelworks and railways. But when we visit these places, we find our own personal associations, being pleasantly surprised by how far-removed our experience was from the pre-supposed notions we had of the place beforehand.

The cathedral town of **Ripon** has a tapestry of rich historical tradition mostly missed by those rushing through to attend the famous race-meetings, or taking the children to the Lightwater Valley Theme Park.

The town's history goes back to 886, when its charter was granted by Alfred the Great, and the people of Ripon are proud of their traditions - every night at 9pm a hornblower, in tricorn hat and full regalia, still sets the watch as one has for centuries, sounding the ancient horn at each corner of the market cross and in front of the Mayor's house. This tradition is also considered the oldest form of burglar insurance in the world (by most Yorkshiremen anyway!) - householders paid a premium of twopence per door per year, and if any break-ins occurred after the setting of the watch, the Wakeman was obliged to re-imburse them for their loss. The 13th century dwelling that the Wakeman owned is still standing in the Market-place, but of course the insurance is dealt with by the companies we now associate such matters with, and the title of Wakeman has changed to that of Mayor. The Town Hall houses the treasures of these traditions, from the ancient wild ox horn given by King Alfred himself to the latest charter granted by Elizabeth II in 1974, amongst other interesting artifacts.

Their greatest pride and joy is, of course, the imposing Cathedral of St Peter and St Wilfrid, also charmingly titled the Cathedral of the Dales - not as graceful nor as extensive as York Minster, but its very solidity, a mixture of Saxon and Perpendicular architecture, commands the attention. There is something very characteristic of Yorkshire in its austerity and the grey millstone grit from which it is made. It appears to have almost monolithic proportions when viewed from the narrow little streets of the town and is probably best viewed 'broadside on' from across the River Skell, especially at night, when it is illuminated.

The cathedral was founded by St Wilfrid in 669, by the site of a wooden monastery that had been built by Eata, Abbot of Melrose. Its treasures are many and deserving of a visit. Those interested in pageantry should visit Ripon in August, when St Wilfrid's Feast takes place, and the Saint himself (or rather a possible lookalike) parades through the streets on a white horse.

The markets in Ripon take place on Thursdays and Saturdays, heralded by the ringing of the Corn Bell. There are 12 race days a year that take place on the **Garden Racecourse**, which is considered to be one of the most beautifully land-scaped in the country - the attractions of the town are certainly varied.

Many people would prefer to opt for a days visit to the elegant Water Gardens of **Studley Royal**, rather than the noisier amusements of **Lightwater Valley**, situated nearby. These are one of the last surviving examples of a Georgian green garden, its classical temples, follies, views and lakes are a delight to see. It is a National Trust property, along with the even more famous nearby **Fountains Abbey**, the pride of all the ecclesiastical ruins of Yorkshire

Fountains was one of the wealthiest of the Cistercian houses and is arguably one of the most beautiful, as well as the largest in Britain.

It was founded in 1132, with the help of Archbishop Thurstan of York, and the first buildings housed just 12 monks of the order, who had first described the site as,

"A place of thorns and rocks, a better dwelling for wild beasts than for men."

Under the guidance of Geoffrey of Clairveaux, the very rocks they had spoken of were used to build a stone monastery. Over the centuries the buildings increased, even spreading across the River Skell itself, which passed under the infirmary.

Under John of York in the 13th century, the number of monks greatly increased and the building of the most influential of Cistercian houses reached its peak in the 15th century, with the grandiose designs of Abbot Marmaduke Huby, whose beautiful tower still stands as a reminder of how rich and powerful Fountains became under the sway of his ambitions. In fact, the Abbey was run on such business-like lines that at its height, Fountains owned extensive lands throughout Yorkshire, had eight sister houses, traded widely in lead and wool and had an income of about a thousand pounds a year, a very substantial sum indeed.

The Dissolution hit the Abbey as it did all the powerful religious houses. The abbot was hanged, the monks scattered, and its treasures

Fountains Abbey

taken off or destroyed. The stonework, however, was left largely intact, possibly due to its remote location.

In 1579, Sir Stephen Proctor pulled down some out-buildings, in order to construct **Fountains Hall**, which still stands in the Abbey's grounds.

This lovely, tranquil tourist spot, with the opulence of Studley Royal and the magnificence of Fountains, is one of the most popular National Trust sites in Yorkshire, and visitors coming here will easily understand why.

North of Ripon, on a minor road off the A61, is the stately home of **Norton Conyers**, owned by the Graham family since 1624.

One of the earliest stories of the family, concerns Sir Richard Graham, who fought on Cromwell's side at Marston Moor in 1644, where he suffered the misfortune of becoming gravely wounded, losing consciousness in the saddle. He escaped the foray due to his horse, which had the good sense to carry him back the thirty miles to the Hall, stopping for no-one, until it finally came to a halt at the foot of their staircase. It was reputed to have placed a hoof on the bottom step, where the heat generated by its exertions, burnt a mark into the wood.

Norton Conyers other claim to fame is possibly more well-known, for it was here that Charlotte Bronte heard the story of "Mad Mary", supposedly a Lady Graham, who had been locked up in an attic room, now tantalisingly inaccessible to the public, on whom she eventually based the character of Mrs Rochester in her novel "Jane Eyre", and several features of the Hall were used in the narrative.

Visitors to the hall will also see the famous painting of Sir Bellingham Graham on his bay horse, as Master of the Quorn Hunt. It is rumoured that ownership of the painting was based on the throwing of a pair of dice. Obviously Sir Bellingham's luck must have been in that day! The Grahams are an interesting set of characters indeed.

One mile west of Thirsk on the A61 Ripon road, we came to the attractive village of **Carlton Miniott**. Close by Thirsk railway station on the edge of the village, we found the impressive former coaching inn, the **Old Red House**, which has been run since 1983 by Mary and Tony Degazon. The inn dates from the mid-1800s, and inside, it retains much of its original character and atmosphere. As well as a range of traditional beers, Mary and Tony serve a fine selection of first-rate bar meals. They also have twelve en-suite guest rooms available, some within the original building and some within an adjacent annexe. All are extremely well appointed, with one being specially furnished for disabled guests.

Whilst staying here we would also recommend the **Dog and Gun**

Old Red House

Inn, an impressive village inn and restaurant which lies a couple of miles west of Thirsk on the A61 Ripon road. Since taking over in early 1992, Keith and Eileen Salter have successfully created an atmosphere which is welcoming for both visitors and regulars alike. The bar retains much of its 18th-century character and offers a good range of bar snacks and traditional beers. The large and stylish conservatory to the rear contains the inn's 50-seater 'Poachers Restaurant' where a first-rate lunchtime and evening menu is served which features everything from scampi to steaks. Vegetarian dishes and special children's meals are also available, with traditional roast lunches being served on Sundays.

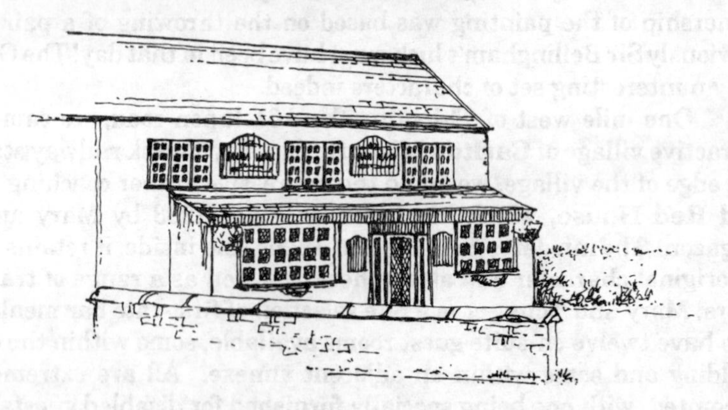

Dog and Gun Inn

Another place to visit if travelling around the area of the A1 trunk route and the B6267 Thirsk to Masham road, is the quiet and picturesque village of **Pickhill,** where we found the popular country inn, the **Fox and Hounds**. It is not known when the inn was built, but it is documented as having been sold as an 'inn, granary and blacksmith's shop' in 1823. The present proprietors Owen and Peggy Jones have been successful at creating an atmosphere which is cosy and welcoming for both visitors and local alike. They serve fine traditional hand-pulled beers (including the local Hambleton Ale) and a wide-ranging bar meals menu which features the wonderful house speciality, homemade steak and kidney pie.

Our next stop enroute was the town of **Thirsk,** famous as the home of veterinary surgeon Alf Wight, better known as James Herriot. We parked right next to the surgery he shared for so many years with the redoubtable Seigfried and his brother Tristram, which is located next door to the British Legion clubhouse.

The history of this market town dates back to the Domesday book, when William the Conqueror gave the manor of Thirsk to one of his barons, Robert de Mowbray.

One interesting piece of information we discovered refers to a visit made to the town at Easter in 1747 by John Wesley, who was reported as

James Herriott's Surgery, Thirsk

finding the town "full of holiday folk drinking, cursing, swearing and cockfighting. I did not stop at all, but rode on to Borobridge!" Looking around this peaceful little town these days, such a description seems difficult to imagine, but perhaps the stalwart Dr Wesley arrived on a race day!

There are eight race-days a year at Thirsk, which are well attended, mostly by the larger population at Northallerton, and the well-off farmers hereabouts, as well as the visitors wishing to sample an intrinsic part of Yorkshire life. On travelling through the areas between the Dales and the North Yorkshire Moors, one is constantly reminded of the great tradition of horse-breeding that the county is famous for, and the tradition runs deep. The traveller and writer Daniel Defoe wrote,

"Whatever part of England you go to, through the farthest corners west and southand whatever inn you come to, 'tis two to one but the hostler is a Yorkshire man; for as they are bred among horses, 'tis always the first business they recommend themselves to"; the sheer numbers of race-courses and stud farms in Yorkshire. and especially around Thirsk, would seem to bear testimony to this.

Opposite the railway station on the western outskirts of Thirsk, we called in at the celebrated furniture workshop and showroom, **The Treske**

St Mary's, Thirsk

Shop. This handsome 200 year-old former maltings' building stands behind a row of redbrick houses on the north side of the A61 Ripon road. (For a fine 40 page colour catalogue, telephone (0845) 522770.) The Treske workshop produces classic modern furniture using traditional methods of manufacture and British hardwoods such as oak, ash, elm and beech. The workshop is unique in that it keeps direct control over every aspect of the manufacturing process 'from forest floor to home delivery'.

Visitors are welcome to watch the skilled wood machinists and cabinet makers at work, and afterwards can view the finished pieces in the many showrooms.

One mile east of Thirsk town centre, close to the point where the A170 Helmsley road meets the minor road to Felixkirk and Boltby, we found the splendid bed and breakfast establishment run by Jean Adlington. Jean's impressive house, **Plump Bank**, stands within two acres of attractive landscaped gardens and has magnificent views over the surrounding countryside. She has three spacious letting rooms available (two double, one twin), all equipped with en-suite facilities and appointed to a good modern standard. Jean provides her guests with delicious Yorkshire breakfasts, first-class hospitality, and an atmosphere which is friendly and relaxed. (Evening meals are available at the nearby Carpenters Inn in Felixkirk.) Children are welcome, but no pets. Open all year round.

Plump Bank

One-and-a-half miles northwest of **Thirsk**, on the minor country road leading towards Newsham, we stopped at the splendid bed and breakfast establishment, **Woodhill Grange**.

This spacious residence is situated in the heart of rural Herriot country, and it may be helpful to telephone the owners, John Haigh and Sara Wissenbach (0845) 522237, for directions. Sara has a background in hotel management and John is keenly involved in country sports, and together they have refurbished the Grange to offer truly first-rate farm-house accommodation. The house and outbuildings are occupied by a number of charming animals including horses, terriers, beagles and a Vietnamese pot-bellied pig, and for guests wishing to bring their own mounts, stabling is offered in the courtyard.

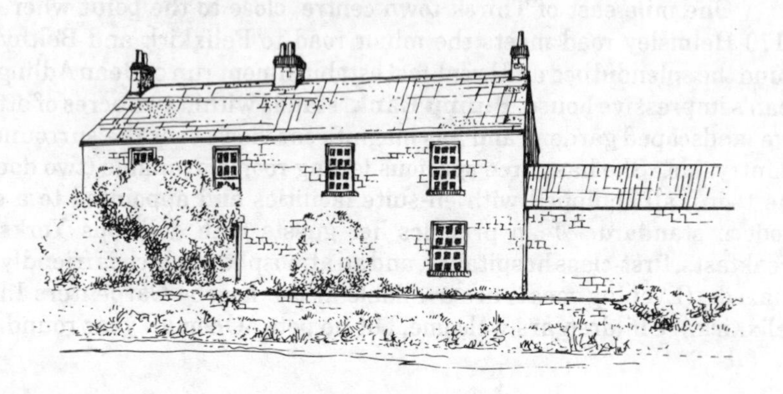

Woodhill Grange

The minor country roads to the east of Thirsk lead to the picturesque hamlet of **Balk**, home of the renowned furniture and craft workshop, **The Old Mill**. (It is located between Bagby and Kilburn, just south of the A170 Scarborough road.) The workshop occupies a 300 year-old corn mill which has been tastefully renovated to provide working and showroom space for fourteen highly-skilled craftspeople.

Each of the senior makers is responsible for the design and manufacture of a unique collection of handmade furniture, and in all, six different ranges are produced, all individually crafted in either oak, walnut, mahogany, cherry, chestnut or ash. Visitors are invited to tour this fascinating workshop and view the finished work in the showroom.

One mile south of Thirsk, we made a point of visiting the attractive village of **Sowerby**. In a fine position overlooking the Greens, we found **Doxford House**, an excellent bed and breakfast establishment which is owned and run by Helen and John Proudley.

The Old Mill

This handsome double-fronted Georgian residence has been comprehensively modernised and offers a number of comfortable guest rooms, all equipped with en-suite shower- or bathroom and beverage making facilities. Look out for the Yorkshire Roses carved on the door surrounds and in the ceiling corners. The house is set within a beautiful shrub-filled garden which leads onto paddock containing a number of charming farmyard animals. The bedroom on the ground floor is also suitable for disabled guests.

Doxford House

The **Yorkshire Gliding Club**, based at Sutton Bank near Thirsk, has been established for many years and provides all the facilities demanded in modern gliding. The club operates seven days a week and, between April and September, offers holiday tuition and short residential courses. The maximum number of people on each course is ten with two professional instructors. This ensures that individual attention is given and a friendly atmosphere maintained at all times.

The club makes a basic charge which covers all accommodation, food and course organisation. Actual flying is then charged at normal club rates. On-site facilities include a centrally-heated, circular clubhouse with lounge and dining room. The circular layout and the site position give incredible panoramic views of the countryside around. Anyone interested in learning to fly is sure to find the course both energetic and worthwhile. Members from other clubs can make use of the aero-tows and may attempt to beat the Gliding Club's record of 30,200 feet!

Yorkshire Gliding Club

Other places to visit whilst in Thirsk are the spectacular Thirsk **Church of St Mary**, a splendid example of Perpendicular Gothic architecture, the racecourse , for those interested in horse-racing, and **Sutton Bank Top** (mentioned in Chapter 2).

Taking the country road leading northeast out of Thirsk, after three miles we reached the attractive village of **Felixkirk**. Here, we found the impressive 17th-century country free house, the **Carpenters Arms**, which is owned by Paul and Lorraine Donohoe. The inn is renowned for its food and offers an excellent menu which combines traditional Yorkshire cooking with the finest continental cuisine. There is an extensive choice including mouthwatering steaks, salmon, monkfish, game and a number of adventurous daily specials. Traditional Yorkshire lunches are served on Sundays. The restaurant area has a magnificent stone fireplace and overlooks

the nearby Hambleton Hills. The hillock to the front of the inn is also believed to contain the ruins of an ancient castle.

The Carpenters Arms

The Old Oak Tree at South Kilvington is a real find for those looking for a first-rate country inn and restaurant. Situated beside the old A19 one-and-a-half miles north of Thirsk, this handsome pantiled building was originally constructed as a farmhouse in the 18th-century. Today, it is owned by partners Sue Bland and Mark Edon who have recently comprehensively refurbished the interior. The bar is decorated with interesting memorabilia, and to the rear, both the Victorian Parlour and Conservatory Restaurant have been furnished with great style.

The Old Oak Tree

The restaurant offers an extensive á la carte menu every lunchtime and evening (except Mondays). Booking is advised on Friday and Saturday evenings

If wishing to stay in this area, one place we can recommend is **Thornborough House Farm**, a delightful farmhouse bed and breakfast establishment run by Tess and David Williamson. This 206-acre working mixed farm is set in the heart of rural Herriot Country a short distance northeast of the village, so it may be advisable to telephone the owners for accurate directions. The Williamson's 200 year-old farmhouse is approached along an attractive driveway and across a private bridge. Inside, it has been tastefully decorated and refurbished to a high modern standard; the three comfortable and spacious guest rooms are all beautifully appointed, and one has the added benefit of en-suite facilities. Tess has lived at Thornborough House Farm all her life and is well practised at providing her guests with the warmest Yorkshire hospitality.

Thornborough House Farm

Tess and David also have a number of self-contained holiday cottages available which stand in different locations within a few minutes drive of the farm. These **Herriot Country Holiday Homes** provide first-rate self-catering accommodation for between two and eight people, and are all clean, comfortable and fully equipped with such appliances as washing machines, microwave ovens and colour televisions. (One of the cottages is a delightful former school house which stands on the lower slopes of the Hambleton Hills in Sutton-under-Whitestonecliffe, three miles east of Thirsk.) The farmhouse and cottages provide an ideal base for exploring the wonderful North Yorkshire countryside with its many beauty spots and places of historic interest.

All those interested in fine furniture, paintings and porcelain should make a point of finding **Sion Hill Hall** near the village of **Kirby Wiske**, six miles south of Northallerton. This fine neo-Georgian mansion was designed in the style of Lutyens by the famous York architect Walter Brierley. Completed in 1913, it is one of the last country houses to be built before the Great War ended the construction of such servant-intensive houses. Its main present-day function is to house the collection of artefacts which was acquired over sixty years by Herbert W Mawer. The Mawer Collection can be viewed in the afternoons of the first Sunday in the month between May and October and by pre-arranged groups at other times.

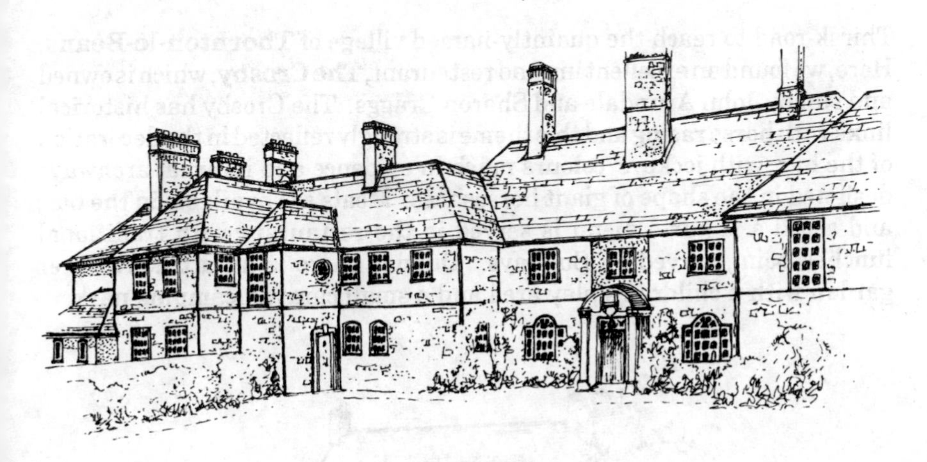

Sion Hill Hall

In the heart of nearby **Maunby** stands the impressive **Buck Inn**, which dates back to the late 18th century. Margaret Shaw, landlady of this cosy and characterful inn, has lived in Maunby all her life and took over the Buck Inn several years ago. The ale here is first class and a good atmosphere prevails. Linda has been the chef here since Margaret took over, and her cooking is superb. The delicious menu is chalked up daily on the blackboard and has to be seen to be believed. The Buck Inn serves food at lunchtimes on Friday, Saturday and Sunday and from Tuesday through to Saturday in the evenings.

Three miles southeast of Northallerton, we turned east off the A168

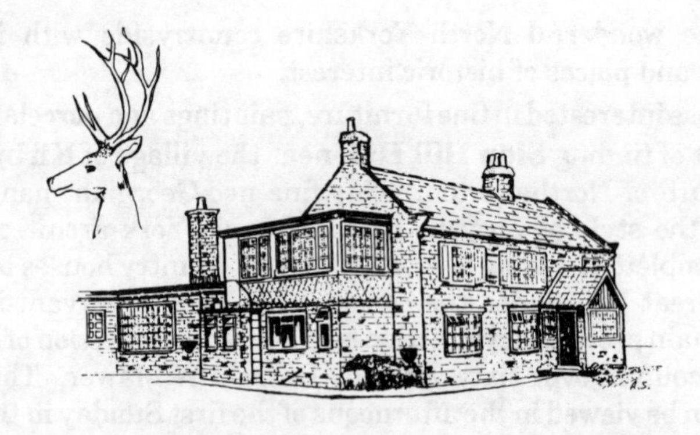

The Buck Inn

Thirsk road to reach the quaintly-named village of **Thornton-le-Beans.** Here, we found an excellent inn and restaurant, **The Crosby,** which is owned and run by John Arundale and Sharon Craggs. The Crosby has historical links with horse racing and this theme is strongly reflected in the decoration of the bar, with jockeys' colours much in evidence and internal archways designed in the shape of giant horseshoes. Meals are available in the bar, and a full á la carte menu is served in the restaurant with traditional lunches being served on Sundays. Outside there is an attractive beer garden with a children's play area and a small caravan/camping park.

The Crosby

Also not far from here to the west, lies the lovely village of **Thornton-le-Moor,** where we visited the **Black Swan,** the friendly pub and eating house run by Tony and Sue Burnley. Built in 1732 as a dwelling house and garth, the building still retains much of its original character with timber-clad ceilings and a relaxed intimate atmosphere. In recent years, the inn has built up an excellent reputation for serving good food and fine traditional ales. Top quality meals are available in the bar and there is also a spacious restaurant area serving an impressive á la carte menu. The two-acre field adjoining the Black Swan is registered as a caravan and camping ground.

The Black Swan

Northallerton, ten miles north-west of Thirsk, has had the dubious distinction for centuries of being famous for it's strong ale. Giles Mornington wrote,

> "North Allerton in Yorkshire does excel
> All England, nay Europe, for strong ale."

- though one may wish on further enquiry to cast as much doubt on his claim as one may on his abilities as a poet!

There is, however, no shortage of inns in the area, which was it is said, one of the favourite haunts of Charles Dickens, who was known to frequent the Old Fleece Inn, a truly Dickensian place, with great oak beams and old-world atmosphere.

On the northern outskirts of the town, we called in at the highly recommended hotel and conference centre, the **Sundial Hotel**. This spacious modern building occupies a peaceful three-and-a-half acre site on the A167 Darlington road, and is the first hotel to be built in the town for over 240 years. We found it to be very professionally run, and from the warm welcome at reception to the efficient attention in the restaurant, the standard of personal service was extremely high. In total, there are 28 bedrooms, all equipped with excellent facilities - private bathrooms, showers, colour televisions, in-house movies, direct-dial telephones, beverage making facilities, hair dryers and trouser presses. Top quality meals are served in the air-conditioned comfort of the hotel's Winston's Restaurant, and on the terrace or in the piano bar, guests can relax with a drink while listening to live piano music.

The Sundial Hotel also provides an excellent service for business guests. Conference facilities are available for groups of up to 150 delegates in rooms which are fully equipped with telephone, television and electrical points. When combined, the suites are also suitable for large presentations and industrial displays. Fax machines are available for delegates' private use, and a full range of catering packages can be tailored to the individual requirements of the organiser. The hotel lies within six miles of the main A1 north/south trunk route and provides a good base for exploring the Yorkshire Dales and North York Moors.

The Sundial Hotel

Northallerton is the county town of the North Riding, and is an important market and shopping centre. There are many old buildings of interest, including an ancient Grammar school, medieval church and a15th century almshouse.

It is an important rail and road junction, and its market days draw the most prosperous farmers in all Yorkshire. The hotels and inns are well-booked at this time, as casual visitors should be warned. On observation, one can see the seating accommodation in these venues is generous in its proportions, as opposed to the more flimsy offerings of city establishments, giving new meaning to the reference that the local agriculture is "widely based", so the natives themselves would wryly comment!

Those looking for truly exceptional guesthouse accommodation in this area should make a point of finding **Porch House** on the northern outskirts of the town. (It is situated in Northallerton's High Street opposite the parish church and next to the police station.) This historic residence is probably North Yorkshire's oldest surviving private house to remain in continuous use throughout its life. The land on which the building stands was purchased by Richard Metcalfe in 1584, and soon after he built an early vernacular crook beam house which now comprises the southern part of the building. This original house had a thatched roof and was constructed of cobbles bound with dung and chaff. These primitive walls were almost four-feet thick at the base, and when they were replaced by one-foot thick brick walls some years later, the original 'tunnel' doorway became the porch that can be seen today. In the years that followed, the house was rebuilt with a timber frame, and then in the 18th-century, the brick-built north end was added and the entire building was re-roofed with pantiles. The present-day guesthouse is owned and run by Peter and Shirley Thompson. They have been careful to preserve the original character and charm of the building whilst providing their guests with the very best in modern Yorkshire hospitality. Inside, the atmosphere is cosy and welcoming, and the guest rooms are tastefully decorated and appointed to a very high standard.

Porch House

We followed the course of the River Wiske (A167) to the south of Northallerton and after three miles came to the village of **North Otterington**. Here, we called in at **Wellfield House Farm**, a 350-acre working mixed farm which

Wellfield House Farm

also offers first-rate farmhouse accommodation. The farm has a flock of 300 breeding ewes and is set in a pleasant riverside position with fine views over the surrounding countryside.

The delightful 17th-century farmhouse has been carefully refurbished to provide three well-appointed letting rooms, one of which also has en-suite facilities. Apart from delicious Yorkshire breakfasts, owner Dorothy Hill provides evening meals by prior arrangement. Guests are welcome to walk around the farm and meet the animals. Open all year round.

A truly outstanding place to eat, and indeed to stay, is **McCoys** Restaurant and Hotel at the **Cleveland Tontine Inn, Staddlebridge.**

McCoys Restaurant

Run by brothers Eugene, Tom and Peter McCoy, this superb establishment stands in an unusual position at the junction of the A19 and the A172 Guisborough road and enjoys a view of the nearby Mount Grace Priory with its ancient tower and ghostly ruined arches. The original inn dates from 1804 when it was constructed to meet the needs of travellers on the newly opened Thirsk to Yarm turnpike. Today, the old courtyard and stone-built stable block still remain which, along with the fortified exterior, give the building a unique romantic atmosphere.

Inside, however, the character is very different. The ground floor houses the main restaurant and is designed to reflect the bourgeois extremes of the 1930s and 40s.

Here, you will find huge fading mirrors, vast parasols, beautifully designed furniture and great vases of flowers. However, it is the food that is even more opulent. Perhaps most easily described as classic French, the menu includes such delicacies as wafer-thin ravioli filled with lemon- and truffle-scented langoustine. (No wonder this has been the Egon Ronay *Restaurant Of The Year* on more than one occasion. However, expect to pay £30 to £40 per head including wine.) Alternatively, the bistro in the cellar offers a less extravagant but nonetheless excellent menu for around half the price. McCoys also operates as a small hotel and has six wonderfully comfortable guest rooms, decorated in a welcoming and homely style.

Two miles northeast of Northallerton, a short detour off the A684 took us to the historic village of **Brompton**. Here, we called in at the splendid pub and eating house, **The Village Inn**, which is run by Geoff and Joan Barber, and their two sons, Phillip and Mark.

The Village Inn

The inn dates from the 18th-century and at one time was a regular stopping point for carters carrying locally-made linen from Brompton to the dying factories at Osmotherly. Since the present owners took over in 1982 they have completely transformed the inn from a small two-roomed pub into a thriving modern establishment. During this refurbishment, care was taken to ensure that the building's original character and charm were retained, and today, the inn possesses an atmosphere which is cosy and welcoming.

Over the years, the Barbers have accumulated a fascinating collection of antique china which includes over 200 teapots, 150 cow creamers, plus numerous toby jugs and miniatures which can be seen throughout the inn. The Village Inn also has a fine carvery restaurant offering traditional English food in pleasant surroundings. There is also an extensive range of main courses available including such items as Chicken Kiev, beef Bourguignon, Tandoori chicken and a number of daily specials on the blackboard. On Sundays, excellent value traditional roast lunches are served which feature the local delicacy, Yorkshire pudding with onion gravy. The Village Inn also has a number of comfortable letting rooms available for those wanting top quality overnight accommodation.

Four miles north of Northallerton on the A167 Darlington road, we came to the charmingly named village of **Lovesome Hill**. Those looking for farmhouse accommodation of the highest standard, lying within easy reach of the Dales and the North Yorkshire Moors, should look for the **Lovesome Hill Farm.** This 165 acre working mixed farm with its impressive 19th century farmhouse is owned by two delightful hosts, Mary and John Pearson.

Lovesome Hill Farm

Mount Grace Priory

They have three comfortable and spacious letting rooms available, one with en-suite facilities, and a charming guest's lounge whichopens on to an attractive garden with a patio and croquet lawn. Guests are provided with hearty farmhouse breakfasts and, by prior arrangement, with delicious evening meals. Further accommodation is under construction in the farm out-buildings.

Two miles west of Northallerton on the A684 Bedale road, we came to the attractive village of **Ainderby Steeple**. This is the home of the fine old inn and eating house, the **Wellington Heifer**, which has been run since 1987 by Norman and Dorothy Boynton. This handsome building dates from the mid-18th century and inside, much of its original character has been retained. Norman and Dorothy serve an excellent range of beers and a selection of top quality bar food which is renowned throughout the area. The extensive menu includes starters, grills, fish dishes, vegetarian meals and a choice of mouthwatering daily specials. There are also two well-appointed letting rooms available which are equipped with en-suite facilities. Children welcome.

The Wellington Heifer

Little Holtby Farmhouse at **Leeming Bar** provides excellent overnight accommodation, both for through travellers and for those looking for a touring base in the beautiful Vale of York. This fully refurbished former working farm is situated just off the main A1, two miles northeast of Bedale on the A684 Northallerton road. The farmhouse has lovely gardens and provides spectacular views across rolling countryside to Pen Hill. Owner Mrs Dorothy Hodgson always provides her guests with a warm welcome and superb Yorkshire hospitality. She has four beautifully decorated guest rooms available, three with en-suite facilities and the fourth with its own private bathroom. All are immaculately furnished and appointed to a good modern standard. Children welcome.

Little Holtby Farmhouse

Three miles west of Northallerton, midway between the A684 and the B6271 at **Yafforth**, we made a point of calling in at the **Yafforth Equestrian Centre** at Broomfield Farm. When Ian and Susan Chapman bought the farm in the early 1980s, they initially carried on running it as a dairy and stock-rearing operation. However, in 1985, changes in the economic climate led them to found the equestrian centre which over the years has proved to be extremely popular with all those interested in horses and riding. As part of their continuing programme of improvements, the Chapmans have built a large indoor arena, 23 timber stables, and in 1989, opened Broomfield Court, a small friendly hotel with six guest rooms all equipped with en-suite facilities, televisions, controllable central heating and tea/coffee making facilities. The hotel also has a tastefully furnished lounge and a pleasant dining room serving fine traditional English cooking. Susan Chapman is a fully qualified riding instructor and organises instructional rides for people of all ages and levels of experience. She also arranges one- and two-hour hacks through the beautiful surrounding countryside, instruction in breaking and schooling, and educational visits for parties of local schoolchildren who come to learn about the working lives of horses, past and present. Activities at the centre also include learn-to-ride holidays, riding improvement holidays, and a number of non-riding activities such as cycling, walking and four-wheel-drive tours of 'hidden' Yorkshire.

Yafforth Equestrian Centre

Travelling out west from Northallerton, on the B684, is the town of **Bedale**, which holds many places of interest for the curious traveller.

This little market town is described as the ideal base for exploring the Yorkshire Dales and the Moors, and indeed, situated as is on the B684, connecting the two expanses and conveniently close to the A1, it well deserves its claim.

It has a curving main street, dominated by the Parish church at it's north end. Opposite is Bedale Hall, with its Georgian ballroom and local museum. Tourists can also seek out the 18th century Leech House, (so called because it was once used by the local apothecary to store his leeches) situated by Bedale Beck.

A place well worth making the effort to find in **Bedale** is **Kirk's** at 12a Market Place. This fascinating establishment is situated above Cockburns' butchers, with three large showrooms. Here, Russell Kirk and his mother Gloria show an interesting range of Edwardian and Victorian pine furniture, curios and giftware. Russell is a member of the Guild of Master Craftsmen and offers a selection of reproduction furniture made entirely of pine which can be made to customer's specific requirements. He also offers a pine stripping and furniture restoration service. Visitors are very welcome to browse. Open daily 9.30am to 5pm. Closed all day Sunday and Thursday afternoons.

A fine artist-painter living in **Bedale** is **Andrew Lawrence Woodhouse**. Now retired, Andrew originally trained at Leeds College of Art and at London's Goldsmiths College before going on to develop a career as a teacher. Today, he works in oils and watercolours and is particularly

known for his landscapes depicting North Yorkshire moorland and village scenes. He is also an accomplished portrait artist and undertakes special commissions of all descriptions. Many fine examples of Andrew's work, many at surprisingly affordable prices, can be viewed in his studio which is located to the rear of his home, Windsor House at No. 86 Southend. He also has work on show in the Dales Gallery, Bedale and at Centre Peace in Northallerton, and Plummers Restaurant & Wine Bar, Bedale.

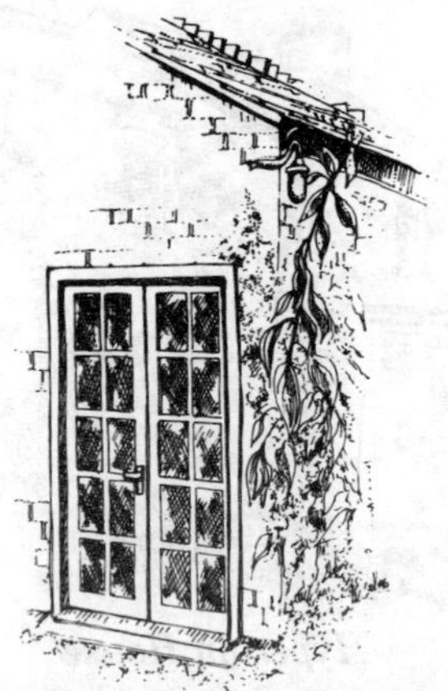

Andrew Lawrence Woodhouse Studio

In the same vein, the fascinating **Dales Gallery** is situated in the heart of **Bedale** and can be found in the courtyard near the church at No. 17 North End. The gallery is owned and personally-run by two former teachers, Ken and Chris Godden.

Dales Gallery

Half-a-mile from the centre of **Bedale** on the B6285 Burneston road (and within two miles of the A1), we found **Hyperion House**, a bed and breakfast establishment run by Mrs Sheila Dean. This charming ivy-clad residence was named by a local man who won a considerable amount of money on the racehorse *Hyperion* and then bought the house on the proceeds.

Hyperion House

It was constructed at the turn of the century, extended during the 1960s and now offers three spacious double bedrooms, all with hot and cold washbasins. Mrs Dean's breakfasts are renowned; she offers a choice of a dozen cereals, home-baked bread and a generous traditional cooked dish. Unsuitable for smokers, young children and pets.

An unusual and intriguing place to visit in the Bedale area is the working dairy farm, **The Big Sheep and The Little Cow at Aiskew**. (Situated one mile east of Bedale on the site of a soon-to-be-restored water mill). Visitors can be sure to receive first class attention from an interested and enthusiastic staff. Experience the animals at close quarters and find out about the high quality milk which is produced by the farm's sheep and Dexter cows (Britain's smallest breed). The excellent-value admission charge includes a 45-minute guided tour, a pony ride, cheese tasting and an ice cream made from sheep's milk. Home-produced milk, cheese, yoghurt, honey , woollens and gifts are available for sale. Open daily 10am to 6pm, Easter to end September. Winter visits by special arrangement. Large groups at discounted rates and prior arrangement(see reference guide for details and phone number).

Five miles northwest of Bedale, the minor roads to the north of the A684 led us to the attractive village of **Arrathorne**. Here, we called in at

The Big Sheep and Little Cow

the country hotel, **Elmfield House**, which is owned and run by Edith and Jim Lillie. This handsome traditionally-furnished building is set within its own secluded grounds and enjoys magnificent views over the surrounding rolling countryside. The hotel has a solarium, games room, a spacious lounge with residents' bar, and a pleasant dining room where guests can enjoy delicious home-cooked meals. There are also nine spacious bedrooms, all with en-suite facilities, direct-dial telephones, satellite TV and beverage making facilities. The two bedrooms on the ground floor are also suitable for disabled guests.

Elmfield House

One place not to be missed whilst in this area is **The Thorp Perrow Arboretum** which is situated on the Well road near the village of **Snape**.

Founded in 1927, this unique private collection of rare and exotic trees was the creation of one man, Colonel Sir Leonard Ropner, the present owner's father. Sir Leonard travelled all over the world collecting rare and unusual species for Thorp Perrow, and today the hundreds of trees he enthusiastically collected are in their prime. The arboretum was initially Sir Leonard's private hobby and visitors were not encouraged; however, after he sadly died in 1977, his son, Sir John Ropner, took the decision to open the 85-acre arboretum to the public and it is now gradually becoming known by visitors from all over the world. This tranquil and peaceful haven is set within 1000 acres of parkland and is home to some of the largest and rarest trees and shrubs in England. Enthusiasts and casual visitors alike come to admire the specimen trees and to enjoy the woodland tree trails, grassy glades, spectacular wild flowers and beautiful lakeside walks. Special attractions include the Milbank Pinetum (a collection of conifers planted from 1840 to 1870), an attractive rustic picnic area, and the formal gardens in front of the great house. Catalogues of the collection, maps of the tree trails and fascinating archive material on the origins of the arboretum are available in the recently-opened information centre and tearoom. Open dawn till dusk, all year round. Adults £2.00, children, OAP £1.00.

Two miles northwest of Bedale on the A684 Leyburn road, we came to the delightful village of **Little Crakehall**. Here, we found **Crakehall Water Mill**, a recently-restored 17th-century corn mill containing machinery dating from the 18th- and 19th-centuries.

Crakehall Water Mill

Thorp Perrow Arboretum

Today, stoneground wholemeal flour is once again produced by two pairs of millstones driven by a breast-shot water wheel powered by Crakehall Beck. Visitors can view the fascinating interior, buy the flour, or enjoy a delicious homemade tea in the grounds. Open 10am to 5pm, Easter to September. (Closed Mondays and Fridays.) The owners also have a holiday cottage available which sleeps four.

In the village of **Crakehall** (listed in the Domesday book as *Crachell*), if looking for outstanding bed and breakfast accommodation, one should make a point of finding the **Old Vicarage**, the first house on the right when approaching from Bedale. This fine Victorian residence was built of stone in 1842 and subsequently extended in 1887. Today, it is owned by Jane and Peter Young who provide their guests with welcoming overnight accommodation (their Yorkshire breakfasts are wonderful). They have six spacious letting bedrooms available, two with en-suite facilities and all with colour televisions, shaver points, hair dryers and beverage making facilities. Open all year round.

Old Vicarage

Also at **Crakehall** is the Museum of Badges and Battledress. Others interested in the production of those famous Yorkshire ales could take a trip to the Theakston's Brewery at **Masham**, 9 miles south-west on the B6268.

In the village of **Thornton Watlass**, three miles north of Masham, we visited one of the most outstanding bed and breakfast establishments we have yet discovered. **The Old Rectory** is a listed part-Georgian, part-Victorian country residence which stands within three-quarters of an acre of beautiful secluded gardens. Here, Olivia and Richard Farnell provide their guests with a wonderful welcome and a standard of accommodation that is truly superb. This memorable establishment has recently won the "England For Excellence" Award, and was lauded as the best bed and breakfast in the country. Their three double guest rooms are beautifully furnished (one has an antique half-tester) and each has a private bathroom and beverage making facilities. There is also a luxurious sitting room and a separate dining room where guests are served delicious homemade breakfasts. This lovely building, which is surrounded by gardens and hidden by profusions of wisteria, jasmine, clematis and climbing roses, was recently described in a newspaper article as being "as sumptuous as the country's best country house hotels". It's log-fires and other first-rate facilities would certainly seem to indicate this. Recommended. Unsuitable for smokers.

The Old Rectory

On the B6267, midway between the A1 and Masham, we came to the picturesque village of **Nosterfield**. Here, we stopped to call in at the surprising establishment, **The Industrious Cottage**, which is run by Mary Walker, produces exclusive handwoven materials and garments from the wool of locally-bred sheep. After washing, dying and carding the raw fleeces, she hand-spins the wool into yarn which is then woven into original fabrics and items of clothing. Mary specialises in soft woollen materials and also provides private tuition in weaving and spinning. Visitors are welcome to view the production process and to purchase the finished garments. Telephone to confirm opening times.

Midway between Bedale and Leyburn, we turned north off the A684 to reach the lovely village of **Hunton**. Here, we called in at the **Countryman's Inn**, a first-rate pub, restaurant and guesthouse which has been

Industrious Cottage

run since 1984 by Pauline and David Robinson. The inn has recently been refurbished to a high standard and now offers six letting rooms (four double, one twin, one luxury four-poster) which are all equipped with en-suite bathrooms and beverage making facilities. (Accommodation unsuitable for pets and children under fourteen.) The Countryman's Inn also serves the finest traditional Yorkshire beers and an excellent range of mouthwatering home-cooked meals. Look out for the interesting collection of teapots in the restaurant area.

Countryman's Inn

Further on down the B6108, is the village of **West Tanfield**, where the once powerful Marmion family (sounding rather like characters from a C. S. Lewis novel) dream on in the alabaster splendour of their tombs, which reside in the church there, guarded by the forbidding presence of the Marmion Tower.

Going out of West Tanfield on the Masham Road we came across **Glebe Buildings**, the workshop of **Frank Jobling**. Frank, a fine craftsman, is a wonderful character and chatted with us enthusiastically about his work, making garden furniture, bird tables and nesting boxes. He is delighted to let visitors to the workshop watch him as he works, using pine, iroko, elm, mahogany and other hardwoods for his solidly constructed, built-to-last garden seats and picnic tables. Frank has been at Glebe Buildings for 16 years now, and can turn his hand to the individual requirements of all his customers, whether it's for a private garden or a busy pub.

Frank Jobling

Going northwards the other way, one would have come to **Jervaulx Abbey**, one of the great Cistercian sister houses to Fountains.

The name Jervaulx is a french derivation of Yore or Ure Vale, just as Rievaulx is of Rye Vale. The first Abbot of Jervaulx was John de Kinstan, who was travelling from Byland with a group of 12 monks, when he was reputedly shown the site through a vision of the Virgin and Child.

Jervaulx eventually amassed enough wealth to own half of the Ure Valley, but its glory was shattered during the Dissolution, when it came under severe persecution, due to the fact that the last Abbot, Adam Sedbar, had caused Henry VIII particular displeasure by his criticisms.

Despite its ruination, Jervaulx's haunting, ivy-clad walls have been described as "romantick in decay". Its grounds have been transformed into one of the most beautiful of gardens, the shattered walls providing interesting backdrops for its sculptured trees and colourful plants and shrubs.

Jervaulx Abbey

Whilst here, we also made a point of calling in at the impressive country house hotel, **Jervaulx Hall**, which stands adjacent to the Abbey. Originally constructed as a private residence, the Hall stands within extensive landscaped grounds containing beautiful lawned gardens and woodland walks. In recent years, owners John and Margaret Sharp have carried out a number of important improvements to the building whilst always taking care to preserve its original character and atmosphere. There are now ten luxurious double bedrooms, all with en-suite bathrooms and appointed to the highest modern standards. (The room on the ground floor is particularly suitable for elderly or disabled guests.) The hotel's elegant restaurant serves a range of imaginative dishes, prepared using locally-sourced vegetables, soft fruit, meats and game.

Catterick, is famous for two things - its racecourse and its RAF and army garrison (visitors may wish to take a trip to the Regimental Museum there).

Jervaulx Hall

This was always a soldiers' town, as far back as Roman times, known in those days as Cataractonium. Visitors to the town will no doubt on their journeys see a road, named rather incongruously, Trafalgar. The connections with Nelson and the town of Catterick are not immediately obvious. but are explained by the fact that Alexander Scott, a vicar of Catterick in 1816, was at Nelson's side when he died at the famous battle. Another connection may be that Lady Tyrconnel, the Admiral's sister-in law, lived at nearby **Kiplin Hall**, a Jacobean country home famous for its beautiful interior plasterwork and medieval fishponds.

The hall contains many memories of Nelson and Lady Hamilton, and on display in the Blue Room, is a folding library chair from the Admiral's cabin on the Victory.

There is a 15th century church here, which boasts a window panel depicting the visit to ancient Cataractonium of the Emperor Paulinus, over 1,300 years ago, when he baptised thousands of Christian converts in the nearby River Swale.

Beside the A6136, one-and-a-half miles north of Catterick Village, we found the **Tudor Hotel and Restaurant** at **Brompton-on-Swale**. This impressive establishment dates from the turn of the century and stands in extensive grounds within a quarter-of-a-mile of the main A1. The hotel has six spacious guest rooms, all tastefully decorated and equipped with en-

Tudor Hotel and Restaurant

suite facilities. Perhaps most impressive, however, is the adjoining restaurant which, with its high walls, half-circled ceiling and fine acoustics, was built to house a church organ. Today, the restaurant offers first-class imaginative cuisine including traditional lunches on Sundays (booking essential). Light meals and genuine real ale are also served in the bar. Look out for Joshua, the African grey parrot who welcomes guests to reception.

A couple of miles to the east of Brompton-on-Swale, is the picturesque village of **Scorton**, where we visited the delightful free house, **The White Heifer**. The inn stands in a splendid position overlooking the village green and is owned and run by a great character, Malcolm Mableson, a retired Royal Naval Lt. Commander.

The White Heifer

Millgate, Richmond

The building has been an inn since 1790 and inside, it has lost none of its original character and charm with beamed ceilings and pleasant traditional surroundings. Malcolm provides a warm welcome for both visitors and regulars alike who are attracted by the fine ales and pleasant company; the conversation often focuses on the cricket team which regularly plays on the adjacent village green.

Richmond, north-west of Catterick, is yet another place with a rich and fascinating history. Alan Rufus, the first Earl of Richmond, built the original castle here in 1071. The site, 100 feet up on a rocky promontory, with the River Swale passing below, is imposing indeed, and in a well-chosen position for its defence. The former county of Richmondshire (which locals still refer to) of which this town was the capital, once occupied a third of the North Riding. As befits its status, the castle is large in its proportions, the keep rising to 109 feet in height with walls 11 feet thick - the lords of this castle obviously believed in tight security. The other side is afforded an impregnable defence by means of the cliff and the river.

With such an inspiring setting, it is hardly surprising that there is a legend that King Arthur himself is buried here, reputedly in a cave beneath the castle.

The story goes that a simple potter called Thompson once stumbled across an underground passage which led to a chamber where he discovered the King and his knights lying in an enchanted sleep, with Arthur's horn and the sword Excalibur placed nearby, in the midst of a hoard of priceless treasures.

The potter reached out to touch them, but withdrew in fear on hearing a huge voice which called out,

“"Potter, potter Thompson. if thou hadst either drawn the sword or blown the horn, thou hadst been the luckiest man alive”.

The terrified man fled, leaving the treasure behind. Predictably, the passage was never located again, and the potter probably spent many hours afterwards, no doubt to the encouragement of many a flagon of strong ale, telling his comrades and others of the tale.

Also in Richmond, is the **Regimental Museum of the Green Howards**, the north riding's infantry regiment, based in the old Trinity Church in the centre of the cobbled market square.

The centre of Richmond has an excellent selection of pubs, retaurants, cafes as well as an impressive choice of accommodation. Here are a few of the ones we selected, on starting from the vantage point of the castle.

Nearby, in a quaint old part of town overlooking the Green, we found the **Old Brewery Guest House**, a former inn which has been tastefully refurbished in luxurious Victorian style by the present owners Jan and George Scott. The spacious and beautifully appointed bedrooms are all equipped with en-suite bath or shower and beverage making facilities. Jan provides delicious evening meals by arrangement, as well as lunches and home-baked afternoon teas on summer weekends. The guesthouse enjoys magnificent views of the castle ruins and is close to the River Swale with its impressive falls known locally as 'The Foss'. Ask for details of special winter breaks.

Old Brewery Guest House

We found the **Black Lion Hotel** in the wonderfully-named Finkle Street, a narrow side street which runs off the Market Square. This fine old coaching inn was built in the 17th-century and for the past twenty years has been owned and personally-run by the Foster family. Inside, it still retains much of its original character and atmosphere with low beamed ceilings, attractive wooden bars and pew-style seating.

The Black Lion Hotel

Richmond Castle

The Black Lion offers four traditional hand-pulled ales (including Camerons) and is featured in the *Good Beer Guide*; it also offers a wide-ranging selection of first-rate meals, seven days a week. The inn also has thirteen comfortable letting rooms available, all equipped with hot and cold washbasins, televisions and beverage making facilities.

The appropriately-named **West End Guest House** stands in Reeth Road on the western edge of Richmond, ten minutes walk from the centre of town. Originally built as a farmhouse around 1840, this handsome stone-built residence still retains much of its traditional character and charm. Inside, it has been thoroughly and tastefully modernised by the present owners Kath, Trevor and Ross Teeley; the five centrally-heated letting bedrooms all have en-suite facilities, colour televisions, shaver sockets and beverage making facilities.

West End Guest House

The guesthouse has a residents' licence, and in addition to delicious home-cooked breakfasts, provides three-course evening meals if required. The Teeleys have recently converted an adjacent barn to provide four beautifully-equipped self-catering units, each sleeping up to four people.

In the heart of the town, we called in at the impressive **Turf Hotel** in Victoria Road. (The hotel gets its name from its long association with the local horse-racing fraternity.) This imposing 18th-century building has a delightfully grand façade which suggests that it was once a lot larger than its present size. Over the years, it has been carefully refurbished so as to retain much of its original character and charm. Inside, the large bar is split into two areas: one side a comfortable and relaxing lounge and the other containing a selection of lively traditional pub games. Both have great atmosphere and offer a warm welcome to visitors and regulars alike.

For those wanting a light meal, a good selection of top quality bar snacks is served here; alternatively, a more elaborate á la carte menu is offered in the hotel's first-class restaurant which is open to residents and non-residents alike. The Turf Hotel also has five comfortable letting bedrooms available (two family, two double, one twin), which are all appointed to a good standard and equipped with colour televisions and first-rate modern facilities. Cots available. Packed lunches can be ordered by those wishing to explore the many beautiful upland areas and places of historic interest which lie within a few hours' drive of the hotel. Open all year round.

Turf Hotel

Those wanting a delicious snack or light meal in this picturesque town should make a point of finding **Willows Restaurant and Coffee Shop** in Grey Friars Arcade in King Street.

Willows Restaurant & Coffee Shop

This first-rate establishment has been run since 1989 by sisters Dale and Rhona Peacock and was once owned by their great aunts, Mollie and Alice Fawcett, who were well-known local celebrities in their day. The speciality of the house is oven-baked jacket potatoes, served with a wide range of mouthwatering fillings. Willows is open six days a week and seven days a week during the summer months serving delicious morning coffees, lunches, afternoon- and high teas.

We also made a note of the charming family-run guesthouse, **Windsor House**, which is owned by Karen and Jeff Pedley. This handsome three-storey brick building dates from the 17th-century and can be found in the old part of town at No. 9 Castle Hill. Inside, much of the building's original character and charm are still in evidence; the atmosphere is cosy and welcoming, and the eight comfortable bedrooms are all centrally-heated and equipped with tea/coffee making facilities and colour televisions. \
Appetising home-cooked evening meals are served in the dining room (which is licensed for residents) .

Windsor House

Situated half-a-mile to the west of Richmond's centre, is the intimate country house hotel, **Howe Villa**, which stands within magnificent landscaped grounds overlooking the River Swale. (For accurate directions, telephone the owners Anita and Tommy Berry 0748 850055.) This fine country residence was constructed around 1823 by Henry Cook, a local businessman who operated a nearby paper mill. Today, Howe Villa offers five beautifully appointed guest rooms, all with en-suite bathrooms, colour televisions and beverage making facilities. The hotel has an excellent reputation for the quality of its food and offers an imaginative table d'hôte menu which on the day we visited featured gratin of seafood and rack of

lamb with pine nuts and spring onions.

Howe Villa

Easby Abbey, situated outside the town's boundaries, on a minor road off the B6271, is a low-built monastic ruin which looks down to the River Swale.

It was formerly occupied by a community of Pre-monstratensian, or "white" canons (so-called because they modelled themselves on the Cistercians), founded in 1155. The order were of more modest leanings than the Cistercians, and the building certainly possesses none of the grandiose lines of Rievaulx and Fountains, although the riverine setting is typically in common. Easby's claim to fame is that in 1346, the English army led by Henry de Percy and Ralph de Neville, marched from here before defeating the Scottish forces led by David II, who was later imprisoned in Richmond Castle.

Whilst in this area, we were recommended to pay a visit to **Broken Brea Farm** near **Easby**. This attractive 270-acre working farm also offers luxurious self-catering accommodation, farmhouse bed and breakfast, fresh farm produce and a private coarse fishery. Three delightful self-catering cottages have recently been converted from the farm's former outbuildings. Each is furnished to a very high standard with full gas-fired central heating, open plan lounge/dining area with colour satellite television, fully-equipped fitted oak kitchen, and modern bathroom with shower and bath.

In the heart of lovely rolling countryside three miles northwest of Richmond, we also found **Mount Pleasant Farm**, a 300-acre working livestock farm which also provides first-rate farmhouse accommodation.

Broken Brea Farm

(The farm is located near the village of **Whashton** just off the Richmond to Ravensworth road.)

This handsome stone-built farmhouse was constructed in 1850 and has been lived-in by the Chilton family since the 1880s. Today, Peter and Christine Chilton provide superb hospitality and a standard of accommodation that is truly outstanding. The stable block adjacent to the farmhouse has been tastefully converted to provide four luxurious letting units, each with its own front door. Each has also been given a special farmyard name: the 'stable' is a family room, the 'carthouse' a double, the 'bullpen' a two-room suite ideal for families, and the 'piggery' a room which has been specially equipped for wheelchair users. In the farmhouse itself there is also a spacious twin room with attractive pine beams.

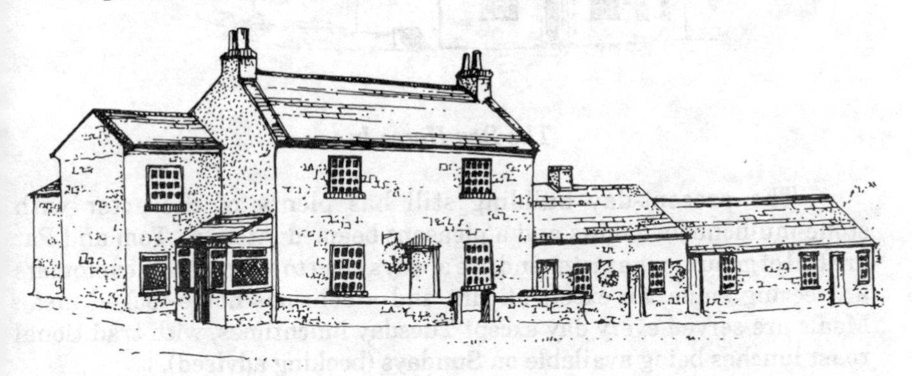

Mount Pleasant Farm

Residents also have access to a comprehensively-equipped laundry room and to an attractive garden with a barbecue area and a children's play space. The largest cottage is situated on first-floor level and sleeps eight people in two double and two twin bedrooms; the other two are on ground-floor level and each sleep four in one double and one twin room. (One cottage has been specially modified for wheelchair users.) Owner Clive Simpson also provides excellent quality bed and breakfast accommodation in the main farmhouse and personally manages the farm shop which sells an excellent range of fresh produce including fruit, vegetables, bacon, dairy produce and health foods. A recent addition to the facilities at Broken Brea is a peaceful three-acre lake stocked with thousands of carp, roach, tench, bream, perch, rudd and gudgeon. This is situated beside the River Swale and offers half- or whole-day coarse fishing at reasonable cost.

Six miles northwest of Richmond, a minor road led us to the peaceful village of **Gayles**. Here, we visited the **Bay Horse Inn**, a first-rate pub and eating house run by Tom and Pat Rennoldson. This Grade II listed inn was built in the early 17th-century and was once used as a shooting lodge by the Dukes of Northumberland.

The Bay Horse Inn

The present-day building still has plenty of character with stone-mullioned windows and a pleasant beamed interior. Tom and Pat are full of genuine character and are always keen to supply their customers a cheering smile, an excellent pint and a delicious home-cooked meal. Meals are served every day except Tuesday lunchtimes, with traditional roast lunches being available on Sundays (booking advised).

One mile to the north-west of Gayles and six miles northwest of

Scotch Corner, we took the country roads to **Dalton** and discovered **Dalton Grange**, a delightful farmhouse bed and breakfast establishment which is run by Susan Anderson. The house dates from the 19th-century and is set within a ninety-acre working dairy farm which is surrounded by beautiful rolling countryside. Inside, there is a cosy residents' lounge, a separate dining area, and two spacious and beautifully-appointed letting bedrooms, both of which have lovely views over the surrounding North Yorkshire landscape. Susan is a host who genuinely enjoys caring for her guests; she serves an excellent farmhouse breakfast and will also provide an evening meal if given prior notice. Open all year round.

Dalton Grange

Travelling up towards Darlington, we made a detour to **Clow Beck House** in **Croft-on-Tees**, three miles south of the town. This well appointed farmhouse forms part of a working farm and lies within twelve minutes drive of the A1 five miles northeast of Scotch Corner. Owners Heather and David Armstrong offer first-class hospitality in a tranquil setting overlooking open countryside and the River Tees. All bedrooms are decorated in an attractive country style and are furnished to a high modern standard with beverage making facilities and hot and cold washbasins (one also has en suite facilities). Croft-on-Tees was the home of Lewis Carroll for over 25 years and is ideally situated for reaching the beautiful Yorkshire Dales.

Travelling north up the A1 from Scotch Corner, lovers of trains and all connected with the history of the railway, will enjoy a visit to **Darlington**, so famous for its part in the history of the golden age of steam, and one end of the renowned Stockton-Darlington line.

The first passenger train, hauled by Stephenson's "Locomotion"

Clow Beck House

started to travel the line in 1825. This famous engine is on exhibition at the Darlington Railway Centre and Museum.

Before the onset of the railway, Darlington had been a market town, but after the line was established, it quickly grew as a centre for the building of the new engine, an industry which now has sadly declined.

However, the Darlington Railway Preservation Society still carry out restoration work on old engines, and visitors calling in at the old railway goods shed can see their concerted efforts to return their recoveries to their former glory.

Darlington Railway Centre and Museum
"Pacific" Class Locomotive

The Museum also runs "steam weekends", where tourists and enthusiasts alike can take a nostalgic trip on one of their famous locomotives. Visitors who are interested are advised to telephone for details first.

What many people might overlook in the great shadow of Darlington's railway tradition, is the fact that, being situated on the great North Road travelled upon since the Romans, it is also an archaeological site of some note, famous for the Piercebridge Roman bridge and Stanwick Fortifications.

The advance of human transport is ever present in the town of Darlington, from the days of the marching Celtic tribes and Roman Legions, through to the pioneering days of steam, up to the present day, and the sound of jets overhead from the RAF base and nearby Teeside Airport at Egglescliffe.

CHAPTER 7

The Yorkshire Dales

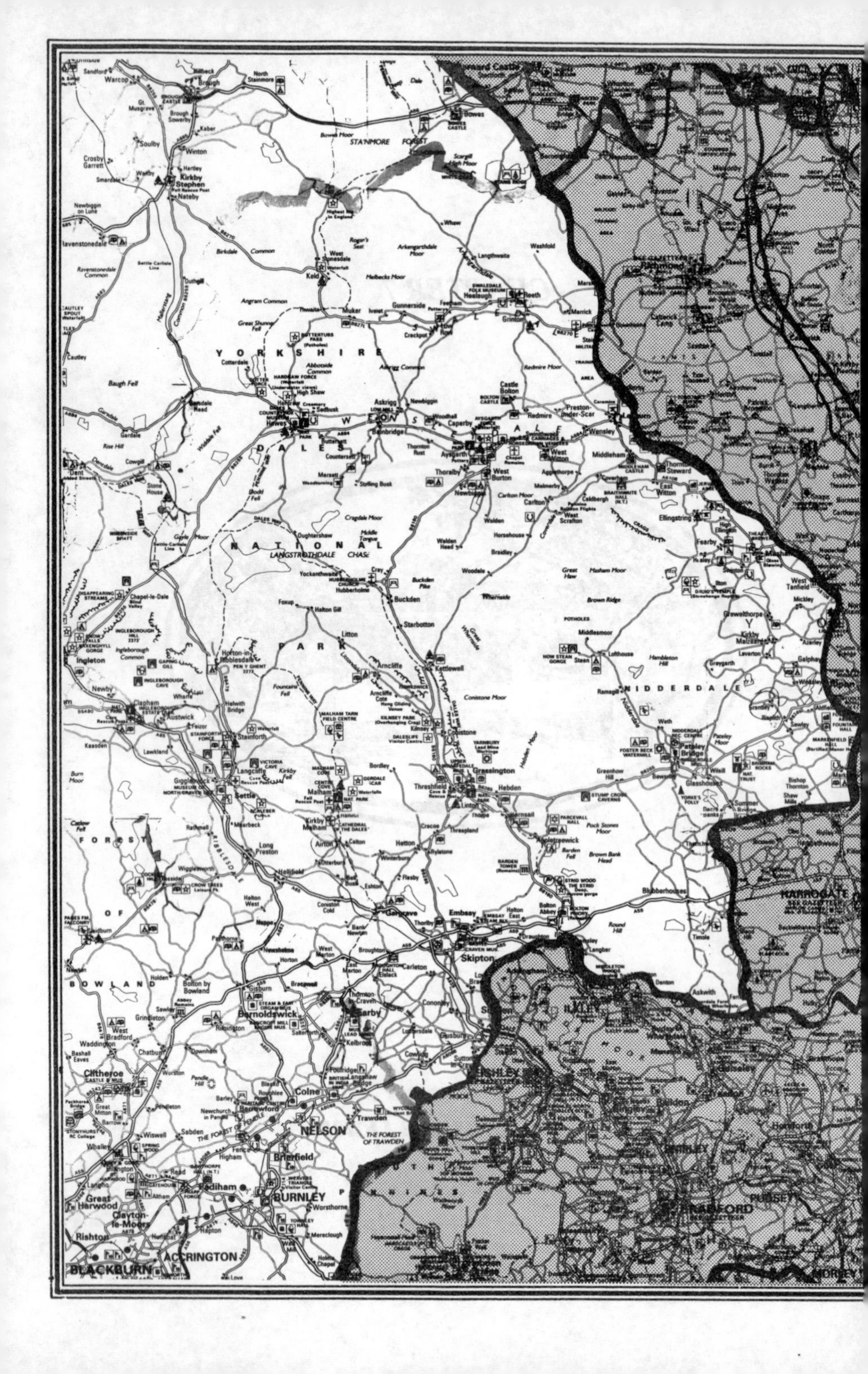

YORKSHIRE DALES NATIONAL PARK
WENSLEYDALE
LANGSTROTHDALE CHASE
NIDDERDALE
FOREST OF BOWLAND
STAINMORE FOREST
Brough
Warcop
Kirkby Stephen
Nateby
Winton
Soulby
Crosby Garrett
Ravenstonedale
Bowes
Keld
West Stonesdale
Thwaite
Muker
Gunnerside
Healaugh
Reeth
Grinton
Richmond
Catterick Camp
Hawes
Askrigg
Bainbridge
Aysgarth
Carperby
Redmire
Castle Bolton
Wensley
Preston-under-Scar
Leyburn
Middleham
West Witton
West Burton
Thoralby
Carlton
East Witton
Masham
Kettlewell
Buckden
Starbotton
Hubberholme
Yockenthwaite
Arncliffe
Litton
Conistone
Grassington
Threshfield
Hebden
Pateley Bridge
Lofthouse
Middlesmoor
Ingleton
Clapham
Austwick
Horton-in-Ribblesdale
Settle
Giggleswick
Langcliffe
Malham
Kirkby Malham
Long Preston
Hellifield
Gargrave
Embsay
Skipton
Bolton Abbey
Ilkley
Harrogate
Gisburn
Barnoldswick
Earby
Colne
Nelson
Barrowford
Brierfield
Burnley
Padiham
Clitheroe
Whalley
Great Harwood
Clayton-le-Moors
Rishton
Accrington
Blackburn
Bradford
Pudsey
Keighley
Shipley
Guiseley
Slaidburn
Waddington
Chatburn
Bolton by Bowland
Dent
Cowgill
Sedbergh
Garsdale Head
Trawden
THE FOREST OF TRAWDEN
Worsthorne
Sabden
Pendle Hill
Blubberhouses
Denton
Askwith

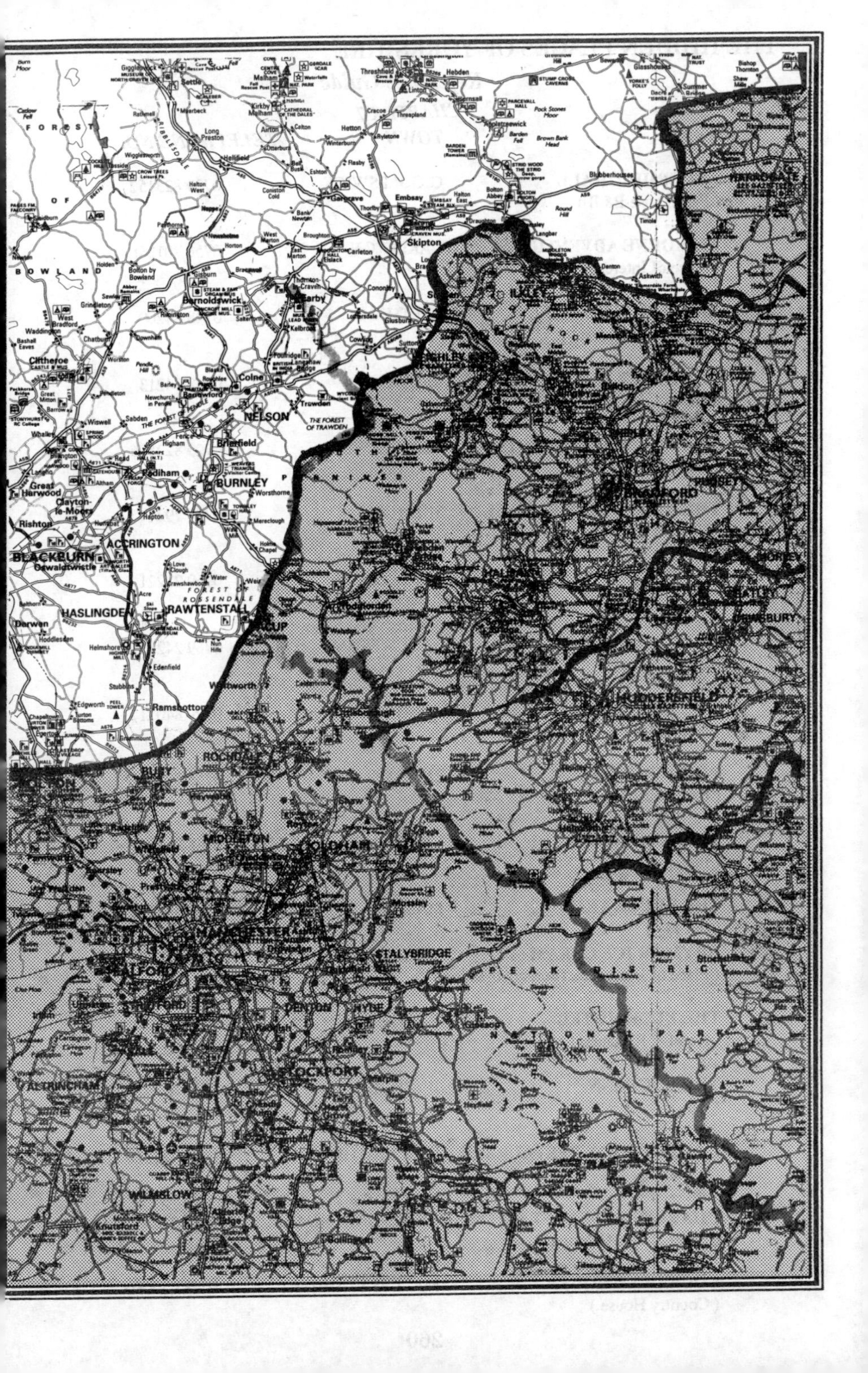

Settle
Malham
Kirkby Malham
Threshfield
Hebden
Linton
Cracoe
Threapland
Hetton
Rylstone
Airton
Calton
Winterburn
Flasby
Long Preston
Hellifield
Wigglesworth
Otterburn
Gargrave
Embsay
Skipton
Halton West
Coniston Cold
Bank Newton
Broughton
West Marton
East Marton
Elslack
Carleton
Thornton-in-Craven
Earby
Kelbrook
Barnoldswick
Gisburn
Bolton by Bowland
Sawley
Grindleton
West Bradford
Waddington
Chatburn
Clitheroe
Downham
Worston
Pendle Hill
Great Mitton
Barrow
Pendleton
Sabden
Wiswell
Whalley
Newchurch in Pendle
Barrowford
Colne
NELSON
Trawden
THE FOREST OF TRAWDEN
Foulridge
Brierfield
Higham
Padiham
BURNLEY
Worsthorne
Mereclough
Great Harwood
Clayton-le-Moors
Rishton
Hapton
ACCRINGTON
BLACKBURN
Oswaldtwistle
Love Clough
Crawshawbooth
FOREST OF ROSSENDALE
HASLINGDEN
RAWTENSTALL
Darwen
Hoddlesden
Helmshore
Edenfield
Stubbins
Edgworth
Turton Bottoms
Ramsbottom
Wentworth
BURY
ROCHDALE
MIDDLETON
OLDHAM
MANCHESTER
SALFORD
STALYBRIDGE
Mossley
DENTON
HYDE
STOCKPORT
ALTRINCHAM
WILMSLOW
Knutsford
Bollington
ILKLEY
KEIGHLEY
Baildon
SHIPLEY
BRADFORD
PUDSEY
HALIFAX
Todmorden
HUDDERSFIELD
BATLEY
DEWSBURY
MORLEY
HARROGATE
Blubberhouses
Bolton Abbey
Appletreewick
Burnsall
Barden Fell
Brown Bank Head
Pock Stones Moor
Glasshouses
Askwith
Langbar
Denton
PEAK DISTRICT NATIONAL PARK
BOWLAND
FOREST OF
DERBYSHIRE

Reference Guide

CHAPTER 7

NAME	*TOWN*	*TELEPHONE NO.*
ACCERHILL HALL (Farmhouse B&B)	GIGGLESWICK	0729 823152
AIRBORNE ADVENTURES (Place of Interest)	CARLETON	0756 701566
ARKLESIDE HOTEL (Hotel & Restaurant)	REETH	0748 84200
THE BLACK BULL (Inn)	REETH	0748 84213
THE BLACK HORSE HOTEL (Hotel & Inn)	GIGGLESWICK	0729 822506
THE BLACK HORSE HOTEL (Hotel & Inn)	SKIPTON	0756 792145
THE BLACK SWAN HOTEL (Hotel & Inn)	MIDDLEHAM	0969 22221
THE BLUE LION (Inn)	EAST WITTON	0969 24273
THE BOARS HEAD HOTEL (Hotel & Inn)	LONG PRESTON	0729 840217
BONDCROFT FARM (Farmhouse B&B)	EMBSAY	0756 793371
THE BRIDGE INN (Inn)	GRINTON-IN-SWALEDALE	0748 84224
THE BRUCE ARMS (Inn)	MASHAM	0765 689372
BRYMOR ICE CREAM (Place of Interest & Tourist Attraction)	MASHAM	0677 60377
THE BUCK HOTEL (Hotel & Restaurant)	REETH	0748 84210
THE BUCK INN (Inn)	BUCKDEN	0756760 228
CARTER KNOX RESTAURANT (Restaurant)	LOW LAITHE	0423 711306
CHARLES BATHURST HOTEL (Hotel & Self-Catering)	ARKENGARTHDALE	0748 84265
COCKLAKE HOUSE (Country House)	MALLERSTANG	07683 72080

CONISTON HALL (Tea Room, Restaurant & Place of Interest)	CONISTON COLD	0756 748136
COVER BRIDGE INN (Inn)	EAST WITTON	0969 23250
THE CRAVEN HEIFER (Hotel)	STAINFORTH	0729 822599
CROSS KEYS RESTAURANT (Inn & Restaurant)	EAST MARTON	0282 843485
DALESWAY CARAVAN PARK (Caravan Park)	EARGRAVE	0756 749592
THE DEVONSHIRE HOTEL (Hotel & Inn)	GRASSINGTON	0756 752525
DOUG MOORE BOATBUILDERS (Boat Hire & Boat Builders)	BARNOLDSWICK	0282 815883
DRAUGHTON HEIGHT RIDING (Riding School)	DRAUGHTON	0756 710242
EASTFIELD LODGE (B&B)	LEYBURN	0969 23196
EASTWOODS FISH REST. (Restaurant)	SKIPTON	0756 795458
THE FELL HOTEL (Hotel)	BURNSALL	0756 720209
THE FLYING HORSESHOE (Hotel, Restaurant, Self-Catering, Caravan and Camping Site)	CLAPHAM	05242 51229
FOLD FARM (Farmhouse B&B, and Self-Catering)	KETTLEWELL	0756 760886
THE FORESTERS ARMS (Inn)	GRASSINGTON	0756 752349
THE FOX AND HOUNDS (Inn)	WEST BURTON	0969 663279
THE GEORGE AND DRAGON (Inn)	AYSGARTH	0969 663358
THE GEORGE INN (Inn)	THORALBY	0969 663256
THE GOLDEN LION (Hotel)	LEYBURN	0969 22161
GRANGE FARM (Farmhouse B&B and Bunkhouse Barn)	HUBBERHOLME	0756 760259
GRASSFIELDS COUNTRY HSE. (Hotel)	PATELEY	0423 711412

GRASSINGTON HOUSE HOTEL (Hotel)	GRASSINGTON	0756 752406
HACKNEY HOUSE (Guest House)	REETH	0748 84302
HIGH GREEN HOUSE (Country Guest House)	THORALBY	0969 663420
HOLGATE HEAD (Wolsey Lodge Hotel)	KIRKBY MALHAM	07293 376
HOWGILL LODGE BARN (17th Century Barn Accomodation)	BARDEN	0756 720655
KEARTON GUEST HOUSE (Guest House, Restaurant & Shop)	THWAITE	0748 86277
KENT FURNITURE (Place of Interest)	GRASSINGTON	0756 753045
KILGRAM GRANGE (Country House B&B)	JERVAULX, MASHAM	0677 60212
THE KINGS ARMS HOTEL (Inn & Restaurant)	ASKRIGG	0969 50258
THE KINGS HEAD (Public House)	GUNNERSIDE	0748 86261
LINDON HOUSE (Guest House)	AIRTON	0729 830418
THE LONG ASHES INN (Inn)	THRESHFIELD, SKIPTON	0756 752434
LOW RAISGILL COTTAGE (B&B)	RAISGILL	0756 760351
LUCYFOLD TEA ROOMS (Tea Rooms)	GRASSINGTON	0756 752414
THE MAD HATTER (Tea Shop and B&B)	MASHAM	0765 689129
THE MARTON ARMS HOTEL (Hotel & Inn)	THORTON-IN-LONSDALE	05242 41281
THE MAYPOLE INN (Inn)	LONG PRESTON	0729 840219
THE MILL RACE TEASHOP (Tea Shop & Place of Interest)	AYSGARTH FALLS	0969 663446
THE MILLER'S HOUSE HOTEL (Hotel)	MIDDLEHAM	0969 22630
MOORGARTH HALL (Country House Hotel)	INGLETON	05242 41946

MOSS COTTAGES **(Self-Catering Cottages and Centre for Staff/Management Training)**	**KEASDEN**	**05242 51584**
NAPPA HALL **(Farmhouse B&B)**	**ASKRIGG**	**0969 50260**
NEW BUTTS FARM **(B&B)**	**HIGH BENTHAM**	**05242 41238**
THE NEW INN **(Inn)**	**APPLETREEWICK**	**0756 720252**
THE NEW INN HOTEL **(Hotel & Inn)**	**CLAPHAM**	**05242 51203**
NEWBIGGIN HOUSE **(B&B and Self-Catering Cottages)**	**NEWBIGGIN**	**0969 663583**
OLD SCHOOL WORKSHOP **(Place of Interest)**	**MIDDLEHAM**	**0969 23056**
OXNOP HALL **(Farmhouse B&B)**	**LOW OXNOP**	**0748 86253**
THE PALMER FLATT HOTEL **(Hotel, Inn & Restaurant)**	**AYSGARTH**	**0969 663228**
PASTURE HOUSE **(B&B)**	**COLSTERDALE, HEALEY**	**0765 689149**
PEN VIEW **(Farmhouse Guest House)**	**THORALBY**	**0969 663319**
THE PUNCH BOWL INN **(Inn with Accomodation)**	**UPPER SWALEDALE**	**0748 86233**
THE RED LION INN **(Inn)**	**LANGTHWAITE**	**0748 84218**
THE RIDDINGS **(Country Guest House)**	**LONG PRESTON**	**0729 840231**
ROOKERY COTTAGE **(B&B)**	**EAST WTTON**	**0969 22918**
ROOKHURST COUNTRY HOUSE **(Country House Hotel)**	**HAWES**	**0969 667454**
ST. GEORGE'S COURT **(Farmhouse B&B)**	**HIGH GRANTLEY**	**0765 620618**
SAWLEY ARMS **(Inn & Restaurant)**	**SAWLEY**	**0765 620642**
SCALEGILL **(Self-Catering Accomodation)**	**KIRKBY MALHAM**	**0729 830293**
SCAR CLOSE FARM **(Farmhouse B&B)**	**AUSTWICK**	**0729 823496**

SPORTSMAN'S ARMS HOTEL (Hotel & Resaturant)	WATH-IN-NIDDERDALE	0423 711306
STACKSTEADS FARM (Farmhouse Accomodation)	INGLETON	05242 41386
STOW HOUSE HOTEL (Country House Hotel)	AYSGARTH	0969 663635
SWALEDALE POTTERY (Pottery)	LOW ROW	0748 86377
SWALEDALE WOOLENS (Place of Interest)	MUKER	0748 86251
TAN HILL INN (Inn)	KELD	0833 28246
TARNEY FORS (Guest House & Tea Room)	HAWES	0969 667475
THE TEMPEST ARMS (Hotel & Restaurant)	ELSLACK	0282 842450
THORNSGILL GUEST HOUSE (Guest House)	ASKRIGG	0969 50617
THE TRADDOCK (Country House Hotel & Restaurant)	AUSTWICK	05242 51224
THE WATERFRONT (Music Bar & Discotheque)	SKIPTON	0756 790121
WATERSHED MILL ARTS (Place of Interest)	SETTLE	0729 825111
THE WHEATSHEAF (Inn)	CARPERBY	0969 663216
WILLOW RESTAURANT (Restaurant)	PATELEY BRIDGE	0423 711689
THE WOODLANDS (Country House Hotel)	GIGGLESWICK	0729 822058
WOODLANDS (B&B)	BEWERLEY	0423 711175
YORKSHIRE DALE COTTAGES (Self-Catering Cottages)	HIGH SHAW, HAWES	0969 667359

CHAPTER 7

"Up Hill, Down Dale..."

The huge expanse of the Yorkshire Dales, one of the favourite haunts of the redoubtable traveller Wainwright, in fact stretches over the three counties of Lancashire, Yorkshire and Cumbria. Devotees of the Pennine Way walks can be seen trudging along at most times of the year in army and navy hiking boots, like pilgrims travelling towards John Bunyan's Celestial City, (hail, snow and other natural disasters permitting). Considering the magnetic appeal this place must have, what exactly must it be that brings these stalwarts back to the place with such regularity? They would probably reply by singing the praises, Wainwright fashion, of such natural glories as Malham Cove, Hardraw Force, Fountains Fell and the cryptically named Lovely Seat. With such evocative names, how could one not be drawn to investigate the curiosities of Rogan's Seat, Middle Tongue and the villages of Muker and Crackpot?

The main attraction of the area has to be the natural wonders of its caves, waterfalls and outstanding geological features, and the best way to explore it has to be a combination of car and hiking gear.

Approaching from Richmond, there is a wealth of sights to see and curious villages to explore in the upper Swaledale area, which starts at the village of **Marrick**, chiefly noted for its abbey - a stern looking Benedictine nunnery founded by Roger de Aske. This is an area of soft wooded hillsides and lush riverside meadows, but as the dale climbs towards Grinton the lower dale gives way to the wilder scenery of its western section.

One mile southeast of Reeth on the B6270 Swaledale road, we came to the picturesque village of **Grinton**. Standing in a magnificent position near the bridge over the River Swale, we found the first-rate inn and eating house, the **Bridge Inn**, which is owned and run by Trevor and Margaret Hird. The building was originally constructed as a farmhouse in 1610 and remained so until the early 1700s. By the middle of the 18th-century, however, it had grown into a full-blown coaching inn serving the busy Swaledale east-west route. Since taking over in early 1992, Trevor and Margaret have undertaken a major and sympathetic programme of refurbishment. The two bar areas have been decorated in attractive traditional style and have a relaxed and welcoming atmosphere. A good range of fine traditional hand-pulled beers is available here, as well as an extensive bar meals menu which offers everything from filled baps and jacket potatoes to pan fried halibut in tarragon and white wine sauce. Upstairs, there are seven letting bedrooms, again all recently refurbished and equipped with hot and cold washbasins and good modern facilities. Most also have magnificent views over the surrounding hills and moors. Being local people, Trevor and Margaret provide their guests with a genuine welcome and the finest Yorkshire hospitality, making this an ideal base for exploring the many beautiful attractions of North Yorkshire.

The Bridge Inn

The village of **Reeth**, considered the capital of Upper Swaledale, is poised at the juncture of the Swale and its main tributary, Arkle Beck. The town was noted in the Domesday Book, whilst everything else in the area was written off as "waste land" (which no doubt caused the surrounding villagers to breathe a sigh of relief, having escaped the threat of taxation). Until the end of the 19th century, a total of four fairs were held here annually, as well as the weekly market. Today the annual agricultural show in September, held in the sprawling village green, is still a magnet for farmers from the entire length of the dale and beyond. Along the top of the green is High Row, with its inns and shops and outstanding Georgian architecture, reflecting the affluence of the town in the 17th century when the trade in wool and lead was booming.

In the centre of the village, we called in at the **Black Bull**, which is run by Bob and Liz Sykes. This 300 year-old inn retains many of its original features including low ceilings, winding passages and a wonderful old fireplace in the bar which was featured in the film *It Shouldn't Happen To*

A Vet. The bars serve traditional hand-pulled beers and a range of home-cooked meals which includes the celebrated 'Black Bull Breakfast'. There is also a relaxing residents' lounge and ten well-appointed letting rooms, three of which have en-suite bathrooms.

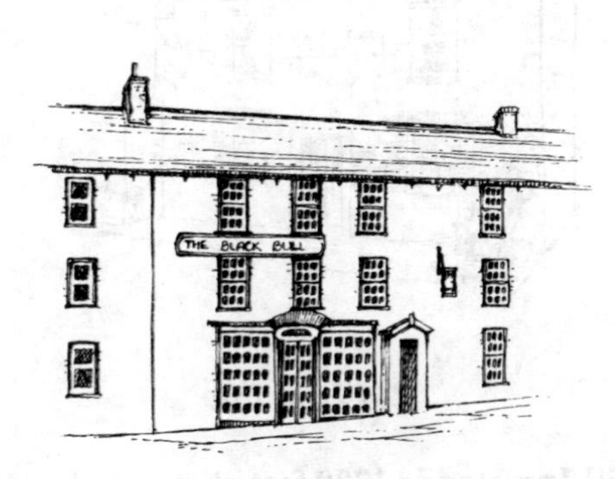

The Black Bull

Taking a detour up the wild, remote dale of Arkengarthdale, where one can see the ridge at Langthwaite, featured in the title sequence of "All Creatures Great And Small".

There are villages here that were established long before mining dominated the area, with such wonderful Nordic names as Booze, Arkle Town, Eskeleth and Whaw. The mines still scar the hillsides here, the ruins of smelting and crushing mills scattered here and there, like blackened ghosts of a long-dead industrial past. Most of the mines were owned by Charles Bathurst, Lord of the Manor in the 18th century, and namesake of the CB Hotel.

One mile beyond Arkle Town, the narrow Arkengarthdale road led us to the tiny hamlet at **Langthwaite**. Here, we visited the 17th-century inn, the **Red Lion**, which stands beside the old drovers' route to Tan Hill. Rowena Hutchinson became the licensee in 1979 after the inn had been in her family for fifteen years. Today, it is still full of genuine character with timber beams, pew-style seating, and to the rear, an intimate snug area where children are welcome at lunchtimes. Rowena provides an excellent pint of traditional ale and a range of first-rate bar meals all year round. Look out for the photographs of the leading characters from the Herriot series which were taken in the bar.

Red Lion Inn

The **Tan Hill Inn** stands 1732 feet above sea level and is renowned as the highest inn in England. It occupies one of the remotest sites in thecountry, four miles north of **Keld** on the northernmost border of North Yorkshire. Alec and Margaret Baines have managed to bring some extra comfort to the inn since they acquired it in 1986. Inside, the bar has open beams, stone-flagged floors and a welcoming fire which burns every day of the year.

Tan Hill Inn

An excellent pint of hand-pulled Theakston's is served (in winter, it has been known to freeze in the pipes), along with a fine selection of bar food. There are also seven comfortable and well-appointed en-suite bedrooms available. Open all year.

The charming **Arkleside Hotel** is a 17th century country house which was converted to a hotel in the Edwardian era. Set in beautiful Swaledale with breathtaking views over the dale, it is the perfect setting to relax and step back in time.

Arkleside Hotel

The present owners, Malcolm and Sylvia Darby, have done much to bring the establishment up to the standard of a modern top-class hotel. The eight individually decorated bedrooms are beautifully appointed and equipped with televisions and courtesy trays. There is also a charming drawing room, a conservatory bar, and a restaurant serving an excellent five-course dinner menu which regularly features traditional Yorkshire recipes, fresh fish and locally produced cheeses. Open March to December. Unsuitable for children under 12.

Hackney House in Reeth is a guesthouse which offers the very best in old-fashioned hospitality. Proprietor Mrs Dorothy Hodgson has been providing good food and first-rate accommodation for her guests since 1968. Her house was constructed around 1900 on the site of former artisans' cottages and is situated in the heart of the village on the northern side of the B6270 Swaledale road. Inside, the atmosphere is homely and relaxing; all the letting bedrooms are comfortable, well-appointed and are equipped to a good modern standard. Dorothy is renowned as a warm and friendly host, and many of her guests return to Hackney House again and again. She is also known for providing splendid Yorkshire breakfasts, and

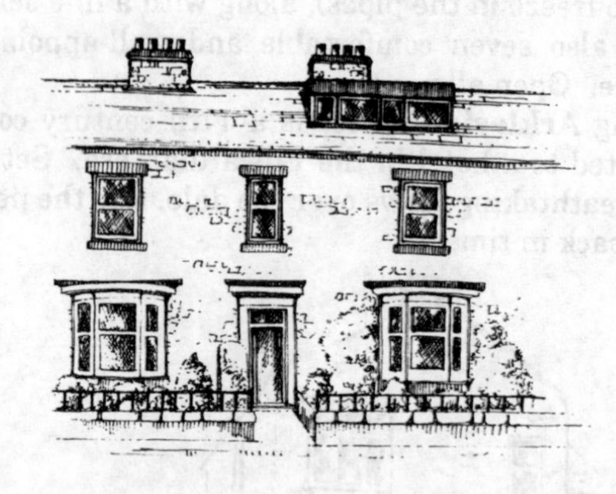

Hackney House

by arrangement, evening meals.

The **Charles Bathurst (or C.B.) Hotel** lies in the heart of beautiful Arkengarthdale, three miles northwest of Reeth on the Tan Hill road. The hotel takes its name from Charles Bathurst, a very wealthy man who in the mid-17th century had many lead mining interests in the area and who at one time owned most of the Dale. At that time, this remote spot lay near the crossroads of two ancient drovers' routes and so an inn was constructed to serve the needs of the passing trade.

Today, the building is owned and personally-run by a charming couple, Brian and Beryl Hopkins. When they took over in 1987, the hotel was in poor condition but thanks to a great deal of effort, it has been comprehensively refurbished and now stands as a monument to their hard work. Inside, the modern establishment retains much of the character and atmosphere of the original inn.

There is a cosy bar area which serves a fine range of hand-pulled beers and bar snacks and an elegant wood-panelled restaurant which offers a good choice of more elaborate dishes. The hotel also offers a number of letting bedrooms (six double, one single), all with en-suite facilities. These are all tastefully-appointed and have magnificent views across the Dale to the Duke of Norfolk's shooting lodge and beyond. Brian and Beryl also have two lovely self-catering suites available which are similarly well-equipped with all the modern facilities one would require. Open all year round.

CB. Hotel

The Buck Hotel can be seen at the top corner of the village green as you enter Reeth from the east. This handsome hotel and restaurant is a former coaching inn which once had a number of adjoining stables and outbuildings. Today, it still retains much of its original character and

Buck Hotel

charm with beamed ceilings in the bar, open log fires and a pleasant welcoming atmosphere. Owners Nigel and Susan Fawcett pride themselves in providing a wide range of fine traditional hand-pulled ales which Nigel keeps to perfection. Top quality meals are served in the bar and restaurant at lunchtimes and in the evenings, or for a more romantic

atmosphere, diners can choose to eat in the relaxed intimacy of the Bucks private supper room. There are also ten spacious guest rooms, all with en-suite bathrooms, colour televisions and tea/coffee making facilities; some also have views overlooking the village green. All in all, the Buck Hotel provides a first-rate base for exploring the northern Dales.

Whilst in Reeth, one can visit the **Swaledale Folk Museum**, once the old Methodist Sunday School, and now the home for exhibits of local farming methods, crafts, mining skills and historical facts relating to these. One can learn about local pastimes, the impact of Wesleyan Methodism and the exodus of the population when the mines closed, forcing local families to move away to the industrial areas of the southern Pennines.

Climbing the valley, travelling west, the terrain becomes more forbidding by the mile, sparsely populated by gritstone cottages, unchanged since the days when the Norsemen gave the places their names. Three miles from Reeth is the village of **Healaugh**, norse for "high forest clearing", with Low Row just beyond and its inn, the Punch Bowl, where weary travellers could stop for rest and refreshment after carrying their burdens along the Corpse Way.

The Punch Bowl

Looking for refreshment on this route, we decided to stop at the **Punch Bowl Inn at Low Row**. This splendid pub and hostelry stands in a magnificent position overlooking the River Swale and has been run since 1990 by Pete Grant and Pete Roe. They have already done much to improve the range and quality of facilities that are available to touring visitors, walkers, cavers and mountain bikers, and now offer bed and breakfast accommodation, rooms for small groups, and good value bunkhouse places. Food is served in the bar, as well as three course evening meals for pre-booked parties. Mountain bikes and caving lamps are available for hire, and there is also a busy programme of live music events.

A few yards from Ye Olde Punch Bowl Inn, we came to another of **Low Row**'s interesting enterprises, the **Swaledale Pottery**, which has been run since 1976 by Juliet and Martin Bearpark. Here, they produce a range of attractive hand-thrown domestic stoneware in a variety of glazes and styles. All items are dishwasher and microwave proof, and being handmade, each has its own subtle individuality. Visitors are welcome to browse around their showroom which is situated on the main B6270 Richmond to Kirkby Stephen road and is open daily except Sundays. As well as producing pottery for the showroom, Martin undertakes special orders and large commissions. Items from the Swaledale Pottery are also available at the Pot Shop in Reeth.

Swaledale Pottery

Travelling along the B6270, we were drawn to the signposts for **Crackpot** through curiosity and decided to take a detour, just to say that we had been there. It is located on a country road that winds through the lovely green hills to Wensleydale, its main attraction being the sad and lonely ruins of Crackpot Hall, which looks like a likely spot for the location of *Lorna Doone*. The Hall was abandoned in the 1950's due to subsidence caused by local mining activity. Although only the wonderful prospect over the river indicates its former glory, it is well worth a visit to view the wonderful position it occupies, at the head of a sweeping valley. The mines nearby have also long been abandoned, although the blacksmith's forge still remains largely intact behind the crumbling walls.

The nearby village of **Gunnerside**, "Gunnar's Pasture", was once the land where a Viking chief guarded his livestock. Later, it became known as the "Klondyke of Swaledale", although it was the centre of the boom in lead-mining rather than gold, and the Old Gang Mines were the most famous in Yorkshire. The paths and ways here are mainly those trodden by the many successions of miners, travelling to their work. The valley's sides are still scarred with mine-workings, but these are now an established part of their character, and by no means detract from the grandeur of the gorge

Crackpot Hall

and the expanse of Melbeck's Moor that leads from it.

In the village, one can visit tearooms that offer such delights as "Lead Miners' Bait", and the delicious Gunnerside cheese-cake, made from a recipe handed down from the mining days.

Those wishing to stay in a genuine Swaledale farmhouse should make a point of finding **Oxnop Hall** which is situated midway between **Gunnerside** and Muker, just to the north of the B6270. This magnificent 17th-century Grade II listed farmhouse stands at the heart of a 600-acre working livestock farm stocking beef cattle and Swaledale sheep. Inside, the building is full of original character with beamed ceilings, mullioned windows and charming decoration. The letting bedrooms are all equipped with en-suite bath/shower and beverage making facilities and have spectacular views over the surrounding upland scenery. Owners Annie and John Porter provide their guests with a warm welcome, delicious farmhouse breakfasts and evening meals by arrangement. Unsuitable for pets.

Oxnop Hall

In a wonderful position adjacent to Gunnerside Gill, we discovered the delightful pub and eating house, the **Kings Head**, which in summer is adorned in attractive hanging flower baskets.

The Kings Head

This fine 17th-century inn has a cobbled courtyard and has a traditional character with stone-flagged floors, beamed ceilings, pew-style seating and an attractive panelled bar. As well as the finest local ales, William and Elsie Whitehead offer an excellent choice of bar meals, both at lunchtimes and in the evenings. On the day we visited, the menu included home-made ratatouille, rump steak and breaded chicken in curry mayonnaise.

An old stone bridge leads into the village of **Muker**, which consists of a collection of grey stone cottages and a church, dating back to the reign of Elizabeth 1, built by the parishioners to bring an end to the tedious journey along the Corpse way to the mother church at Grinton. Local family names, such as Harker, Alderson and Fawcett feature prominently on the gravestones, as they do still living in the village today.

Again, local specialities are on offer in the local tea-rooms, such as Swaledale Curd Tart, Yorkshire Rarebit and Deep Apple Pie with Wensleydale Cheese. The main crafts revolve around the wool provided by the hardy Swaledale sheep, in great demand by carpet manufacturers and for jumpers worn by the fell walkers and climbers.

One place to visit here is the local enterprise, **Swaledale Woollens**, which was established in 1974 to revitalise the local cottage industry of hand-knitting and crocheting woollen items using fibre from the famous Swaledale breed of sheep. In the decades leading up to the Second World War, many generations of miners' and farmers' families supplemented their incomes by producing and selling knitted and crocheted items such as sweaters, cardigans and socks. However, this practice was steadily dying out until Swaledale Woollens set up their base in the 1970s.

Swaledale Woollens

Today, their cottage shop provides a thriving centre for the collection, display and sale of hand-knitted woollen garments and cloth. (There is also stock of various natural yarns on cone or in packs for those who do their own hand or machine knitting.) Visitors are welcome to call in at the centre to view the fascinating exhibition on the Swaledale sheep, a breed which is renowned for its hardiness, its excellent mothering qualities and for its tendency to remain on a given area of open hillside, thus making shepherding easier. A wide selection of locally designed and produced sweaters, cardigans and other items is on sale at the centre which is open daily (please telephone 0748 86251 to confirm times). An efficient mail order service is also available.

Further on, the tiny village of **Thwaite** stands amidst the panoramic scenery of Kisdon Hill, Great Shunnor, High Seat and Lovely Seat, and is the last stop for the stout-hearted climbers looking for a challenge. The name is of ancient origin, as are most in this region, coming from the Nordic "thveit", meaning a clearing in the wood, although the woodlands that once provided shelter and fuel for the Viking settlers have long since gone.

An excellent place to stay in this remote location is the renowned private guesthouse and restaurant which is owned and run by Jacqui and Ian Danton. **Kearton Guest House** has thirteen tastefully decorated bedrooms all with hot and cold washbasins and tea/coffee making facilities. The lounge and bar are full of traditional character, and the licensed restaurant is known throughout the area for its imaginative and wide-ranging menu which on the day we visited featured the house speciality, spiced gammon cooked in orange and peach juice. The Pennines rise directly to the rear of the building making this an ideal base for walkers and touring visitors alike. Closed January and February.

Kearton Guest House

From the mountainous scenery of Thwaite, the scene changes completely on arriving at **Keld**.

This is a place where the rushing sound of water is ever present, the word "Keld" meaning "a spring" in Nordic. The little cluster of stone buildings here stand at the earliest stages of the Swale, and at this point it is Yorkshire's most exuberant river. For lovers of green woodlands and breathtaking waterfalls, and who wish to observe these wonders in relative isolation, Keld is definitely the place to go. It gives an impression of a place apart, untouched by the modern age. This is the last outpost of civilisation in Swaledale, but having arrived here, who would wish to go any further! It occupies a hollow in the hills and is surrounded by inhospitable and barren moorland. Horse and carts were the only means of transport until a rather infrequent bus service was introduced. This truly can be defined as a hidden place, although it is today something of a crossroads for long distance walkers and the curious motorist searching for a tranquil break in his travels.

One should definitely take time to walk the short distance to one or more of Keld's scenic offerings. Wain Wath Force can be found alongside the Birkdale road, and Catrake force, with its stepped formation, can be reached from the cottages on the left at the bottom of the street in Keld - the most spectacular of the falls in the region. Following a rough lane at the bottom end of the street, this soon becomes a lovely woodland walk, from which there is a short detour to Kisdon Force, which is confined to a narrow channel through which the young river thunders.

Truly outstanding country house accommodation is offered by Greta and Archie Naysmith at their superb home, **Cocklake House,** which lies near the village of Outhgill within the little-known dale of **Mallerstang,** six miles west of Keld. This genuinely hidden place can be found four miles south of Kirkby Stephen and just to the west of the B6259 Garsdale Head road and the Settle to Carlisle railway. Cocklake House was built between 1660 and 1670 by Lady Anne Clifford as a gatehouse to Pendragon Castle. The castle stands on top of an artificial knoll three hundred yards from the house and is said to have been founded by Uther Pendragon, father of King Arthur, who attempted to create a moat around it by diverting the course of the River Eden. After many centuries of neglect, Lady Anne carried out a major programme of restoration, though sadly the castle fell into decline once again following her death in 1676.

Since moving to Cocklake House in 1987, Greta and Archie have carried out a series of tasteful improvements to their home. They now have two luxurious letting bedrooms available for guests, both spacious, beau-

Waterfalls, Keld

tifully decorated and equipped with their own en-suite bathrooms. Those fortunate enough to stay here are provided with superb accommodation and wonderful hospitality. As well as a fine English breakfast, guests have the option of having delicious evening meals which are prepared using fresh locally-sourced ingredients and are enjoyed in the relaxed informal atmosphere of the dining room. Most of the rooms in Cocklake House command breathtaking views of Pendragon Castle and the rocky fells above Mallerstang making this a truly outstanding base for walking and for touring the Eden Valley, the Yorkshire Dales, the Lake District and beyond. For accurate directions, telephone the owners on 07683 72080 - it's certainly worth making the effort to find.

Cocklake House

Travelling back through Thwaite, is **Shunnor Fell** and then **"Buttertubs Pass"**, one of the highest and most forbidding mountain passes in the country.

The Buttertubs themselves are an outstanding natural feature and are well known to walkers and travellers. They are a series of closely packed vertical potholes, not linked by a series of passages as potholes usually are, but freestanding, bearing only a slight resemblance to the objects after which they are named. There is a tale that farmers, on their way back from Hawes market, would hang their unsold butter there in baskets, until they passed by there again on the way back the following week.

Yorkshire Dales Country Cottages is the collective name for the six wonderful self-catering holiday cottages owned and personally run by

Mrs Brenda Stott. These can be found in a beautiful peaceful location on her small Dales farm at **High Shaw**, Simonstone, two miles north of Hawes on the Buttertubs road. The cottages sleep between two and ten people and are all English Tourist Board three or four key commended. All are equipped with washing/ironing facilities, colour televisions, duvets and pillows and central heating and all are individually prepared and maintained to the highest standard under the personal supervision of the owner. (Full information on each property is available on request.) Trout fishing

Yorkshire Dales Country Cottages

is available to guests on the nearby River Ure/Cotter.

After Buttertubs, a snake-like road leads through the mountains to **Hawes** and Upper Wensleydale. Hawes is not a particularly old town, springing up as it did from the coming of the Settle - Carlisle railway in the 1870's. There was an older town here once though, as one can see in some of the street names indicating ancient trades, such as Dyer's Garth, Hatter's Yard, Printer's Square and Cooper's Garth. For more information on these old local trades, take a trip to the **Dales Countryside Museum**, based in the old railway station, which tells the story of how man's activities have helped to shape the Dales' landscape, with historical information on domestic life, the lead-mining industry, hand-knitting and other local trades.

Hawes is also renowned for its rope-making industry, and at the Hawes Ropeworks, one can still see the trade being practised, with the experienced ropers twisting cotton and man-made fibres to make halters, picture cords, dog leads and clothes- lines.

There is also a Wensleydale cheese factory here, based in Gayle Lane, which, due to health regulations, is not open to tourists, although the cheeses are available in the little family-run shops around the market-place.

Hawes' greatest attraction, though, has to be the nearby **Hardraw Force**, at 98 feet the highest unbroken waterfall in England above ground. Access can be gained through the Green Dragon Inn for a small fee. It is located in an amphitheatre-like surround of limestone crags, where Hardraw Beck plunges over the edge in a breath-taking cascade, behind which, due to an under-cut in the cliff, walkers can gain access to the back of the waterfall, as both Turner and Wordsworth did, an adventure not to be missed!

Another impressive waterfall, **Cotter Force**, is located three miles out of Hawes, following the Sedburgh road, accessible through fields - an effort well spent. The stream passes through the tiny hidden village of Cotterdale, before it transforms into a magnificent display of giant steps of limestone over which the water drops gracefully, overshadowed by leaning boughs of trees.

Hawes' streets are usually inhabited at any time of the year by the stout-hearted walkers travelling the Pennine Way, which of here, makes its way across the sparsely populated Langstroth Chase, through the middle of the Dales to Malham, Todmorden and across Howarth and Saddleworth Moor to Kinder Scout in the Peak District.

Two miles southwest of **Hawes**, on the B6255 Ingleton road, we found the delightful guesthouse and tearooms, **Tarney Fors**. This handsome Grade II listed Dales Longhouse with its beautiful south-facing terrace and garden, is surrounded by dramatic rolling hills and provides an ideal base for exploring the area by car or on foot. Owners, Sue and Alan Harpley provide first-class accommodation and charming hospitality. They have three centrally-

Green Dragon Inn

heated double bedrooms available, with either en-suite or private faciities. All with TV, shaver points, tea and coffee making facilities and spectacular views of the fells. They also serve delicious breakfasts, teas and evening meals in their superb beamed dining room with its working range and stone-flagged floor. Also available is **Tarney Barn**, a two-bedroomed self-catering apartment which adjoins the farmhouse.

Tarney Fors

On leaving Hawes, we turned south onto the minor Kettlewell road and within a mile reached the delightful hamlet of **Gayle**, home of the magnificent **Rookhurst Georgian Country House Hotel**.

Rookhurst Georgian Country House Hotel

Resident proprietor Iris Van Der Steen and her staff provide their guests with superb hospitality and the finest traditional English cuisine which is prepared using fresh locally-grown ingredients. Unsuitable for children under twelve.

Wensleydale is richer, kindlier and more verdant than Upper Swaledale, as the quality of its ewes-milk cheese would suggest. It is the only one of Yorkshire's dales not to be named after the river that flows through it, but rather after the town of Wensley, where the lucrative trade in the cheese began in the 13th century, before the Plague wiped out its population. Before this, the dale was known by the ancient name of Yore Dale, after the river Yore or Ure that flowed through it.

It was the monks of the affluent nearby Jervaulx Abbey who started the trade in the cheese, although the farming communities took over when its popularity became apparent.

Wensleydale is also the home of the greatest concentration of waterfalls in the dales, and travelling along the B684, five miles from Hawes, is the market town of **Askrigg**, and the natural wonder of Mill Gill Force.

Once an important market town before Hawes took over, Askrigg is now better known as the main location for "All Creatures Great and Small", in which it is known as Darrowby. The house opposite the ancient church serves as Skeldale House, and the King's Arms as the Drover's Arms. The bewitching little church here, nestling amidst surrounding trees, makes a particularly good subject for one's photographic skills.

An ideal base for touring the surrounding countryside is **Thornsgill Guest House** in Askrigg, owned and run by Mollie and Colin Gilyeat. It's a handsome Victorian house, full of character and with a welcoming and friendly atmosphere.

Thornsgill Guest House

Mollie is an excellent cook and the emphasis, morning and evening, is on good Yorkshire home cooking - and lots of it! - served in an attractive, cosy (and licensed) dining room. There are three spacious, beautifully decorated bedrooms and Thornsgill is open all year round. While Mollie thrives in the kitchen, Colin has his own workshop behind the house, where he makes just about anything from all kinds of wood.

Being avid watchers of "All Creatures Great and Small", we couldn't go to Askrigg without visiting **The King's Arms Hotel** in the Market Place, better known to viewers as the Drovers Arms. It was here that William Turner stayed in the early 1800's, while he painted scenes of the surrounding countryside. Liz and Ray Hopwood, the owners, describe The King's Arms Hotel as a 'country' Georgian Manor House, and have lovingly preserved its history and character. The Hotel is beautifully and thoughtfully furnished, a true period piece, and it has won many accolades for its excellent traditional English cuisine and superlative wine list. This was a real treat!

The King's Arms Hotel

Across the river lies **Bainbridge**, once known to the Romans as Virosidum, where they built a succession of forts on Brough Hill, now an overgrown grassy hummock located on private land. In Norman times, this was a hunting forest, and the Forest Horn is still sounded at 9pm each evening between Holyrood (September 27th) and Shrove Tuesday, an ancient custom introduced to guide travellers though the forest.

Nearby **Semer Water** is a lovely location - an isolated lake steeped in myth. It is said that a town lies beneath its depths, cast under water by a curse.

A poor traveller once sought shelter here, but was turned away by the affluent inhabitants, eventually seeking shelter with a shepherd in the nearby hills. The next day, he stood on the hill above the town and laid this curse

> "Semerwater rise, Semerwater sink.
> And swallow all the town save this little house,
> Where they gave me food and drink."

A great flood engulfed the town completely, which was never seen again. A curious postscript to this tale is that during a drought, the level of the lake dropped to reveal the remains of a Bronze Age town, thereby proving the truth behind the legend.

Just outside Askrigg, on the **Carperby** Road, we came to the most unusual and splendid **Nappa Hall**, ancient seat of the famous Metcalfe Family of Wensleydale and now the home of Patsy and Ken Thompson. Nappa Hall is described as a castellated house - or a fortress - which dates back to the 15th century. Today Patsy and Ken still work the 450 acres of picturesque farmland at the foot of dramatic cliffs and Nappa Scar. Through the summer, after the lambing season, they let out three rooms for bed and breakfast. Don't expect all the mod cons - that would spoil its charm - but you will be assured of fine hosts, comfort, good hearty food and tranquility.

Nappa Hall

Heading on to **Carperby**, we found the exceptional country inn and hotel, **The Wheatsheaf**, which is run by Max and Sheila Mackay. Inside, there is a delightful little 'snug' bar and a residents' lounge with a superb 17th-century arched fireplace stretching the full length of one wall. The dining room serves first-class continental and traditional English dishes.

There are also eight beautifully appointed bedrooms, some with four poster beds, all with en-suite facilities, colour televisions and beverage making facilities. In 1941, James Herriot and his wife Helen spent their honeymoon here.

The Wheatsheaf

Travelling back to the B684 will bring one to **Aysgarth**, famous for its pottery and the spectacular Aysgarth Falls. Here, the river thunders through a rocky gorge and drops some 200 feet over three huge slabs of limestone, the falls being divided into Upper, Middle and Lower Falls, particularly exhilarating after a heavy rainfall. Nearby stands Yore Mill, in its time a corn mill, flax mill and wool-spinning and stocking-making factory. Now it houses the **Yorkshire Carriage Museum**, with its comprehensive collection of horse-carriages, farm carts, fire engines, hearses and even a haunted cab!

In an elevated position above the falls, we found the impressive **Stow House Hotel** which is jointly run by Mike and Irene Sullivan and David and Louise Burton. This imposing country house hotel was built in 1876 as a vicarage for the Reverend Fenwick William Stow of Aysgarth from whom it takes its name. In recent years, the building has undergone a major refurbishment and now offers nine luxurious bedrooms (one with a four-poster), all equipped with en-suite bathrooms, colour televisions and beverage making facilities. All rooms also enjoy magnificent views over Wensleydale and Bishopdale. The hotel's elegant dining room is open both to residents and non-residents and offers first-rate continental and traditional English cuisine. Afternoon tea can be taken here or on the terrace. Guests are welcome to use the hotel's private lawn tennis court, croquet lawn and golf practice facilities.

Stow House Hotel

Should one seek refreshment after one's walks around this area's scenic delights, in a location overlooking the River Ure, is the celebrated **Mill Race Teashop**. This impressive café and tearoom is housed in a former corn and flax mill which was built by the Birkbeck family in 1784. A major conversion was completed in 1984 and the building now includes a specialist bakery in the basement area where the delicious home-made cakes and pastries for the café are produced. The menu includes specialist teas, coffees, set teas and a number of mouthwatering light meals including salads, jacket potatoes and Wensleydale ploughman's lunches. Joyce and Mike Smith also run the impressive **Dales Park Café** which is situated within the nearby Aysgarth Falls Visitors' Centre. Open Easter to 1st November.

Mill Race Tea Shop

The **George and Dragon Inn at Aysgarth** lies only a short walk from the famous falls and is an ideal base for exploring the wonderful unspoilt landscape of Upper Wensleydale. This pleasant family-run inn can be found on the edge of the village midway between the market towns of Leyburn and Hawes on the A684 cross-Pennine route. Originally constructed in the 17th-century, this lovely old building is now Grade II listed. Inside, it still retains much of its original character with timber-beamed ceilings, antique furniture and an open log fire in the bar. The inn is owned and personally run by Ken and Madeline Naylor along with their daughter and son-in-law , Alison ad James. They have done much to preserve its unique atmosphere and charm. No fruit machines or modern pub games here; instead, the bar is decorated with interesting artefacts and pencil sketches of local people drawn by Ken who is an accomplished arts graduate.

James is responsible for keeping the inn's excellent range of traditional cask-conditioned ales and he always takes great care to ensure they are served in prime condition. The selection of bar food on offer is of a similar outstanding quality. On the day we visited, we had a choice of twenty main courses including turkey filled with asparagus and lemon sole filled with crab meat. A good variety of vegetarian dishes is also always available, along with salads, sandwiches and light snacks.

Ken and Madeline also have a number of beautifully appointed guest rooms available. These are all centrally heated and are equipped with private en-suite facilities, colour televisions and tea/coffee making facilities.

George & Dragon Inn

The hosts offer the warmest Wensleydale hospitality and a delicious full English breakfast which is guaranteed to set you up for a day in the Dales. Enquire about the special breaks which are available out of season and over the Christmas and New Year period. The George and Dragon is open all year round and welcomes pets by prior arrangement. Visa and Mastercard welcomed subject to a small surcharge.

Just to the east of Aysgarth, we turned south off the A684 to reach the scenic Wensleydale village of **Thoralby**. Here, we called in at the pleasant small-scale guesthouse, **Pen View**, which stands in a wonderful position overlooking Pen Hill and Bishopsdale. The Bailey family have lived here since the house was built in 1978 and are experienced at providing their guests with a warm welcome and excellent hospitality. They have four comfortable guest rooms available, with central heating which are all equipped with TV etc. Delicious breakfasts and evening meals, prepared using home-produced ingredients wherever possible are served in the licensed dining room overlooking the magnificent views of the Dales. They also have a lounge (with TV) in which guests can relax and meet other residents. Children and pets are most welcome. Pen View Guest House has an ETB approved 2 crown rating.

Pen View

Here, we can also recommend the community's last remaining pub, the **George Inn**, which dates back to 1732. This wonderful establishment is run by Maureen Evans, her mother and her daughter who together provide a welcome and a standard of hospitality which is difficult to match anywhere.

The George Inn

Customers are offered a fine range of well-kept ales and a selection of appetising bar meals which come in agreeably generous portions. There are also two spacious letting bedrooms available, both comfortable, attractively decorated and equipped to a good modern standard. Beware, Maureen's breakfasts are amongst the largest and most delicious we have found.

Also in **Thoralby**, is the small family-run guesthouse, **High Green House**, which stands on the edge of the village green. This handsome Grade II listed Georgian residence is surrounded by an attractive walled garden and enjoys magnificent views over Bishopsdale. Owners Pat and Ted Hesketh have been careful to preserve the original character of the

High Green House

building despite carrying out a tasteful modernisation. The three comfortable guest rooms all have en-suite or private bathrooms, colour televisions and tea/coffee making facilities, and the ground-floor room is also specially adapted for elderly or disabled guests. Excellent traditional Yorkshire breakfasts are served in the dining room, with four-course evening meals being available if required. Open Easter to early November.

North of Aysgarth is **Castle Bolton**, known predictably enough, for its castle. It was built in 1379 by Richard le Scrope, Lord Chancellor of England to Richard II, and a personal friend of Chaucer, who is said to have used him as a model for the Knight's Tale. It is, in fact, a luxurious fortified manor house, which dominates the rows of stone cottages in the village. Today, it is still impressive, with its gaunt towers and huge Guest Room, which serves today as the Castle Tea-room. It is still occupied by Harry Orde Powlett, a direct descendant of the first Lord Scrope. Its halls and galleries are remarkably well-preserved, some of the private apartments having been the home of Mary Queen of Scots between 1568 - 69. The view from the battlements is awesome, if rather exposed to the full force of the winds.

Castle Bolton

Midway between Leyburn and Hawes, near the Aysgarth Falls, is the **Palmer Flatt Hotel**. We could have happily settled in here for several days, since it is ideally placed for exploring the best beauty spots of Wensleydale and, for more relaxing days when you don't want to travel too far, it also offers free trout-fishing rights to residents, gentle walks from the doorstep to breathtaking scenery, or horse-racing at nearby Middleham.

As far back as the crusades a hospice stood on the site where the Palmer Flatt Hotel is now, hence its name, which was taken from the pilgrims who returned from the Holy Land bearing palm branches. The oldest part of the Hotel was built in the mid 1700's and a private house was built on to it in the 1830's. Nowadays it is all one property, with twelve lovely bedrooms, a very pretty and reasonably priced restaurant, and two relaxed and comfortable bars. Guests and non-residents are all warmly welcomed by Val Hansard and her son Mark, who own and run the Hotel. They have been careful to maintain all the old character of the building, with its stone walls and timbers, and are justifiably proud of the spectacular views from the Hotel grounds, from where we looked across the beautiful countryside to Bolton Castle.

Palmer Flatt Hotel

One and a half miles south-west of West Burton, on the B6160 Kettlewell road, we stopped in the tiny hamlet of **Newbiggin in Bishopdale** to visit **Newbiggin House,** a delightful bed and breakfast establishment run by Mr and Mrs Proctor. This handsome creeper-clad residence was constructed of local stone in 1924, and today provides charming and peaceful accommodation for visitors to the area. The Proctors have two comfortable letting bedrooms available (one twin, one single), and provide Yorkshire breakfasts that are second to none. They also own two self-catering holiday cottages, both rated as "three key, commended": the adjoining Newbiggin House Cottage, which sleeps two people, and overlooks the attractive garden, and Beech Cottage, which sleeps five, and overlooks the village green in Thoralby, one mile to the north.

Newbiggin House

Midway between Leyburn and Bainbridge on the A684 Wensleydale road, is the delightful village of **West Burton**, noted for having its own waterfall. In a wonderful position overlooking the village green, we found the impressive country inn, the **Fox and Hounds**, which is run by Norma and Alan Fish. This 200 year-old former coaching inn is a focal point for local walking, touring and social activities, and in recent years has acquired an excellent reputation for providing good food, traditional ales and first-class accommodation. The eight well-appointed guest rooms are situated around a cobbled courtyard to the rear and are all equipped with en-suite facilities, colour televisions and tea/coffee making facilities.

Fox and Hounds

The nearby village of **West Witton** is known for its annual feast of St Bartholemew, patron saint of the Parish Church, which takes place on August 24th each year. The effigy of "Owd Bartie" is carried through the village followed by the chant,

"At Pen Hill Crags he tore his rags
At Hunter's Thorn he blew his horn
At Capelbank Stee he brake his knee
At Grassgill Beck he brake his neck
At Wadham's End he couldn't fend
At Grassgill End he met his end"

It is unlikely that the origins of the festival are anything other than pagan, although some monumental, if ill-fated, journey by a warrior of some sorts would seem to be indicated. The effigy is eventually burned at Grassgill End at the culmination of three days of festivities.

Travelling through the quiet, pretty village of Wensley, one will eventually come to **Leyburn**, the main market and trading centre of the middle dale, as its wide cobbled market places, bordered by high, affluent -looking buildings, would seem to suggest. Its name is a corruption of Le Bourne, as it is called in the Domesday Book, or "Stream by the Clearing", and the nearby area of escarpment known as the Shawl was occupied as far back as prehistoric days.

The town has many famous connections, one of which is the fact that Lord Nelson's surgeon, Peter Goldsmith, once lived in the Secret Garden House in Grove Square. Another can be discovered on a visit to the War Memorial, where one will see the name of flight lieutenant Alan Broadley DSO, DFC, DFM, the famous "F" for Freddie, of Dam Buster fame.

Much of the imposing architecture dates from the 1700's, and such buildings as the Grove Hotel, the Sandpiper Inn and Sanderson's Paint shop (once the family home of Frances L'Anson of "Sweet Lass of Richmond Hill" fame) are worth investigation.

Overlooking Leyburn's ancient Market Square we found the impressive **Golden Lion Hotel** which is owned by Anne and Richard Wood. This handsome building was constructed of local stone in 1765 and for the next 120 years operated as a coaching inn known as 'Fothergills'. The present-day hotel provides an ideal base for exploring the beautiful countryside and many places of interest which lie within the Dales National Park. The fifteen comfortable bedrooms all have beverage making facilities and televisions, and most also have en-suite bathrooms. An extensive range of delicious home-cooked dishes is served in the oak-panelled dining room, and in the lounge bar, bitter is served which is brewed by Richard and named after his son, Oliver John.

Golden Lion Hotel

Just off the market place and adjacent to the church, we called in at **Eastfield Lodge**. This substantial Victorian hotel was built around 1835 for a wealthy industrialist who was involved in the Stockton to Darlington railway project. It is now owned by Janet and Barry Atkinson who in the short time since taking over in May 1992 have undertaken an ambitious refurbishment programme. They now have eight spacious en-suite bedrooms available which, along with the attractive south-facing dining room, lounge and garden, have magnificent views over lower Wensleydale.

Eastfield Lodge

The Shawl lies to the west of the town, a mile-long limestone scarp along which runs a footpath with panoramic views. One legend says that it gained it's name from the fact that Mary Queen of Scots dropped her shawl here during her flight from Bolton Castle, though a more likely explanation is that the name is a corruption of the one given to the ancient settlement here. The eccentric Victorians held Their Tea Festivals atop this limestone terrace, with marquees, music and dancing.

The Spring is probably the best time to visit the town, for it is at this time when both the Swaledale and Wensleydale Festivals take place, as well as the prestigious Dales Music Festival.

Historic **Middleham** is entered via a fascinating castellated bridge, that almost looks like the ones that one would normally see spanning a castle's moat. James Herriot commented about the place, "When it comes to sheer historical associations, I think Middleham is perhaps the winner".

The famous castle was the stronghold of the powerful "Kingmaker" Neville family, and favourite home of Richard III; it earned the title of the "Windsor of the North", drawing Kings, Queens, Lords and Ladies in their medieval pageantry. However, on the death of Richard at Bosworth Field, the great castle was reduced to ruins, much of its stone being used to create buildings for the town below. The recent discovery of the Middleham Jewel near the ruins, which was sold for £1.3 million, brought new interest in this most romantic of medieval castles - a replica is on display in the office at the entrance to the building. There is the site nearby of another, earlier castle, unusually close to the main one.

Middleham itself has two market places, some splendid Georgian and Victorian buildings, and a profusion of racing stables, for which the town is renowned. There is also an old stepped cross in the main market, known as the Swine Cross, which once bore the White Boar emblem of Richard III, hence the name. There is also a very lovely parish church outside the town, with an inscription over the door that tells us the church was built by Thomas, Lord of Aylesbury. This spot is quiet and idyllic, with sheep grazing in the graveyard on the brow of the hill that sweeps down to the Coverdale valley, the sort of place that Wordsworth would have been inspired by.

Also in the town, a short distance from the cobbled village centre, we came across a fascinating establishment, the **Old School Arts Workshop**. This former village school was constructed in 1869 in elaborate Victorian Gothic style and has an unusual central tower topped with a castellated parapet and a raised bell arch. Following the school's closure in 1977, the building (which is now Grade II listed) was allowed to fall into disrepair until it was purchased in 1981 by Peter and Judith Hibbard. They restored and converted it into a modern study centre which today offers courses in sculpture, painting and related arts. Visitors are invited to look around the gallery exhibitions and bookshop, and to visit the workshop's pleasant tearooms.

Old School Arts Workshop

Looking for somewhere to stay here, we found the impressive hotel and restaurant, **The Miller's House Hotel,** which is owned and personally-run by Judith and Crossley Sunderland. This handsome Georgian residence was built in 1726 in a sheltered position just off the market square. Inside, it has been extensively refurbished to bring it up to the standards of a modern first-class hotel.

Miller's House Hotel

delightfully named 'Orange Boodle'. Middleham is a major racehorse training centre (three Grand National winners have come from here) and the hotel offers special breaks for enthusiasts which include tours of local stables and visits to the races.

In a superb position overlooking the town square, we can also recommend the **Black Swan Hotel**, a handsome Grade II listed building which retains much of its original 17th-century character. Proprietors Sue and George Monday have seven beautifully decorated guest rooms available, all with private bathrooms and first-rate modern facilities; two also

Black Swan Hotel

have four-poster beds. Top quality meals (including the house specialities, steaks and 'tipsy' casseroles) are served in the bar and main dining room. To the rear, there is also an attractive beer garden which backs onto Middleham Castle.

Approximately midway between Masham and Leyburn on the A6108, we came to the delightful village of **East Witton**. Here, we called in at the impressive inn, the **Blue Lion**, which is run by Paul and Helen Klein. Originally built as a coaching inn around 1840, the interior has a truly welcoming atmosphere with an open fire, stone-flagged floors and unusual curved timber seating in the bar. Here, an excellent range of traditional hand-pulled beers is served along with a selection of top quality, freshly-prepared bar meals. Alternatively, customers can enjoy first-class cuisine in the elegant candlelit restaurant. The Blue Lion also has nine spacious guest rooms available which are all beautifully appointed and equipped with en suite facilities.

The Blue Lion

Standing beside the old bridge in East Witton, the **Cover Bridge Inn** is a marvellous example of a traditional Yorkshire inn. This fine establishment lies within the grounds of the Jervaulx Estate, two miles southeast of Middleham on the A6108 Leyburn to Ripon road. With parts dating back to the 16th-century, the inn is now listed as a building of special architectural interest. Inside, there are low beamed ceilings, huge open fireplaces and a relaxed and genuine atmosphere. Owners Jim and June Carter serve fine draught beers (Theakstons, John Smiths), and there is a cosy little restaurant which is open every day of the week. There are also three comfortable and well-appointed letting bedrooms which are available all year round.

Cover Bridge Inn

Should one wish to stop over in this picturesque village (reputed to have the longest village green in England), we can recommend **Rookery**

Cottage, an exceptional bed and breakfast establishment which has recently been converted from four almshouses and has parts dating back to the 16th-century. The cottage has been refurbished to luxurious standards . The dining room is oak panelled with open fires and there are two magnificent beamed guest rooms, both sharing beautiful bath/shower room offering every modern comfort. Owners Ursula and Ronnie Bussey provide their guests with wonderful Yorkshire hospitality and a delicious breakfast which regularly includes locally-grown mushrooms, trout and smoked salmon. Booking strongly advised.

Rookery Cottage

Connoisseurs of ice cream might not be able to resist stopping at a particular location, one mile southeast of the ancient Abbey at Jervaulx. Here, one can find **High Jervaulx Farm**, home of the celebrated **Brymor Real Dairy Ice Cream**. The company was founded in 1984 by Brian and Brenda Moore in the village of Weeton on the edge of Wharfedale. The new ice cream was such an instant success with the public that the company soon began to outgrow its original production facility; however, restrictive planning regulations meant that instead of being able to expand on the existing site, new premises had to be found in a different location. This was finally achieved and in February 1992, Brian and Brenda finished installing their new production equipment and moved their herd of pedigree Guernsey cows to their new home at High Jervaulx Farm. The Moores and their staff now make ice cream, frozen yogurt, sorbets and special diabetic desserts in over thirty different flavours using fresh whole Guernsey milk, double cream and the finest natural Italian fruit flavours. In their 'Big Country' range, they also use nuts and other special ingredients imported from the USA and Canada. Visitors are welcome to tour the farm, meet the animals, and view the ice cream production process. They are also able to purchase delicious cones, sundaes and ice cream gateaux (which can be specially decorated 'while-you-wait') from the helpful and knowledgeable staff. Altogether, a fascinating and mouthwatering place to visit.

Brymor Ice Cream Parlour

Past the sleeping ruins of Jervaulx, lies **Masham**, possibly most famous as the home of the celebrated Theakston's Brewery.

In older days, the town built its wealth on the quality of its sheep, with a breed of sheep named after the town. It was the site of great cattle and sheep fairs in days gone by. The Masham Sheep Fair takes place each September and is never to be missed by serious sheep breeders.

The company of T & R Theakston have been brewing "Old Peculier" strong ale here since 1827, sometimes known as "Lunatic Broth" for obvious reasons. There is a Brewery Visitors centre, where you can learn how the brew is made and watch the coopers going about their trade. There is also an interesting display of the traditional pub games and why not visit the White Bear pub within the complex, where the purest form of the ale is sold! Due to the popularity of these tours, however, it is advisable to book in advance to avoid disappointment!

Tucked away off the main market place in the town, we discovered the **Bruce Arms**, a superb inn and eating house which has been run since 1988 by David and Jean Young. The building has been a pub since 1783 and was once owned by Lord Aylesbury. As well as good ales and hospitality, David and Jean offer an extensive range of home cooked meals which on the day we visited included such items as home-made steak and kidney pie and vegetable curry. There are also three well-appointed guest rooms available, and to the rear an attractive beer garden has views over the village cricket field.

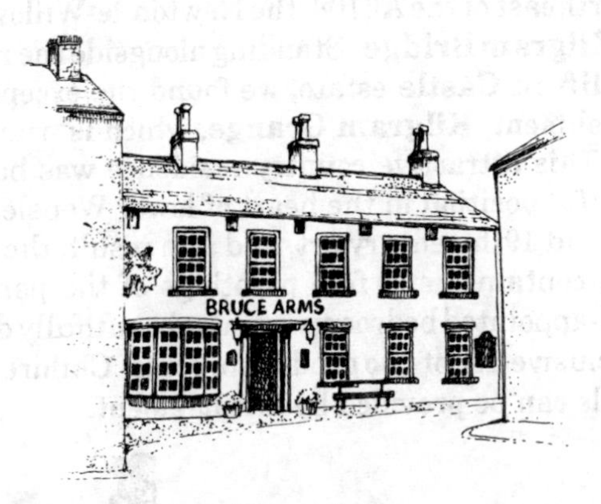

Bruce Arms

Also on **Masham**'s attractive market place, we found the **Mad Hatter Tea Rooms**, a delightful establishment serving delicious Yorkshire teas and light meals. The tearooms have been run since 1990 by Margaret and Brian Boshier and inside, they have successfully managed to create an atmosphere which is welcoming and full of traditional character. The menu offers a choice of eight different teas, several blends of coffee and a number of old-fashioned soft drinks including sarsaparilla and dandelion and burdock. There is also a wide range of mouthwatering cakes, scones and snacks including welsh rarebit and open sandwiches. Open daily except Thursdays. Margaret and Brian also have two spacious en-suite letting rooms available which overlook the market square.

Mad Hatters Tea Rooms

One mile northeast of the A6108, the Newton-le-Willows road crosses the River Ure at **Kilgram Bridge**. Standing alongside the river within the grounds of the **Clifton Castle** estate, we found the exceptional bed and breakfast establishment, **Kilgram Grange**, which is run by Carol and Tony Marshall. This attractive country residence was built during the 1850s in a delightful position in the heart of lower Wensleydale. Tony is a dealer in 18th- and 19th-century art, and as a result, the guests' lounge and dining room contain many fine paintings of the period. The four spacious and well-appointed bedrooms are also beautifully decorated, with guests having exclusive use of two good bathrooms. Children are welcome, and evening meals can be provided by arrangement.

Kilgram Grange

Only a couple of miles to the south of **Fearby**, is the mysterious **Druid's Temple**, an interesting place to stop off at. This is, however, not a meeting place constructed by pagan worshippers for magical rites as it would seem, but rather a charming folly, built in the 1820's by William Danby of the nearby Swinton Estate. His project was intended to provide work for local unemployed people, and could be compared to a rather more complete version of Stonehenge (scaled down) - it is considered one of the best druidical follies in the country.

Colsterdale is one of the lesser known dales but the visitor who takes time to drive or walk along its quiet roads and pleasant pathways will be both delighted and surprised. Although only short compared with others, this is a gem set in an area of small, family farms and interesting villages.

Pasture House stands alongside the little road that leads, eventually to a dead-end at the head of the dale. It was formerly owned by Leeds

City Council who had plans to use the area as a reservoir. The discovery of porous rocks or, as the locals have it, - " a plug hole" in the valley floor prevented this happening and the house was bought by Gerry and Avril Scott.

Druids Temple

There are wonderful views from every window in the house and guests staying in any season will be enchanted by the scenery. A silent, proud memorial to the Leeds "Pals" Regiment - decimated at the Somme in World War I - stands on the opposite hillside.

Pasture House is centrally heated, has excellent facilities and offers evening meal, bed and breakfast. All bedrooms have colour televisions, hot and cold water and tea-making facilities. There is fishing (fly only) and pony trekking within 3 miles of the house and, of course, incomparable walking in the area. Gerry Scott won the Grand National in 1960 on Merryman II and a collection of photographs of the event provides an "ice-breaking" talking point in the entrance hall.

Pasture House

Should one feel like some excitement on one of the white-knuckle rides at the **Lightwater Valley Leisure Park** (which boasts the world's only underground roller-coaster), it can be located only 6 miles to the south of Masham on the 6108.

And for those desiring more sedate pleasures, the tranquility of **Kirkby Malzeard**, accessible via country roads, may be more to your taste.

Here is a village which holds many interesting secrets, starting with the the Anglo-Norman church of St Andrew, noted for the abundant evidence of witchcraft that is connected with it.

The north-eastern corner of the churchyard was favoured by practitioners of the black arts for conducting their strange rituals and charms.

One famous witch of the area was Janet Burneston, who, in 1639, was tried in a local court for placing a dead man's skull under the bed of a man she wished to influence. The kindly magistrates however did not choose to burn her at the stake as one may have expected, but instead she was given a severe reprimand and asked to restore the skull back to its rightful owner, should he need it on Resurrection Day!

One other amusing story concerns one Christopher Pinkney, who claimed to have heard voices telling him to break the windows of the church, a sacrilegious act at the very least. The local plumber informed the local magistrates of his deed, whereupon Pinkney's wife revealed that she had also heard the ghostly voice. After some days of investigation it was discovered that the gullible Pinkney's "Voice from the Lord" had in fact been the plumber himself, who had devised the scheme to gain a lucrative commission for the replacement of the church windows!

Not far from here, midway between Ripon and Pateley Bridge, we turned north off the B6265 to reach the splendid farmhouse accommodation which is offered by Mrs Sandra Gordon at **Old Home Farm**, half-a-mile south of **High Grantley** village.

St George's Court

St George's Court is a development of five top quality letting bedrooms which were converted from the farm'soriginal outbuildings in 1990. These are set around a lovely courtyard and provide accommodation of great character and charm combined with the modern comforts of central heating, en-suite bathrooms, colour televisions and beverage making facilities.

Set within twenty acres of grounds and standing over 200 yards from the nearest road, St George's Court offers a truly relaxed and tranquil environment from which to escape the rigours of the modern world. The rooms all enjoy wonderful views over the surrounding woods and farmland which guests are welcome to explore on foot. There is also a fascinating half-acre pond within the grounds where wildlife and natural flora are encouraged to flourish. Mrs Gordon is a charming host who is renowned for providing delicious home-cooked breakfasts which she prepares from fresh, locally-sourced produce. St George's Court lies within two miles of Fountains Abbey and is an ideal base for exploring the beautiful countryside and many places of interest this part of Yorkshire has to offer.

Less than three miles from here (and within a couple of miles of Fountains Abbey as the crow flies), we came to the attractive small village of **Sawley**, home of the renowned inn and restaurant, the **Sawley Arms**. This fine establishment has been owned and personally run by Mrs June Hawes since 1968 and in this time, she has built up a first-class reputation for home-cooked food, drink and a quality of service which is second to none. Built in the early 18th-century, this handsome stone-built country inn has lost none of its original character and charm. Inside, there are open log fires, antique furniture and an atmosphere which is truly relaxed and welcoming.

Sawley Arms

As well as a bar serving fine traditional ales and an excellent selection of first-rate bar meals, the Sawley Arms also has a tastefully-furnished split-level restaurant. Here, customers dine in cosy intimate surroundings and enjoy a standard of cooking which is unrivalled in the area. June specialises in creating imaginative new dishes and is famous for her interesting soups and desserts. On the day we visited, these included superb meringue swans, apple pie and the mouthwatering 'Amaretti Schockoladentorte'. In summer, the inn and garden are ablaze with colour; indeed in 1990, June helped the Sawley Arms to become the Yorkshire and Humberside winner of the annual Britain in Bloom competition.

Pateley Bridge, considered one of the prettiest of dales towns, is perfectly situated as a base to explore the reaches of Upper Nidderdale. Considering its size, it is remarkably well-connected by roads, which in fact have been here since the monastic orders established trade routes through the town whilst transporting their goods. A street market whose charter was granted in the 14th century has, however, been abandoned for some time, although the sheep fairs and agricultural shows still take place here.

The Nidderdale Museum is based here, a fascinating record of local folk history, stored in one of the original Victorian work-houses, built in 1863. This museum was winner of the National Heritage Museum of the Year, and gives us an insight into the daily life of folk in this picturesque dale.

A short walk from the Museum is the peaceful village of **Bewerley**. Here, we called in at **The Woodlands**, a spacious and elegant private residence which also offers top quality bed and breakfast accommodation. This handsome Edwardian house stands within its own secluded grounds and enjoys superb views of the surrounding Nidderdale countryside. Since 1986, it has been owned by John and Pauline Shaw; thanks to a lot of hard work, they have managed to create a delightful atmosphere and a standard of accommodation which is truly first-class. The two guest bedrooms are both beautifully furnished and equipped with beverage making facilities; the double room also has a private bathroom and the twin room a private shower room. An excellent traditional English breakfast is served each morning, and for lunches and evening meals, Mrs Shaw is happy to direct guests to one of the many fine eating places which lie within easy reach. A number of lovely riverside and moorland walks start from the house, and the popular centre of Pateley Bridge is only a few minutes away. The larger towns of Harrogate, Ripon and York also lie within easy driving distance making this an ideal base for exploring the many fascinating places of interest the area has to offer. The double room at the Woodlands is available all year round and the twin room from Easter to October.

The Woodlands

The town of Pateley Bridge is filled with quaint, pretty buildings, such as the 17th century Apothecary's House and Sweet Shop. The oldest building is St Mary's Church, a lovely ruin dating from 1320, from which the views of Nidderdale and the surrounding moors are spectacular. Another fabulous vista can be obtained from the aptly named Panorama Walk, the main medieval route from Ripon to Skipton. St Cuthbert's Church was built to replace St Mary's, and is based further down the town. It houses the original bell from Fountains Abbey, rescued after the Dissolution. In nearby Wath Road, is Hawkridge House, where Rudyard Kipling stayed when his god-father was a methodist minister here around 1860.

Tucked away in Park Road, just off the village High Street, looking for somewhere to eat, we found the delightful **Willow Restaurant** which is owned and run by the Hartley family and managed by daughter Helen. The restaurant building dates from the early 1800s and inside, it has a wonderful intimate atmosphere. There is a pleasant bar area and coffee lounge, and a dining area with room for thirty covers. All are tastefully furnished and decorated in an attractive country style. Helen offers her customers a large and imaginative blackboard menu which she changes each week. On the day we visited, the main courses included shark steaks and quail, and there was also a wonderful selection of desserts ranging from the traditional to the more exotic. There was also an excellent wine list which included some fine wines from the New World, and for the whisky-drinking connoisseur, the bar was stocked with a selection of malts. All bread and rolls for the restaurant are baked on the premises and, wherever possible, the dishes are prepared using fresh locally-sourced ingredients. In the short time since taking over in 1992, Helen has gained many new customers who, like the regulars who have been eating here for years, enjoy returning to the Willow again and again. The restaurant is open daily except Mondays and Tuesdays.

The Willow Restaurant

North of Pateley Bridge, we made a point of visiting the splendid **Grassfields Country House Hotel** which stands within its own two-acre grounds on the Ramsgill road. This handsome Georgian building is surrounded by trees and lawns and provides the perfect place for a truly 'get-away-from-it-all' break.

Grassfields Country House Hotel

Despite being comprehensively renovated, the house still retains much of its original character and atmosphere. The nine recently decorated guest bedrooms are spacious and beautifully appointed and enjoy wonderful views over the gardens and surrounding countryside. All rooms have en-suite facilities, shaver points and tea/coffee making facilities. Downstairs, there is an elegant lounge with an open log fire, a cosy bar and a further sitting room with a colour television. Grassfields specialises in wholesome English cooking, dishes are freshly prepared using locally produced meat and fresh vegetables. The resident proprietor, Barbara Garforth, takes a great interest in her guests and is always on hand to provide information on local walks, the many unique attractions of the surrounding area, including Fountains Abbey, one of the National Trust's most visited attractions, and outdoor activities such as clay shooting, horse riding, pony trekking and squash all of which can be arranged by advance notice. Closed December and January.

The impressive **Sportsman's Arms Hotel and Restaurant** can be found in the charming Nidderdale village of **Wath**. Also located at the north of the town. This splendid establishment has been owned and personally run by Ray Carter and his family since 1979. The hotel building dates from the 17th-century and is set in beautiful secluded grounds within a quarter of a mile of Gouthwaite Reservoir, a paradise for those interested in birdlife. Tastefully decorated and furnished throughout, the Sportsman's offers seven comfortable guest bedrooms, each beautifully appointed and equipped to a high modern standard. The hotel also has a spacious residents' lounge and a fully licensed bar with a truly relaxed and friendly atmosphere.

Sportsman's Arms

Ray prides himself in the superb standard of cuisine which is served in the Sportsman's elegant restaurant. Open both to residents and non-residents, this top class eating place offers a range of mouthwatering dishes which are carefully prepared using only the finest locally-sourced fish, meats, fruit and vegetables. On the evening we visited, the menu included 'fresh fillet of Whitby turbot on a bed of saffron noodles in a creamed chive sauce' and 'breast of duckling roasted pink in a natural sauce with oranges, Cointreau and a passion fruit tartlet'. Meals can be complemented by a bottle from the carefully chosen wine list and finished with a wonderful dessert such as Ray's famous 'Sportsman's summer pudding' which has been a perennial favourite since he first opened the restaurant in 1979.

Not far from this particular area, Ray Carter's brother Charles runs the exclusive **Carters Knox Manor Restaurant** which is situated at **Low Laithe** on the B6165 Pateley Bridge to Harrogate road. Surrounded by beautiful Nidderdale countryside, the restaurant building was constructed around 1750 as Knox Mill, a flax mill which operated until the early years of this century. Today, this handsome structure has been transformed into unique eating place where diners can enjoy a top quality light meal, lunch or full dinner. The menu offers an imaginative range of starters, fish dishes, main courses and puddings, all made from fresh local produce wherever possible. (Each day, there is a delivery of fresh fish from Whitby Market.) There is also a first class wine list and excellent facilities for catering for private functions such as wedding receptions and special parties. The restaurant is open at lunchtime and in the evening, seven days a week and also offers a top quality outside catering service.

Carters Knox Manor

When we visited in late 1992, we heard of Charles Carter's plans to offer guest accommodation at Knox Mill. Please telephone the restaurant for further information.

One interesting curiosity of the area is the **Brimham Rocks**, some three miles from the town. These strange rock formations rise to heights of over 20 feet above the open moorland, almost like some giant sculptor has left them in order to work on them at some later date. The huge outcrops of dark millstone grit were carved out millions of years ago by glacial action, and were given fanciful names by Victorian visitors, such as Dancing Bear, Oyster Shell and Indian's Turban.

Visitors to this area with a sense of adventure should not miss out on a trip to the **Stump Cross Caverns**, a spectacular cave system discovered in 1853. This labyrinth of limestone caves are richly decorated with stalactites and stalagmites, with landscaped paths for public access. The formations have such names as "Sleeping Cat", "Hawk", "Wedding Cake" and the "Sentinel", a stalagmite some nine and a half feet high. Only the upper level is available to tourists, the lower levels being the more hazardous domain of the potholers, nicknamed "Hell", due to the conditions down there. Researchers still have not entirely charted the extent of the system, and the visitor centre keeps an up to date record of all the latest finds. Lovers of pre-history will be fascinated by the wolverine cave, where the bones of bison, reindeer, wolves and wolverines were discovered.

A drive further west will bring you to **Grassington**, known as the capital of Upper Wharfedale. In many ways this is a typical dales village, with the ubiquitous market square. It is rooted in Celtic history and was mentioned in the Domesday book, later being a centre for the lead-mining industry.

Grassington is also the economic centre of Wharfedale, with the greatest concentration of shops, hotels, industrial complexes, business centres and supermarkets in the area.

The Foresters Arms is a delightful former coaching inn which stands in an attractive roadside position in the heart of historic Grassington. This is an establishment which has just about everything; fine hand-drawn ales, delicious home-cooked bar meals (on the day we visited, the menu included giant Yorkshire Pudding filled with steak and mushrooms), a relaxed atmosphere and a number of spacious letting bedrooms. These are all well-appointed and equipped with hot and cold washbasins and tea/coffee-making facilities. Proprietor Mrs Richardson is a wonderful host who over the years has made the Foresters into an ideal base for touring the surrounding area.

The Foresters Arms

The impressive **Devonshire Hotel** stands in a wonderful position alongside the cobbled square in Grassington's main street. This handsome old stone-built inn dates from the 18th-century and was once a regular stopping place on the busy cross-Dales coaching route. In recent years, the building has undergone a programme of careful renovation to bring it up to the standard of a first class modern hotel whilst still retaining its original character and atmosphere. The bar has a beamed ceiling and an open fire, and serves a fine selection of traditional cask-conditioned ales. An excellent selection of meals is served both here and in the hotel's splendid restaurant. On the evening we visited, the range of dishes on offer included the starters 'ham paté with strawberry marmalade' and 'scallops grilled with Gruyere cheese', and the main courses 'pan fried monkfish with courgette and truffle' and 'mignons of beef with wholegrain mustard sauce'.

Devonshire Hotel

The menu also featured delicious char-gilled steaks, a choice of maginative vegetarian dishes and a number of less elaborate bar snacks. The guest bedrooms at the Devonshire Hotel are all spacious, tastefully urnished and equipped with with en suite bathrooms with showers, colour elevisions and tea/coffee making facilities. The rooms at the front look out over Grassington's cobbled square and the 'Littondale' room features a handcrafted four-poster bed. There is also an attractive function suite for special celebrations, details of which can be obtained from the general nanager, Anne House.

Nearby, we also found the impressive **Grassington House Hotel**, a handsome early 18th-century residence which today is listed as a building of special architectural interest. Grassington House is owned and personally un by Gordon and Linda Elsworth, two fine hosts who have successfully created an atmosphere which is truly relaxed and welcoming. The hotel has eleven elegant guest bedrooms, all equipped with en-suite facilities, elevisions and beverage making facilities. Top quality light meals are available in the bar, and an impressive table d'hôte menu is served in the hotel's splendid Georgian restaurant.

Grassington House Hotel

Looking for refreshment in the centre of town, we found the truly delightful **Lucy Fold Tearooms**. This impressive black-and-white painted establishment stands opposite the Black Horse Hotel, a short distance to the north of the village square. Proprietor John Cross provides his customers with delicious morning coffees, light lunches, afternoon and high teas. Among the range of mouthwatering items on offer are home-baked cakes and pastries, sandwiches, salads and jacket potatoes. As well as the more usual Earl Grey and Darjeeling, John offers a first-class range of specialist teas including passion fruit, lemon and orange, and camomile.

Open daily except Mondays, March to November (though open Bank Holidays). Also closed Tuesdays, December to February.

Lucy Fold Tearooms

On the northern edge of Grassington, we made a point of calling in a the fascinating workshops and showroom which are the home of **Kent Traditional Furniture**. Since moving here in 1986, the firm has won a rural development award for the refurbishment of their premises which stand in a superb position overlooking Grassington and the Wharfdale valley. Founders Janet and Paul Kent and a dozen skilled craftspeople currently produce a range of traditional hand-crafted solid oak furniture which is shipped to all parts of the country.

Kent Traditional Furniture

Each piece is made from carefully selected fully-seasoned oak and carries the firm's famous signature, a hand-carved White Rose which is discreetly added as a final seal of approval. Visitors interested in finding out more about traditional methods of furniture making are welcome to call in at the Moor Lane showrooms which are open seven days a week. Open days are also organised which include tours of the workshops, and inspection of the beautiful finished pieces of furniture.

The **Fell Hotel** stands in a wonderful elevated position overlooking the village of Burnsall, three miles downriver, with its picturesque bridge over the River Wharfe. It can be found three miles southeast of Threshfield, just off the B6160 Upper Wharfedale road. Originally constructed as a private residence for a wealthy 19th-century landowner, this splendid establishment is privately run by proprietors Jim and Jean Cobbett. The hotel has recently been comprehensively refurbished and now offers thirteen en-suite bedrooms all of which have colour televisions, beverage making facilities and magnificent views across the fells. There are two lounges; one overlooking the river, the other with an open fire, bars serving traditional hand-pulled ales and offering an extensive bar menu lunch times and evenings, a spacious restaurant offering first-class table d'hote and a la carte cuisine, much of which is prepared from locally-produced ingredients.

The Fell Hotel

The countryside around the town is lush and verdant, with cultivated fields that sweep up the valleys' sides, and such places as the Queen's View, Kilnsey Crag and Trollers Gill near Appletreewick are well within reach. A little further on, downriver from lovely Burnsall, is the stately ruin of

Bolton Abbey

Barden Tower, another residence of Lord Henry Clifford, owner of Skipton Castle. It was built in the 15th century, but allowed to fall into rack and ruin until the famous Lady Anne Clifford undertook its repair in 1657. Nearby is the attractive Barden Bridge, a 17th century arch, now designated as an ancient monument.

If you are looking for an excellent bed and breakfast establishment in this location, you could do no better than **Howgill Lodge Barn**, at **Barden**. Situated just off the B6160 between Bolton Bridge and Grassington, it may be advisable to telephone the owners, Ann and Bernard Foster (0756) 720655, for directions. The accommodation is located in a converted 17th-century barn which was completely renovated by Bernard and a team of willing helpers in 1986. Today, not only do the guest rooms enjoy panoramic views, but they are also equipped with ensuite facilities, colour televisions and tea/coffee making facilities. Ann and Bernard are North Yorkshire born and bred, and as well as excellent accommodation, they offer their guests superb local hospitality.

Howgill Lodge Barn

Further on downriver, the wide river bed suddenly narrows into a confined channel of black rocks, where its waters thunder through in a white frothing rage that are exhilarating to the senses. This is known as **the Strid**, so-called because heroic types down the ages have attempted to leap its width as a test of bravery (or foolhardiness). Some way on, the spectral ruins of **Bolton Abbey** come into view. This was, in fact a 12th century Priory, sister to Fountains, accessible through "The Hole in the Wall". Its sad, graceful arches make the perfect subject for atmospheric photographs, and a wonderful backdrop to the many diversions the nearby river has to offer.

The peaceful village of **Appletreewick** is overlooked by the craggy expanse of Simon's Seat, while Burnsall Fell rises beyond to some 1661 feet. Its single street, situated on the side of the hill appears as if to be sliding down towards the valley bottom. The lead mines on the northern slopes were the property of the monks of Bolton Abbey. This was also the home of William Craven, almost legendary Lord Mayor of London, who returned to spend much of his amassed wealth on improvements and additions to the town's fine old buildings. The cottage where he was born was largely furnished by the similarly legendary Bob Thompson of Kilburn.

Near the village, in a splendid position overlooking the River Wharfe on the edge of Pockstones Moor we found the **New Inn**, a 300 year-old hostelry which is run by beer expert, John Pitchers. As well as a choice of traditional draught ales, John offers his customers a huge selection of bottled beers from around the world. He currently holds the title 'William Younger Grand Master', and his inn was named the CAMRA 'Pub of the Season' in Autumn '87 and Spring '90. He also provides a good range of wholesome bar meals and has four comfortable letting rooms available all year round.

One curious and eerie story of the area, concerns a young motor-cyclist who was travelling the country roads, and was later to be seen over-

The New Inn

taking a lady motorist in a state of panic on the outskirts of the town. Concerned, the lady questioned the young man, who told her that he had been pursued down the lanes from the hamlet of **Skyreholme**, a short way back, by a huge fearsome dog which he had been unable to lose, until it had disappeared down a side lane. The villagers added further mystery to the tale by informing the young man that no such lane had existed at the point he had described for over a hundred years. What they decided not to tell the distressed youth, was that the Skyreholme area is reputed t be haunted by Barguest, a spectral hound of legend - an encounter with this beast is usually held to be a precursor to death. So take care - should one hear an eerie baying or the padding of huge paws on the road whilst taking a quiet picnic in this lovely area, you might be advised to beat a hasty retreat!

Half a mile along the B6160 to the north of Threshfield, we noticed a sign to **Long Ashes Inn and Park** and turned off onto a winding road which led to an attractive woodland estate. At the end, we discovered an unexpected hidden gem, an excellent inn and eating place, managed by Yvonne Smith,situated conveniently near to a leisure centre and caravan park. The Inn has recently been beautifully refurbished, and provides first class ale, food and a pool table. There is also an excellent function room adjacent which caters for up to 70, and besides weddings and other functions, can be used by visiting coach parties.

Mrs Smith ensures her visitors receive a warm welcome, and we can heartily recommend a trip to this excellent establishment whilst in the area. The Inn is open all year round.

Long Ashes Inn

The lovely Upper Wharfedale village of **Kettlewell**, travelling north of Grassington, provides an ideal base for exploring the dramatic beauty of the Dales whether by car or on foot. It lies five miles north of Grassington on the B6160 Wharfedale road midway between Skipton and Wensleydale. Those looking for a self-catering holiday cottage or for superb farmhouse bed and breakfast accommodation in this wonderful part of the country should make a point of finding **Fold Farm** on the eastern edge of the village. (For accurate directions, telephone the owners Barbara and Clifford Lambert (0756) 760886.) Fold Farm is a typical Dales hill sheep farm covering 350 acres of unspoilt upland to the south of Kettlewell Beck. The Lamberts have converted some of the farm's original stone-built outbuildings into five superbly equipped holiday cottages which sleep from two to seven people and which are now English Tourist Board four key commended. All the cottages have beamed ceilings and open fires (coal and logs can be purchased at the farm), as well as a range of up-to-date equipment which is truly impressive. The modern kitchens are fully fitted and equipped with top quality appliances including a washing machine and (except for the smallest cottage) a dishwasher. The sitting areas all have colour televisions and carefully chosen furnishings, and the bathroom facilities are similarly well-appointed.

Mrs Barbara Lambert also offers delightful bed and breakfast accommodation at the main farmhouse. This unique residence is believed to be a late medieval timber-framed 'open hall' and is thus one of the most important houses in Upper Wharfedale. Parts of the building date back to

Fold Farm

the 15th-century, in particular the enormous oak structure which comprises the main hall. There is evidence to show that this was encased in stone in the 17th-century, and then was subsequently refenestrated in the 19th-century. The modern interior is full of ancient character with exposed stone walls, original timber beams and stone-mullioned windows. There is also a unusual spiral stone staircase which leads to the beautifully decorated letting bedrooms on the first floor. The wonderful historic atmosphere of the house coupled with the Lamberts' excellent hospitality makes this a very special place to stay. Fold Farm is open all year round and offers a range of special off-season breaks.

We carried on up the B6160 into the heart of Upper Wharfedale until we reached the small Dales village of **Buckden**. In a dramatic position facing the village green with the 2,300-foot Buckden Pike as a backdrop, we found the **Buck Inn**, an impressive Georgian coaching inn which is renowned for its good food and accommodation.

The present owners, the Hayton family, have done much to enhance the inn's original interior in recent years. The bar has a genuine traditional atmosphere, and a fine residents' restaurant has been created in the courtyard where local wool auctions were once held. The inn also offers fifteen beautifully-decorated bedrooms which are all equipped with en-suite facilities, colour televisions and direct-dial telephones.

Buck Inn

If you are looking for bed and breakfast accommodation in what must be one of the most central locations in the Dales National Park, try **Low Raisgill Cottage** near **Hubberholme**. This beautifully restored 16th-century cottage is situated in the tiny hamlet of Raisgill and can be reached by turning west off the B6160 Upper Wharfedale road after Buckden and taking the minor road towards Hawes. (For accurate directions, telephone the owner, Mrs Middleton (0756) 760351.) Inside, the cottage is full of wonderful character; the bedrooms are all beautifully appointed and equipped with private bath and beverage making facilities. Set within the breathtaking landscape of Langstrothdale, this truly is an ideal place for walkers and touring visitors. Vegetarians welcome.

Low Raisgill Cottage

Following the sign at Buckden for Hubberholme off the B6160, you will find **Grange Farm** where you will find two forms of accommodation. Your friendly hostess Mrs Falshaw provides an excellent bed and breakfast service within her homely farmhouse, where the rooms are cosy and welcoming and a hearty breakfast will set you up for the day. Outside, the converted stables and coach-house form a bunkhouse barn which sleeps up to 18 people and provides full self-catering facilities including bedrooms, a drying room, central heating, kitchen, dining and recreation room on the first floor and showers, washrooms and toilets downstairs. Ideal for large parties or several families.

Six miles west of Grassington, lies the area of geological interest known as **Malham**. I can fondly remember field trips to the place when I was a schoolgirl, and the thrill of ascending the steep mountainous path to the awesome view from the limestone pavement on top, not one for the faint-hearted!

There is much spectacular scenery in this area, as the many sightseers who come here will testify. A trip to Malham can transport one to an older age. There are old mine workings below Pike Daw Hill and Langscar Gate, under which run a complex system of tunnels and caverns , indicated by the remains of a lonely smelt mill. At Langscar are also the traces of an important Iron Age settlement , In fact, should one have a vivid imagina-

Malham Cove

tion, it is not too hard to view the place as these early settlers saw it. The lynchets, or cultivation terraces of these early settlers are still to be seen flanking the hillsides of Malham Beck, adding further to the primitive feel of the place, their drystone walls indicating a primitive husbandry long since gone.

But it is the ancient glacial grandeur of Malham Cove itself that gives the greatest feeling of the past. One can almost imagine the mammoth and bison that must have grazed its slopes once, the caves of its limestone cliff occupied by cave-bears and mountain lions. The limestone outcroppings and scree could almost be the remains of their bones, standing out starkly from the tough grass that flanks the huge escarpment.

The way to the Cove is approached from the Langcliffe road beyond the last buildings of Malham village, down a path alongside the beck that leads through a scattering of trees; as one walks on through these, the 300 foot limestone amphitheatre emerges into view in the most dramatic fashion. This is the most spectacular section of the Mid-Craven fault, and as recently as the 1700's, a massive waterfall cascaded over its edge, higher than Niagara Falls! Sadly these days, the water disappears through potholes at the top called water-sinks, and reappear through a cavern mouth at Aire Head near the village. A steep path leads to the limestone pavement at the top, with its distinctive 'clints' and 'grykes', where water has carved a distinctive natural sculpture through the weaknesses in the limestone.

From here it is not too far to reach the equally inspiring **Gordale Scar**, a huge gorge carved by glacial melt water. An impressive waterfall leaps in two stages from a fissure in its face. Further on is another waterfall known as Janet's Foss, beside which is a cave which Janet, a friendly fairy is reputed to inhabit!

Three miles north of the scar, is Malham Tarn, a glacial lake, possibly best viewed in the winter to truly get that feel of prehistoric Ice Age grandeur. Not far from here is Malham Tarn House, where such famous names as Ruskin, Darwin and Charles Kingsley (Author of 'The Water Babies') received inspiration.

Two miles south of Malham village, is the wooded ecclesiastical town of **Kirkby Malham**, with its ancient church and Norman font. The register here bears the signature of Oliver Cromwell, when he witnessed a wedding here. The church was possibly also used as a garrison by his forces during the Civil War.

An exceptional place to stay if stopping off here is Holgate Head. (The house lies on the eastern side of the road between the A65 and Malham.)

This fine establishment is a member of the Wolsey Lodge group of private country homes which offer top quality accommodation and hospitality to paying guests. Holgate Head is a handsome stone-built residence set within 3 acres of garden, paddocks and woodland. Inside, there are many interesting features including superb 17th century oak panelling and a wonderful stone fireplace in the hall/sitting room. An impressive staircase leads to the three guest rooms which are all beautifully appointed and equipped with en-suite facilities.

Holgate Head

If you happen to be looking for self-catering holiday accommodation in this area, we can recommend **Scalegill**, a renovated water mill which is situated a short distance from the source of the River Aire in the heart of beautiful Malhamdale.

Scalegill

This impressive conversion stands at the end of a sweeping half-mile driveway and can be reached from the Kirkby Malham to Hanlith road. A mill on this site was recorded in the Domesday Book and it was subsequently owned by the monks of Fountains Abbey who used the water power to grind their corn. Today, Scalegill offers three cottages and four apartments, all individually decorated and equipped with the full range of modern facilities. Open all year round.

Aireton, or Aire Town, based as it is on the idyllic River Aire, is a lovely village built mainly by Quakers, dating from 1700.

In this idyllic location, we found **Lindon House**, a delightful seven-bedroomed guesthouse which has recently been converted from an old stone-built barn. This fine establishment lies in Aireton, and can be reached by turning north off the A65 midway between Skipton and Settle. The bedrooms all have hot and cold washbasins, shaver points and beverage making facilities, and downstairs, there is a spacious residents' lounge with exposed beams and a colour television.

Lindon House

Proprietor Joan Robinson provides her guests with the warmest hospitality, a delicious Dales breakfast and an optional evening meal which is personally prepared by her son Ian (a trained chef) using local ingredients wherever possible.

Not far to the west of Aireton, is the tree-sheltered village of **Long Preston**, with its maypole around which traditional dances take place each Spring.

It might not, therefore, be surprising to know that the village boasts an inn called the **Maypole Inn**, a fine pub and eating house which was named 'Pub of the Season' in 1988 and 1992 by CAMRA's local district. The Maypole dates from the 17th-century and despite being added to over the years, still retains much its original character with an open fire in the bar and an interesting list of landlords dating from 1695 to the present. Proprietors Robert and Elspeth Palmer have built up a reputation for superb pub food; portions are generous and the choice of dishes (including vegetarian and children's meals) is truly excellent. There are also six letting bedrooms available which at the time we visited were being fitted with en-suite facilities.

The Maypole Inn

In 1991, Tony and Di Hague acquired **The Riddings**, a small country manor and estate, and subsequently turned it into a truly superb country guest house. The house stands at the end of a half mile long driveway in a magnificent elevated position overlooking the Ribble Valley and can be reached by turning north off the A65 just to the northwest of Long Preston. The building is now Grade II listed and is believed to have been built around 1708. Many of its original features remain including ornate internal plasterwork, delicate mosaic, parquet floors and even a servants' call system. The main south-facing reception rooms (now the guests' lounge and dining room) have French doors opening onto delightful formal gardens from where outstanding views over the Ribble valley can be enjoyed. Tony and Di have carefully modernised the house so as to retain its unique character and atmosphere. The bedrooms all have private washing facilities, colour televisions and beverage making facilities, as well as superb views over the surrounding countryside. Two of the bedrooms also have either a bath or shower en-suite. In one of these, the facilities are hidden behind what appears to be solid oak fitted bedroom units; when guests open what looks like the wardrobe, they walk through into a lovely en-suite area.

An unusual feature of The Riddings is that guests dine together at one enormous table, an idea which works surprisingly well and adds to the informal atmosphere of the establishment.

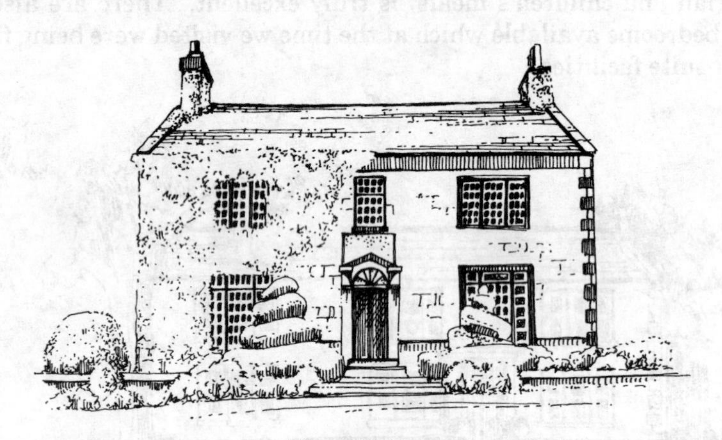

The Riddings

Tony and Di specialise in good English cooking and offer their guests generous breakfasts and four-course table d'hôte dinners in the most genial of surroundings. On the day we visited, the menu included leek and potato soup, beef in ale and lemon meringue pie followed by cheese and biscuits. After dinner, guests are welcome to take a stroll in the wonderful ten-and-a-half acre grounds. These contain a huge variety of specimen trees and shrubs, ornamental ponds, a charming stone summerhouse and an area of designated wildlife gardens. In addition, there is the attractive formal garden, a walled kitchen garden and a delightful walk through a bluebell wood which contains a series of small waterfalls. The Riddings is ideal for those looking for a luxurious base from which to explore the many delights of the surrounding North Yorkshire countryside.

Also if stopping in this lovely hidden place, one might make a point of calling in at the traditional country inn, the **Boar's Head Hotel**, which is owned and run by the Greenwood family. This impressive establishment began life as a stable block in the early 18th-century and today, it still retains much of its original character and charm. Inside, there are two splendid Victorian bars offering first-class traditional ales and a range of appetising bar meals. Excellent table d'hôte and á la carte menus are also served in the adjacent Kestrel Room restaurant. The Greenwoods also have three comfortable letting bedrooms available, all equipped with en-suite bathrooms, colour televisions and beverage making facilities. Open all year. Children welcome.

Boar's Head Hotel

All along the road here as one nears the Dales town of **Settle**, runs the famous **Settle - Carlisle Railway**, a proudly preserved memento of the glorious age of steam, the line flanked by charming little signal boxes and stations that are a real tourist magnet. This attractive railway was, however, built in the midst of great controversy and even greater cost in both money and lives, earning it the dubious title of "the line that should never have been built". There is a churchyard at St Leonard's in Chapel-le-Dale where over 100 of the workers and miners, who were forced to labour under the most adverse of conditions, lie buried. Today, the trains still thunder through the 21 viaducts, 14 tunnels and numerous bridges they gave their lives for.

The town itself is dominated by one of these huge viaducts, as well as the Castleberg cliff, and is truly worth spending some time in.

Walk along Duke Street and pop into the Naked Man Cafe (so-called due to a relief on the wall of a naked man holding a date plaque to preserve his modesty!) for a cup of tea and a Fat Rascal cake - too many of these and that's just what you'll end up as! There is another tearoom further down named after the famous item of confectionery. Two miles away in Langcliffe is presumably the Naked Man's spouse, the Naked Woman.

Settle's architecture is very distinctive, in the main being Victorian sandstone buildings that all look as if they are born of the railway culture Buildings of note include the arcaded Shambles, originally butcher's slaughter houses, the french-style Town Hall, the Victorian Music Hall, and the oldest building, Preston's Folly, described as an extravaganza of mullioned windows and Tudor masonry, and so-called because the man who created this anomalous fancy impoverished himself in the process! Apart from the grander structures on the main streets, there are charming little side streets with Georgian and Jacobean cottages criss-crossed with quirky little alleyways and ginnels and hidden courtyards and workshops of a time gone by.

In Chapel Street is the **Museum of North Craven Life**, giving us a historical, topographical and geological background of the area.

The features of the surrounding countryside are interesting to say the least - the fascinating **Victoria Cave** has yielded finds of Roman relics, Stone Age artifacts and even 120,000 year old mammoth bones. Other places of interest include the erratic Ebbing and Flowing Well, the very lovely Catrigg Force near Stainforth, numerous unusual geological features and caves (including the grimly titled Dead Man's Cave) and the fascinating Celtic Wall, a defensive structure probably constructed by a local Celtic tribe to help deter invaders.

Wonderful scenery, two National parks and a host of places steeped in history - these are all part of a Yorkshire holiday. Now a new attraction has been added, bringing the work of Dales craftsmen into one centre at **Watershed Mill** in Settle.

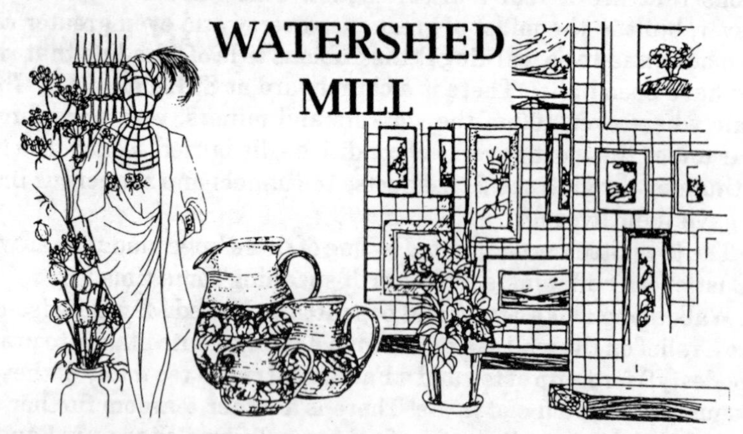

On the banks of the River Ribble, this 1820's cotton mill has been converted by owners Lynne Ridgway and David Wilkinson into the

Dalesmade Centre, a prestigious retail showcase devoted entirely to products made in the Dales, and winner of the 1992 White Rose Award for 'The best newcomer to Tourism'.

Past an imposing entrance with the Centre's logo depicted in glowing coloured glass, the retail space is artistically arranged around a fountain bubbling over pebbles from the nearby riverbank. The displays are sitedto lead the eye from one area to the next with lush plants and natural wood adding to the atmosphere.

Products range from paintings and prints to designer knitwear, jams to jewellery and greetings cards to oak dressers, offering a wide choice of gifts for friends and family or an item of lasting value for your home.

Craft demonstrations are an added feature, with regular exhibitions showing the skills needed to create many of the products on display. During the spring and summer months events are held including Craft Demonstrations, Farm Week, Wool Week, Art Activity Week and Charity Week all part of the unique attractions of Watershed Mill.

In addition to the shopping section there is an Arts Activity Area, originally designed for children, who can dabble with paints and clay and let their imaginations run riot while the family can browse at leisure.

Finally there is Hector's Restaurant, named after the original mill owner. Here the flowery tables and leafy murals reflect the conservatory ambience, and you will find delicious home cooked food and a varied selection of coffees, teas and fruit infusions. Yorkshire specials are the highlights of the week.

There is ample free parking for cars and coaches and easy level access for disabled people. Information on events and workshops during your holiday is available from the helpful staff on 0729 825111.

Open daily (except Mondays October/March, Christmas and Boxing Day and last week in January).

Nearby **Giggleswick** sports several interesting places, including the 15th century church of St Alkelda and the well-known Giggleswick Public School with an observatory that was used by the Astronomer Royal in 1927 to observe an eclipse of the Sun. The green-domed school chapel is a conspicuous landmark, well worth a photograph or two. From Giggleswick Scar, the views across the Ribble Valley to the distinctive promontory of Pen-Y-Ghent are truly awe-inspiring. Here is truly a place to get away from it all, unpopulated and undisturbed for thousands of years, save perhaps, one might fancy, by the spectre of our good friend Mr A. Wainwright, on one of his legendary walks, or one of his pilgrim-like devotees perhaps!

This ancient village once stood on the old coaching road between

West Yorkshire and the Lakes. In 1663, the **Black Horse Hotel** was established on a site adjacent to the historic church behind the market cross and soon became a regular stopping place on this busy cross-Pennine route. Although today, the streets no longer resound to the thunder of heavy horses, the Black Horse still maintains the tradition of welcoming both travellers and locals alike. Owners Peter and Doreen Starkey provide their customers with the very best in imaginative home-cooked food and hand-pulled beers (Peter has won awards for his cellar-keeping). They also have three spacious en-suite guest rooms available which are comfortable and beautifully appointed.

Black Horse Hotel

In a wonderful position at the highest point in the village, stands the **Woodlands Country House Hotel**, a splendid establishment which caters exclusively for vegetarian and non-smoking guests.

Woodlands Country House Hotel

This fine Edwardian residence is situated on the northern side of the old A65 and is set within attractive wooded grounds with magnificent views over the surrounding Ribblesdale countryside. Inside, the atmosphere is spacious and comfortable; the ten guest bedrooms are appointed to a high modern standard with most having en-suite bathrooms, televisions and radios. (One also has a four-poster bed.) Owners Margaret and Martin Lewton and their staff provide their guests with first-rate hospitality and the finest vegetarian cuisine. They are also pleased to cater for vegan and special diets.

Margaret and John Cowperthwaite provide first-rate farmhouse bed and breakfast accommodation at their 100-acre working sheep and cattle farm, **Accerhill Hall**, which is situated a short distance to the west of Giggleswick village. It can be reached by taking the Lawkland/Eldroth exit off the A65 Settle bypass (for more accurate directions, telephone the owners on 0729 823152).

Accerhill Hall

The farmhouse dates from the 17th-century and inside retains much of its original character and charm. The three comfortable letting bedrooms (two family, one single) are all tastefully decorated and equipped to a good modern standard. What is perhaps most special about Accerhill Hall, however, is its spectacular views over Ingleborough, Pen-y-ghent and the dramatic countryside of the southern Dales.

Two miles north of Settle, the B6479 Ribblesdale road reaches the delightful village of **Stainforth**. Look out here for the stone packhorse bridge which is said to have been built by the monks of Sawley Abbey in the 14th-century. Standing adjacent to the bridge we found the **Craven Heifer Hotel**, which is run by Christina Tillotson and her sister Belinda

Nixon. Built over 200 years ago as a stopping place for packhorse traffic between North Lancashire and the Northeast of England, this charming establishment offers good food and traditional ales in a relaxed and intimate atmosphere. There are also three comfortable letting bedrooms available, all equipped with colour televisions, hot and cold washbasins and tea making facilities.

The Craven Heifer

The hidden village of **Feizor** lies three and a half miles northwest of Settle and only two thirds of a mile from the main A65. A Cistercian monastery was founded here in the 12th-century, although today it is home for only thirty permanent residents. Nearby, **Scar Close Farm** offers farmhouse bed and breakfast accommodation with wonderful views of the southern Dales. This 185-acre working farm has three spacious letting bedrooms located in a converted barn which was completely rebuilt in 1985. All rooms have private facilities and are appointed to a first-rate modern standard.

Scar Close Farm

There is also a large guest lounge and a dining room where Mrs Sheila Knowles serves delicious farmhouse breakfasts. The accommodation is open all year round and is English Tourist Board three-crown commended. This other-age atmosphere pervades all of one's journeys around this region, as one travels the roads to **Ingleton**, 12 miles or so to the north-west.

Austwick, which is on the way, is an ancient place of stone cottages and crofts, dry-stone walls, abandoned quarries and patchwork hills. Its name originally meant "Eastern Settlement", as it was known to the Nordic settlers who made it their home.

The largely 17th century buildings, with their elaborately decorated stone lintels, flank what remains of the village green, where the ancient cross stands as a reminder of when this was the head of a dozen neighbouring manors. The most peculiar feature of the area has to be the **Norber Erratics**, eerie black boulders which stand on limestone pedestals, which despite their contrived appearance, are in fact a completely natural feature. They are known as "erratics" because they are anomalous - the grey silurian slate they are composed of usually occurs beneath limestone rather than on top of it. The mystery of their existence is explained by the fact that these huge rocks were originally deposited by glacial action at the end of the last Ice Age.

Another distinctive feature are the Clapper Bridges, medieval structures made from large slabs of rock that span the becks hereabouts, with such eccentric titles as 'Pant', 'Flascoe' and "Wash Dubs'.

Austwick is also the home of the renowned country house hotel, **The Traddock**. This impressive Georgian country house is set within spacious landscaped grounds and is owned by resident proprietors Frances and

The Traddock

Richard Michaelis. In recent years, they have carefully modernised the hotel to bring it up to a luxurious standard whilst still retaining its elegant historic character. The Traddock's twelve guest rooms have wonderful views over the surrounding countryside; most have en-suite facilities and all have colour televisions, direct-dial telephones and beverage making facilities. The magnificent oak-beamed restaurant serves an excellent table d'hôte menu and a carefully-selected range of fine wines.

On this southwestern fringe of the Dales National Park, we visited the village of **Clapham**, a community which for many centuries has been a stopping place for travellers en route between West Yorkshire and the Lake District. Standing on the old A65 midway between Settle and Ingleton, the village has a great deal to offer the visitor including access to the three peaks circular walk and to Clapham's famous Ingleborough Cave, a spectacular show-cave which forms part of the Gaping Gill underground river system. Situated in the centre of the village, the **New Inn Hotel** has been providing hospitality for travellers and locals for over 200 years. This impressive free house and hotel is run by resident proprietors Keith and Barbara Mannion, two charming hosts who take great pride in providing their customers with the very best in food, drink and accommodation. There are two bars at the New Inn, both with open fires and a cosy traditional atmosphere. Here, customers can enjoy a pint of hand-pulled ale or choose from the excellent range of bar meals which are served every lunchtime and evening.

New Inn Hotel

There is also a first-class restaurant for those wanting a choice of more elaborate dishes. Keith and Barbara have thirteen comfortable letting bedrooms available, all equipped with en-suite bathrooms, colour televisions and tea and coffee making facilities. The New Inn is English Tourist Board three-crown commended and provides an ideal base for exploring the many attractions of the surrounding area. Children welcome.

Lying between the Dales National Park and the Forest of Bowman, the **Flying Horseshoe Hotel** opposite **Clapham** railway station provides an excellent base for exploring this dramatic part of the country. The hotel is set within three acres of attractive grounds and can be found a mile and a half southwest of the A65.

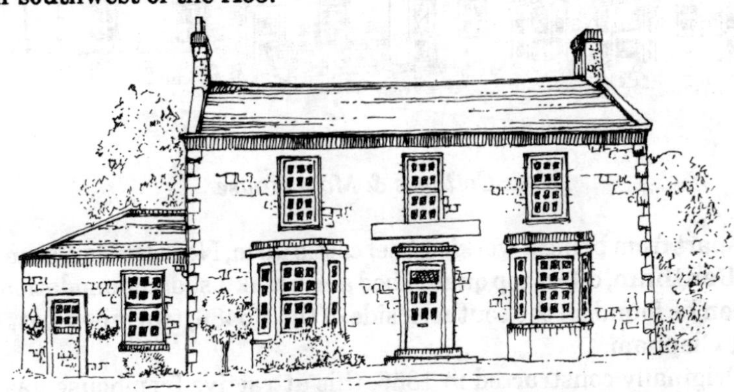

Flying Horseshoe Hotel

Originally constructed in 1845 as a resting place for rail travellers who alighted here before continuing their journey by carriage, today, it is owned and run by Helen and Tony Harris and family, who pride themselves in providing good food, drink and accommodation for customers of all ages (families with children are particularly welcome). Also available are a number self-catering holiday apartments and pitches for fifteen touring caravans and six tents.

At Clapham Village, turning south off the A65 Settle to Kirkby Lonsdale road, one will find the self-catering holiday cottages and residential centre for staff/management training which are situated at **Moss Farm** in the scattered village of **Keasden**. This small farmhouse development lies approximately one mile south of the River Wenning and Clapham railway station and has wonderful views of Ingleborough and Pen-y-Ghent.

Here, there are three beautifully appointed holiday cottages sleeping from six to eight people which are all equipped to the highest modern standards. Moss Farm also doubles as a fully equipped seminar and conference centre which is ideal for training groups of twenty to thirty people in an atmosphere which is secluded, undistracting and supportive.

Moss Cottages & Moss House

Apart from being a working beef cattle farm, **New Butts Farm**, near **High Bentham**, offers top quality bed and breakfast accommodation. The farm can be found on the southern side of the B6480, two miles west of the A65 at Clapham.

Originally constructed in 1856, this attractive farmhouse has magnificent views over Ingleborough and the southwestern fringe of the Dales National Park. Inside, there are six letting bedrooms, all spacious, comfor-

New Butts Farm

-table and equipped with good modern amenities. Some also have en-suite facilities and most have lovely views over the wonderful surrounding countryside. Proprietor Jean Newhouse provides her guests with the finest hospitality and a generous Yorkshire breakfast. She is also happy to provide evening meals by prior arrangement.

Situated approximately one mile south of **Ingleton**, and half a mile from the A65 Settle to Kendal road, we made a point of finding **The Barnstead** at **Stacksteads Farm**. The Barnstead is a building which has been converted from an existing stone-built Dales barn where bunk-style self-catering accommodation is provided for individuals, families and groups. This accommodation is particularly suitable for ramblers, pot-holers, school parties and study groups who come to explore the many local geological and historical places of interest. On the ground floor, there are four rooms which together contain sleeping accommodation for 22 people, as well as a drying room, two showers, washbasins and toilet facilities. On the first floor, there is a large fitted kitchen with cookers, fridge and cooking utensils, a spacious dining and sitting area, and further showers and toilet facilities. The whole of the property is centrally heated and has good access for the disabled. The proprietors, Jim and Mona Charlton, are former publicans who are used to providing warm and friendly hospitality.

The Barnstead, Stacksteads Farm

Originally constructed in 1856, this attractive farmhouse has magnificent views over Ingleborough and the southwestern fringe of the Dales National Park. Inside, there are six letting bedrooms, all spacious, comfortable and equipped with good modern amenities. Some also have en-suite facilities and most have lovely views over the wonderful surrounding countryside. Proprietor Jean Newhouse provides her guests with the finest hospitality and a generous Yorkshire breakfast. She is also happy to provide evening meals by prior arrangement. They also provide bed and breakfast accommodation at their farmhouse, parts of which date back to the 17th-century. They have three bedrooms available (two doubles with en-suite facilities and one twin), and provide good quality evening meals by arrangement. Being situated within one of the most beautiful limestone landscapes in England, Stacksteads Farm provides an ideal base for fell walking or for exploring the many outstanding features which lie within the surrounding area.

This is the area covered by the **Three Peaks Project**, the three peaks being **Whernside, Ingleborough** and **Pen-Y-Ghent** (736, 732 and 694 metres high respectively) It has been designated an area of Special Scientific Interest, mainly due to the need to conserve the swiftly eroding hillsides and paths.

Pen-Y-Ghent

This is an ancient landscape, well worth the efforts to preserve its relic ash woodlands, primitive earthworks and rare birdlife such as peregrine falcon, ring ouzel and golden plover. There are also a great many caves in the area, which add to the sense of romance and adventure one feels in this place. The title Pen-Y-Ghent means 'Hill of the Winds" and Ingleborough Hill originally meant 'Fire Mountain', the reason being that its flat top was used by the Brigantian tribesmen for their signal beacons.

It was here that they were held under siege by the Roman legions, this being the highest Iron Age fortress in Britain and a coveted vantage point.

One mile west of Ingleton, we stopped in **Thornton-in-Lonsdale**, a charming village which stands on the old Leeds-Kendal turnpike and contains the church where Sir Arthur Conan Doyle was married. Standing opposite the church and the old village whipping post, we found the impressive **Marton Arms Hotel**, a fine old inn which has parts dating back to the 13th-century.

Marton Arms Hotel

Today, it is owned by Colin Elsdon and Tim Hazelden who, through a lot of hard work, have made it into a truly first-class establishment. Over fifty malt whiskies are normally available, along with fifteen cask-conditioned ales (such as Black Magic Mild and Pendle Witches Brew). The food here is also of a high standard; the menu features freshly-cooked pizzas, burgers and salads, along with a selection of children's meals and daily specials on the blackboard. The old stables and hayloft of the former coaching inn have recently been refurbished to create eight attractive letting rooms, all but one of which have en-suite facilities. A beautifully designed restaurant will also be open in time for the 1993 summer season.

Ingleton, the 'Beacon Town' of the Dales, one can imagine being the perfect honeymoon location for all lovers of the Great Outdoors and idyllic waterfalls and grottoes. Wainwright described it as simply 'bewitching'. The tributaries Twiss and Doe fall in a succession of cascades to converge as the lovely River Greta, all surrounded by sylvan glens, a fitting location for any of Tolkien's novels.

The town is dominated by the viaduct that spans the river, with typical dales architecture and a cosy little parish church, built in the squat squarish style so common to these once isolated, hidden places. Whilst here, one should not miss out on a trip down the magnificent Ingleborough Cave, with its maze of underground formations, streams and illuminated pools. There is even a picnic area, should one fancy a subterranean snack! Above ground, the four miles of waterfalls called collectively the Ingleton Falls, and which include Pecca Twin Falls, Holly Bush Spout, Thornton Force, Beezley Upper and Lower Falls and Baxengill Gorge, amongst others, should only be attempted with the aid of a pair of stout walking shoes.

If you are looking to stay in this beautiful location, we can heartily recommend the impressive country house hotel, **Moorgarth Hall**, which is run by resident proprietors Henry and Liz Ibberson.

Built in 1891 by the Greenwood family, this elegant Victorian residence stands within its own extensive wooded grounds and is approached along a sweeping tree-lined driveway. The building has recently been comprehensively refurbished and now offers eight spacious and beautifully appointed guest rooms, all with en-suite facilities, colour televisions and magnificent views over the surrounding landscape. (One also has a four-poster bed.) An excellent table d'hôte dinner is served in the hotel's first-class restaurant (also open to non-residents) and there is an attractive guests' lounge and adjoining bar.

Moorgarth Hall

Travelling back down the A65 towards Skipton, the impressive **Coniston Estate** lies in a beautiful position on the banks of the River Aire and can be found on the northern side of the A65 at **Coniston Cold**, travelling back in the direction of Skipton. Within the grounds of this splendid privately-run estate there is a magnificent twenty-four acre lake stocked with 2 to 14 pound rainbow and brown trout. Visiting fly fisherman can fish here by the day, or if they prefer, they can try for wild brown trout on the nearby two-and-a-half mile stretch of the River Aire. The estate also offers clay pigeon shooting facilities for individuals and groups of all levels of experience. Those preferring their fish and game ready-caught should make a point of calling in at the wonderful estate shop where an unrivalled selection of fish (fresh, frozen and smoked), shellfish, venison and game is always available.

Coniston Estate

Visitors are also invited to call in at the estate's delightful tearoom and restaurant which serves delicious morning coffees, lunches, afternoon and high teas between 10am and 6pm, seven days a week.

Not far from here, the impressive **Dalesway Caravan Park** can be found near the River Aire and the Leeds-Liverpool Canal, a mile from the centre of **Gargrave**. (For accurate directions, telephone the owners Brenda and Derek Shuttleworth on 0756 749592.) This small caravan park is set within two acres of attractive grounds and offers sixteen beautifully appointed static caravans, all equipped with flush toilets, hot and cold running water, colour televisions and fully-equipped kitchen areas. There is no shop or club but instead this peaceful and friendly site offers beautiful surroundings with splendid opportunities for walking, fishing, pony riding or just relaxing. Dalesway has been graded a 'five-tick' British Holiday Park and has been awarded the prestigious Rose Award for first-class caravan holiday homes.

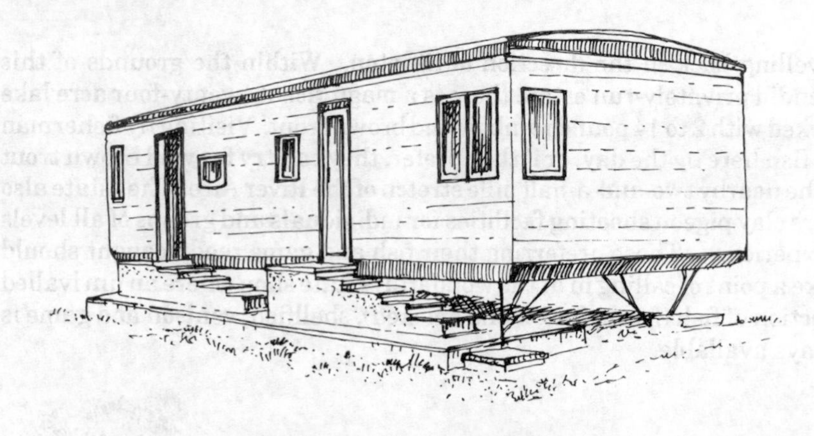

Dalesway Caravan Park

A once-in-a-lifetime trip over the Yorkshire Dales in a hot air balloon is offered by David McCutcheon's enterprising company, **Airborne Adventures**, which is based at **Carleton**, one-and-a-half miles southwest of Skipton. For a surprisingly affordable price, David and his team provide participants of all ages with a three hour adventure which includes a breathtaking hour-long balloon flight over the countryside of northwest Yorkshire (be sure to take a camera). On landing, participants are provided with a champagne reception and a certificate commemorating their flight before being driven back to the starting point. All balloons are inspected annually and issued with certificates of air worthiness, and every trip is piloted by a Civil Aviation Authority certified commercial balloon pilot, so safety is assured.

Airborne Adventures

Midway between Skipton and Earby, is the **Tempest Arms**, a splendid roadside inn, hotel and restaurant which stands on the A56 near the village of **Elslack**, not far from Carleton. Formerly a farmhouse and counthouse, this impressive 200 year-old building is named after the Tempest family who once owned the site and who still live in nearby Broughton Hall. For the last nine years, it has been in the hands of Francis and Joan Boulongne who have done much to improve its attractiveness to both visitors and regulars alike.

The Tempest Arms

First, they constructed the renowned "Bonaparte" restaurant, then in 1990, they added ten first-class letting bedrooms. The stylish oak-beamed restaurant has a reputation for good food and friendly efficient service. Paris-born Francis Boulongne insists on the finest fresh meat, vegetables and fish (he visits the Manchester Fish Market twice a week), and prepares an excellent value three-course set menu as well as many specialist dishes. The ten beautifully furnished guest bedrooms all have private bathrooms, showers, satellite televisions, direct- dial telephones and beverage-making facilities.restaurant has a reputation for good food and friendly efficient service. Paris-born Francis Boulongne insists on the finest fresh meat, vegetables and fish (he visits the Manchester Fish Market twice a week), and prepares an excellent value three-course set menu as well as many specialist dishes. The ten beautifully furnished guest bedrooms all have private bathrooms, showers, satellite televisions, direct- dial telephones and beverage-making facilities.

Nearby, the village of **East Marton** stands at the point where the Pennine Way meets both the Leeds-Liverpool Canal and the A59 Skipton to Clitheroe road. Overlooking the canal, we found the delightful **Cross**

Keys and **Marton Bridge Restaurant**. This splendid 16th century inn and eating place has an attractive front garden with plenty of seating where customers can enjoy peaceful views of the canal and surrounding countryside. Inside, the building is full of character with old timber beams and pillars, stone-flagged floors, long tables and a wonderful open fireplace with a wooden mantle. The restaurant is elegantly furnished and offers an extensive menu of top class dishes. There is also an impressive wine list and a special children's menu.

If you are looking for a day or a week on the water, then we can thoroughly recommend the luxury narrow boat hire centre at **Doug Moore (Boatbuilders) Ltd**. This is run by Doug and Marie Moore from the Lower Park Marina on the B6383 Kelbrook road, four miles from Elslack. They also operate a working boatyard, situated on the summit pound of the Leeds/Liverpool Canal. Here, the waterway climbs out of the industrial backcloth of the Lancashire mill towns and enters into the soaring Pennine hills and dales.

Doug Moore Boatbuilders

There are three types of hire available; daily, short-term or weekly - the choice is yours. The boats are fully equipped with excellent facilities, and on arrival you are given every assistance and full instructions in handling the craft. This will include accompanied help as you tackle the first locks (not applicable for daily hire) and you will soon gain confidence to negotiate these yourself. The boats are both easy to handle and very quiet to operate, making this a pleasurable and gentle way to to see the best of the surrounding countryside.

The shop is stocked with unusual ideas for gifts - many with a nautical theme like painted ware, brassware, books and maps. To be sure of having the appropriate map or guide so you can do your homework before you arrive you can always give Doug and Marie a call and order them beforehand! The telephone number is (0282) 815883.

A visit to the Craven area would not be complete without a trip to **Skipton**, the Gateway of the Dales. Its origins can be traced to the 7th century, when Anglian farmers christened it 'Sheeptown', for reasons which do not need explanation.

The Normans built the first castle here in the twelfth century, and established the markets and fairs here which have carried on ever since, in the wide cobbled market place. There is a homely, inviting atmosphere in this town, and the tempting smell of food pervades the air. Approach at your peril J Stanforth's Pork Pie Establishment, which sells its delicious pies straight from the oven. And at the cost of your waistline, take a trip to Whitaker's 100 year old Chocolate Emporium, with a huge selection of mouth-watering chocolate confections on the ground floor and a friendly tea-shop on the first level. On market days all sorts of local delicacies are on offer, including smoked Wensleydale Cheese and a wide assortment of restaurants and cafes all vie to tempt the hungry travellers through their doors.

A wonderful place to eat in Skipton, especially for lovers of top quality fish and seafood is **Eastwoods Fish Restaurant** in Keighley Road. The restaurant can be found a short distance south of the town centre in a superb position on the brow of the bridge across the Leeds/Liverpool Canal (Pinder Bridge). Inside, the atmosphere is pleasant and welcoming with old beamed ceilings and walls lined with interesting boating memorabilia. Proprietors Mr and Mrs Mills who have owned and personally run Eastwoods since 1978, have developed the extremely successful policy of serving top quality fish at surprisingly reasonable prices. As well as delicious fish and chips, their menu also includes a wide choice of more exotic fish dishes such as halibut, trout and salmon, many of them cooked in mouthwatering sauces. There is also a good selection of non-fish dishes such as gammon and Cumberland sausage, a number of specially prepared vegetarian dishes, a special children's menu and a good range of starters and desserts. The restaurant is also fully licensed and stocks an unexpectedly varied list of wines and beers. A good value set lunch is served on weekdays and there is also a take-away facility next door. All in all, the quality of the food, the generous portions and excellent value make this an outstanding place to enjoy traditional English cooking at its best. Open for lunch, teas and suppers, every day; the restaurant opens on Sunday from 4pm till 9pm and the shop is open from 4pm till 11pm.

Eastwood's Fish Restaurant

Feeling well-fed and rested, one may decide to take a trip to the **Craven Museum**, which boasts Britain's oldest piece of cloth, a Viking tombstone and Georgian and Victorian relics.

In the centre of this historic market town, we called in at the town's oldest inn, the **Black Horse Hotel**. This lovely old building has a long and fascinating history which dates back to the 15th-century. Despite having experienced a number of changes over the years, the purpose of the establishment remains the same: to provide visitors and regular customers alike with the very best in food, ales and hospitality. As well as a full range of bar meals, manager Ron Maxfield and his staff serve a first-class á la carte menu in the recently refurbished Mews Restaurant. They also have five spacious guest rooms available which are all equipped with en-suite facilities and appointed to a high standard.

The Waterfront Music Bar and Discotheque stands in a

The Black Horse Hotel

magnificent position alongside the Leeds/Liverpool Canal in Coach Street, just to the south of Skipton's town centre. With its beautifully renovated architecture, imaginative decoration and great atmosphere, this splendid pub, bistro and nightclub is one of the premier attractions in the area. Formerly a canal-side mill, the building dates from 1710 and is now Grade II listed. The mill's old lifting gear can still be seen on the top floor and there is a lovely cobbled courtyard in front of the entrance which joins the canal to the road.

By day, the Waterfront offers an excellent choice of good food and drink including a fine selection of bottled and draught beers, wines and a bistro menu which includes authentic Italian Lasagne, home-made beef steak pie, shepherds' pie, special house salads and a choice of vegetarian dishes.

The Waterfront Music Bar and Discotheque

Skipton Castle

There is also a good selection of snacks, including sandwiches, soups, jacket potatoes, cold pies, cakes and pasties. A snack menu is available in the discotheque in the evening, when the building takes on a new persona as a lively nightclub with exciting lights, great decor and a tremendous atmosphere.

Through their sheer hard work and talent, proprietors Steve and Sandra Spalding have made the Waterfront into an exceptional place to spend some time in. The building's special features include a sun terrace overlooking the canal and a fascinating interior with mirrored pillars and a unique collection of pictures. The Waterfront offers something for everyone, from those looking for a coffee or a light meal to those wanting a special dinner or an enjoyable evening on the dance floor. Steve and Sandra's work and enthusiasm is reflected in the building's wonderful, vibrant atmosphere making this a special place to visit, to be seen in and to return to over and over again.

The Parish Church of the Holy Trinity is another fascinating venue, built originally in the 12th century and replaced in the 1300's. There is a wealth of interest inside, which is topped by a beautiful oak roof, constructed originally in the 15th century and added to and strengthened in the 1800's. Most of the roof bosses are original and amongst other designs is one of the ancient symbolic Green Man, found in many old churches. Another very old item in the church is the fresco known by the grim title 'The Hand of Death', the contribution of local monks in medieval times. There is also a beautiful oak memorial screen, a 13th century font with its elaborate cover, an ancient stone sedilia and a 16th century choir screen with wonderful carvings. One can spend much time discovering the centuries of artefacts in this place, but the various tombs and memorials are possibly the most interesting.

Apart from the Clifford tombs, is that of the poet Longfellow's father, whose family home was Skipton.

But it is the powerful and courageous Clifford family, the Lords (and Ladies) of Skipton Castle, who draw the imagination of most of the visitors. The Parish Church became the principal burial place of the family after the Dissolution of Bolton Abbey in 1540. The vault under the Sanctuary was built in 1542, following the death of Henry, 1st Earl of Cumberland.

The story of the Cliffords is worthy of a novel in itself, so inspiring and fascinating were their lives. Henry, the 1st Earl's tomb is of black polished marble. Many other tombs of his descendants are here, including the larger- than- life George, third Earl, Elizabeth 1's champion. Perhaps most moving are the memorials to the infant Cliffords, who, due to the high mortality rate, never grew to claim their inheritance. On the north wall of the chancel is the inscription, written by Henry, 5th and last Earl of Cumberland, whose memorial to his three young sons translates,

"On this small memorial, Henry, the father, bewails with much grief, Francis, Charles, Henry, AD 1631."

Many of the tombs were defaced by Cromwell and his men, but defiantly and lovingly restored at a later date by the courageous Lady Anne, Countess of Pembroke, daughter of George the 3rd Earl.

If taking a rest in Skipton, take time to explore this church's many fascinating hidden places, your efforts will be well rewarded.

Of all the castles I have ever visited, **Skipton Castle** is the only one I could ever imagine living in. As soon as we entered the lovely, sea-shell decorated Visitor's Office at the entrance, we knew that this was a place worthy of a great deal of research and exploration.

The first fortress was built here by Robert de Romille in 1090. It suffered severe attacks from the marauding Scots, until a powerful stone structure was devised in 1310 by Robert de Clifford, the 1st Earl of Skipton. The Cliffords were a fighting breed and possibly the best choice Edward II could have made for the defence of this vulnerable region, having earned their spurs in the wars with the troublesome Welsh previously. The spirit of the family is perhaps best exemplified by Walter de Clifford in 1250, who, during a period of disagreement with his king, caused the king's messenger to "eate the King's Writ, Waxe and All"!

In their turbulent history, one can see that the Cliffords feared neither death, nor meting it out - the first Lord Clifford was killed at Bannockburn in 1314, the fourth Lord, another Robert, fought at Crecy in 1346, the sixth Lord died in Germany and the seventh at the siege of Meaux at the age of thirty three. Under Thomas, the eighth Lord, the Cliffords entered the Wars of the Roses on the side of the House of Lancaster. Thomas was killed at St Albans in 1455, and his son John died at Towton in 1461, having earned himself the title of "the Butcher", due to the great slaughter he inflicted on the Yorkist forces, which included the severing of the Duke of York's head and placing it over the gates of the city.

The ninth lord, due to the rage this caused, was forced to flee to the wilds of Cumbria, his lands confiscated, where he tended flocks of sheep, until his power was restored after the Battle of Bosworth. Henry, the tenth Lord, was known as "the Shepherd Lord" (presumably not to his face!) Due to his pastoral upbringing, but this did not prevent him from achieving great honours at the Battle of Flodden, which would account for the very many Scottish cannons that now adorn the castle's battlements.

His son Henry, first Lord of Cumberland, was a great favourite of Henry VIII, and it is a little known fact that, had any of his three sons survived, they would have been designated as successors to the throne, in the event of lack of issue from Henry's own children, Elizabeth, Edward and Mary.

Perhaps due to the portraits we have of them, it is perhaps the images of the flamboyant George, the third Earl of Cumberland and his daughter, lady Anne, that stick in our minds. The third Earl's head and shoulders portrait stays forever in one's thoughts, his strong level stare and monumental shoulders (adorned with armoured shoulder pads that Joan Collins would envy!) convey the personality of a man definitely not to be trifled with. He was Elizabeth's jousting champion, possibly the most revered of her knights, and a notorious gambler and buccaneer. Unfortunately, his extravagant lifestyle left behind massive debts for his daughter, who despite this inheritance, still managed to become known for her many good works. George's extravagance can perhaps be forgiven on viewing the beautiful Shell Room, previously mentioned, with its charming reliefs of the four elements made from the ormer shells and Jamaican coral he brought back from his many sea voyages.

Skipton Castle is lauded as one of the most complete and well preserved medieval castles in England. Despite the heroic nature of its owners, time has been kind to it - the Royalist forces who sought refuge here fared better than most and when Major General Lambert was ordered by Cromwell to 'slight' or make the castle untenable, he wrote back to the Lord Protector that the labourers in charge of the operation, "come late, go early, and stand idle while they are here".

The unshakeable Lady Anne made good the small amount of damage that was undertaken, thereby preserving a monument that gives a great deal of pleasure to visitors today, and living up to her family motto 'Desormais', or, translated from the Norman/French, 'Henceforth!'

Travelling out of Skipton, two miles to the north-east of the town, we went in search of the top-rate farmhouse accommodation which is offered by Mrs Christine Clarkson at **Bondcroft Farm**, near **Embsay**, famous for its steam railway.

Situated on high ground just to the north of the village, the Clarksons' 150-acre working dairy cattle and sheep farm enjoys spectacular views of the surrounding Dales countryside. The 17th-century farmhouse offers a truly friendly and welcoming atmosphere; the three letting bedrooms (two double, one twin) are all tastefully decorated and equipped with hot and cold washbasins. Downstairs there is a pleasant guests' lounge and a

Bondcroft Farm

dining room where Mrs Clarkson serves delicious farmhouse breakfasts and, by arrangement, home-cooked evening meals. In the evenings, look out for Mr Clarkson training his competition sheepdogs.

The nearby village of **Draughton** is the home of the **Draughton Height Riding School** (just follow the 'horse' signs). This riding centre and livery stables is run by Nora Halstead with the able assistance of her chief riding instructor, Clare Christopher, and their band of willing helpers.

Draughton Height Riding School & Livery Stables

For all those interested in equestrianism (whatever their age and level of experience), Draughton Height offers just about everything. As well as expert tuition, accompanied hacks are available through the

wonderful surrounding countryside. The centre also boasts over fifteen mounts and has a recently constructed 100 x 60 feet indoor arena. Open all year round.

Brasses from the tomb of Sir Henry Clifford, 1st Earl of Cumberland

Ilkley

CHAPTER 8

Menston Grange, 1672

Keighley to Castleford

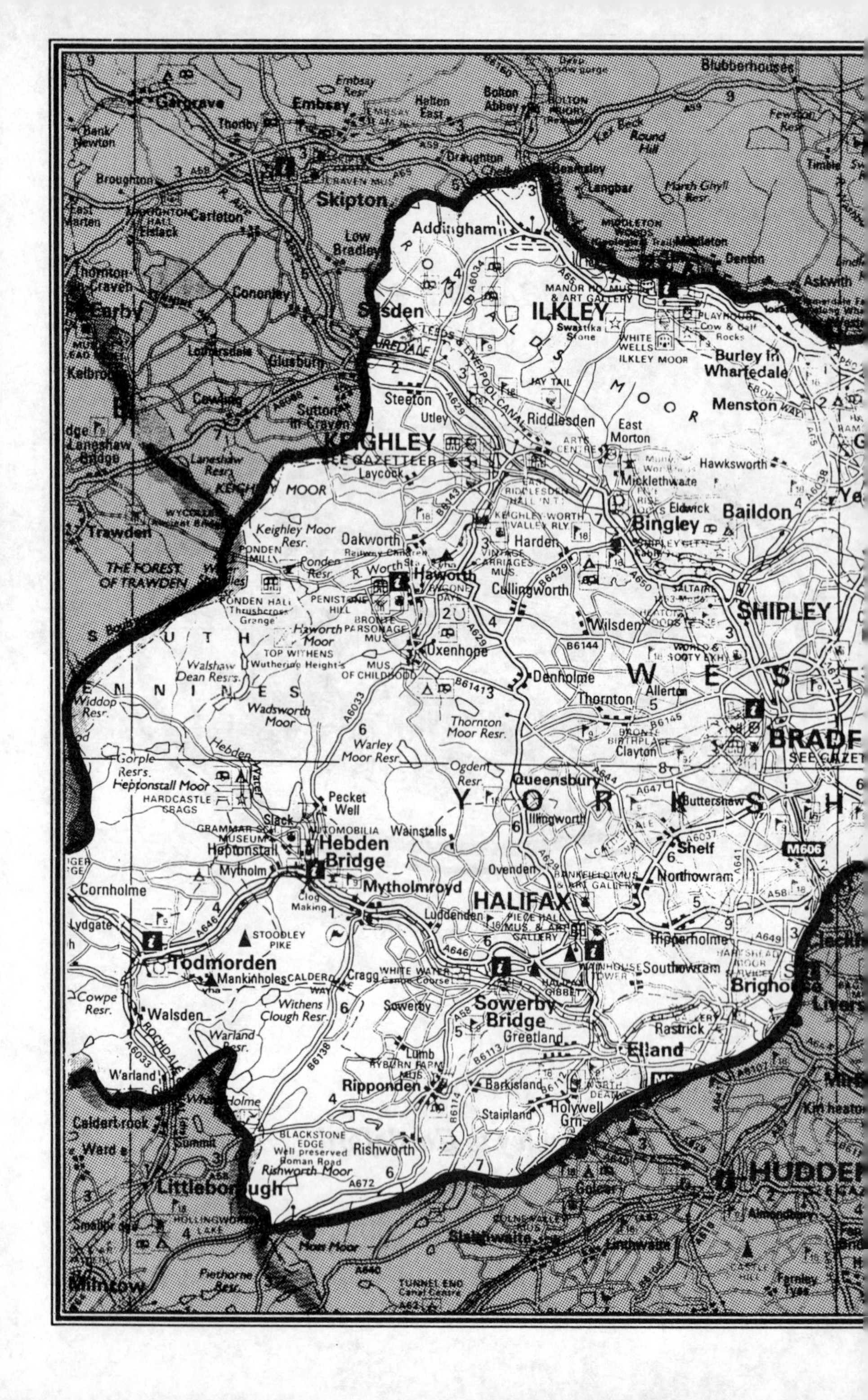

Skipton
Gargrave
Embsay
Bolton Abbey
Blubberhouses
Addingham
ILKLEY
ILKLEY MOOR
Burley in Wharfedale
Menston
Silsden
Steeton
KEIGHLEY
SEE GAZETTEER
Riddlesden
East Morton
Bingley
Baildon
SHIPLEY
Oakworth
Haworth
Cullingworth
Harden
Wilsden
Oxenhope
Denholme
Thornton
Allerton
BRADF
Queensbury
Illingworth
Buttershaw
Shelf
Northowram
HALIFAX
Hipperholme
Southowram
Brighouse
Hebden Bridge
Heptonstall
Mytholmroyd
Todmorden
Walsden
Sowerby Bridge
Greetland
Elland
Rastrick
Ripponden
Barkisland
Holywell Grn
Rishworth
Rishworth Moor
Littleborough
HUDDE
Trawden
Keighley Moor
W E S T
Y O R K S H

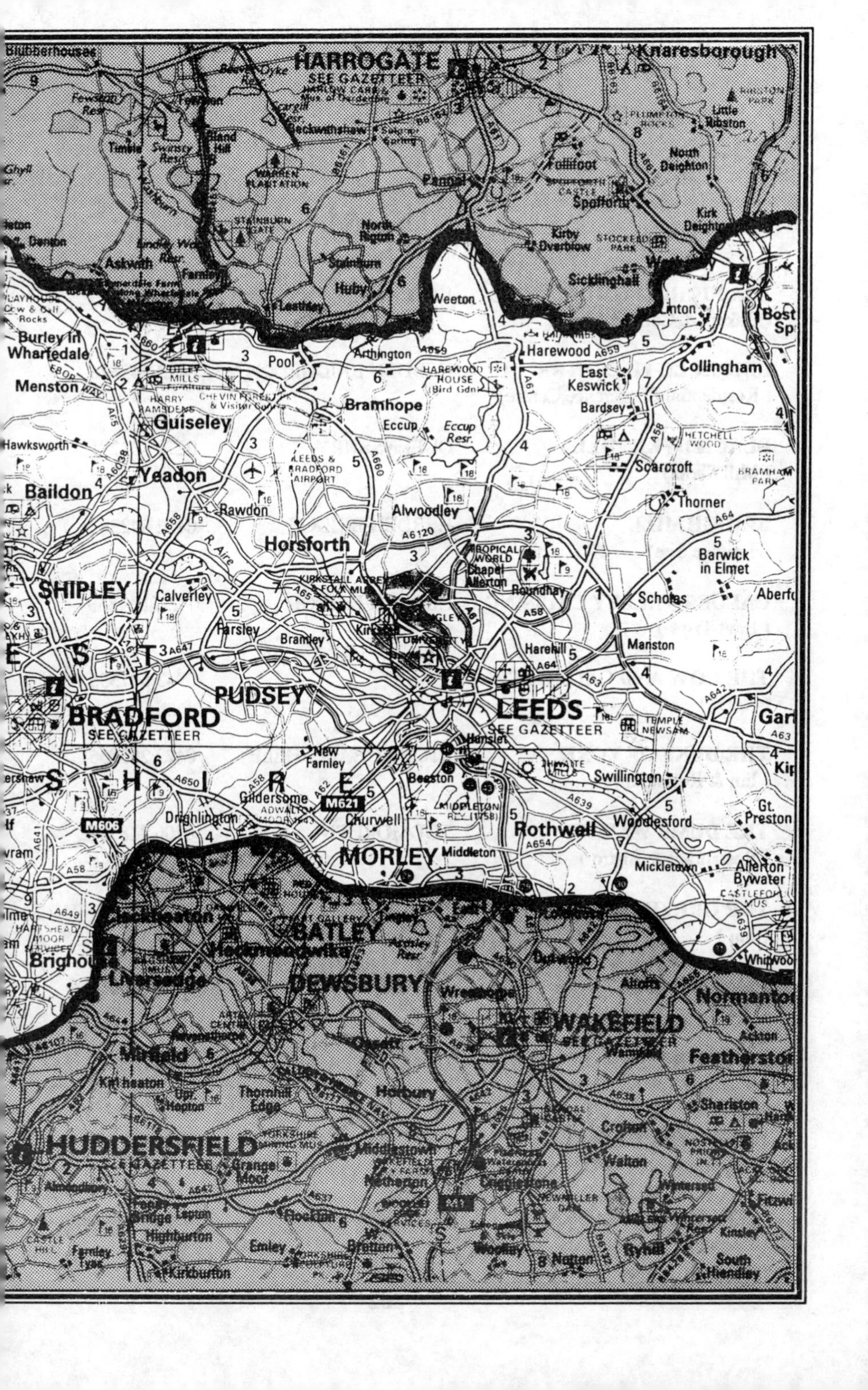

HARROGATE
SEE GAZETTEER
Knaresborough
Beckwithshaw
Little Ribston
North Deighton
Pannal
Follifoot
Spofforth
Kirk Deighton
Kirby Overblow
Sicklingham
Askwith
Denton
Stainburn
Huby
Leathley
Weeton
Burley in Wharfedale
Menston
Pool
Arthington
Harewood
HAREWOOD HOUSE (Bird Gdn)
East Keswick
Collingham
Bardsey
Guiseley
Bramhope
Eccup
Eccup Resr.
Hawksworth
Yeadon
LEEDS & BRADFORD AIRPORT
Scarcroft
Thorner
Baildon
Rawdon
Alwoodley
Horsforth
TROPICAL WORLD
Chapel Allerton
Roundhay
Barwick in Elmet
SHIPLEY
Calverley
Scholes
Farsley
Bramley
Harehills
Manston
PUDSEY
LEEDS
SEE GAZETTEER
TEMPLE NEWSAM
BRADFORD
SEE GAZETTEER
New Farnley
Hunslet
Beeston
Swillington
Gildersome
M621
Churwell
MIDDLETON RLY (1758)
Rothwell
Woodlesford
Gt. Preston
Drighlington
M606
MORLEY
Middleton
Mickletown
Allerton Bywater
BATLEY
DEWSBURY
Normanton
WAKEFIELD
Featherstone
Horbury
Thornhill Edge
HUDDERSFIELD
Crofton
Walton
Emley
Woolley
Notton
Ryhill
South Hiendley
Kirkburton
Highburton
A61
A659
A58
A64
A65
A660
A6120
A647
A650
A639
A654
A642
A63

Reference Guide

CHAPTER 8

ASA NICHOLSON AND SONS (Bakers & Confectioners)	KEELHAM, DENHOLME	0274 833149
BIRCHCLIFFE CENTRE (Residential Conference Centre)	HEBDEN BRIDGE	0422 843626
BLACK DYKE MILL (Mill Shop)	QUEENSBURY	0274 882271
BRIDGE MILL (Heritage Site)	HEBDEN BRIDGE	0422 842382
CALDER VALLEY CRUISING (Boat Trips)	HEBDEN BRIDGE	0422 844833
THE COW AND CALF HOTEL (Hotel)	ILKLEY	0943 607335
THE DUKE OF YORK (Inn & Restaurant)	STONE CHAIR SHELF	0422 205056
THE DUMB WAITER (Restaurant & Bistro)	TODMORDEN	0706 818387
THE GREYHOUND (Inn)	BRADFORD	0532 852427
HEATHER COTTAGE (Tea Room & Guest House)	HAWORTH	0535 644511
LA JARDINIERE (Restaurant)	BOSTON SPA	0937 845625
LAPWATER HALL (Restaurant)	BRADFORD	0274 681449
MERLIN'S RESTAURANT (Restaurant)	SILSDEN	0535 655995

Reference Guide

CHAPTER 8

MOORVIEW HOTEL (Hotel)	ILKLEY	0943 600156
PALM COURT TEA ROOMS (Tea Room)	ILKLEY	0943 602472
PARK LANE RESTAURANT (Restaurant)	ROUNDHAY, LEEDS	0532 663307
RIVERSIDE (Hotel)	ILKLEY	0943 607338
TONG VILLAGE HOTEL (Hotel)	BRADFORD	0532 854646
TOP BRINK INN (Inn & Restaurant)	TODMORDEN	0706 812696
WOODHALL HOTEL (Hotel)	LINTON	0937 587271
YE SLEEPING HOUSE (B&B)	HAWORTH	0535 645992

Kirkstall Abbey

CHAPTER 8

From Keighley to Castleford

At the junction of the rivers Worth and Aire, is the bustling textile and engineering town of **Keighley**. Despite its modern redevelopments, Keighley still retains a strangely nostalgic air of the Victorian industrial Revolution, for it was that era that created the town we know today, beginning at Low Mill in 1780, when cotton spinning first began.

On viewing the grim but fascinating reminders of those days, one can almost see the child workers, cruelly nicknamed "the crooked-legged-uns", trudging through the early morning chill, to begin yet another long day of drudgery.

Despite the reminders of hardship, the labyrinths of ginnels and terraces, amidst the many elaborately decorated mills, hold a great deal of exploration potential. There are delightful carvings, and on one early mill chimney, are three heads, one wearing a top hat; in contrast is the classical French-styled Dalton Mill in Dalton Lane with its ornate viewing gallery.

The centre of Keighley is dominated by impressive Victorian civic buildings and a beautifully set-out covered shopping precinct, where the statue of legendary local giant Rombald stands.

The Parish church also in the centre is famous as the site where Patrick Bronte often officiated at marriages. The graveyard contains 15th century headstones, as well as a crude cross made from four carved heads which is believed to be Saxon in origin.

Above the town, as a means of escaping the industrial past, one might enjoy a walk in Park Woods, taking the cobbled path to Thwaites Brow, which affords magnificent views of the town below.

Outside the town centre is **Cliffe Castle**, which, despite its deceptive name, is in fact a grand late 19th century mansion complete with a tower, battlements and parkland, once belonged to local mill owners, the Butterfields. It now houses a natural history museum, with fascinating information on the local topography and geology of Airedale. The decor is Victorian at its grandest, with magnificent french chandeliers. Predictably, there is also an excellent exhibition of cotton mill memorabilia and history which is well worth a visit.

A short way down the valley is **East Riddlesden Hall**, a National

Trust Property with parts dating back to Saxon times. The main building was constructed in the 1630s by James Murgatroyd, a wealthy Halifax clothier and merchant. It is a dark stone, gabled house with mullioned windows, original central hall, superb period fireplaces, oak panelling and plaster ceilings. The house is furnished in Jacobean style, which is complemented by carved likenesses of Charles Stuart and Henrietta Maria. There are also said to be various ghosts dating from this period and earlier!

East Riddleston Hall also has one of the largest and most impressive timber-framed barns in the North of England, which now houses a collection of farm waggons and agricultural equipment.

Three miles up the towpath of the Leeds/Liverpool canal is **Silsden**, specialising in nail and worsted manufacture, whose centre, despite its industrial connections, has remained remarkably unspoilt.

Opposite the park in Bolton Road, we discovered a truly exceptional restaurant and wine bar which is located in a converted stone-built cottage. **Merlins** is owned and personally run by Chris and Cynthia Sykes and their son Howard who over the years have accumulated a wealth of training and experience in catering to the highest standard. Today, they offer their customers the very best in food and wine, both in the relaxed atmosphere of the bar and in the more formal surroundings of the restaurant.

Merlins Restaurant

Howard is responsible for selecting Merlin's first-class wine list which features examples from some of the world's finest lesser-known vineyards. He also chooses the daily menu for Merlin's first-class á la carte restaurant. This features a variety of English, continental and international dishes which are carefully prepared from top quality ingredients including fresh fish, game in season and meat supplied by a celebrated local butcher. Meals are individually cooked to order and may take a little time to prepare, but the results are well worth waiting for. For those requiring a lighter, more straightforward meal, these are also provided in the bar every evening except Saturdays. The Sykes also organise excellent value monthly gourmet wine-tasting evenings which typically feature a six course meal accompanied by up to seven specially selected wines. Open Monday to Saturday, 7pm to midnight.

But the most famous local attraction has to be **Ilkley Moor**, immortalised in the well-known song, and a must to visit, if only to say that you've been there.

Like any of the Yorkshire moors, Ilkley Moor can look inviting and attractive on a sunny day, but dreary and forbidding when the weather turns for the worse. The river Wharfe runs along the edge of the moor and through the town of **Ilkley**, which is clustered within a narrow section of the valley, in the midst of heather moorland craggy gritstone and wooded hillside.

One of the most beautiful views is from White Wells, where there is a famous spring and a little bench where one can sit and enjoy the spectacular vista of Wharfedale, as well as recover from the long and winding path up!

This place marks the boundary of North and West Yorkshire, and in one's journeys around the Wharfedale area, one will see an odd juxtaposition of modernised towns and croft-like farms enclosed by dry-stone walls.

Ilkley's history is extensive, originally an Iron Age settlement, it was eventually occupied by the Romans, who built a camp here to protect their crossing of the River Wharfe, and who named the town that sprang up Olicana, giving rise to the present name, with the familiar "ley" (Anglo-Saxon for pasture) added. Behind the medieval church is a grassy mound where a little fort was built and in the town's museum are altars carved in gritstone, dedicated to the Roman gods.

The spring at White Wells brought more visitors in the 18th century, and a small bath-house was built, where genteel and elderly patients were encouraged to take a dip in the healing waters of the "heather spa", as it was known.

Early Victorian times saw the development of the hydros - hydropathic treatment hotels, providing hot and cold treatments based on the ideas of

Ilkley

Dr Preissnitz of Austria who, in 1843, opened Britain's first hydro at Ben Rhydding. Similar establishments soon followed, such as those at Wells House (now Ilkley College) and what is now the Craiglands Hotel.

The coming of the railway lines from Leeds and Bradford in the 1860's and 70's, during a period of growth in the Yorkshire woollen industry, saw Ilkley take on a new role as a fashionable commuter town. Wool manufacturers and their better paid employees came, not only to enjoy the superb amenities, but to build handsome villas in West Riding gritstone. If Bradford and Leeds was where people made their "brass", then it was usually Ilkley where they spent it. Even today, Ilkley sports some remarkable and opulent Victorian architecture as proof of this.

A short distance from **Ilkley** town centre, we found the **Moorview Hotel**, a spacious private hotel standing within a large attractive garden which extends between the A65 Leeds to Skipton road and the banks of the River Wharfe. Now AA one-star rated, the hotel is decorated in a pleasant traditional style which reflects its original Victorian character. Most guest rooms have en-suite facilities, and all have televisions and beverage making facilities.

Moorview Hotel

Proprietor Jean Cockburn is a very friendly host who offers her guests the warmest of welcomes and a first-rate Yorkshire breakfast. The hotel is situated only 100 yards from the start of the Dales Way, and within easy reach of Bolton Abbey, Barden Towers and the Bronte Country.

Ilkley's patrons and well-to-do citizens gave the town a splendid Town Hall, library, Winter Gardens, and King's Hall and a sense of elegance is still present along the Grove. It is still a delight to have morning coffee in the famous Betty's coffee house, and discerning shoppers will find a wealth of fashionable clothes, antiques, paintings, and excellent wines. In a tiny garden to the right at the top of the Grove, you will find the remains of one of Ilkley's actual chalybeate springs, sadly no longer running, and a large marble bath dedicated to the memory of Dr Preissnitz. Behind the Grove are pleasant pedestrian areas round the small market square, the lower part of which leads down to a perfectly preserved Victorian arcade complete with beautiful potted palms and balconies.

Whilst here, we made a point of visiting the arcade (Based on South Hawkesworth Street), where the fabulous aroma of freshly ground coffee drew us towards the **Palm Court Tearooms** and restaurant on the first floor. Here, customers can sit reading the daily papers amongst fuchsias and palm trees under the arcade's impressive glass roof.

Palm Court Tearooms

Tony Dobson and his staff provide friendly and efficient table service and a menu which contains a good choice of specialist coffees and teas, cakes and light meals. A wide range of filled baked potatoes, wholemeal pancakes, salads and hot dishes is on offer, as well as a number of desserts and set afternoon and cream teas. Licensed.

The Tourist Information Centre, almost opposite Ilkley's cleverly refurbished station, has an excellent range of maps and guides to help you discover some of the most delightful of hidden places. On your journeys around this town, you should try to make a point of visiting the little **Manor House Museum**, close to the site of the old Roman Fort, an Elizabethan Manor House with an excellent display of the town's long history, but it is useful to note that the museum is closed on Mondays.

But as with many places in the dales and moors, you will have to get on your walking shoes to sample some of Ilkley's real delights. There is a lovely riverside parkland area, and a few hundred metres up from the present main road bridge across the Wharfe, you will come to Ilkley's original hump-backed bridge.

A short distance from the Old Bridge, we found the **Riverside Hotel**, a fine establishment run by Kristine Dobson and her son Kelvin. Open all day, the hotel's public bar has an attractive open log fire and a beer garden which overlooks the River Wharfe. There is also a fine restaurant offering a varied lunchtime menu including traditional roasts on Sundays. Facilities for children include rides, and a riverside cabin selling ice cream, candy floss and snacks.

Riverside Hotel

A huge playground and park stands on the riverbank adjacent to the hotel where rowing boats can be hired for trips between the Old and New Bridges. The Riverside Hotel's restaurant and public bar are open all year round.

Another popular route for walkers is to follow Grove Road to Heber's Ghyll, a natural wooded ravine with a stream which tumbles down the moors, and which has been landscaped with a series of footbridges. Not far from the top of the Ghyll is a moorland path which leads to the Swastika Stone, one of Yorkshire's most curious monuments - a boulder carved with an ancient swastika dating back to Bronze Age times.

For anyone with a love of open spaces and grand landscape, as well as a sense of ancient mystery, few places in the North can equal Ilkley Moor, or more correctly, Rombalds Moor, as it should be known. The Ilkley Moor made famous in the song is, strictly speaking, only the vast tract of ancient open common land which lies within the old township of Ilkley.

The moorland, much of it still covered in heather, is an area of national importance for its archaeology. A series of mysteriously marked cup -and- ring stones, dating, like the Swastika stones from the Bronze age, are a source of puzzlement to the archaeologists. Were they boundary markers, waymarks, ancient symbols of energy or of religious significance? Almost in the centre of the moor is an ancient stone circle, which hints at this being a site of some religious importance. Only the keen walker, armed with a large scale map and a fair amount of stamina, is likely to find them. Closer to home, there is a fine example of a cup-and-ring stone in the lower part of St Margaret's Churchyard on Queen's Road.

Keighley and Worth Valley Railway

Looking at a map of the area, many people's attention is drawn to the curiously named **Cow and Calf Rocks**, which form a striking moor-edge landmark above **Ben Rhydding**, which be reached by footpath from White Wells or Ilkley Tarn, or from the car-park on Cowpasture Road. The Cow is a great gritstone outcrop concealing an old quarry, which is now a popular nursery crag for climbers, whilst the freestanding Calf is a giant boulder. Both give splendid viewpoints.

The splendid **Cow and Calf Hotel** is situated near the rocks on the northern slopes of Ilkley Moor and commands a magnificent position overlooking lower Wharfedale, just to the south of the A65 Leeds to Skipton road. This friendly family-run hotel is owned and personally run by brothers Andrew and Philip Norfolk together with their parents Garfield and Brenda. Since taking over in 1980, they have been successful in bringing the establishment up to the standard of a modern first-class hotel which is now English Tourist Board four crown commended. The hotel is surrounded by an attractive landscaped garden which contains a charming rockery and a collection of rhododendrons which make a stunning display in June. Beyond this, the hotel has direct access onto Ilkley Moor which is an ideal location for rambling and hiking, and is a paradise for all those interested in outdoor pursuits.

Cow and Calf Hotel

Inside, the hotel has twenty individually-decorated bedrooms, all equipped with en suite facilities, colour televisions, telephones, radio alarms and tea/coffee making facilities. Five of these are rated as executive rooms and one, the Norfolk Suite, has a four-poster bed. Perhaps the most striking feature of the guest rooms, however, is the wonderful views they enjoy over the dramatic surrounding landscape. The hotel's Panorama Restaurant also has magnificent views from its large picture windows. Here, diners can enjoy the very best in traditional English and continental cooking in an atmosphere which is spacious and relaxed. The restaurant offers an excellent-value table d'hôte menu, along with an extensive range of imaginative á la carte dishes. At lunchtimes, an innovative lite-bite menu is offered where one can eat in the bar with its attractive open stonework, brass tables and log fire in the winter months; 'Le Jardin' with attractive trellising and indoor plants or more formally in the restaurant.

The newly created Ilkley Moor Suite, with magnificent views again of adjacent Ilkley Moor and the famous Cow and Calf rocks offers ideal facilities for private dining or small meetings for up to 30- people. Look out for the many fine of examples of hand-embroidered fabrics and tapestries which have been personally made by Brenda Norfolk. These attractive samples of Mrs Norfolk's artistic talent can be seen throughout the hotel and should not be missed. Open all year round.

Addingham, lying just two and a half miles on the Skipton side of Ilkley, was a prosperous mill town at the time when Ilkley was just a quiet back-water.

This was mainly due to the availability of ample water-power in the locality. Two large early water-powered mills along the River Wharfe, High Mill and Low Mill, are both now converted to attractive riverside developments.

For serious students of Yorkshire's early industrial history, Addingham repays exploration. Various small mills and industrial buildings demonstrate the evolution in the West Riding of the world's first textile manufacturers. In the 18th century, cottage hand-loom weavers, sharing a common house loft, began to develop the idea of a common workshop - the significant change from a cottage to a factory system. Addingham also has several old inns dating back to the stagecoach days, and it was here that the horses would be changed ready for the long ascent over Chelker Brow into Skipton. There are also some interesting craft outlets, a pottery and antique shops to browse around.

Like Ilkley, there is a fine parish church, and the town is also the starting point for numerous moorland walks, being at the access point for routes through both West and North Yorkshire.

One walk that can be recommended, leads from the centre of Addingham, through a narrow break in the rocks known as Windgate Gate on to Addingham Moor. Not far away, easily reached by footpath across the heather, are the Doubler Stones, a series of strange, wind-carved gritstone rocks standing on the open moorland.

Travelling back along the A65 through Ilkley, one will eventually come to **Otley**, a medieval market town, which keeps its individual character with a busy cobbled market-place, little alleyways and courtyards. There are still ancient mileposts in the wilds of the moors which mark the distance to Otley market. To keep the hoards of merchants and farmers well-lubricated during their financial transactions, a large amount of inns sprang up, some 27 in number, which even for Yorkshire, is something of a record! There is also a large Irish influence in Otley, due to the fact that the busy cattle-market here held an annual hiring, to take on labourers for the harvest, which drew a great many Irish immigrants, hopeful of employment.

One tourist attraction is the plaque and statue of Thomas Chippendale in front of the 17th century Grammar school building in Manor Square, now an antiques centre. The great furniture maker was born in Otley, and was baptised in the Parish Church in 1718.

The Parish church dates from Saxon times, the main body, though, having been constructed in the 11th century. An unusual memorial, close by, is a stone model of Bramhope Railway Tunnel, with its crenellated entrance portals on the Leeds-Thirsk Railway (the present Leeds-Harrogate line), built in the 1830's. Over 30 men lost their lives in the construction, due to inadequate safety precautions, and the model is to commemorate this.

There is still a maypole in Otley on Poole Road, close to the Tourist Information centre. There is an old house next door to the centre which was once an apothecary's shop, and where John Wesley frequently stayed on his visits here.

Otley, like Ilkley, is something of a riverside resort, with a series of lovely promenades and gardens and boating area. Just behind and above the town, dominating the skyline, is Otley Chevin, an area of magnificent woodland and moorland, now an exceptionally fine forest park owned and managed by Leeds City Council. A path, well-signed, leads to the summit of the Chevin, directly from the town centre, an exceptionally steep climb, not to be recommended to those with any heart or respiratory disorders! The alternative is to take a car round the back and park close to "Surprise View", from where there are magnificent views of Wharfedale, looking across to Almscliffe Crag and thickly wooded Norwood Edge. There is a little visitor centre part way up the summit, called the White House, with a small wildlife exhibition and a choice of woodland trails. Guided walks are arranged by the Ranger service during the tourist season. Other walks from Otley take you into Washburndale, that tributary of the Wharfe with its chain of moorland reservoirs, forming Yorkshire's "Little Lake District", whilst a bridal path by the Wharfe begins at the riverside park and takes you to Leathley past Farnley Park where J W Turner spent a number of summers as a guest of the Horton Fawkes family, producing impressive water-colours to repay their kindness.

The scenery in these parts in both idyllic and magnificent - who would think that one is only three miles from the Leeds/Bradford Airport!

Nearby **Bramhope** is notable for its rare example of a Cromwellian

Puritan Chapel, situated on the side of the A660, with a hexagonal font dating from 1673.

Harewood is a village that grew up around the very famous **Harewood House**, and which was moved to its present site in the 1760's.

The House, renowned for its royal connections, was originally owned by Henry Lascelles, a wealthy 18th century merchant, who during his lifetime in fact lived at nearby Gawthorpe Old Hall, across the valley from Harewood. It was his son Edwin, however, who became the first Lord Harewood, inheriting the two estates on his father's death in 1753. It was he who built the Harewood house we know today, commissioning the distinguished architect John Carr of York to mastermind its construction.

Edwin Lascelles was a typical Yorkshireman, and was thrifty despite his great wealth. Although he commissioned Adam and Chippendale to furnish his creation, he constantly reminded them to watch the cost. He was also a remarkably slow payer of bills. In the eight years Chippendale worked for him, Lascelles paid him nearly nothing.

Harewood has the reputation of being one of the first houses to have a bell system fitted for hailing the servants of the house.

Gawthorpe Old Hall was eventually demolished and Capability Brown was brought in to landscape and extend Harewood's grounds. One can only hope that he was paid more promptly than the unfortunate Chippendale!

The Harewood family fortunes had waned by the fifth generation. At this time, Lord Lascelles was living the life of an officer in the Grenadier guards, living on £600 per annum. The family, however, must be in possession of the most remarkable luck, for, during a casual conversation in a London club with his great uncle, the Marquis of Clanricorde in 1916, the Lord became the old man's favourite, and on his death, was left his entire fortune, collection of paintings and his estate in Ireland.

The Lord's luck was further added to when he met, and later married the Princess Royal in 1922, From hereon, the family's fortunes were sealed.

Lord Lascelles died in 1947, and the Princess, only daughter of King George V and Queen Mary, lived on at the house until her death in 1965, when the National Trust acquired the property which we can view today.

The grounds are truly breath-taking, with Royal rhododendron gardens, bird gardens and Tropical Rain Forest area, and certainly not to be missed. The interior is also stunning in its elegance and beauty, as befits its prestigious list of contributors.

Nearby, on the road to Wetherby, one might wish to take a short detour to **Bardsey**, site of a lovely church, with its Anglo-Saxon tower and

Harewood House

later Perpendicular additions.

Boston Spa is another town in the locality, well worth stopping in. It is a gracious, inviting place, whose growth began in 1744, through the discovery of its spring by a labourer called John Shires.

A guidebook of 1853 tells us of the pure and bracing air to be had at Boston Spa, where one might either drink or bathe in the waters, by visiting one of the pump-rooms and variety of baths.

Nowadays, it no longer functions as a spa town, and is better known as a popular fishing ground.

It was in the attractive environment of Boston Spa, that Paul and Susan Tatham chose to open their own very special restaurant, **La Jardiniére**, which can be found in a charming 300 year-old Grade II listed building near the centre of the village.

La Jardiniere

Inside, it has a charming traditional atmosphere with timber-framed walls and ceilings, antique furniture and luxurious drapes. The tables are also delightfully decorated with white linen tablecloths, antique candlesticks and delicate vases of fresh flowers. The restaurant food goes hand-in-hand with these wonderful surroundings; French inspired rather than classical French in nature, head chef Adam Hewitt prepares a range of mouthwatering dishes using top quality ingredients such as beef from Scotland and fresh fish from Yorkshire's North Sea ports. The menu is changed every three to four weeks and features a balanced mix of classic and innovative dishes. For families and early-evening diners, the restaurant has recently introduced an excellent-value three-course 'early bird' menu which is served between 6.30pm and 8pm each evening. This features a choice of half-a-dozen dishes in English rustic style which owe much to the classic recipes of Mrs Beeton. Paul and Susan are both very experienced front-of-house managers and are sure to make a visit to La Jardiniére a rewarding and enjoyable experience. The restaurant is open Tuesday to Saturday evenings; advance booking recommended.

Completely unspoilt by industry is **Wetherby**, situated on the Great North Road at a point nearly midway between Edinburgh and London. Hence, it is renowned for its coaching inns, of which the two most famous were the Angel and The Swan and Talbot. It is rumoured that serving positions at these inns were considered so lucrative, that employees had to pay for the privilege of employment in them!

The centre of the town is of a quaint appearance, in the midst of which is a market place first granted to the Knights Templar, who were allowed to hold a market here every Thursday and an annual fair lasting three days.

Many of the houses in the town are Georgian, Regency or early Victorian. Apart from its shops, quaint galleries, old pubs and cafes, there is also a famous racecourse nearby.

Another feature is the renowned 18th century bridge with a long weir which once provided power for the town's cornmill, possibly dating from mediaeval times.

On leaving Wetherby, we went in search of the truly outstanding country house hotel, **Wood Hall**, which is set within 100 acres of rolling parkland on the northern bank of the River Wharfe. To get there from Wetherby, take the A661 Harrogate road for half-a-mile, then turn left towards Sicklinghall and Linton and Wood Hall, cross the bridge and turn left again, sign-posted to Linton and Wood Hall. In **Linton**, turn right opposite the Windmill public house and follow the estate road for just over a mile to the hotel. The Wood Hall estate has a long and interesting history dating back beyond Oliver Cromwell to early Norman times. In the 1750s, a family of wealthy wool and cloth merchants, the Scotts, acquired it and built a fine Georgian country mansion onto an existing Jacobean wing. In more recent times, the estate was under the ownership of the Roman Catholic Church who ran it as an ecumenical college before in 1988, a new courtyard wing was added and the building was transformed into one of the finest country house hotels in the country.

After enjoying the breathtaking views from the terrace, present-day guests step into the hotel's grand entrance hall with its highly polishedstone-flagged floor and light gracious atmosphere. The hotel's three main public rooms lead from here: the beautifully proportioned

Wood Hall

dining room with its elegant dark wood furniture, white linen-covered tables and superb menu, the luxuriously furnished drawing room with its huge sofas and sumptuous furnishings, and the enormous lounge bar with its warm oak panelling and genuine country-house atmosphere. Each of Wood Hall's forty four luxurious bedrooms has been individually furnished and equipped with en suite facilities and several carefully-chosen extras. Some have private sitting rooms, one has a huge four-poster bed, and most have magnificent views over the valley of the River Wharfe.

A recent addition to the facilities at Wood Hall is an exclusive health and leisure club. This contains a fully-equipped gym, heated pool, spa bath, jogging track, steam room and solarium, and is manned by a fully-qualified fitness instructor. A beauty therapist is also on hand to provide a range of treatments to those in need of a little special pampering. Standing as it does within easy reach of Harewood House, Bramham International Horse Trials, York, Harrogate and the beautiful Dales, Wood Hall provides a truly luxurious base for enjoying the many delights this part of Yorkshire has to offer.

Travelling down the A1 to Castleford, one might think to call in at **Bramham** and nearby **Bramham Park**, one of the loveliest villages in this part of lower Wharfedale.

This is an area of rich, rolling countryside, mature farmland, woodlands and picturesque villages, sometimes called "the Little Cotswolds".

Bramham Park

Bramham Park is one of Yorkshire's most exquisite country houses and is special for a number of reasons. The house itself dates from the Queen Anne era, built by Robert Benson, Lord Bingley, between 1698 and 1710, and superbly proportioned in an elegant and restrained classical style. The finished effect is more French than English, with tasteful gardens, elegant furniture and paintings by such famous artists as Kneller and Sir Joshua Reynolds. In fact, the gardens were modelled on Louis XIV's Versailles, with ornamental canals and ponds, beech groves, statues, long avenues and a prized arboretum with a collection of rare and unusual trees.

Lotherton Hall, six miles to the south, is another stately house, dating from the 19th century, owned by Leeds city council. Originally the ancestral home of the Gascoigne family, it contains many fine features, including a 12th century chapel.

The nearest big town, 9 miles down the A1, is **Castleford**, whose growth has evidently stemmed from it's mining and factories. It is situated at the confluence of the rivers Calder and Aire, once plentiful with salmon, trout and grayling. A well-known verse goes,

"Castleford lasses may well be fair
For they wash in Calder and rinse in Aire"

The happy, rural atmosphere that this verse conjures up has been replaced by a concentration of pottery and glass bottle factories and several collieries for the mining of coal. In 1826, Aire and Calder Navigation opened the Castleford - Goole Canal for the shipping of these goods, although of course these days, this has been replaced by the M62.

Travelling up from here to Leeds on the main roads, one may decide to call in at **Temple Newsam House**, set back off the A 63, at the Garforth turn-off.

A nineteenth century visitor was not really impressed with the house, commenting that,

"This edifice has a great singularity, instead of battlements, a stone gallery surrounds the roof consisting of letters which compose a sentence from the Bible".

He went on to say that the park was melancholy and the furniture old-fashioned without being interesting. Some people can be very difficult to please!

The sentence he referred to, was introduced by Sir Arthur Ingram, and in fact reads,

"All Glory and Praise be given to God The Father The Son and Holy Ghost on High Peace on Earth Goodwill Towards Men Honour and True Allegiance To our King Loving Affection Amongst His Subject Health and Plenty Be Within This House" No doubt that Sir Arthur felt he had covered all eventualities in this long supplication, and therefore felt no need to go to the further expense of adding punctuation!

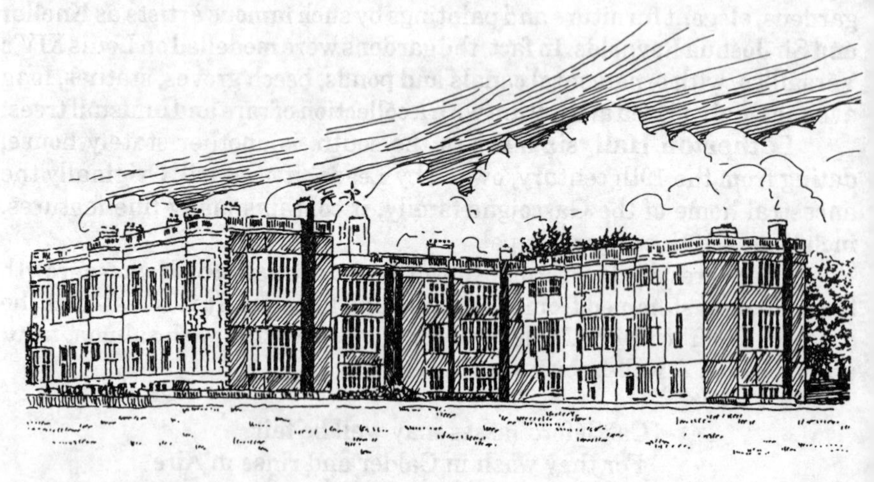

Temple Newsam House

There has been a mansion here of some sorts since couple of Anglo-Saxon thanes, Dunstan and Glunier, set their claim to the land, and since then it has had a great many owners, including the Earl of Pembroke, the Darcy family, the Ingrams and the Marchioness of Hertford. It was purchased in 1922 by Leeds City Council.

In its time, such names as John Carr, the Adam brothers, Chippendale and Capability Brown have contributed to its improvement, and it houses some incomparable collections of antiques within its walls.

The view of the house, if such it could be described as, is impressive. Set amidst huge expanses of rolling grassland, it certainly looks more like a castle than anything else, the visitor who described it as an edifice, though unkind, was understandable in his observation.

The grounds cover 1200 acres, and include the Home Farm, where there is a rare breeds centre. There is ample car-parking and it is worthwhile noting that admission to the grounds is free and that there are concessions for the unemployed, elderly, students and children on admission to the House.

In the north-eastern outskirts of Leeds, we found the suburb of **Roundhay**. A site overlooking the ninth green of the famous Golf Course there is perhaps an unlikely location for a top class eating place, but this is where we found the **Park Lane Restaurant**. This superb privately-owned establishment lies just off the A58, three miles northeast of Leeds city centre. The restaurant is personally-run by owner Robert Williams who has successfully created an atmosphere which is both luxurious and informal; the tables are elegantly furnished with pale pink tablecloths, white china, candlesticks and vases of fresh flowers.

Park Lane Restaurant

Robert has also built up a reputation for providing excellent service, good value for money and truly outstanding cuisine. Open Tuesday to Saturday evenings, and on Sundays for traditional lunch. Booking advisable on Leeds 0532 663307.

The city of **Leeds** is the largest urban development in Yorkshire and can certainly lay claim to being the economic capital of the county. If there is any indication of this, one need only look upon the unsurpassed grandeur of the Town Hall, which has to be seen to be believed.

In the early 19th century, Leeds owed its rapid development as an inland port to the Leeds-Liverpool and Aire and Calder Navigation canals. It therefore formed a central link between Liverpool and Hull, from where goods were exported world-wide. The Canal Basin, which formed the link, rapidly grew, providing extensive wharves, warehouses, boat-building yards and wet and dry docks where boats could be repaired. Although the water trade sadly declined as first the railways, then the roadways took over as the trade routes, interest has been recently been rekindled, as it has in many other cities with this heritage, in the long-neglected warehouses and waterways, with their rich and historical tradition. The Canal Basin has been designated a Conservation Area, and the once derelict buildings redeveloped into sought-after offices and shopping areas, as well as street-shows, markets and landscaped water-side areas.

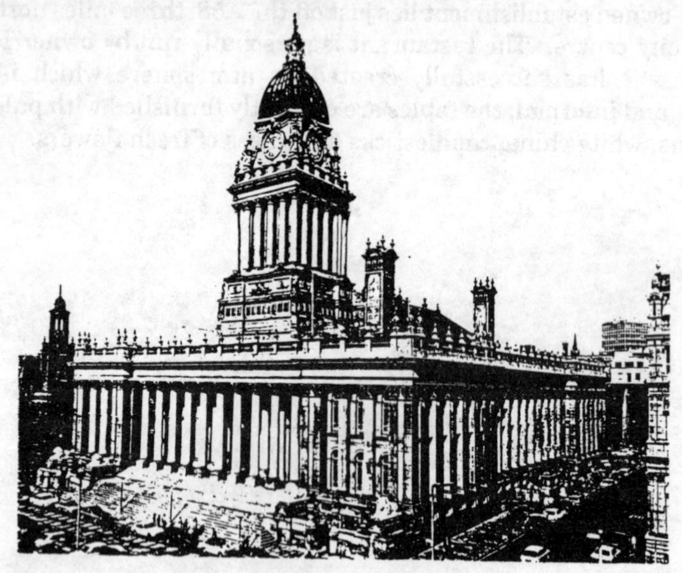

Leeds Town Hall

Leeds City Museum and Gallery

There are many interesting and hidden places in this fascinating area, well worth exploring for their historical value before the developers make a complete transformation.

The Redevelopment Programme has, however, taken pains to maintain as much as possible, and familiar landmarks such as the cargo-cranes, famous buildings and the twin towers (modelled on Italian campaniles) have been preserved as interesting focal points.

The canal itself has also enjoyed a new lease of life in recent years, with a wide variety of leisure craft increasingly evident on its waters

In response to the enormous interest in the site, a trail with an environmental theme is being developed which is available to disabled visitors. A Visitor Centre is housed in the former Canal Office.

Another excellent way to discover Leeds' remarkable early industrial heritage, is to follow the Museum of Leeds Trail along the towpath of the canal through the Kirkstall Valley.

This takes the visitor from the Canal Basin past warehouses and mills, bridges, locks and canal architecture, to the Leeds Industrial Museum at Armley Mill, once the largest textile mill in the world. It now houses a museum of the textiles, clothing and engineering industries of which Leeds is still a major centre. The story of the development of the clothing industry in Leeds is told in a reconstruction of the Jewish tailoring quarter. One of the few surviving water-powered fulling mills in Europe is to be seen, and there are boat-rides along the canal in Summer, whilst a narrow gauge railway winds it's way around the site.

Leeds Town Centre offers a great deal to occupy it's visitors, as well as some of the most beautiful baroque civic architecture in the North.

There is plenty of shopping available, with wonderful arcades and a large market, a regional theatre, Opera House and the City Museum and Art Gallery. The latter houses the Henry Moore Sculpture Gallery, founded by the late sculptor who was born in nearby Castleford. The Museum has been in existence for over 170 years and its collections are amongst the finest outside London. The exhibits range from coins to wildlife, dinosaurs to minerals, costumes to Greek and Roman marbles. The Natural History galleries are especially fascinating and include the largest egg in the world.

Travelling a small way out of the city centre, there are various places of interest, including , at **Fulneck**, a settlement originally founded by a German religious sect called the Moravian Brotherhood in 1742, which has kept much of its 18th century village atmosphere. One of the cottages has been restored and is now used as a museum.

Kirkstall Abbey, to the north-west of the city, is one of the most

Kirkstall Abbey

complete ruins in this part of Yorkshire. Building started in 1152 by the Cistercians and finished within a generation, and Kirkstall is regarded by many to reflect Cistercian architecture at it's most monumental. It was executed with the typical early Cistercian austerity, as can be seen in the simplicity of the outer domestic buildings, but the bell-tower, a 16th century addition was in contravention of the rule that there were to be no stone bell towers, considered an unnecessary vanity.

Nearby **Tong** is interesting for the Tong-Cockerdale Country Park, and area of reclaimed coal mines, ironworks, railways and mill-races which form a lovely semi-natural area with footpaths and walks. The village is situated on a minor road two miles to the south of Pudsey which is itself located midway between Leeds and Bradford.

In Tong Lane, we found the excellent inn and restaurant, **The Greyhound**, which is run by John and Pearl Argyle. This beautifully preserved building dates from the 16th-century and inside, old beamed ceilings and a fine collection of antique toby jugs help to create an atmosphere which is full of great character and charm. John and Pearl offer their customers a friendly welcome and a welcome pint of traditional ale, plus an excellent range of moderately priced bar meals in the charming surroundings of the inn's intimate little dining room. They also have an extensive a la carte menu.

The Greyhound

Also based here is the **Tong Village Hotel**, a large and superbly-appointed hotel surrounded by green belt countryside, yet which is only ten minutes drive from Leeds and Bradford. It can be reached by leaving the M62 at junction 27 and following the A650 towards Bradford; at the second roundabout take the third exit towards Drighlington and then the first left into Tong Lane; the hotel is approximately one mile on the right. The building has a pleasant country house atmosphere with a light and elegant interior and a friendly staff which offer attentive, yet unobtrusive service. In total, there are sixty beautifully decorated guest bedrooms, all with en suite bathrooms, televisions, direct-dial telephones and beverage making facilities. The hotel also has an excellent reputation

Tong Village Hotel

for the quality of its food and wines. A wide selection of imaginative á la carte dishes (including such local specialities as steak and mushroom pie) are served in Lautrec's Restaurant, whilst in the Tavern Bar, a first-rate bar meal can be enjoyed with a glass of wine or traditional ale. On Sundays, the house speciality is a splendid traditional roast lunch. For those keen to relax, there is a sauna, solarium and mini-gym, as well as a beautiful landscaped garden to the rear. The Tong Village Hotel also provides an ideal environment for business users and offers first-rate conference facilities including a photocopying and fax service and a choice of fully-equipped meeting rooms which can seat up to 300 delegates.

Anyone looking for a special night out should make a point of finding the impressive restaurant at **Lapwater Hall** in Westgate Hill, also in Tong.

Lapwater Hall

This fine establishment specialises in providing excellent-value all-inclusive evening meals and traditional Sunday lunches in splendid elegant surroundings. A typical dinner would include a starter, glass of wine, a main course such as chicken Kiev or fillet steak, dessert, coffee and glass of port. (Children's portions are available at half price except on Saturdays.) Meals are accompanied by music from a resident DJ who is only too pleased to accept requests, with diners being able to dance until late. Lapwater Hall welcomes party bookings and also provides catering for weddings and functions of up to 120 people.

Bradford is a city with a lot of entertainment to offer its visitors, with a number of interesting museums. Amongst these is the National Museum of Photography, Film and Television, which houses one of the largest cinema screens in the world.

The city has an excellent, pedestrianised centre, indoor market and a wide choice of Asian restaurants and supermarkets, selling everything you might need for cooking that authentic curry for discerning friends.

Possibly unfairly, Bradford has not received a very good press over the years, and hence recently, the EDU (Bradford Economic Development Unit) has been set up to oversee the redevelopment of Bradford's historical and cultural past.

One area of focus is **Little Germany**, the historic merchants' quarter, with its tall, handsome warehouses situated behind the Cathedral. The father of composer Frederick Delius plied his wares from one of these buildings.

Salt's Mill, built in 1853 by the cloth manufacturer Titus Salt (whose name conjures up thoughts of Dickensian novels) is a very impressive building, modelled on a 15th century Italian palace. Through sponsorship by local businessmen, the mill's interior has been beautifully transformed into the world's biggest Hockney art gallery.

Many others, such as the Victorian Merchant's House, have been transformed into prestigious office space, and other areas such as Bradford's stretch of the Aire Valley are also being targeted for redevelopment and conservation with business sponsorship help.

The fact that Bradford has a Cathedral is an indication of its historical importance as a city. The first evidence of worship on the site comes from the remains of a Saxon preaching cross, showing that Christians may have worshipped here since the mission of Paulinus to Northumbria in 627 AD. In Norman times, there may have been a wooden church here, and there was a stone church in the year 1327, which was probably burnt down in a Scottish raid. Bradford was involved against the Royalists in the Civil War, and the church was the focal point, being the highest point from where musket fire could be returned.

After the battle of Adwalton Moor in 1643, Bradford was besieged. The defenders hung woolsacks on the church tower to protect it from cannon fire. This did not protect the town from capture, but on 3rd March, 1644, John Lambert's army drove out the Royalists and then defeated a Royalist counter attack on March 25th.

As Bradford's wealth grew, due to the increasing trade in wool and cloth, so did the church, until in 1919, the city was granted it's own diocese, and major extensions took place.

The Cathedral contains many items of interest, including beautiful stained glass windows (some of which were designed by no less than William Morris), carvings and statuary. The old parts of the building are well worth exploring for their curiosities, and the door and steps used that lead to the famous tower from which the defenders of the city made their stand is still on public view.

In a magnificent elevated position four miles southwest of Bradford city centre, we found the famous **Black Dyke Mill**, in **Queensbury**. This working textile mill was founded in 1819 by entrepreneur John Foster and was named after his father-in-law's farm.

Black Dyke Mill

Today, it stands looking out over the surrounding valleys which for over 150 years sheltered the homes of first his outworkers and then his mill workers. John Foster, and later his son William, embody the very spirit of the Industrial Revolution, their family motto *'Do Right and Fear No One'* suggesting the high Victorian standards of the day. Recent massive investment in new technology has revitalised the mill and its present output of top quality cloth such as mohair ensure that its fabrics ultimately bear internationally-known labels of distinction. Visitors to the mill are welcome to call in at the celebrated **Mill Shop**. This is situated in the old stable block, across the car park from Prospect House, John Foster's home from 1827. Here, visitors can browse through shelves and racks full of trousers, sweaters, skirts, scarves and hats, all for sale at special mill shop prices. The mill shop attracts about 20,000 visitors each year, many of whom come to buy the famous worsted suit lengths. Black Dyke Mill is also famous for its brass band which was founded by John Foster and which in recent years has won a number of international accolades. Their many recordings are also available in the mill shop.

The towns to the north of Bradford, **Shipley**, **Saltaire** and **Bingley**, are interesting for a number of reasons. Although Shipley is mainly industrial, **Shipley Glen** is a very popular area for tourism, with its tramway, a narrow woodland valley with steep sides and huge millstone grit boulders, flanked by a plateau of moorland. There is a Japanese Garden with lake, created in the1890's, as well as various amenities for visitors, such as tea-houses, gift-shops, etc.

Saltaire was the model village created by the famous Titus Salt for the workers at his mill. Despite sounding like a dour Dickensian character, Salt was a very benevolent employer, and determined to provide his workers with everything essential for a decent standard of living, unlike many of the other unfortunate mill-workers who were forced to live in poverty and squalor. The facilities in the village were designed to cater for all his people's needs, health, leisure and education - but no public houses. Their spiritual needs were attended to by the elegant Congregational church, built in Roman classical style, with its lovely campanile tower, described as the most beautiful Free Church in the North of England. Salt's statue stands in nearby Robert's Park, (where swearing and gambling were banned) above the figures of a llama and an alpaca, whose wool he importedfor spinning in his mills. The houses are of mixed styles, in accordance with the tastes of his workers, who he consulted beforehand; Victoria Road, with its trees and elegant houses is probably the most famous.

The Victoria Boat House was built in 1871 and has been beautifully restored, with an open fire, pianola, wind-up gramophone, all recreating a traditional parlour atmosphere, which serves cream teas and runs special Victorian Evenings in fancy dress.

Saltaire

Saltaire also has an unusual Reed Organ Museum with a collection of over 45 instruments, including harmonicas and an American organ, which are demonstrated, also being available for visitors to try.

Bingley is a medieval town renowned for its staircase locks on the Leeds-Liverpool Canal, the "Three-rise" and "Five-rise", which each take at least take half an hour to negotiate. They were built in the 1770's and designed by John Longbotham of Halifax, with much of the mechanism still in workable order. The lock gates are of English Oak and are built to withstand 90,000 gallons of water. This area has some lovely walks, leading into the centre of Bingley via a path with the curious title of "Treacle Cock Alley". The history of the town is fascinating, mostly for the eccentricity of its inhabitants as much as anything.

In 1875, a writer called James Burnley described the incumbent of the local church as a "ritualistic firebrand - who froths and fumes and endeavours to frighten the people into penitential exercises". This did not appear to have a great amount of suppressive influence on the people of Bingley, whom he described, apart from their other numerous leisure activities, as "fond of indulging in practical jokes. If they can induce a greenhorn to fetch a pennorth o' strap oil from the grocer's or the second edition of Cock Robin from the booksellers, their delight is unbounded". This sounds as if the unfortunate Mr Burnley had been on the receiving end of their humour himself on occasion.

One fact that is worth noting if in this area of rich industrial towns, is that the heritage of grandiose Victorian and earlier buildings have provided many venues for museums and exhibition halls, information for these being available from the local tourist information offices.

In the south-eastern corner of the South Pennine Heritage area, we found a truly first-rate inn, **The Duke of York**, which is situated between Halifax and Bradford at **Stone Chair, Shelf**, which is close to the junction of the A644 and A6036.

This 17th-century former coaching inn still retains much of its original character with oak-beamed ceilings, open fireplaces and a fascinating collection of antique brassware and china whisky jugs. The Duke of York offers a lively atmosphere, seven different cask-conditioned ales, a good selection of malt whiskies and a varied menu of home-cooked meals including sandwiches, jacket potatoes, steaks, fish, grills and an imaginative choice of Indian dishes. These are served every lunchtime and evening, with an excellent traditional roast lunch also being available on Sundays.

The Duke of York

Owners Pat and Steven Whitaker also have eleven charming letting bedrooms available, all with en suite facilities, colour televisions and tea/coffee making facilities. Five are in the inn, with the other six being situated in converted weavers' cottages nearby.

Nearby **Halifax** has more than its fair share of these, and the large and beautiful **Piece Hall** is probably the most impressive. It possesses a large quadrangle, in which the excellent Sunday market is held, colonnades and balconies, under the shadow of which are interesting shops and commercial outlets. There is also an art gallery with a varied programme of contemporary exhibitions and workshops. Built in the 17th century, it was originally utilised for the selling of cloth, and in the 18th, after having been allowed to fall into disrepair, was renovated with the permission of Lord Ingram. The existing hall was replaced in 1779, in the midst of great rejoicing and celebration, and has been the centre of trade, in one way or another, ever since.

Piece Hall, Halifax

The Town Hall is another notable building, designed by Sir Charles Barry, who also designed the Houses of Parliament. There is an attractive Borough Market, constructed in cast-iron and glass, with an ornate central clock. In Gibbet Street stands a grisly reminder of the past - a replica of a guillotine. In the 18th century, Halifax was renowned for its executions of felons, hence the saying "from Hull , Hell and Halifax, Good Lord Deliver Us".

Halifax has the largest Parish Church in England, of almost cathedral sized proportions, which dates from the 12th and 13th centuries, although most of the present building is from the 15th century. There is a lovely wooden ceiling which was constructed in 1635, and visitors should look out for "Old Tristram", a life-sized wooden effigy of a beggar, reputedly based on a local character, which was once the church poor box.

There are a lot of hidden places in old Halifax to explore,. From Shear's Inn, an old weavers inn below the centre, one can walk up the cobbled Boy's Lane, very little changed from Victorian times, or trace out the ancient Magna Via, a medieval path to the summit of Breacon Hill.

Of museums, the **Calderdale Industrial Museum**, which houses still-working looms and mill-machinery, the **"Horses at Work Museum"** at Dobbin's Yard and the **Bankfield Museum** are worthy of a visit.

Shibden Hall and Park, about two miles out of town, is somewhere very special that should not be missed. The Old hall itself lies in a valley on the outskirts of the town and is situated in 90 acres of parkland, The distinctive timber-framed house dates from 1420 and is deliberately furnished to reflect the various periods of its history. There is a particularly good collection of 17th and 18th century furniture and various domestic items. The 17th century barn behind the Hall houses a fine collection of horse-drawn vehicles and the original buildings have been transformed into a 19th century village centre with a pub, estate-worker's cottage, and saddler's, blacksmith's, wheelwright's and potter's workshops.

Shibden Hall

Between Halifax and Keighley is a wide expanse of moorland, including Heptonstall Moor, Haworth Moor and Keighley Moor.

On the way out to these, on a day's drive, one first comes to the mill-town of **Hebden Bridge**, characteristic by the stepped formation of its houses, which are stacked one on top of the other up the hill, reminiscent of a cornish fishing village.

Its unusual perspectives have provided an excellent tourist spot - once filled with factories producing trousers and corduroy, it is now a place of bookshops, antique shops, restaurants and a market, all open on Sundays.

One can walk up the hill to **Stoodley Pike**, an awe-inspiring place with the best views of the moor. One can also visit **Automobilia**, a traditional moorland textile mill converted to house a remarkable collection of Austin and Morris cars, motoring memorabilia, early cycles and motorbikes. The museum also has an unusual hire service, and for a fee, you can glide along the Pennine roads in an Austin seven or Morris Eight to the envy of passers-by

Automobilia

Originally opened in 1804 following ten years of construction, the impressive Rochdale Canal was the first to cross the Pennines. Today, this remarkable feat of engineering is gradually being restored by the Rochdale Canal Trust who hope to have the work completed in time for its 200th birthday. The seven-mile Calderdale section between Sowerby Bridge and Todmorden is now fully reopened; this contains nineteen locks and passes through some of the loveliest countryside and small industrial communities in West Yorkshire. The best way to explore this stretch of the canal is to take a barge trip from Hebden Bridge Marina with Calder Valley Cruising, an efficient and enthusiastic company who run regular trips using both powered and horse-drawn narrow boats and barges.

Another of the attractions in Hebden Bridge is the **Birchcliffe Centre**, a unique residential and conference centre which is located in Birchcliffe Road, just to the north of the town centre. Standing on a hillside overlooking the town, this former Baptist chapel and Sunday school was one of the largest and most impressive of its time when it was completed in 1899. The magnificent old chapel was converted into a conference hall and office space in 1977 which enabled it to take on a new role whilst leaving its exterior character virtually untouched. Since then, the conference hall has played host to the BBC's *Clothes Show*, the AGM of a large building society and a large number of smaller events including private functions and wedding receptions.

Calder Valley Cruising

In 1980, conversion work began on the old Sunday school building to provide sleeping accommodation for up to 62 guests. These are accommodated in large four-berth Scandinavian-style rooms which are all equipped with en suite facilities. Delicious English and continental breakfasts and dinners are served in the dining room on the basement floor, and packed lunches are also available if required.

Birchcliffe Centre

Today, the Birchcliffe Centre is used by all kinds of groups, families and individuals who come to use the excellent study and leisure facilities provided by the Centre, the town and the surrounding area. It is also located within a mile of the Pennine Way and is often used as a stopping

Hebden Bridge

point on this scenic long-distance walk.

A little known fact is that Hebden Bridge was one of the first purpose-built industrial towns in the world. It has seen many changes of fortune and today stands as a proud monument of an era which changed the entire world.

The town retains its early character with mills lining every waterway and its unique houses seeming to cling to the hillsides.

Local conservationists have saved many of its ancient mills and converted them them for a wide range of new uses. Be sure not to miss the oldest and most attractive, **Bridge Mill**, at the very heart of the town in St George's Square. Once the Lord of the Manor's corn mill, it was first built by royal charter in 1314. Reconstructed many times after river floods and even civil war damage, it has now been converted to speciality shops, craft workshops, an excellent Italian restaurant, Il Mulino (ie. the Mill). The Innovation licenced cafe, with its tranquil riverside terrace, serves a delicious selection of home-made foods and is famed for its authentic Breton Galettes - hot savoury pancakes with a choice of tasty fillings, each a meal in itself.

On the south side of the town, the historic 200 year old Rochdale Canal crosses the river by means of a huge stone aquaduct, a well protected ancient monument still in daily use as boats pass back and forth through the locks. A little way alongthe towpath, the **Hebble End Craft Work-**

shops are a must for all visitors to the town. An internal street within this finely restored former factory leads to a collection of small workshops where craftsmen and women demonstrate their skills and sell their wares. Glassblowers, artists, wood-carvers, cabinet-makers, leather-workers.... and so much more can be seen. Special commissions are produced to order for that special present.

Bridge Mill

Only one and three quarter miles from the village, one will find Hardcastle Crags, a National Trust property. This steep, thickly wooded valley has a distinctly Alpine feel to it, with dense areas of oak, birch and pine woods, with some interesting and rare wildlife. There are way-marked trails to follow, one of which leads past Slurry Rock, where local children once slid down on their clogs. The three mile valley leads to Blake Dean, with its waterfalls and paths, up to Widdop Reservoir and on to Haworth.

Whilst in this area, one should not miss out on a visit to **Heptonstall**, a lovely, quiet and traditional moorland village, filled with winding, cobbled streets of cottages with mullioned windows, courts, inns and chapels. Cats gaze serenely at any passers-by from the window, adding to the tranquility of the place. There is a famous old Grammar school, which houses an exhibition of Heptonstall's textile past, medieval cobbled paths and the wonderful ruined church of St Thomas a Becket, which dominates the skyline. The blackened ruins are haunting, the graveyard compelling in its mystery, amongst which is the gravestone of Sylvia Plath, the American novelist. The crooked towers in their state of decay, are charming - may they never collapse, as they threaten to!

Curious travellers may feel compelled to visit the cheekily-titled

Slack Bottom. The inhabitants hereabouts must have had a ribald sense of humour - the surrounding hills have been given such names as Back of Behind, Too To Hill, and others that cannot be mentioned here!

Travelling further west, we turned south off the A646 Halifax to Burnley road at Todmorden to go in search of the **Top Brink Inn** which is situated in the pleasant old village of **Lumbutts**. This splendid establishment is a Free House and was bought by the present owners Jim and Dilys Ashton in 1991. They run the Inn along with their family, Martin, Mark and Paula. Martin is a trained chef and it is for its food that the Top Brink Inn is best known with people coming from miles around to sample the delights of the kitchen. Among the renowned specialities are T-- Bone steaks, homemade steak pie, prime gammon and delicious Cumberland sausages. On Sundays an excellent value traditional roast lunch is also offered which is extremely popular.

In the short time that they have been in charge, Dilys and Jim have totally transformed the building (which was previously known as the Dog and Partridge) into a truly first-rate inn. Today, the bars have been sympathetically restored and offer an excellent range of traditional ales in an atmosphere which is comfortable and welcoming, there is that extra special touch with fresh flowers on the bars and the window sills, all adding to a relaxed and intimate ambience.

Outside, there is a spacious car park and an attractive beer garden which is ideal for walkers and families with young children. At the time we visited an impressive conservatory was being planned which will add greatly to the attractiveness of this already first-class establishment.

Top Brink Inn

A restaurant offering delicious food, fine wines and remarkably good value for money is the **Dumb Waiter** in nearby **Todmorden**. This delightful bistro can be found three miles southwest of Hebden Bridge in Water Street, just outside Todmorden's town centre. Inside, you will find umbrella lamp shades hanging from the ceiling, interesting prints on the walls and an atmosphere which is completely relaxed and congenial. The restaurant is owned and personally run by hard-working husband and wife team Colin and Wendy Sweet, two former teachers who have embarked on a second career. Together they prepare and serve a truly imaginative series of dishes, many of which are suitable for vegetarians. Open Wednesdays to Sundays, 12pm to 2pm and 7pm to 10pm. Recommended.

The Dumb Waiter

Travelling across the moors on the B6033, will bring one to that most popular of Yorkshire tourist spots, **Haworth**.

Once a bleak, moorland town, in a dramatic setting that fired the romantic imaginations of the Bronte sisters, it has been transformed into a lively, attractive place, with wonderful tea-houses, street theatre and antique and craft shops. It is, however, worth exploring the ginnels and back roads off the steeply rising High Street, to get a feeling of what the place was like in the days of the Brontes.

One might also choose to take the leafy paths on the outskirts of the town that lead over stone bridges and sparkling streams, past grey stone mills, with the occasional steam train rushing past. **The Worth Valley Steam Railway** sheds are always fascinating. When we visited in the summer, there were a team of men working on a huge engine, manipulating it with a combination of chains attached to the old steam driven crane, still in good working order.

Today, Haworth is a very different place to how it must have been in the Brontes' day. It was then a thriving, industrial town, squalid amidst the smoke from its chimneys, filled with the noise of the clattering looms, which were rarely still.

Near the centre of Howarth, we found the wonderful tea rooms and guesthouse which are run by Jeanne Wilson and her staff. Formerly two weavers' cottages, **Heather Cottage** dates from the 17th-century and is now Grade II listed; inside, it has original stone-flagged floors and a charming traditional atmosphere. The menu offers an outstanding range of delicious home-cooked food, toasted sandwiches, jacket potatoes, salads and desserts, as well as delicious home-baked cakes and pastries. Jeanne also has three beautifully-appointed en-suite letting bedrooms available, all with central heating colour televisions and beverage making facilities. Open all year round. Children and pets welcome.

Heather Cottage

The Parsonage, built in 1789, is the focus of most Bronte pilgrimages. The Bronte Society have restored the interior to be as close as possible to how it was when the sisters were here. There are exhibitions and displays of contemporary material, personal belongings, letters and portraits, as well as a priceless collection of manuscripts, first editions and memorabilia in the newer extension.

Bronte enthusiasts can sit in the **Black Bull**, where Branwell sent himself to an early grave on a mixture of strong Yorkshire ale, opium and despair (although the last two are not available here these days, we can heartily recommend the ale!)

Bronte Parsonage

The Post Office, from where the sisters sent their manuscripts to London publishers, is still as it was, as is the Sunday School at which they all taught. Sadly the church which they all attended, no longer exists, although Charlotte, Emily and Branwell, with the exception of Anne, who is buried in Scarborough, all lie in a vault in the newer church, which dates from1879.

Apart from being the home of the Brontë Sisters and the Keighley & Worth Valley Steam Railway, Howarth provides an ideal base for exploring the many delights of West Yorkshire. Those looking for first-class bed and breakfast accommodation in this delightful town should make a point of finding **Ye Sleeping House** in Main Street at the foot of Howarth Hill. Here, Mike Hutchison provides the warmest hospitality and an enormous full English breakfast. All guest bedrooms have washbasins, remote-control colour televisions, tea/coffee making facilities and many extras. Enquire about the Mike's special Victorian weekends which take place during December and feature a full traditional Christmas dinner on the Saturday evening which comes complete with crackers, hats and lots of surprises.

The countryside around Haworth inspires the modern visitor as much as it did the Brontes, a landscape that recurs in their novels, as an escape from their often drab and uninteresting lives. This is excellent walking country, and if you should get the chance, it is worth taking a trip via the Penistone Hill Country Park, following the rough track by old moorland farms, to the Bronte falls and stone footbridge, for so long one of the sisters' favourite walks. If you are feeling energetic, you may wish to

Ye Sleeping House

continue on to the romantic, deserted ruins of Top Withins Farm, said to have been the inspiration for the setting of "Wuthering Heights".

Near the junction of the A644 and B6145, in between Howarth and Bradford, we found the wonderful family-run bakery and tearoom, **Asa Nicholson's**, in **Keelham** near **Denholme**. The business dates back to 1898 when young Asa Nicholson turned his hand to baking after he was unable to earn a living in the quarrying industry. After many years of successful growth, the present-day bakery is still run by Asa's grandson and great-grandson. Visitors to the shop and tearoom can see the staff busily at work through the modern bakery's viewing windows. Apart from over 100 retail lines, the Nicholsons provide a wide range of delicious light meals, beverages and desserts in their busy tearooms. They also offer an efficient wholesale service.

A S A Nicholson & Sons

CHAPTER 9

Heptonstall

Huddersfield to Pontefract

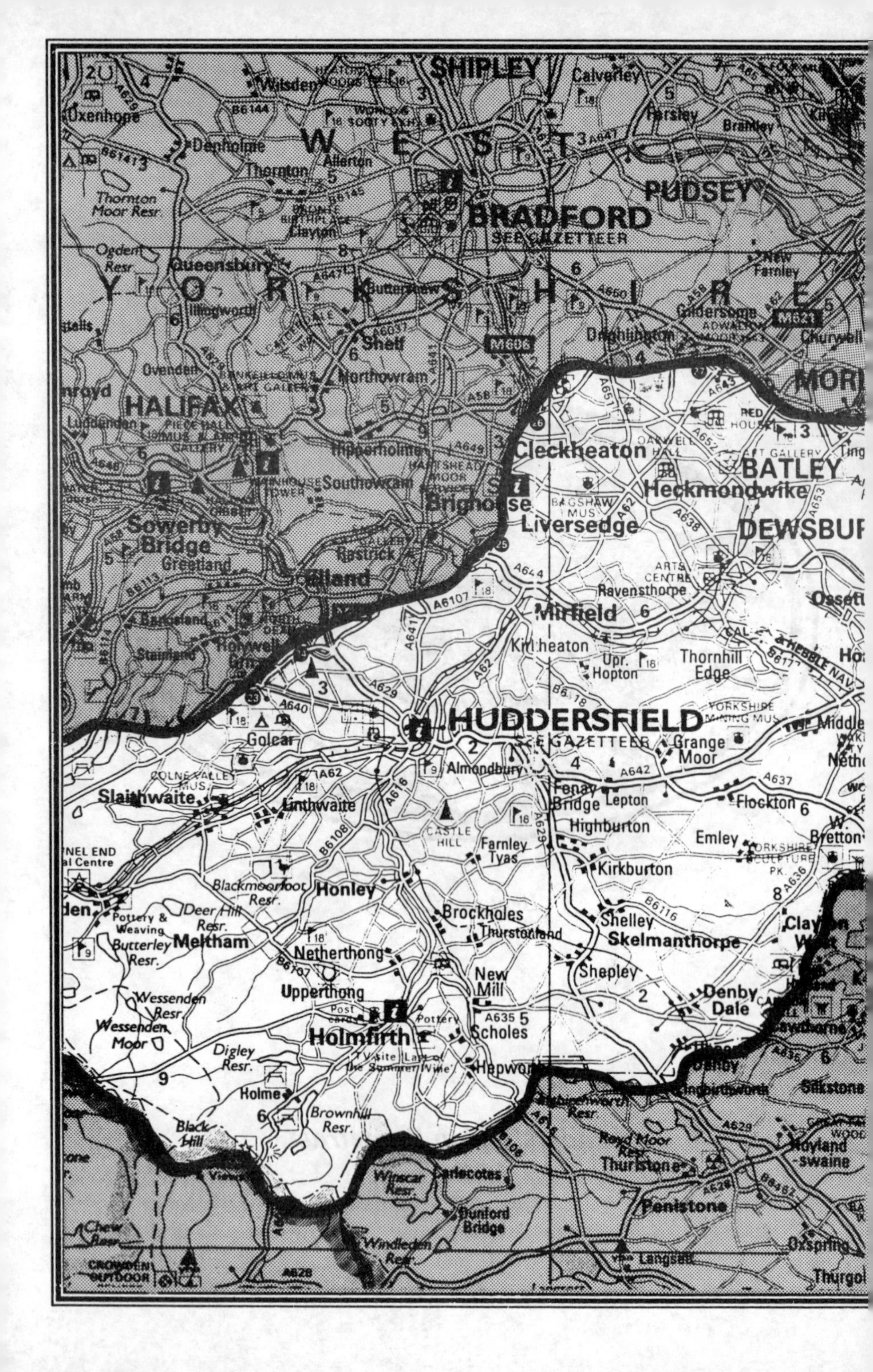
SHIPLEY
Calverley
Wilsden
Oxenhope
Denholme
WEST
YORKSHIRE
Allerton
Thornton
Thornton Moor Resr.
PUDSEY
BRADFORD
SEE GAZETTEER
Clayton
Ogden Resr.
Queensbury
New Farnley
Illingworth
Gildersome
Drighlington
Shelf
Ovenden
Northowram
HALIFAX
Luddenden
Hipperholme
Cleckheaton
BATLEY
Southowram
Heckmondwike
Brighouse
Liversedge
DEWSBURY
Sowerby Bridge
Greetland
Rastrick
Elland
Ravensthorpe
Mirfield
Kirkheaton
Upr. Hopton
Thornhill Edge
HUDDERSFIELD
Golcar
Grange Moor
Almondbury
Slaithwaite
Linthwaite
Fenay Bridge
Lepton
Flockton
Highburton
Emley
Farnley Tyas
Kirkburton
Blackmoorfoot Resr.
Honley
Deer Hill Resr.
Brockholes
Shelley
Meltham
Butterley Resr.
Thurstonland
Skelmanthorpe
Netherthong
Shepley
Upperthong
New Mill
Denby Dale
Wessenden Resr.
Wessenden Moor
Holmfirth
Scholes
Digley Resr.
Hepworth
Holme
Brownhill Resr.
Black Hill
Silkstone
Royd Moor Resr.
Thurlstone
Winscar Resr.
Carlecotes
Penistone
Dunford Bridge
Windleden Resr.
Oxspring
Langsett

Barwick in Elmet
Chapel Allerton
Roundhay
Scholes
Aberford
Church Fenton
Saxton
Barkston
Harehill
Manston
Little Fenton
Old Micklefield
LEEDS
SEE GAZETTEER
Garforth
Sherburn in Elmet
Hunslet
South Milford
Kippax
Swillington
Ledsham
Monk Fryston
Rothwell
Woodlesford
Gt. Preston
Middleton
Fairburn
Hillam
Mickletown
Allerton Bywater
Burton Salmon
CASTLEFORD
Lofthouse
Outwood
Ferrybridge
Wrenthorpe
Altofts
Normanton
WAKEFIELD
SEE GAZETTEER
Ackton
Pontefract
Warmfield
Featherstone
Purston Jaglin
Darrington
Sharlston
Crofton
E. Hardwick
High Ackworth
Walton
Wentbridge
Ackworth Moor Top
Crigglestone
Wintersett
Thorpe Audin
Fitzwilliam
Kirk Smeaton
Woolley
Kinsley
Badsworth
Ryhill
Campsall
Notton
South Hiendley
Upton
Hemsworth
Royston
Carlton
South Kirkby
Hampole
Grimethorpe
Cudworth
Clayton
Hooton Pagnell
BARNSLEY
Gt. Houghton
Brodsworth
Thurnscoe
Hickleton
Marr
Worsbrough
Darfield
Billingley
Dearne
Barnburgh
Wombwell
Bolton upon Dearne
Adwick-upon-Dearne
High Melton
Birdwell
Brampton

Countryside Centre, Tunnel End

Reference Guide

CHAPTER 9

DEARDEN GALLERY (Art Gallery)	OSSETT	0924 265000
ELM CREST GUEST HOUSE (Guest House)	EGERTON	0924 530990
HIGHLIFE (Place of Interest)	HOLMFIRTH	
WHITE CROSS FARM (B&B)	EMLEY	0924 848339
WHITELEY'S GARDEN CTRE. (Garden Centre)	MIRFIELD	0924 495944
YORKSHIRE SCULPTURE PK. (Sculpture Park)	WEST BRETTON	0924 830302

Ackworth Friends' School

CHAPTER 9

Huddersfield to Pontefract

Huddersfield may seem an unlikely place to begin a tour of this region, but its streets and Yorkshire stone buildings, blackened with years of industrialisation, have an honest, no-nonsense charm that have a certain appeal.

It has a gritty, industrial atmosphere, with steep, often cobbled streets, a mixture of terraced houses, older millstone grit cottages and larger Victorian dwellings, some interesting pubs and a skyline dominated by the scars and marks of its industrialisation. The wealthy lords of the manor hereabouts were the Ramsdens, and much of the grand architecture in the centre is due to their efforts. There is a very impressive railway station, designed by James Pigott of York and built between 1846-50. Other buildings of interest include the Italianate Town Hall, the neo-Gothic Parish Church of St Peter and Bryam Arcade. The Brook Street market is another pleasant place to wander around.

The outskirts of the town are interesting, and many visitors may decide to head towards the highest point in the area, **Castle Hill**, about two miles south of Huddersfield. It is considered one of the most important archaeological sites in Yorkshire. The hill, a high moorland ridge overlooking the Colne and Holme Valleys has been occupied as a place of defence since Stone Age times, circa 20,000 BC, by what are believed to be Neolithic herdsmen from mainland Europe - simple tools, flints, bone needles, combs and pottery have been unearthed to substantiate this. The magnificent ramparts of the Iron Age Fort, built here in 600 BC can still be seen, later destroyed by fire. In 1147, the Normans restored the earthworks, building a motte and bailey castle here, which was apparently used as a base for hunting. The hill was also used as a beacon during the times of the Armada and also during the Napoleonic wars. At present, it is crowned with the Jubilee Tower, built in 1897, to celebrate Queen Victoria's reign. It stands at just under 1000 ft above sea level and apart from offering wonderful panoramic views of the valleys, it also houses an exhibition of the hill's long history.

The **Elm Crest Guest House** in Queens Road, **Edgerton** is an ideal stopping place for those looking for quiet and friendly accommodation in the northwestern suburbs of Huddersfield. This handsome Victorian residence is located on the A629, one mile from the city centre and within easy reach of the M62, junction 24. Owner Derek Gee offers guests the warmest of welcomes and the very best in home-cooked cuisine. Derek is a keen chef and is justifiably proud of the Elm Crest's reputation for excellent food (Les Routier and Michelin listed). The guesthouse stands within a large attractive garden and has eight letting bedrooms, all beautifully decorated and appointed to a high modern standard. English Tourist Board 'three crown' rated.

Elm Crest Guest House

Nearby **Almondbury Village** has a charming old part with several interesting 17th century buildings. The Church of Old Hallows dates from the 13th century, with lovely 15th century stained glass windows. However, if you get the chance, look up at the ceiling and observe the wonderful carved bosses, representing the instruments of passion, in grotesque faces, a half-moon, a face with two tongues and a head with three eyes and two noses.

Golcar, less than three miles from Huddersfield was once an important woollen weaving centre, and one can still see the weavers' cottages with their long mullioned windows. It is also the home of the Colne Valley Museum, based in 19th century cottages converted to their original state. One loom chamber has been turned into a gas-lit cloggers' workshop, whilst the ground floor is a Victorian parlour. The village is also the start of the 12 mile Colne Valley circular walk along paths and old tracks between moorland farms to Marsden and beyond - an interesting place to discover the hidden places of the Valley which can be done in stages, sometimes using public transport. A booklet explaining it is on sale in the museum.

Whilst in the area, many will no doubt feel compelled to visit **Holmfirth**, better known as the location of the television series "Last Of The Summer Wine", and despite the commercialisation, their trip will not be disappointing.

Visitors can take a trip past the real Sid's Cafe, Nora Batty's cottage and sit in the famous pub. The rest of the town offers a network of side lanes, courts and alleyways, and with some interesting shops and cafes besides. The terraces of weaver's cottages are typical of a town famous for its production of wool textiles. As with so many of these moors villages, there is a lot of water surrounding it, in the form of streams, tarns and reservoirs, and in its time, Holmfirth has suffered three major floods, of which the flood of 1852 was the worst. The nearby Bilbury Reservoir burst its banks, killing 81 people and destroying mills, cottages and farms at the cost of 7,000 jobs. A pillar near the church records the height of the waters.

The lovely Georgian church was built in 1777-8 in neo-classical style to the designs of Joseph Jagger. The gable faces the street and the tower is constructed at the eastern end against a steep hillside. Also in Holmfirth is the delightful Holmfirth Postcard Museum (above the library) based on nearby Balmforth's - the country's leading producers of the traditional saucy seaside postcard. The displays also include cards from over nearly a century, including patriotic cards form World War One, less sentimental ones from World War Two and a moving audio-visual documentary presentation of the 1852 flood.

Whilst in Holmfirth, it is well worth finding the interesting retail outlet, **High Life**, which is run by Chris Howlings. This unusual establishment stands at river level behind the bus station and the Old Bridge Hotel in **Norridge Bottom**.

High Life

Holmfirth

During the last century, the rooms above the shop were occupied by Irish tinkers and the adjacent building was the home of a notorious brothel. The modern shop offers a carefully selected range of jewellery and crafts, some locally-made and some from such exotic locations as Bali, Thailand, Mexico and Morocco. Other items on display include scarves, rugs, purses and batik work, as well as a wide selection of fascinating books on subjects ranging from local history to philosophy and art.

The small surrounding villages, such as **Upperthong**, **Netherthong** and **Hepworth** are also worthy of exploration, and **Denby Dale**, eight miles to the east, is famous for its production of gigantic meat pies, a tradition which was started to celebrate King George III's recovery from mental illness. Several have been produced since then, to celebrate such occasions as the battle of Waterloo and the repeal of the Corn Laws. One of the most recent was in 1964, when the pie measured 18ft long and weighed six and a half tons. The last one was in 1987, the dish now on display just outside the village.

Travelling north, the minor country roads to the south of the A642 Wakefield to Huddersfield road led us to the lovely village of **Emley**, three miles east of Kirkburton. On the outskirts of the village we found **White Cross Farm**, a working farm which also offers first-rate farmhouse bed and breakfast accommodation. The house which originally occupied the site was constructed in the 11th-century and was inhabited by Cistercian monks from Byland Abbey near Helmsley. The splendid present-day farmhouse was rebuilt during the 16th-century and was once the home of a Royalist captain who was captured by Cromwell following the fall of Wakefield on Whit Sunday, 1644.

White Cross Farm

The present owner, Marie Gill, offers her guests comfortable farmhouse accommodation and wonderful Yorkshire hospitality.

Bretton Hall, a handsome neoclassical mansion built in 1720, is in the private grounds of Bretton College. This superbly landscaped estate of enclosed parkland and mature trees is open to the public and contains miles of walks, lakes and gardens. Part of the gardens is taken up by the **Yorkshire Sculpture Park**, a unique outdoor setting for permanent and changing exhibitions of important works of sculpture. The Park was founded in 1977, and as well as being known for its major exhibitions, it is also famous for its permanent collection of sculptures by artists such as Henry Moore, Elizabeth Frink and Barbara Hepworth. At certain times it is possible to see sculptors working on site; it is also possible to actually create a piece oneself in one of the public sculpture workshops. In recent years, the Yorkshire Sculpture Park has taken a further step forward by opening an Access Sculpture Trail which has been specially designed for disabled and elderly people. There is also disabled access to the park shop and Bothy Café. The Country Park is open daily and is best reached from the small car park and visitor centre which is situated just off the A637 north of junction 38 on the M1. The entrance to the Sculpture Park is in West Bretton, a short distance further north.

Yorkshire Sculpture Park

Mirfield, to the south-west of Dewsbury, has some interesting buildings and a popular canal basin from where there is a summer waterbus service to nearby Brighouse, of brass-band fame. The town also has it's

Bronte associations; Emily and Charlotte went to Roe Head School near here and Emily based her novel "Agnes Grey" on Blake Hall, where she was governess.

If you happen to be a keen gardener, a truly top class garden centre can be found beside the A62 near Mirfield, between Dewsbury and Huddersfield. **Whiteleys Garden Centre** in Leeds Road was named the Regional Garden Centre of the Year by the Garden Centre Association for three years in succession between 1988 and 1990. (The trophy is now on permanent display at Whiteleys who were named outright winners when the competition came to an end in 1990.) The centre is owned and managed by Dennis and Linda Whiteley who, along with their twenty friendly and well-trained staff, strive to offer their customers the widest range of top quality plants that is available anywhere. The centre employs a flair for display more commonly seen at the Chelsea Flower Show and takes great pride in introducing new and unusual varieties of garden and house plants. Dennis and Linda have successfully created a relaxed and unpressured environment, both in their indoor showrooms and in their beautifully maintained outdoor plant areas. They also offer their customers an enormous range of garden furniture, barbecues, terra-cotta pots, floral art arrangements, books and gifts. Whiteleys Garden Centre is open every day until 8pm throughout the spring and summer, and can be found on an attractive green-belt site on the northern side of the A62 Huddersfield to Leeds road. It is easily reached by taking exit 25 off the M62, driving south for one mile, then picking up the eastbound A62 for another mile.

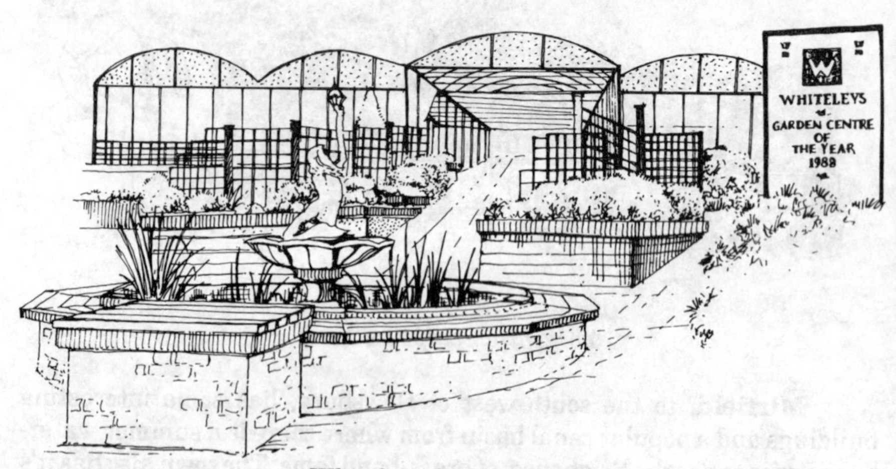

Whiteleys Garden Centre

Three miles to the north, lies **Dewsbury**, which probably has even less of a reputation as a tourist magnet than Huddersfield. It is an extremely old town which once had considerable influence. It remains the centre of Yorkshire's heavy woollen industry, filled as it is with old mills and warehouses. It has one of the region's oldest town centres with an imposing Town Hall (1888-9) designed by Henry Ashton and George Fox. It also has a number of other notable public and commercial buildings and it has a substantial shopping centre with a famous market.

The Church of All Saints is situated, according to legend, at the point where Saint Paulinus baptised converts in the river Calder. It dates from the 12th century, although the tower was designed by the eminent York architect, John Carr, in 1767. The interior is interesting, with several intriguing features, including fragments of an Anglo-Saxon Cross and coffin lids. It is, however, best known for its custom of tolling the Devil's Knell on Christmas Eve to ward off evil spirits - the bell is known as Black Tom. Patrick Bronte was the curate of Dewsbury between 1809-11 and Charlotte taught at Wealds House School nearby which was run by Miss Wooler, who later gave her away when she married.

One place of interest to visit whilst in the town, is **Crow Nest Park**, a landscaped park, also containing a Victorian mansion, which contains the **Dewsbury Museum of Childhood**, which has a reconstructed classroom and a wonderful display of toys and dolls.

North of the town, is **Batley**, with its pleasant cobbled market-place, handsome Town Hall and Library. The Central Chapel in the Square, built in 1869, was known as "Shoddy Temple" because of the amount of business done by local textile merchants on the steps after Sunday morning service (shoddy is a cloth made from old rags reworked with new wool - a technique of recycling materials to make a cheaper cloth, hence the association with the term of abuse "shoddy"). The technique was discovered by Benjamin Law, known as the "Shoddy King", who lies buried in the Church.

Batley is also the home of the **Bagshaw Museum**, which has extensive collections of ancient Egyptian and oriental artifacts, as well as natural and local history displays - definitely not to be missed if visiting the area.

Nearby is Oakwell Hall, a remarkable Elizabethan timber Manor house, furnished exactly as it would have been in the 17th and 18th centuries. It has a carefully recreated Jacobean herb garden, wildlife garden, arboretum and 87 acres of parkland. It also has strong Civil War and Bronte connections.

Thornhill, two miles to the east, is an old village connected with the

Savile family who built Thornhill Hall in Rectory Park. The hall was burnt down in 1648, when Royalist forces were besieged by Parliamentary forces under Colonel Charles Fairfax. The village contains a fine church with a Gothic interior and several interesting buildings dating from the 17th century.

The attractive town of **Ossett** is situated midway between Wakefield and Dewsbury, close to junction 40 of the M1. Here, we made a point of calling in at the **Wellgate Centre**, a new development of eleven shops and offices which has been carefully designed and constructed to blend in with the original architecture of the old town. The Centre is built around a well which was discovered on the site during construction and which has now been turned into an attractive wishing well.

The impressive **Dearden Gallery** is located in a renovated mill, just south of **Ossett**'s town hall. This carefully restored 'shoddy mill' ceased its original operations in 1986 and now forms the perfect environment for exhibiting works of art in a variety of styles. Within its well-lit interior, there is a fascinating display of original works by local painters and craftspeople, as well as a large collection of reproductions and limited-edition prints, many at surprisingly affordable prices. Exhibitions are changed every six to eight weeks to ensure a fresh and varied selection.

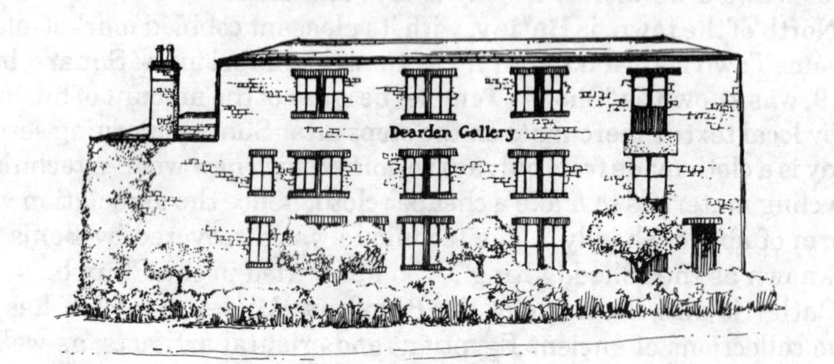

Dearden Gallery

Travelling in an easterly direction, the next big town is **Wakefield**, one of the oldest towns in Yorkshire, which was a focal point even in Anglo-Saxon times.

The town stands on a hill guarding an important crossing of the River Calder, which has been a major routeway ever since those times.

Its strategic importance was further emphasised during the Wars of the Roses. When the Duke of York was defeated in the Battle of Wakefield in 1460, it gave rise to the song "The Grand Old Duke of York". There is also a strong argument that Robin Hood came from here - according to the Court Rolls, one Robin Hode lived here in the 14th century with his wife Matilda before fleeing to become an outlaw.

Wakefield is also well-known for its cycle of medieval miracle plays, which explore New and Old Testament stories in vivid language. The cycle is performed on the precinct in front of the Cathedral as part of the city's annual festival.

There are three main streets, Westgate, Northgate and Kirkgate ("gate" being Nordic for street or road), which still run exactly where they did in medieval times. The tiny Chantry Chapel on Chantry Bridge (the old Wakefield Bridge) dates from the mid 14th century and is one of the only four such examples of bridge chapels - and the best - in England. It was believed to have been originally built by Edward IV to commemorate the brutal murder of his brother Edmund.

Chantry Chapel, Wakefield

This modern city, close to the great Yorkshire coalfields, remains an important industrial and administrative centre, and until 1974, was the county town of the West Riding. The status that this brought the town is evident in some of the grand architecture that can still be seen. Just north of the centre, on the site of the medieval town (where there are still old inns and courtyards) are some stately Georgian and Regency terraces and squares. There are fine civic buildings too, most notably the Town Hall, the County Courts and the huge County Hall, a beautiful building with a sumptuous interior, and the recently restored Edwardian Theatre Royal. The town centre is mostly pedestrianised and dominated by the Cathedral with its 247 ft spire - the highest in Yorkshire.

There are some award-winning shopping centres, and much more to see in this lively, friendly town.

The Elizabethan Grammar School, in Brook Street near the market, has been superbly restored as an exhibition centre and small art gallery. **The Wakefield Art Gallery** in Wentworth Terrace is located in an attractive former Victorian vicarage and houses an important collection of contemporary British artists. **The Wakefield Museum** is located in a 19th century building in Wood Street, originally a music saloon and public rooms and later converted into a Mechanics Institute. It houses a collection of local archaeology, history and social history of Wakefield from Pre-historic times to the present day. There is also an excellent permanent display of exotic birds and animals collected by the noted 19th century traveller and naturalist Charles Waterton, who lived at nearby Walton Hall , a house built on an island on a lake.

Other museums to visit are the **Stephen G Beaumont Museum**, which houses an unusual exhibition of medical memorabilia, and the **Yorkshire Mining Museum** at **Overton**.

Those looking for more outdoor diversions, could take a walk through Thornes Park, with its lovely open parkland and gardens. The remains of an early motte and bailey castle can be discovered amidst the shrubbery here.

The satellite village of **Heath** is well-worth a visit for its beautiful village green and magnificent houses built for the wealthy merchants of Wakefield. These include Heath House, built in the 1740's for James Paine, architect of Nostell Priory, and Heath Hall built by John Carr.

Sandal is now an attractive suburb of the town, with a remarkably well-hidden castle, which should be visited by all lovers of medieval history. This Norman motte and bailey structure was a stronghold for the Norman Manor of Wakefield, captured from the Saxons, that covered most of the Calder Valley. This was the scene of the historic battle of Wakefield which was fought in the midst of a snowstorm in December 1460, when the Duke of York was killed by Lancastrian forces and his head displayed at Micklegate Bar in York. There is a Victorian monument to the battle on Castle Road, where flowers appear each year to commemorate the battle.

The castle was garrisoned by Charles 1's forces during the Civil War, and after a siege was demolished on the orders of Parliament. Little now remains apart from the foundations of this once impressive fortress.

Nearby is **Pugneys Country Park**, an area of man-made lakes created out of old mine subsidence areas where land has been cleverly reclaimed and restored for various leisure activities. Other areas of similar interest nearby are Newmillerdam, a nature and water reserve, based around an old mill dam, Wintersett Reservoir and the walks along the old Barnsley Canal.

No doubt though, that **Nostell Priory**, some six miles south-east of Wakefield on the A638 Doncaster road, is one of the most popular tourist venues in this area. The word "priory" is misleading, and evokes the picture of an ecclesiastical structure, although it is in fact a large Palladian building that was built on the site of an old Augustinian priory. The land was originally owned by Ilbert de Lacy, and donated by his son Robert to the order in the 1100's, who dedicated it to St Oswald. The monks here were a mining fraternity and worked the local seams. At the time of the Dissolution, the Priory was owned by Sir Thomas Gargrave, Speaker of the House of Commons at the time of Elizabeth 1. It passed through various hands, the original building being used, until 1733, when Rowland Winn commissioned James Paine to build a new house near the old priory, which was then pulled down. Paine was only 19 at the time and this was his first large project. Paine also met his wife, Sarah Jennings of Wragby, whilst working on the Priory.

A further wing and extensions to the riding school and stables were added by Robert Adam in the time of Sir Robert's son, the fifth baronet, and more help was enlisted by James Rose, Antonio Zucchi and Thomas Chippendale.

The interior of the house is truly beautiful, with some of the most skilfully executed of Chippendale's works, including the fascinating Doll's house, made in 1735, with some intricate and tiny pieces of furniture made by the great craftsman still inside. Of Nostell's many art treasures, perhaps the celebrated portrait of Thomas More and his Family by Holbein, is the most famous. The grounds are also of outstanding beauty, with rose gardens, a lake, a summer house, beautiful trees and the 16th century Wragby Church.

Facilities include a large adventure playground and picnic area, a craft centre in the stables, camp-site for tents and caravans, excellent coarse-fishing and a conference and banqueting suite located in the converted riding school.

The Priory is still the home of Lord and Lady St Oswald, although the main part was donated by the late Lord St Oswald in 1953.

At nearby **West Hardwick** is the Top Farm Agricultural Museum

Nostell Priory

Wragby Church

and craft centre, a traditional Yorkshire farm sporting some fascinating relics, such as old farm machinery, traction engines, old tractors and rare breeds of farm animals. There is also a restaurant and Yorkshire's only barn dance centre.

The rich, rolling countryside hereabouts is the home for many a picturesque village, and lovely **Ackworth**, with its famous 18th century Quaker School, is one of these. Here, there are some lovely 18th and 19th century houses, as well as some notable Georgian almshouses. There is also a Victorian church at High Ackworth with a 15th century tower. One sad reminder of the village's old history is the Plague Stone situated at the cross roads, where the unfortunate natives were required to leave money in vinegar in exchange for food. A couple of miles south-east, lies the equally picturesque village of **Badsworth**, famous as the burial place of Sir John Bright, Cromwell's right hand man at the battle of Selby and the siege of Pontefract, whose grave can be located in the lovely 15th century church. A mile to the south is Upton Beacon, with wonderful views as far as Derbyshire and the Lincolnshire Wolds.

Although the industrial heritage of the towns here may not be hidden, it could be said that much of their ancient and inspiring history is, and **Pontefract** must be amongst the foremost of these.

Shakespeare alluded to the town in his plays as "Pomfret", a place of influence and power, often visited by kings and their followers.

The great shattered towers of the castle still stand atop the crag to the east of the town. It was built by Ilbert de Lacy in the 11th century, one of the most formidable fortresses of the Norman forces. In medieval times, it passed to the House of Lancaster and became a Royal Castle. Richard II was imprisoned here and tragically murdered in the dungeons on the orders of Henry Bolingbroke, as described in the play by Shakespeare.

The Castle became a major Royalist stronghold during the Civil War, after which it was destroyed by Cromwell, and it remains today, a gaunt

Ackworth Friends' School

ruin with only sections of the inner bailey and the lower part of the keep surviving intact. There is an underground chamber, part of the dungeons, where prisoners carved their names, that they might not be forgotten completely. Perhaps even the unfortunate King Richard may have lived here for the years he was imprisoned within these very walls. The oldest pats are the foundations of St Clement's Church and part of the 12th century bailey wall with the postern gateway. The Keep, or Round Tower, dates from the 13th century and was hewn from the solid rock.

Many of the streets of this town evoke memories of its medieval past, with such names as Micklegate, Beast Fair, Shoe Market, Salter Row and Ropergate. Sadly, though, modern development has masked much of old Pontefract, but behind the surfeit of 20th century civilisation, lies a fascinating array of historical relics and architecture. There are still many old Georgian buildings, winding streets and the old Butter-cross, the focal point around which the weekly street market revolves.

But the most famous product the town has to offer, has to be the celebrated Pontefract Cakes. Liquorice-root has been grown here since monastic times, and was possibly the monks' one weakness and indulgence in a life otherwise dominated by abstinence! A few roots of the plant are still grown in the local park for the sake of continuity, and naturally, the cakes and liquorice allsorts are a firm favourite with the tourists. In Salter Row is an ornate Art Nouveau building which now houses the Information Centre and museum, which gives more information on the liquorice industry. In here there is also an impressive model of the castle and how it looked in its hey-day, plus more information about Pontefract's medieval past and local industries such as pottery and glass-making.

Curious as it may seem, this part of the West Riding is noted for the quality of its rhubarb, and at one time was even exported to France to improve the quality of its champagne!

Nearby **Knottingley** is an industrial town, once an important inland port on the River Aire for the wool industry. If driving in this area, one might make a point of stopping off at Fairburn Ings, where there is a 600 acre nature reserve, reclaimed from old pit-sites, and newly greened. The reserve is run by the RSPB, and has informative display boards to aid in the observation of the local water-fowl.

CHAPTER 10

Chapel of Our Lady, Rotherham

Doncaster to Sheffield

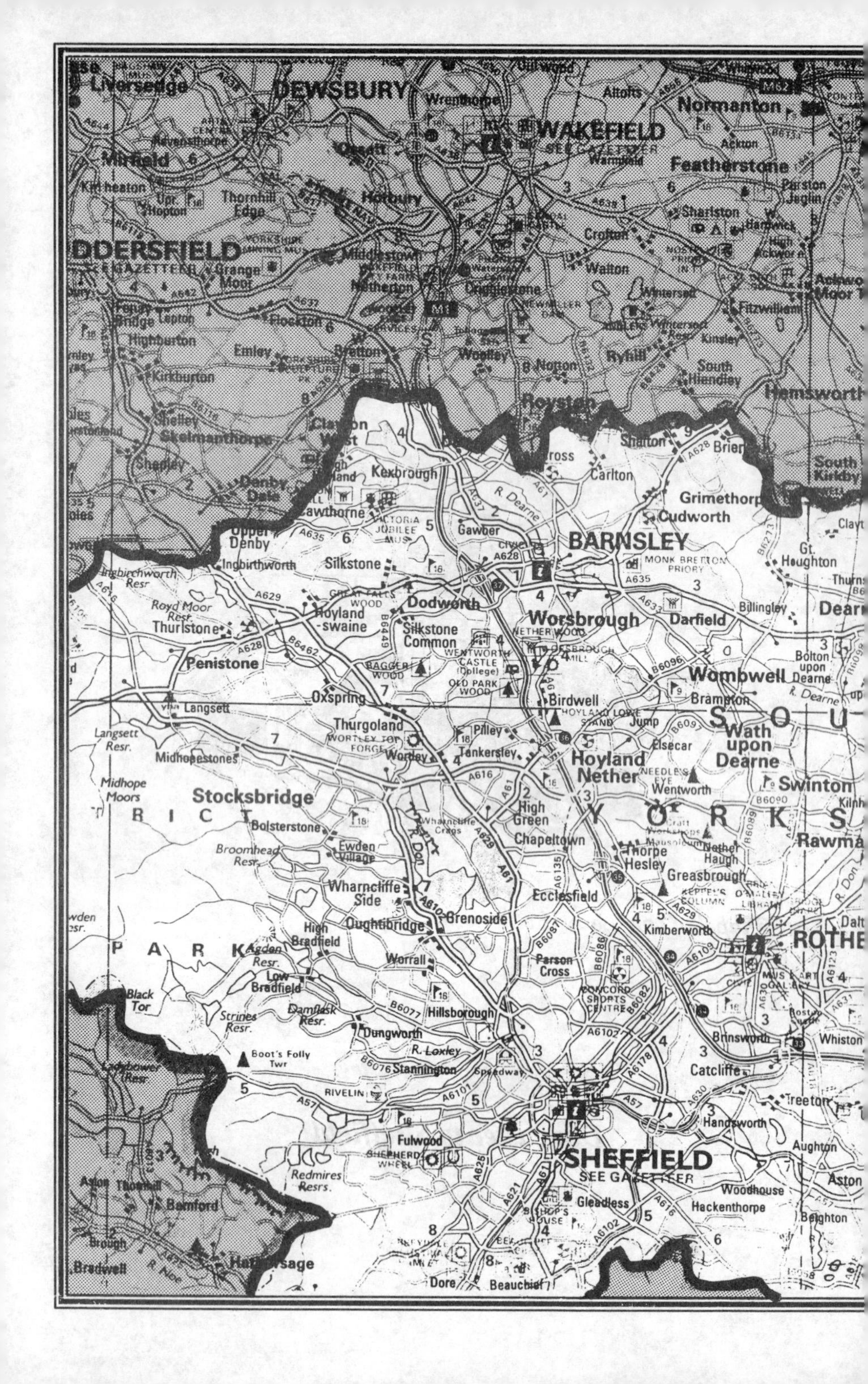
Liversedge
DEWSBURY
Wrenthorpe
Altofts
Normanton
WAKEFIELD
SEE GAZETTEER
Mirfield
Ravensthorpe
Ossett
Ackton
Featherstone
Kirkheaton
Thornhill Edge
Horbury
Sharlston
Crofton
Middlestown
Grange Moor
Netherton
Walton
Crigglestone
Flockton
Fitzwilliam
Lepton
Highburton
Emley
Bretton
Woolley
Notton
Ryhill
Kinsley
South Hiendley
Kirkburton
Hemsworth
Shelley
Skelmanthorpe
Clayton West
Royston
Shafton
Brierley
South Kirkby
Shepley
Denby Dale
High Hoyland
Kexbrough
Carlton
Grimethorpe
Cawthorne
Cudworth
Upper Denby
Gawber
BARNSLEY
Gt. Houghton
Ingbirthworth
Silkstone
MONK BRETTON PRIORY
Ingbirchworth Resr.
Royd Moor Resr.
Thurlstone
Hoyland -swaine
Dodworth
Worsbrough
Darfield
Billingley
Silkstone Common
WENTWORTH CASTLE (College)
Bolton upon Dearne
Penistone
Wombwell
Birdwell
Brampton
Oxspring
Langsett
Jump
Thurgoland
Pilley
Elsecar
Wath upon Dearne
Langsett Resr.
Wortley
Tankersley
Hoyland Nether
Midhopestones
Swinton
Midhope Moors
Stocksbridge
Wentworth
High Green
Chapeltown
Bolsterstone
Ewden Village
Broomhead Resr.
Thorpe Hesley
Nether Haugh
Greasbrough
Rawmarsh
Wharncliffe Side
Ecclesfield
High Bradfield
Oughtibridge
Grenoside
Kimberworth
Agden Resr.
Worrall
Parson Cross
Low Bradfield
Black Tor
Damflask Resr.
Hillsborough
Strines Resr.
Dungworth
R. Loxley
Brinsworth
Whiston
Boot's Folly Twr
Ladybower Resr.
Stannington
Catcliffe
RIVELIN
Treeton
Fulwood
Handsworth
SHEPHERD WHEEL
SHEFFIELD
SEE GAZETTEER
Aughton
Redmires Resrs.
Aston
Thornhill
Bamford
Gleadless
Woodhouse
Hackenthorpe
Beighton
Brough
Bradwell
Hathersage
Dore
Beauchief
R. Don
R. Dearne
R. Noe

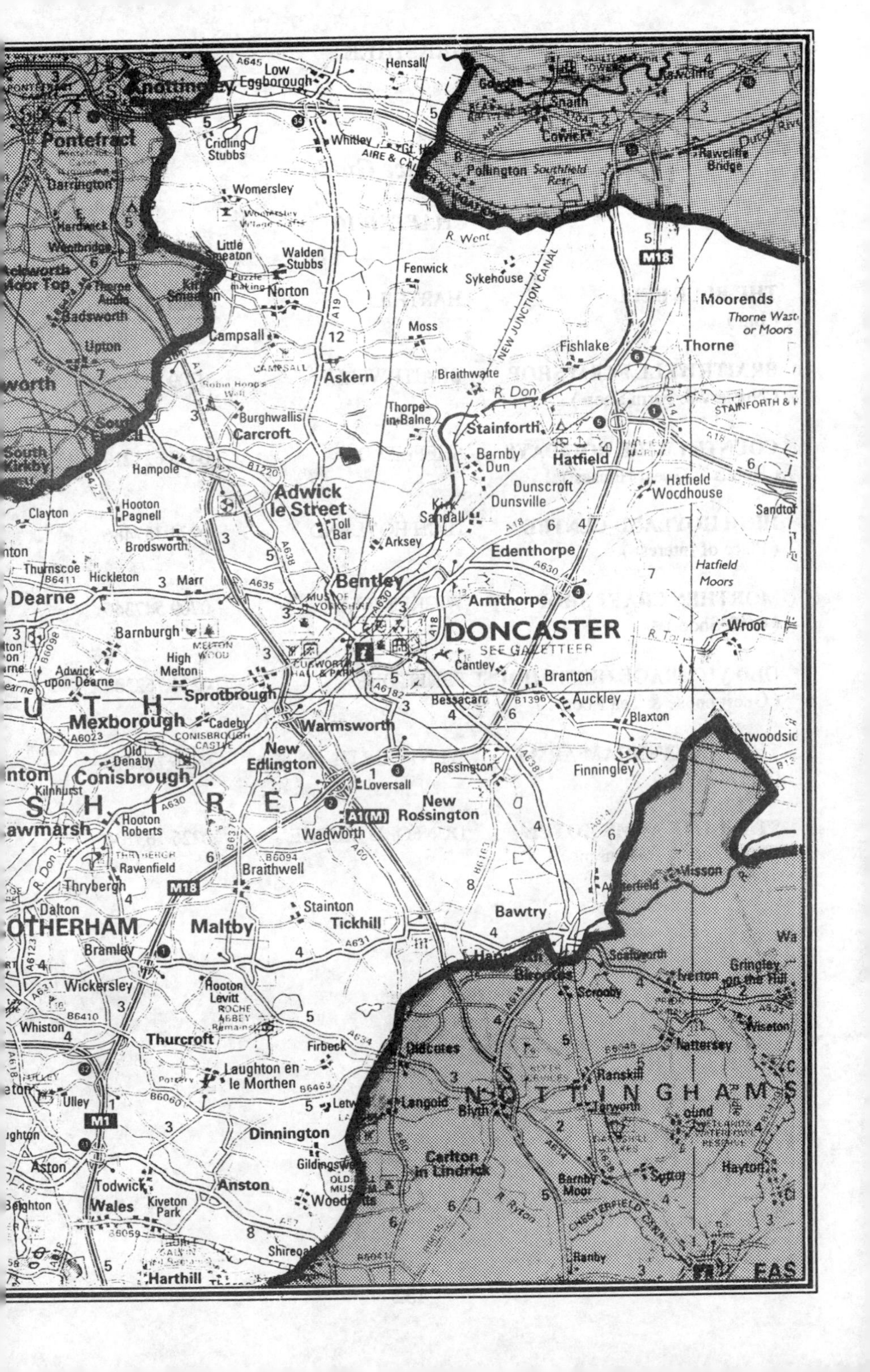
Pontefract
Knottingley
Low Eggborough
Hensall
Snaith
Cowick
Pollington
Rawcliffe Bridge
Cridling Stubbs
Whitley
AIRE & CALDER NAVIGATION
Womersley
Little Smeaton
Walden Stubbs
Darrington
Wentbridge
Badsworth
Upton
Norton
Fenwick
Sykehouse
NEW JUNCTION CANAL
Moorends
Thorne Waste or Moors
Thorne
Fishlake
Campsall
Moss
Askern
Braithwaite
R. Don
Burghwallis
Carcroft
Thorpe in Balne
Stainforth
Hatfield
Hampole
Barnby Dun
Dunscroft
Dunsville
Hatfield Woodhouse
Adwick le Street
Clayton
Hooton Pagnell
Kirk Sandall
Toll Bar
Arksey
Brodsworth
Edenthorpe
Hatfield Moors
Thurnscoe
Hickleton
Marr
Bentley
Armthorpe
Dearne
Wroot
Barnburgh
DONCASTER
SEE GAZETTEER
High Melton
Cantley
Adwick upon Dearne
Branton
Sprotbrough
Bessacarr
Auckley
Mexborough
Cadeby
Warmsworth
Blaxton
Conisbrough
New Edlington
Rossington
Finningley
Loversall
SOUTH YORKSHIRE
New Rossington
Hooton Roberts
Wadworth
Ravenfield
Braithwell
Thrybergh
Dalton
Stainton
ROTHERHAM
Maltby
Tickhill
Bawtry
Misson
Bramley
Wickersley
Hooton Levitt
Roche Abbey
Gringley on the Hill
Scrooby
Whiston
Thurcroft
Firbeck
Oldcotes
Wiseton
Laughton en le Morthen
Ranskill
Ulley
NOTTINGHAMSHIRE
Langold
Blyth
Torworth
Dinnington
Carlton in Lindrick
Gildingwells
Todwick
Anston
Barnby Moor
Hayton
Wales
Kiveton Park
Woodsetts
CHESTERFIELD CANAL
R. Ryton
Harthill
Shireoaks
Ranby
M18
M1
A1(M)

Reference Guide

CHAPTER 10

THE BLUE BELL (Inn)	HARTHILL	0909 770391
BRAITHWELL FARM SHOP (Nursery & Farm Shop)	BRAITHWELL	0709 812328
COUNTRYWIDE HOLIDAYS (Hotels & Guest Houses)	SHEFFIELD	0433 621219
HIGH HOYLAND CENTRE (Place of Interest)	HIGH HOYLAND	0924 387486
MORTHEN CRAFT SHOP (Craft Shop)	WICKERSLEY	0709 547346
OLD VICARAGE GUEST HOUSE (Guest house & Tea Rooms)	PENISTONE	0226 762206
THE ROCKINGHAM ARMS (Inn & Hotel)	WENTWORTH	0226 742075
STANHOPE ARMS HOTEL (Hotel, Inn & Restaurant)	DUNFORD BRIDGE	0226 763104

Town Centre, Rotherham

CHAPTER 10

Doncaster to Sheffield

There are not many people who would consider a holiday in these parts, but as ever, Yorkshire holds yet more surprises and hidden places.

Doncaster was yet another important Roman Town, known as Danum, and was chosen by them because it was the lowest crossing point on the River Don. Budding archaeologists may be interested to know that there is a well-preserved piece of Roman road just west of Ardwick le Street, and that many of the churches have Saxon connections.

Doncaster has strong roots in several non-conformist religions - the Quaker Meeting House at Warmsworth was one of the earliest in the district. George Fox visited it and held rallies at nearby Balby. It is also worth noting that John Wesley came from **Epworth** and William Bradford, one of the Pilgrim Fathers who sailed with the Mayflower, was baptised at **Austerfield**.

The town also has some impressive public buildings, including the Mansion House, the Parish Church and the Corn Exchange. The Mansion House was built in 1748, and was designed by James Paine, to be the only civic mansion house outside London and York. The Parish Church was rebuilt in 1858 by Sir Giles Gilbert Scott as an outstanding example of Gothic revival architecture. The lively shopping centre is enhanced by a stately Corn Exchange building and a market which takes place every Tuesday, Friday and Saturday.

Doncaster was also one of the most important centres for the production of steam trains - both the Flying Scotsman and the Mallard, two of the fastest and most advanced engines of their day, were built in the town.

There is no-one connected with the racing fraternity that has not heard of the St Leger, one of the oldest classic races, which has been held at Doncaster since 1776. Doncaster, in that Yorkshire tradition provides a magnet for all horse racing enthusiasts and there are a total of twenty-six meetings held a year, including National Hunt Flat Races.

The town has a wealth of galleries and museums for people seeking more aesthetic pleasures. The **Doncaster Museum and Art Gallery** is based in Chequer Road, in a modern building it has used since 1964, although the actual gallery was founded in 1909. It houses impressive collections of archaeology, regional natural history, geology, local history,

European fine art, paintings and sculpture, costumes, militaria and special exhibitions. Within the gallery is the collection of the King's Own Yorkshire Light Infantry, introduced in 1987, including uniforms, medals and equipment. Queen Elizabeth, the Queen Mother, visited in 1988, in her capacity as their Colonel-in-Chief.

The Museum of South Yorkshire Life at **Cusworth Hall** appeals to a great range of ages and tastes. Cedar and strawberry trees, larches, cypress, fig, yew and bamboo all grow in the pleasure gardens around this imposing mansion. The building sports fine ornamental doors and windows and palladian pavilions, in one of the finest examples of early Georgian architecture. The interior is adorned with elaborate plasterwork, panelling and carved marble chimney pieces. There are permanent displays that chronicle the way of life over the last 200 years of the people of South Yorkshire. It has an interesting collection of children's dolls, whalebone corsets and decorated chamber pots!

Cusworth Hall

About 12 miles east of Doncaster, near Hatfield is the **Sandtoft Transport Museum**, Britain's largest collection of preserved trolley and motor buses. Here one can ride on an authentic working trolley bus system, which had all been phased out by 1972, but which are to be revived in the near future.

The areas around Doncaster are full of nature reserves and conservation sites, with places such as **Denaby Ings**, **Potterie Carr**, **Sandall Beat** and **Thorpe Marsh**. Twelve miles to the north west is **Howell Wood Country Park**, which was originally planted as an 18th century game reserve. Today, it is 140 acres of delightful woods, streams and ponds, with special consideration for the disabled. The wildlife includes jays, woodcocks, stoats, weasels, brown hares, foxes etc. The Park also has an unusual ice-house used by former residents of Burntwood Hall to preserve food. It consists of a cylindrical well 18 feet deep, packed with ice from the adjoining lake. Its double brick walls and shade from the overhanging oak trees helped to keep the ice frozen for up to three years. To the north west of here is Campsall Park, which consists of 90 acres of a former country house estate with a surrounding lake and picnic area.

At **Skelbrooke**, seven and a quarter miles north west of Doncaster's town centre, sign-posted from the A638, is **Robin Hood's Well**. Skelbrooke is featured in many Robin Hood stories, and was reputedly frequented by the outlaw and his companions. It is distinguishable by the elaborate well-head cover designed by the famous Vanburgh, of Castle Howard fame. It is also rumoured that Robin Hood married Maid Marion at St Mary Magdalene's Church at nearby **Campsall**.

Barnbrough, five miles west of Cusworth, is known as the Cat and Man town, famous for sporting a cat on its coat of arms, a motif that also reappears on the Norman church tower. The story connected with this is that in 1477, a ferocious wildcat was killed by Sir Percival Cresarce, who apparently died later from the injuries he incurred during his confrontation.

Stainforth is an attractive area to the north of Doncaster well worth exploring. It was once an important trading centre and inland port on the River Don, as the main thoroughfare for the Stainforth-Keadby canal, which still has a well- preserved dry dock and 19th century blacksmith's shop. The area is built on low, marshy ground, drained by Dutch engineers in the 17th century to produce rich peaty farmland. The place has retained the air of a quiet backwater, a little-explored area of narrow lanes, pretty hamlets, drained by slow moving dykes and canals. The rich peat resources are commercially exploited in part, but are also the home of a great deal of natural wildlife.

The area of **Sprotborough** also holds some interest for those searching for items of interest. There is a fine medieval church dedicated to St Mary, which amongst other things has some unusual burlesque pew carvings, said to represent the marital joys and disappointments of a family in Tudor times, and reported as having been executed by a local craftsman in lieu of his tithes.

The **Boat Inn** at **Lower Sprotborough** is famous for having ben the place where Sir Walter Scott wrote the novel "Ivanhoe". This is a magnificent coaching house, for many years the family seat of the Copley family, their family crest still visible over one of the windows.

Not far to the south of here, lies magnificent **Conisbrough Castle**. Overlooking the River Don, its mighty white stone keep towers over an impressive medieval fortress, which at one time stood at over 100 feet high, and is considered one of the finest examples of Norman architecture. Much of the circular keep now lies in ruins, but one can still walk through the remains of several rooms, including the 1st floor chamber, with its huge open fireplaces, giving one a fascinating insight into the lifestyle in Norman times.

Twelve miles down the A630, is **Rotherham**, whose past, again, is linked with iron. As far back as Roman times, in fact, iron has been worked here. They built a fortress here to protect their workings, at Templebrough on the banks of the Don, which included a granary and a bath house. Relics from the site, which was discovered around a hundred years ago, are on show at the **Clifton Park Museum**.

Conisbrough Castle

In the Middle Ages , the monks of Rufford Abbey also prospected for and smelted iron. They also planted orchards, and even today, despite the proximity of so much heavy industry, agriculture is still important to the area and three quarters of it still remains rural.

However, it is the heavy industry, all connected with the iron ore resources, that brought Rotherham its prosperity. The famous Walker family struck on the idea of making cannons, and their wares were used in the American War of Independence and the Battle of Trafalgar. They were also responsible for Southwark Bridge in London.

Famous inventors were also born in Rotherham - Sir Donald Colman Bailey, inventor of the Bailey Bridge used in World War Two was born here, and Edward Crimes, the inventor of the household screw-down tap was also from these parts. It was also an important ceramics centre, and a range of the famous Rockingham wares are on display in the Clifton Museum.

Nearby, the village of **Wickersley** is the home of the **Morthen Craft Workshop**, a fascinating place to visit for all those interested in living country crafts. It can be reached by turning south off the A631 midway between Rotherham and Maltby, onto the B6060 at Wickersley and then turn west into Morthen Lane. Open all the year round with car park, tea room and herb garden, visitors can browse the crafts and stone sculpture gallery. Both skilled crafts people, the owners Sylvia and Brian also have pre-booked evenings for groups (between 10 and 50); these include a demonstration on topics varying from herbs to jewellery making, followed by refreshments. All visitors can be assured of a warm welcome.

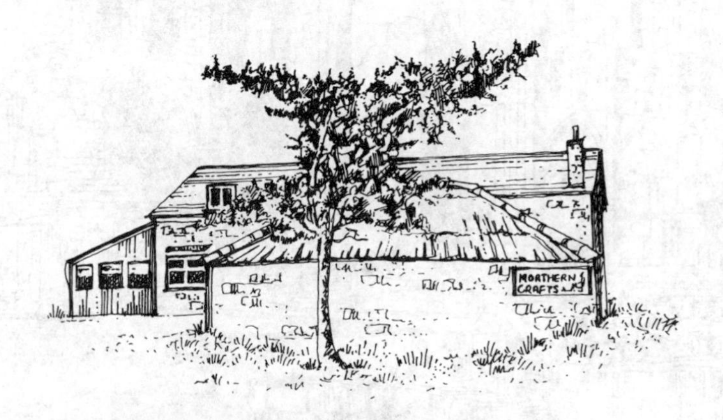

Morthen Craft Workshop

As far as ecclesiastical buildings are concerned, Rotherham also has more than its fair share - the **Parish Church of All Saints** is widely regarded as being one of the finest perpendicular buildings in Yorkshire, and dates from the 15th century, although there is evidence of an earlier Saxon Church on the site.

Inside, is the Chapel of Jesus built in 1480 by Thomas Rotherham,

Roche Abbey

who, after having been educated at Eton and Cambridge, became first Bishop of Lincoln, then Lord Chancellor and was, at the time of his death, Archbishop of York. He was responsible for the founding of the College of Jesus in 1483, although little of this remains now, as it was closed in 1547 during the Dissolution. The College was closed at this time, as was the 15th century Chapel of Our Lady on Rotherham Bridge, which consequently became an almshouse, a jail and even a tobacconists.

Travelling out of the town, beyond **Maltby**, are the beautiful remains of **Roche Abbey**, a ruined Cistercian house situated in an idyllic riverine setting. The story of the monks' dismissal at the hands of Henry VIII's men is filled with pathos, for an on-site auction of all their treasures and effects was held, and the monks were forced to look on as Henry's favourites and other well-off personages haggled over their sacred artefacts. Their departure was followed by an almost complete devastation of the Abbey, so that today, there are only two graceful fragments upstanding to attest to the building's former glory. A guilt-ridden participant later commented in regard to the auction.

"What should I do", he confessed "might I not as well as others have some Profit of the Spoil of the Abbey? For I did see all would away".

The locals of Rotherham recorded how even the frugal cells of the monks themselves were ransacked for what little they contained, even to the point of the doors themselves being carried away. What was not sold or stolen, was pulled down or defaced. Michael Sherbrook, a native of Rotherham and rector of Wickersley, recorded how, from his memories of the bells pealing from the towers of Roche, "It would have pitied any Heart to see what tearing up of Lead there was , and plucking up of Boards, and throwing down of the Sparres...and all things of price, either spoiled, carped away or defaced to the uttermost". The guilty participant earlier quoted was in fact the self-same rector's father, in response to his son's questioning regarding his part in the spoiling.

The foundations that remain of the great House, give one a clear picture of the ordered existence of the Cistercian lifestyle, the monks based on the east of the building and lay brethren to the west. One can also still see the clever drainage system, the engineering of which dictated the locations of all Cistercian houses, which caused them all to be sited next to fairly flat stream beds, which could be harnessed and diverted to their purposes.

The surrounds of the decayed Abbey were landscaped in the 1770's by Capability Brown, as part of the grounds of Sandbeck Hall, home of the Earls of Scarborough.

Should one feel inspired by the great Capability Brown to do a little creative gardening yourself, three miles north of the Abbey is the delightful village of **Braithwell**, home of the unusual nursery and garden centre, the **Braithwell Farm Shop**, which can be found at Ashton Farm on the High Street. Owners Peter and Rita Dunstan are fourth generation farmers who specialise in growing unusual varieties of garden plants. Among the many rare and original species on offer, they are particularly well-known for their 'Green Goddess' variety of arum lily. The plants are grown in the field behind the farm shop where customers are welcome to browse and choose from the large selection on show. A wide range of conservatory plants is also available, along with a great deal of friendly expert advice.

Braithwell Farm Shop

On the edges of Rotherham, are two wonderful 18th century buildings, **Boston Castle** and **Clifton House.**

Boston Castle was built by the Earl of Effingham as a shooting lodge. It was so-called due to the Earl's sympathies with the American War of Independence, recalling the Boston tea-party, and the drinking of tea was strictly forbidden within its walls. Unfortunately, the house is not open to the public, although the environs of Boston Park in which it stands, offer excellent views of the surrounding countryside.

Clifton House was the home of the influential Walker family, the head of which, Joshua Walker, was known as the Iron Master. It now houses the Clifton Park Museum, based in lovely parkland and was built in 1783. It's collection of Rockingham pottery includes the spectacular Rhinoceros Vase, which stands at almost 4ft high. The Rockingham Kiln, established by Joseph Flint in 1745, can still be visited at Blackamoor Road in nearby

Swinton. Clifton House also houses an authentic Victorian kitchen, still crammed with crockery, pots and pans, and which has retained that 19th century feel. On the 1st floor, is a reconstructed Victorian child's bedroom.

A short walk from here on Drummond Street, is the **York and Lancaster's Museum**, which tells the history of the regiment from 1758 to it's disbandment in 1968. There is an exhibition of almost 1000 medals.

The small town of **Tickhill**, further on from Maltby, was once a place of great note in medieval times, with a castle of its own. Here, one can see the remains of an Augustinian Friary and a medieval millpond. The Buttercross, erected in 1777, was part of the impressive Church of St Mary the Virgin, largely rebuilt in the 15th century. The Parish Rooms were originally part of St Leonard's hospital, which date from 1470. The plaster and timber walls have been used for many purposes over the years, including a school.

There are little more than the foundations remaining to tell of the former glory of Tickhill Castle, once one of the most influential castles in England at the time of the legendary Richard the Lionheart. It was considered one of the most technically advanced of such structures, and was donated by the king to his notorious younger brother. John. The castle was besieged twice in Richard's time and withstood a three week siege, led by Thomas, Lord of Lancaster, and his baronial rebellion. Tickhill was garrisoned by both sides at times during the Civil War, and was probably rased afterwards to prevent it's further military use.

The scars that South Yorkshire's industrial past left behind, have, for the large part been covered without a trace, and this reclamation can be seen to it's best at the **Rother Valley Country Park**, an area of restored and replanted countryside and lakes, with extensive leisure facilities. Bedgreave New Mill within the Park, contains a restored water wheel and a visitor centre.

Despite its closeness to the M1, the picturesque village of **Harthill** retains an atmosphere which seems far from today's fast-moving world. (The village lies a mile east of the motorway, midway between junctions 30 and 31, less that two miles from the Country Park) Harthill has won the area's Village In Bloom competition on several occasions and it is also well-known as a centre for traditional village activities such as Morris dancing. The focus for these activities is the renowned village pub, **The Blue Bell**, which is run by George 'Barry' Cartlidge and his wife June. Traditional folk music evenings take place in the pub's recently opened function rooms, and there is also a large landscaped beer garden with a pond containing Barry's prize-winning collection of Koi carp.

The Blue Bell

The **Chesterfield Canal** is another of the area's industrial inheritances that has been converted to recreational use, with lovely walks along the 46 miles of its length.

Marked on the map and only a short drive from Rotherham, is the **Thrybergh Country Park**, based around the reservoir there, and a well-known venue for fishing enthusiasts. In a similar vein, is the Firsby reservoir, noted for its wildfowl and birdlife.

Six miles north west of Rotherham, on the B6090, one might make a point of calling in at the **Rockingham Arms** in **Wentworth**, a splendid example of a 17th-century country inn with ivy clad walls and a wonderful traditional atmosphere.

The Rockingham Arms

Standing on the northern edge of Wentworth Park, the inn's interior is decorated in charming rural style with open log fires burning in the winter months. There is a cosy dining room and family room where children are welcome. The bar offers a fine selection of traditional hand-pulled ales, including Youngers and Theakstons. There are also thirteen comfortable newly decorated letting bedrooms in the quaint stone cottages opposite the main building.

Those interested in the beginnings of the industrial revolution, should also take a trip to nearby **Elsecar**, now transformed into a remarkable industrial village, and a designated conservation area. The village was developed in the 18th and 19th centuries by the Earls of Fitzwilliam of nearby **Wentworth Woodhouse**. It has a fine church, stone cottages, a flour mill built in 1842 which now houses a craft centre and a series of workshops, warehouses, a canal and a train station now housing a major heritage centre. One can also follow a Heritage Trail around the village. The showpiece at Elsecar is the Newcomen Engine, a late 18th century steam powered beam engine and the only one of its kind in the country to have been retained on its original site. Its original purpose was to drain water from the local mines, which it did until 1923. At maximum power, the engine could pump out 400 gallons of water a minute.

It was the local Fitzwilliam family who made most money from the local mine workings, and it was at Wentworth Woodhouse that they spent it, a palatial 18th century manor, set in lavish grounds, with one of the longest facades in England. It is not open to the public, but can be enjoyed from the public paths that run through the park. There is plenty to see and do nearby, in the shape of craft workshops, reached through the Hauge Lane garden Centre, ornamental gardens to the west of the house with a grotto tunnel and bear pit. A number of follies and monuments, dating from the 18th century, are also on the estate. **Hoober Stand** is a 100 ft monument that was erected at the highest point of the borough to commemorate the suppression of the Jacobite Rebellion, whilst Keppels Column, just across the way, rises to 115 ft, in remembrance of the acquittal of Admiral Keppels, court-marshalled for failing to beat the French in 1778. There is also the Needles Eye in Lees Wood, which consists of a tower pierced by a carriage way. The story goes that it was built after a wager by the Marquis of Rockingham to prove he could drive a horse and carriage through the eye of a needle. The Wentworth Mausoleum, not open to the public was constructed in 1788 in memory of the second Marquis.

At **Worsborough Mill Museum**, south of Barnsley, there is a restored corn mill where flour is still ground by water power in the traditional way, using mill-stones. There has been a mill here since Norman times, and it was mentioned in the Domesday Book, the present structure dating from 1625. A steam-powered mill was added in 1843, and was still working up to the 1960's. Both mills are still in working order, and are two of the features of the 130 acre Worsborough Park on the banks of the River Dove.

Not many would associate the very Yorkshire town of **Barnsley** with being a 'hidden place', however, as with so many of the places in this character-filled county, one would not need to scratch too far below the surface to find many interesting venues to visit and experience. It is its wealth of coal that has shaped the town and the lives of the inhabitants, the proximity of its mines are of vital importance to the iron and steelworks of its neighbours.

The satellite towns and villages are steeped in history and myth. The village of **Monk Bretton** is famous for its ruined priory, the only remaining settlement of the Cluniac Order of monks.

It started in 1154, colonised from the wealthy Pontefract Priory, although a dispute later led to a rift between the two. It achieved independence in 1281, which led to its affiliation with the Benedictine Brotherhood. The plan of the priory, which includes the foundations of both infirmary and guest house, is unusually complete. The Prior's lodgings, based on the first floor of the west claustral stage are particularly interesting due to the fine detailed chimney piece. Also of interest are the two gatehouses and the curious administrative building in the outer court, one of the few that have survived in this country.

North of Barnsley, in the midst of rolling wooded countryside, is the village of **High Hoyland**, with the Church of All Hallows, which stands on a hilltop, commanding the best views for miles around.

An interesting development took place here, when the Church was made redundant; the building has continued to give pleasure to people for a decade in its later role of residential **Activity Centre**. Disabled facilities were included when a charitable trust carried out the conversion. Available to diverse groups, school parties, choirs, bird-watchers, etc, administration is now in the hands of nearby Bretton Hall College.

Nearby **Cawthorne** is a pretty village with a 16th century church that sports an octagonal font rescued from Roche Abbey. Here is the location of the Victoria Jubilee Museum, with its remarkable collections of natural and local history exhibits, founded in a local cottage in 1884 and expanded in the year of the Queen's Golden Jubilee.

Nearby is the **Cannon Hall Country Park and Hall**. At one time the house here was nicknamed Roast Beef Hall, due to the generous hospitality of its 19th century owner, Sir Walter Spencer Stanhope. It is a typical Georgian house, solid, dignified and above all, comfortable, set in beautiful and serene parkland. Now a museum, the hall's rooms are furnished in a variety of styles from Jacobean to Victorian. Most sumptuous is the Jacobean ballroom, with its oak-panelled walls, minstrels' gallery and elaborate fireplace. There is an interesting glassware collection which amongst other things, contains such oddities as glass rolling pins and walking sticks. Cannon Hall also houses the Regimental Museum of the 13th and 18th Royal Hussars, whose part in the Charge of the Light Brigade in 1854, is recalled in a series of stirring displays.

Silkstone, not far away, is a historical village that dates from Anglo-Saxon times. A visit to the church reveals a sad reminder of the exploitation of child labour in the grim days of the Industrial Revolution, for here is a monument to the 26 children who drowned in the Husker Pit Disaster of 1838.

Penistone forms a gateway to the Peak District, a small South Yorkshire town with a character all of its own. It is situated 700 ft above sea level, in the midst of moorland landscape, and has an agricultural heritage that it is careful to preserve. It has some interesting public buildings, including the 17th century Dissenters' Chapel, an 18th century Cloth Hall, and a Parish Church with a 15th century tower, where ancestors of the poet Wordsworth are buried.

In the village, on Shrewsbury Road, opposite the ancient parish church we found the **Old Vicarage Guest House and Tearooms**, a fine old building set within beautiful mature gardens.

Old Vicarage Guest House

(The adjoining village post office is housed in the Old Vicarage's former coach house). Owners Joyce and Paul Clibbens have six beautifully-appointed guest rooms available, some with en suite facilities. They also run an attractive tearoom which offers delicious home-made cakes and snacks including their celebrated cinnamon teacakes and the 'Penistone Parcel', a mouthwatering savoury surprise invented by Joyce. Evening meals are available for guests, including special weekend dinners which feature recipes from around the world.

A relatively short distance away, is the lovely hamlet of **Langsett**, and then on to the scenic beauties of Ladybower Reservoir and the heart of the Peak District. Nearby, Thuristone contains some charming examples of Pennine weaver's cottages, and west, just north of the busy Woodhead pass, lies **Dunford Bridge**, a hidden place that nestles in a deep fold of the surrounding hillsides, where once the trains halted before entering the now redundant Woodhead tunnel.

Nearby, situated below Thurlstone Moors on the northeastern edge of the Peak District National Park, we came across the first-rate hotel, pub and restaurant, the **Stanhope Arms Hotel**. This fine establishment lies on the Windle Edge Road and can be reached either by turning north off the A628 near Salter's Brook Bridge or west off the B6106 midway between Holmfirth and Penistone. The building stands a short distance from the source of the River Don and is a former hunting lodge which was once owned by Cannon Hall. The present-day hotel provides an ideal base for exploring this dramatic part of West Yorkshire.

The Stanhope Arms Hotel

The five guest bedrooms, one of which is a luxurious bridal suite, are all equipped with en suite bathrooms and are appointed to a good modern standard. The hotel also has a pleasant bar which is open to non-residents and an impressive restaurant which serves generous full English breakfasts, lunches and top quality evening meals. The hotel stands next to the old Woodhead Tunnel and has close associations with the famous Thurlstone Owl Sanctuary which is situated only a short distance away.

On the A629 road, south-east of Penistone, at Thurgoland, is the only ironworks of its kind in Britain still on its original site, **Wortley Top Forge**, which dates from the 17th century. Complete with its dam, sluices and waterwheels, it also has a rare example of an 18th century water-powered forge hammer.

It is perhaps the unexpected nature of these places, amidst so much industrialisation, that makes South Yorkshire such a rewarding area to explore.

Aston, a few miles to the north east of the city of Sheffield, has a collection of Georgian buildings that give an air of grace and elegance to the town. One of them, a former rectory, was the home of the reverend William Marshall, author, poet, musician and friend of Thomas Gray. It is reputedly for the reverend, that Gray wrote the famous 'Elegy'. The house was designed by the celebrated John Carr, and is a place of ornamental plaster ceilings and copious fireplaces, in which Marshall would play his coelestinette and pentachord, or devise a new dramatic scene for 'Caractacus' or 'Elfrida'.

The once greatest steel-making town in the world, **Sheffield**, is another example of this unexpected aspect of the South Yorkshire area.

I can recall my first view of the town, nesting comfortably in the middle of the basin in which it is situated, with a great sense of nostalgia. Having travelled on the back of a motorbike along the Snake Pass from Manchester in bleak, snowy conditions, I can honestly say I have never been so pleased to see a town in my life, if only because it heralded the possibility of a warm place in which to thaw out!

Viewed from the hills, as I first saw it, Sheffield does not, on the surface seem a likely venue for the sight-seer, nor does it seem to have retained the aura of a great steel town, for that matter.

But its busy, modern heart still, on closer observation, finds time to recall the history of its days as a steel-making capital. There is no where in the world that you will not find some item made of Sheffield steel, and such a heritage has made a deep mark indeed.

Sheffield is not often accredited with the fact that it contains more parks within its boundaries than any other European city, second only to Glasgow - the rich steel barons of the town needed somewhere to promenade their ladies after all! At Weston Park, is the City Museum, with the world's greatest collection of cutlery, dating from the Paleolithic Age to the present day (I must admit to experiencing a rather amusing mental image of a Sheffield caveman poised over a mammoth steak, delicately holding the precursors to the familiar heavy steel knife and fork we know so well!)

The Kelbrook Island Museum, which is located on Penistone Road was voted Museum of the Year in 1982, and provides an opportunity to see the River Don Engine "in steam" - a magnificent engineering wonder.

Nearby, is one of the few buildings of national importance left unused in Sheffield, **The Globe Works**. It was built in 1825 by cutlery and tool manufacturers Henry and William Ibbotson. Here is an unusual example of an industrial building which also incorporates a domestic residence. The interior includes a magnificent circular staircase and fine plaster mouldings, which have now been adapted to provide prestigious office accommodation. The original factory areas have been given over as craft workshops, and other additions, such as a visitor centre, restaurant and public house are hoped to make this beautiful building a busy tourist attraction as well. The whole of the Kelbrook Island area has, in fact been designated a conservation site by Sheffield City Council.

Globe Works

In the heart of **Whitley Woods** is the Shepherd Wheel, a water-powered grinding shop which dates from the 16th century, restored to full working order. Even older is the **Bishop's House** in **Meersbrook Park**, so-called because it was once occupied by brothers John and Geoffrey Blythe, Bishops of Salisbury and Lichfield and Coventry respectively, and which was built in the 15th century. It stands in a grove of trees at the highest point of the park, a simple L-shaped structure that is the most complete example of a black and white timbered house in Sheffield.

Whitley Woods are part of a 10 mile Round Walk through public open spaces in the south and south western districts of the city. The signposted way starts at Endcliffe Park and leads by wooded paths to **Graves Park**, at 300 acres, the largest of Sheffield's parks.

The Park, gifted to the city in 1926 by Alderman J G Graves, houses a Rare Breed Survival Centre, with a number of rare domestic breeds on show, the adjacent Norton Nursery and **Chantryland**, Sheffield's First theme park. There is a famous plant Associated with and created at the Nursery , namely the Chantryland Viola, created by H D Widdowson and now grown all over the world, which speaks of the reputation of this celebrated horticultural centre, that regularly holds places in the finals of the "Britain in Bloom" competitions.

The name of Chantry was originally that of Britain's most prolific sculptor, Sir Frances Leggot Chantry, known in his lifetime as "Sculptor of the Great". Born at Norton, he achieved such status that he was, on his death interred at Westminster Abbey. In celebration of his works, part of Chantryland has been dedicated to a Sculpture Trail, created by local artists in cooperation with the famous Graves Art gallery. Here, there are permanent exhibits, such as the Green Man sculpture by Rod Powell and several temporary ones.

Sheffield's Nature trails do not attempt to hide their industrial links, but rather seek to make use of them, as on the **Rivelin Nature Trail**, where one will see hundreds of discarded mill grinding wheels lying by the river's edge. Evidence of heavier industrial relics can be found on the city's East End Trail.

Since Victorian days, the citizens of Sheffield have sought an escape from the hustle and bustle of the busy steel town in the wonderful Botanical Gardens, located on the western edge of the city. They occupy 19 acres and comprise of rose gardens, rockeried, heather gardens, wilderness area, as well as many specialist and rare trees and plants. An unusual feature is an entire area set aside for the disabled.

The beautiful glass and metal 19th century structures no longer contain exotic botanical specimens as they did in Victorian times, but now house an aquarium and aviary.

As befits a city of the former glory and stature of Sheffield, it has a Cathedral, whose possibly most famous feature is the Famous Te Deum Window, designed by Christopher Webb, depicting Christ, surrounded by his prophets and apostles. Considered in a similarly reverential manner by devotees of the game of snooker, let us not overlook the famous **Crucible Theatre**, so often the venue for the game's many well-attended finals and sponsored events, and situated in the heart of the city.

Three and a half miles south west of the city, is the **Abbeydale Industrial Hamlet**, once one of the largest water-powered industrial sites on the River Sheaf (from where Sheffield got its name). One of the best preserved monuments of the Industrial Revolution, Abbeydale was famous for the production of scythes and other agricultural tools. The works closed in 1933, but today the workshops have been reconstructed to present a complete picture of foundry work in the 19th century. Fast flowing water and abundant iron ore and coal ensured Sheffield's prominence as a steel production area. Abbeydale was enabled to retain its position as a self-contained community, whose craftsmen lived alongside their workshops in terraces cottages, each of them producing as many as seven dozen scythes a day. There are regular demonstrations of their craft that take place each day, a must for all those who truly wish to get a real flavour of South Yorkshire's industrial heritage, and long may it be appreciated!

We left Sheffield and headed out on the A625 down the Hope Valley and across the border into Derbyshire (the subject of another book in the Hidden Places Series) where we found a great place to stay if you find yourself on the border between the two counties an area loved by walkers in particular.Countrywide Holidays Association was established 100 years ago and pioneered the first walking and special interestholidays.The association now own a total of 13 houses in beautiful locations throughout the British Isles , many with special or historic interest. Moorgate is one such house , situated in the tranquil village of Hope with the finest Peak District countrside literally on its doorstep.Recently refurbished to a high standard,the whole house is centrally heated and most rooms now provide en-suite facilities.The wonderful surrounding scenery is dotted with picturesque stone villages to explore, and visitors to Moorgate will find many places of interest within easy reach.Activity and special interst holidays are available by prior arrangement.For full details and a brochure phone them on 061 225 1000.

We do hope that you have enjoyed reading the book as much as we have compiling it .and we would like to thank all the proprietors and managers of the places we have visited for their kind hospitality. We would be grateful if you mentioned the fact that you found them via the Hidden Places, and if you do find somewhere not already mentioned please let us know and we will be happy to consider it when the book is reprinted.

Meanwhile we leave you to discover the hidden delights of the beautiful county of Yorkshire.

TOURIST INFORMATION CENTRES

IN
YORKSHIRE AND HUMBERSIDE

Barnsley
56 Eldon St
Barnsley
S .Yorks S70 2JL
0226 206757

Bedale
Bedale Hall
N > Yorks DL8 1AA
0677 424604

Beverley
The Guildhall
Beverley HU17 9AU
0482 867430

Boroughbridge
Fishergate
N .Yorks YO5 9AL
0423 323373

Bradford
National Museum of
Film & T>V.
Princes View
W.Yorks
0274 753678

Bridlington
25 Princes St
Humberside YO15 2NP
0262 673474

Brigg
The Buttercross
Market Place
Humberside DN20 8ER
0652 657053

Cleethorpes
42-43 Alexandra Rd
Humberside DN 35 8LE
0472 200220

Danby
The Moors Centre
Lodge Lane Danby YO21 2NB
0287 660654

Doncaster
Central Library
S>Yorks DN1 3JE
0302 734309

Easingwold
Chapel Lane
N. Yorks YO6 3AE
0347 21530

Filey
John St
N. Yorks YO14 9DW
0723 512204

TOURIST INFORMATION CENTRES
IN
YORKSHIRE AND HUMBERSIDE

Goole
Goole Library
Carlisle St
Humberside DN14 5AA
0405 762187

Grassington
National Park Centre
Hebden Rd
N.Yorks BD23 5LB
0756 752774

Grimsby
National Fishing Heritage Ctr.
Alexandra Dock
Humberside DN31 1UF
0472 342422

Halifax
Piece Hall
W. Yorks HX1 1RE
0422 368725

Harrogate
Royal Baths
Crescent Rd
N,Yorks HG1 2RR
0423 525666

Hartshead Moor
M62 Service Area
Brighouse W. Yorks
HD6 4 JX
0274 869167

Hawes
Dales Museum
Station Yard
N.Yorks
DL8 3NT
0969 667450

Haworth
West Lane
Haworth
W.Yorks BD22 8EF
0535 642329

Hebden Bridge
Bridge Gate
W.Yorks HX7 8EX
0422 843831

Helmsley
Market Place
N.Yorks YO6 5BL
0439 70173

Holmfirth
Huddersfield Rd
W. Yorks HD7 1JP
0484 687603

Hornsea
75 Newbegin
Humberside HU18 1PA
0964 536404

Hull
Central Library
Albion St
Humberside HU1 3TF
0482 223344

Also at
King George Dock
Hedon Rd
0482 640852

TOURIST INFORMATION CENTRES

IN

YORKSHIRE AND HUMBERSIDE

Ilkley
Station Rd
W. Yorks LS29 8HA
0943 602319

Knaresborough
35 Market Place
N.Yorks HG5 8AL
0423 866886

Leeds
19 Wellington St
Leeds LS1 4DG
0532 478301

Leyburn
Thornborogh Hall
N.Yorks DL8 5AD
0969 23069

Malton
Old Town Hall
Market Plac
N.Yorks YO17 OLH
0653 600048

Northallerton
Applegarth Car Park
N.Yorks DL7 8LZ
0609 776864

Otley
8 Boroghgate
W.Yorks LS21 3AH
0943 465151

Pateley Bridge
Southlands Car Park
N.Yorks
0423 711147

Pickering
Eastgate Car Park
N.Yorks YO18 7DP
0751 73791

Richmond
Friary Gardens
Victoria Rd DL10 4AJ
0748 850252

Ripon
Minster Rd
N.Yorks HG4 1LT
0765 604625

Rotherham
Central Library
Walker Place
S.Yorks S651JH
0709 823611

Scarborough
St Nicholas Cliff
N. Yorks YO11 2EP
0723 373333

Scotch Corner
Service Area A1
Richmond N.Yorks
0325 377677

TOURIST INFORMATION CENTRES
IN
NORTH YORKSHIRE AND HUMBERSIDE

Scunthorpe
Central Library
Carlton St
DN15 6TX
0724 282301

Selby
Park St N.Yorks
YO8 OAA
0757 703263

Settle
Town Hall
N.Yorks BD24 9EJ
0729 825192

Sheffield
Town Hall
Union St S12HH
0742 734671
Railway Stn
Sheaf St
0742 795901

Skipton
Victoria Sq
N.YorksBD23 1JF
0756 792809

Thirsk
Kirkgate
N.Yorks YO7 1PQ
0845 522755

Wakefield
Town Hall
Wood St
W.Yorks WF1 2HQ
0924 295000

Wetherby
24 Wesgate
W.Yorks LS22 4NL
0937 582706

Whitby
Langborne Rd
N.Yorks YO21 1YN
0947 602674

York
De Grey Rooms
Exhibition Sq
N.Yorks YO1 2HB
0904 621756
Also at
Railway Stn
0904 643700

Travel Office
Rougier St
0904 621756

A-Z Index Yorkshire

An alphabetical listing of the major

Towns & Villages featured in this guide

THE HIDDEN PLACES

If you would like to have any of the titles currently available in this series, please complete this coupon and send to:

M & M Publishing Ltd
Tryfan House, Warwick Drive
Hale, Altrincham
Cheshire, WA15 9EA

Somerset, Avon and Dorset	☐	£ 5.90 inc. p&p
Norfolk and Suffolk	☐	£ 5.90 inc. p&p
Yorkshire	☐	£ 5.90 inc. p&p
Devon and Cornwall	☐	£ 5.90 inc. p&p
	☐	£ 5.90 inc. p&p
Cumbria	☐	£ 5.90 inc. p&p
Southern and Central Scotland	☐	£ 5.90 inc. p&p
Sussex	☐	£ 5.90 inc. p&p
Hampshire and the Isle of Wight	☐	£ 5.90 inc. p&p
Gloucestershire & Wiltshire	☐	£ 5.90 inc. p&p
Nottinghamshire, Derbyshire & Lincolnshire	☐	£ 5.90 inc. p&p
Oxfordshire, Buckinghamshire & Bedfordshire	☐	£ 5.90 inc. p&p
Lancashire & Cheshire	☐	£ 5.90 inc. p&p
Hereford & Worcester	☐	£ 5.90 inc. p&p
Set of any Five	☐	£ 25.90 inc. p&p

NAME..

ADDRESS...

....

.................................Post Code...

Please make cheques/postal orders payable to: M & M Publishing Ltd